500

5~Ingredient Desserts

500

5~Ingredient Desserts

Decadent and Divine Recipes for Everyday Cooking

Robert Hildebrand and Carol Hildebrand

FAIR WINDS
PRESS
GLOUCESTER, MASSACHUSETTS

Text © 2005 by Robert Hildebrand and Carol Hildebrand

First published in the USA in 2005 by

Fair Winds Press, a member of

Quayside Publishing Group

33 Commercial Street

Gloucester, MA 01930

09 08 07 06 05 1 2 3 4 5

ISBN 1-59233-172-6

Library of Congress Cataloging-in-Publication Data

Hildebrand, Robert.
  500 5-ingredient desserts : decadent and divine recipes for everyday
cooking / Robert Hildebrand and Carol Hildebrand.
      p. cm.
  Summary: "Simple dessert recipes using only five
ingredients"--Provided by publisher.
  ISBN 1-59233-172-6
  1. Desserts. 2. Quick and easy cookery. I. Title: Five hundred
five-ingredient deserts. II. Hildebrand, Carol. III. Title.
  TX773.H48 2005
  641.8'6--dc22

Cover design by Mary Ann Smith

Book design by Leslie Haimes

Printed and bound in USA

Contents

Introduction

Is it really possible to make a spectacular dessert from just five ingredients? The notion seems the ultimate in incompatibility. On the one hand, we've got the concept of dessert, in all its lush, decadent, swoony goodness. On the other hand, there's the simplicity and peace of mind inherent in a short ingredient list.

But, as it turns out, simplifying how we make and think about dessert does not have to rob it of its decadence. In fact, simplifying dessert recipes can help bring the simple pleasure of cooking back into our lives. Who doesn't like the idea of having a cookie jar filled with homemade cookies or capping a dinner party with a suitably sumptuous sweet that looks a lot more complicated than it really is? The 500 recipes in this book allow you to do just that, by emphasizing simple, creative ideas that help us fit a little cooking for love into our busy schedules.

In developing these recipes, we tried to stay away from ingredients that aren't readily available in our local supermarkets and corner grocers. You should be able to make these desserts easily and without a lot of fuss—allowing you to spend less time shopping and more time cooking and enjoying your creations. And by keeping away from exotic or hard-to-find ingredients, rest assured that you can make these desserts without spending a lot of time (or money) on specialty ingredients you'll use only once.

The Recipes

By distilling recipes down to one or two distinctive flavors, we can bring a new simplicity to dessert that lets the cook off the hook from complex, demanding recipes without sacrificing the taste and extravagance of a fancy dessert.

There are several principles that we used to help build luscious desserts using only five ingredients.

PRINCIPLE #1: **Clever use of packaged goods.** Cooks have been relying on packaged staples such as cake mix since Betty Crocker and Duncan Hines first picked up a mixing spoon, but that's only the beginning. We headed out to our local supermarkets in search of other packaged basics that can serve as a springboard to inspired cookery. Frozen puff pastry, for example, is a vital basic in many of our desserts, such as the Poached Pear Praline Napoleon. This stuff is the real deal, a product that's so good that it's not really worth the hassle of making from scratch.

Cookies, too, make an excellent base in many pudding and trifle-like dishes such as the Sicilian Trifle Parfait, while prepared pie doughs have progressed by leaps and bounds, from "acceptable if you have to use them," to "almost as good as my great Aunt Marion makes." Meanwhile, prepared mixes such as cappuccino and chai tea provide piquant flavoring to many desserts, such as Chai Tea Ice Cream.

PRINCIPLE #2: **Make the ingredients work harder.** Self-rising flour works well for many cakes, while sweetened condensed milk helps us cut the need for sugar in some recipes.

PRINCIPLE #3: **Think beyond baked goods.** Dessert vistas widen dramatically when you step away from the standard notion of confections such as pies, cookies, and cakes. There are the spoils of the freezer—frosty delights such as sorbets, granitas, and ice creams—as well as other cool confections such as homey puddings and their more elegant cousins, custards and flans.

PRINCIPLE #4: **Make friends with fruit.** Yes, we know. For many people, fruit is as about as desserty as a hearty slice of haggis. We blame this phenomenon on too many traumatic memories of moms trying to bamboozle their kids into believing that an apple was every bit as yummy and acceptable as a chocolate chip cookie. But fruit has taken a bad rap, and truly delicious desserts can be built around peaches, plums, cherries—even apples. Our Poached Peaches with Melba Geleé, for example, is the sort of dessert that might come out of an upscale restaurant, but it's easy to make and certainly has the extravagant taste sensation we associate with dessert.

PRINCIPLE #5: **Nobody complains when the dessert is chocolate.** Good chocolate is an excellent one-ingredient dessert all on its own, but it combines so marvelously with so many other flavors that it's a cinch for a great dessert base.

A Word about Our Recipe Counts

Every recipe in this book has five or fewer ingredients, not counting salt, water, and fat (butter, shortening, and/or oil).

CHAPTER ONE

Pantry Basics

Since desserts are often more of a pleasant option than a real necessity, it's not a real given that you'll be able to count on having a deep pantry full of dessert esoterica. Most people won't be so annoyingly efficient as to have homemade, prebaked pie crusts in their freezer (Yes, Mom, we're looking at you), but on the other hand, there are a few things that it's helpful to keep in your pantry if you plan on serving the sweet course with any regularity.

Here are the things we like to keep on hand.

> All-purpose flour
> Self-rising flour
> Granulated sugar
> Confectioners' sugar
> Brown sugar (light and dark)
> Baking powder
> Baking soda
> Chocolate (semisweet and unsweetened; be extravagant.
>   Get the best-quality you can afford.)

Vanilla extract

Vanilla sugar (See "Making Vanilla Sugar" below.)

Frozen puff pastry dough

Purchased or homemade frozen pie crusts

Unsalted butter

Making Vanilla Sugar

Place 8 cups of granulated sugar in an airtight jar with 2 split vanilla beans. Seal for 2 weeks. The sugar will be permeated with the vanilla flavor. Keeps indefinitely.

Or, if you need the vanilla sugar right away, substitute regular sugar mixed with 1 teaspoon vanilla extract for each cup of sugar needed.

Making Cinnamon Sugar

Although you can buy cinnamon sugar, it's easy to make yourself. Simply substitute 1 teaspoon cinnamon mixed with 1 cup sugar for each cup of sugar needed.

About Self-Rising Flour

Self-rising flour is simply flour with baking powder and a little salt already mixed in. It can be found in any supermarket, but you can also make it yourself. Here's how.

    4 cups all-purpose flour

    2 tablespoons baking powder

    2 teaspoons salt

Sift all ingredients together and store in a tightly sealed container.

Greasing Pans

Many of these recipes call for the pan to be greased. We usually use either shortening or nonstick cooking spray.

Specialty Ingredients

Some recipes call for specialty items. Although there are a couple of ingredients in this book that you will need to find in gourmet stores or perhaps online, the vast majority are available at larger supermarkets in our areas. Many of the ingredients we specify are convenience foods, often intended by their manufacturers for other uses. For example, we use chai latte mix not to make a beverage, but as a flavor base for tarts, mousses, and torte fillings. We have sought out quality products that provide convenience to our readers when shopping and cooking. We find that it is often easier, and less expensive, to use a product that already contains a variety of ingredients than shopping for the individual components. Pumpkin pie spice mix is one such example.

Here's a list of some of the specialty ingredients we call for in various recipes, along with a notation if we did not find it readily available in supermarkets. Some of the things on this list, such as eggnog, may be widely available seasonally, but hard to find the remainder of the year.

Andes mints

Amoretti cookies (Usually these are found in gourmet stores.)

Apple pie spice

Blood orange juice (This is available in some supermarkets or at gourmet stores.)

Café Vienna coffee mix (This is made by General Mills.)

Canned piña colada mix

Canned plums in syrup

Caramel sauce

Chocolate condensed milk (You'll find this in some supermarkets.)

Chocolate cookie pie crust (Oreo brand is the most common.)

Chocolate sauce

Coffee syrup (Usually this is found near the chocolate syrup in the supermarket.)

Cookie ladyfingers

Crème fraîche

Crepes

Dried lavender (It's available in health food stores.)

Egg nog

Fig tart and bar filling

Frozen phyllo dough

Fudge sauce

Green tea

Key lime juice

Mascarpone cheese

Nabisco Famous Chocolate Wafers

Nutella (This is a chocolate-hazelnut spread found near the peanut butter in the supermarket.)

Plum wine (Depending on your state laws, this will be sold in the supermarket or in liquor stores.)

Powdered cappuccino mix

Prepared custartd (Check the pudding section of your local super market.)

Powdered chai latte mix

Powdered daiquiri mix

Pumpkin pie spice

Quinces (These can be found in grocery stores in season.)

Rolled wheat (It's usually available in health food stores.)

Spiced and sweetened pumpkin pie filling (Libby's brand is the most common.)

Sponge or cake ladyfingers

Sweetened chestnut puree (Check gourmet stores or seasonally in grocery stores.)

Sweetened shredded coconut

Basic Equipment

Dessert making tends to rely on some more specialty equipment than basic day-to-day cooking, but some of these items also come in handy in other situations. (The little individual ramekins that many flan and custard recipes call for are very helpful for holding small helpings of items such as applesauce or cottage cheese, for example.) We generally rely on the following items to build our desserts.

Stand mixer

Hand mixer

One set dry goods measuring cups

One set measuring spoons

Liquid measuring cups (We like a metered 2-cup measure and the same in the 4-cup amount.)

Rubber spatulas

Layer cake pans (You'll need to have two, either 9 inch or 10 inch.)

Pie pans (Two or three are plenty.)

Springform pan (If you can, buy a set of 4 inch, 8 inch, 9 inch, 10 inch, and 12 inch.)

Cookie or baking sheets (Three or four is a good number to own. Size 9 x 13-inch baking sheets are standard.)

Pastry bag

Soufflé dish (It's good to have a 1 quart and 2 quart.)

Small ramekins (6 or 8 ounce—A set of eight is good to have.)

9 x 13-inch pan (This is for sheet cakes and bars.)

Wire whisk

Rolling pin

Set of stainless steel mixing bowls

Cooling racks

Ice cream maker

9 x 9 inch square baking pan (Choose either metal or pyrex.)

CHAPTER TWO

Techniques and Terms

In a perfect world, we'd all have fond memories of a grandmotherly type with a bun and a ruffled apron who taught us all the little tricks that make up good cookery. The reality is that many of us got nothing in the way of culinary instruction during our formative years. With that in mind, here are some tips and techniques that will help you turn out desserts to die for.

Creaming

The beginning step in many cake, brownie, and quick bread recipes is creaming fat and sugar together. The idea is to create a smooth, light, and fluffy mixture of whatever fat you are utilizing (typically butter or shortening) and sugar. This step provides several key benefits to a good batter.

- It provides a uniform distribution of the sugar in the batter.
- It adds air, and thus leavening, to the batter.
- It begins the emulsion process by which the fat and liquids in the batter are combined into a smooth mixture.
- It prevents the development of gluten when the flour and liquids are added, thus making the cake tender.

To cream, the fat should be at room temperature, especially if it is butter. Use the paddle attachment of a stand mixer (or a hand mixer) and beat the fat until creamy and smooth. Add the sugar and cream until light and fluffy—6 to 8 minutes. You may begin at high speed, but most of the mixing should be done on medium for maximum air incorporation.

After creaming the fat and sugar, typically eggs are added, one at a time, beating to fully absorb each into the batter before adding the next. Liquids and sifted dry ingredients are then added alternatively in batches.

Folding

Folding describes the introduction of a light, airy, whipped product into a more dense mixture. Typical uses for folding include adding whipped cream or whipped egg whites to cake batters and mousses. The idea is to combine the two products into one completely homogenous mixture while still keeping as much of the air (and thus the lightening and leavening properties) in the whipped product as possible.

To fold, you will need a rubber spatula. Add about one-quarter of the whipped product to the heavier batter and stir it in with a vigorous motion. You are in essence "sacrificing" the air in this to lighten the batter. Now add the remaining whipped product to the bowl and combine by gently scraping along the bottom of the bowl with the rubber spatula toward you, up and over. Turn the bowl a quarter turn with each stroke. Continue until the mixture is thoroughly combined. This motion turns the mixtures over on top of each other and allows them to combine in a gentle way.

Measuring Dry Ingredients

The best way to measure dry ingredients, such as flour, is to dip the measuring cup into the bin and level the top with the back of a knife. It is not good to tamp down the dry ingredient into the cup.

Making Soufflés

It is easy to make a great soufflé.

To prepare the baking dishes, butter the insides of the dishes on the bottom and sides with soft butter. Add some sugar and rotate the dish until the bottom and sides are coated in sugar. Use a paper towel to clean the rim of the dish. You may choose to attach a parchment paper collar to the dish to allow the soufflé to rise higher than the dish with straight sides.

See the information on folding for adding the whipped egg whites to the custard base.

After filling the soufflé dishes, drop them gently on the counter or tap the bottoms with a knife to release any trapped air pockets.

Blind Baking

The idea behind blind baking a tart shell is to bake the shell, either partially or fully, prior to filling it, in order to keep the bottom of the shell nice and flat. If you were to just bake an empty shell, the bottom would puff up. This method is used when the filling either is not cooked in the tart shell at all, or when the filling needs less cooking time than the tart shell.

After you have made the tart shell and frozen it solid, line the inside of the tart shell, bottom and sides, with foil. Fill the center with 2 to 3 cups (for a large tart) of dried beans, uncooked rice, or metal pellets (pie weights), which are sold in cooking stores expressly for this purpose. Bake to the desired degree of doneness, then remove the foil, with the weights still in it. You can save the whole setup for the next tart.

To partially bake a shell, preheat the oven to 375°F (190°C, gas mark 5). Put the pie weights in the shell to keep the dough from bubbling and bake for 20 minutes. Let cool.

To fully bake a shell, preheat the oven to 375°F (190°C, gas mark 5). Put the pie weights in the shell to keep the dough from bubbling and bake for 20 minutes. Then remove the weights from the shell and bake the empty shell for an additional 10 minutes, until the shell is a pale golden brown. Let cool.

Crimping Pie Dough

Crimping pie dough allows a nice, high edge to keep the filling in the pie and in a two-crust pie seals the top and bottom crusts together. There are tools to do this and many styles of crimping. The basic technique is to pinch the dough gently between thumb and forefinger to make a scalloped edge, turning the pie dish as you go. Don't be hung up on perfection; with a little practice you will have a beautiful pie.

CHAPTER THREE

Cakes

Why bake a cake from scratch when the supermarket is filled with pretty good mixes? Because you're missing so much if you just stick to the boxes. Cake mixes are useful, but they're just not as good as a homemade cake. (Full disclosure: We do use cake mixes as ingredients in several recipes in this book.) The thing is that it is pretty darn easy to make most cakes. There are a couple of simple techniques to master, and you are on your way.

Cakes run the gamut, from the homey delight of a thickly frosted layer cake to the desserty elegance of Warm Fallen Chocolate Soufflé Cake in a Phyllo Nest (page 30). In this chapter, you can choose from basic cakes such as loaf cakes or fancier cakes such as genoise, a light, moist cake that is actually quite easy to make. Then there are the tortes, which almost all have a high impress-the-guests factor.

All in all, no matter what recipe you choose, we're sure the result will, er, take the cake.

Apple Spice Cake

1 cup (255 g) **applesauce**

1 package (20 ounces, or 560 g) **yellow cake mix**

3 teaspoons **apple pie spice**

2 **eggs**, lightly beaten

1/2 cup (120 ml) vegetable oil

1 cup (235 ml) water

1/2 cup (70 g) **raisins**

Preheat the oven to 350°F (180°C, gas mark 4). Grease a 9 x 13-inch baking pan.

Combine all ingredients in a mixing bowl and beat, using the paddle attachment of a stand mixer, on medium speed for 2 minutes. Pour the batter into the prepared pan.

Bake for 30 to 35 minutes, until a tester inserted into the center of the cake comes out clean. Cool in the pan.

YIELD: Serves 12 to 15

ADD IT! Sprinkle cinnamon sugar over the top of the cake just after it comes out of the oven.

Banana-Sour Cream Loaf

This is a classic method of using up the bananas that have gone around the bend in terms of ripeness.

1 1/2 cups (300 g) **sugar**

3/4 cup (150 g) shortening

3 **eggs**

1 cup (225 g) mashed **banana** (about 2 bananas)

1 cup (230 g) **sour cream**

2 cups (250 g) **self-rising flour**

Preheat the oven to 350°F (180°C, gas mark 4). Grease two 5 x 9-inch loaf pans.

Combine the sugar and shortening in a mixing bowl and beat until fluffy—4 to 5 minutes. Add the eggs, one at a time, beating after each addition until well combined. Stir in the banana and sour cream, then mix in the flour until combined. Pour the batter into the prepared pan.

Bake for 45 to 50 minutes, until a tester inserted into the center of the cake comes out clean. Turn the cake out onto a rack to cool completely.

YIELD: Serves 10 to 12

Lemon-Yogurt Cake

The more naturally flavored the yogurt you use, the better this cake will turn out. This makes a sturdy and neat loaf that travels well.

> 1 cup (225 g) lemon **yogurt**
> 2 **eggs**
> 1 cup (200 g) **sugar**
> 2 teaspoons **baking soda**
> 2 cups (250 g) **all-purpose flour**
> 1/2 teaspoon salt

Preheat the oven to 350°F (180°C, gas mark 4). Grease and flour a 10-inch bundt pan or tube pan.

In a large mixing bowl, combine the yogurt, eggs, and sugar, beating until smooth.

Sift together the baking soda, flour, and salt and mix into the yogurt mixture until just thoroughly combined. Pour the batter into the prepared pan.

Bake for 40 to 45 minutes, until a tester inserted into the center of the cake comes out clean. Turn the cake out onto a rack to cool completely.

YIELD: Serves 12 to 14

Summer Plum Upside-Down Cake

Wait until you can get plums in season and bursting with ripeness.

     3 pounds (1.5 kg) **plums** (about 8 plums), halved and pitted

     1 cup (2 sticks, or 225 g) butter

     2 cups (400 g) **sugar**

     2 **eggs**

     2 cups (250 g) **self-rising flour**

     1/2 teaspoon salt

     1 cup (235 ml) **milk**

Preheat the oven to 350°F (180°C, gas mark 4).

In a mixing bowl, cut together 1/2 cup (1 stick, or 112 g) of the butter with 1 cup (200 g) of the sugar. Sprinkle over the bottom of a 9-inch round cake pan. Top this mixture with the plums, cut sides up.

In a large mixing bowl, using a mixer on medium speed, cream the remaining butter and sugar for 5 minutes, until fluffy. Add the eggs, one at a time, beating well after each addition.

In a separate bowl, sift together the flour and salt and add this mixture alternately with the milk, beating to combine after each addition. Spoon the batter on top of the plums and smooth the top.

Bake for 30 to 35 minutes, until a tester inserted into the center of the cake comes out clean. Allow to cool just for a minute or 2 and then turn the cake out onto a serving plate.

YIELD: Serves 8

Piña Colada Upside-Down Cake

If you dream of fruity tropical drinks and a lovely sunset walk, try this cake!

1 can (13 ounces, or 370 g) **pineapple rings**
Water
1 cup (225 g) packed **light brown sugar**
1/2 cup (1 stick, or 112 g) butter
1 package (6 ounces, or 170 g) **coconut pudding mix**
1 package (20 ounces, or 560 g) **white cake mix**
1/4 cup (60 ml) vegetable oil
2 **eggs**

Preheat the oven to 350°F (180°C, gas mark 4). Lightly grease a 9-inch spring-form pan and line the bottom with parchment paper.

Drain the pineapple, reserving the juice. Add enough water to the pineapple juice to make 1 1/2 cups (355 ml) total liquid and reserve.

In a mixing bowl, cut together the sugar and the butter. Spread this mixture evenly over the bottom of the pan. Arrange the pineapple rings over the sugar mixture.

In the bowl of a stand mixer, combine the pudding mix and cake mix. Add the oil and eggs. Add the reserved pineapple juice. Mix together using the paddle attachment of a stand mixer until thoroughly combined—about 3 minutes. Pour the cake batter over the pineapple.

Bake for 35 to 40 minutes, until a tester inserted into the center of the cake comes out clean. Allow to cool in the pan for 15 to 20 minutes, then remove the side of the pan. Flip the cake onto a serving plate and remove the bottom of the pan and the parchment paper, rearranging the pineapple if need be.

YIELD: Serves 10 to 12

Carrot Cake Loaf

This is an easy-to-make loaf that you can dress up with some easy Cream Cheese Frosting (page 496).

    1 cup (110 g) shredded **carrot**

    2 cups (250 g) **self-rising flour**

    1 1/2 cups (300 g) **sugar**

    1 cup (235 ml) **milk**

    1/2 cup (120 ml) vegetable oil

    2 teaspoons **apple pie spice**

Preheat the oven to 350°F (180°C, gas mark 4). Grease a 9 x 5-inch loaf pan.

Combine all ingredients in a mixing bowl and beat, using the paddle attachment of a stand mixer, on medium speed for 2 minutes. Pour the batter into the prepared pan.

Bake for 50 to 55 minutes, until a tester inserted into the center of the cake comes out clean. Turn the cake out onto a rack to cool completely.

YIELD: Serves 10 to 12

Chocolate Hidden Delight Cake

2 packages (8 ounces, or 225 g, each) strawberry **cream cheese**

1/2 cup (100 g) **vanilla sugar** (See "Making Vanilla Sugar" on page 12.)

4 **eggs**

1 package (20 ounces, or 560 g) **devil's food cake mix**

1/2 cup (120 ml) vegetable oil

1/2 cup (120 ml) water

1 cup (175 g) **semisweet chocolate chips**

Preheat the oven to 350°F (180°C, gas mark 4). Grease and flour a 12-inch bundt or tube pan.

Combine the cream cheese and sugar in a mixing bowl. Beat until completely smooth—7 to 8 minutes. Add 2 of the eggs, one at a time, beating well after each addition. Set aside.

In another mixing bowl, combine the cake mix, the remaining 2 eggs and the oil and water. Mix for 4 to 5 minutes, until the batter is smooth. Fold in the chocolate chips. Pour the batter into the prepared pan. Spoon or pour the cream cheese mixture in a ring on top of the cake batter.

Bake for 45 to 50 minutes, until a tester inserted in the center of the cake comes out clean. Cool in the pan for 15 minutes, then turn the cake out onto a rack to cool completely.

YIELD: Serves 12 to 15

Chocolate-Yogurt Pound Cake

This cake is moist, rich, and delicious.

> 8 ounces (225 g) semisweet **chocolate**, cut into small chunks
>
> 1/2 cup (1 stick, or 112 g) butter
>
> 1 1/2 cups (300 g) **sugar**
>
> 3 **eggs**
>
> 1 cup (8 ounces, or 245 g) **vanilla yogurt**
>
> 2 cups (250 g) **self-rising flour**
>
> 1/2 teaspoon salt
>
> 1/2 cup (120 ml) water

Preheat the oven to 350°F (180°C, gas mark 4). Grease and flour a 10-inch tube pan.

Put the chocolate in a stainless steel mixing bowl and place the bowl over a pan of simmering water. Stir every few minutes until the chocolate is melted and smooth. Set aside.

In a large mixing bowl, using a mixer on medium speed, cream together the butter and sugar until light and fluffy—5 to 6 minutes. Add the eggs, one at a time, mixing well after each addition. Add the yogurt and mix well. Add the melted chocolate and mix well.

In a separate bowl, combine the flour and salt. Add the flour mixture to the butter mixture and mix to combine, then add the water and mix until the batter is smooth. Pour the batter into the prepared pan.

Bake for 55 to 60 minutes, until a tester inserted into the center of the cake comes out clean. Turn the cake out onto a rack to cool completely.

YIELD: Serves 12 to 14

German Chocolate One-Pan Cake

This cake was pounced upon with great glee by many neighbors at one of our tasting parties. Fisticuffs were narrowly averted.

1 package (20 ounces, or 560 g) **German chocolate cake mix**

1/2 cup (120 ml) vegetable oil

1 cup (235 ml) water

2 cups (250 g) chopped **walnuts**

2 cups (150 g) sweetened **shredded coconut**

1/2 cup (1 stick, or 112 g) butter

8 ounces (115 g) **cream cheese**

1 pound (about 2 1/2 cups, or 300 g) **confectioners' sugar**

Preheat the oven to 350°F (180°C, gas mark 4). Grease a 9 x 13-inch baking pan.

In a large mixing bowl, combine the cake mix, oil, and water until thoroughly combined.

In a separate bowl, combine the walnuts and coconut. Sprinkle them in the bottom of the prepared pan. Pour the cake batter over the nuts.

In a saucepan, melt the butter over low heat. Place the melted butter in a mixing bowl. Add the cream cheese and sugar and mix thoroughly—4 to 5 minutes. Put this mixture into a piping bag and pipe in lines on top of the cake batter. Draw a knife through the cream cheese mixture to create a marbling effect.

Bake for 50 to 55 minutes, until a tester inserted into the center of the cake comes out clean. Cool completely in the pan and cut into squares.

YIELD: Serves 15

Warm Fallen Chocolate Soufflé Cake in a Phyllo Nest

This one is spectacular to serve at a dinner party—the awe and mystique factor is huge. You don't need to disclose just how easy it is to make.

1/2 cup (1 stick, or 112 g) butter

4 sheets frozen **phyllo dough** (14 x 18 inch, or 35 x 45 cm), thawed

6 ounces (170 g) **semisweet chocolate**, cut into small chunks

6 **eggs**

1 1/2 cups (300 g) **sugar**

1/2 cup (30 g) **all-purpose flour**

Prepare six 6- to 8-ounce ramekins by spraying them each with nonstick cooking spray and tucking in a strip of parchment paper (1/2 x 8 inch, or 1 x 20 cm) so that the ends hang out opposite sides.

In a saucepan, melt the butter over low heat. Lay a sheet of phyllo dough out on a flat surface and brush with the melted butter. Cover with another sheet of phyllo and repeat until all phyllo is used up, finishing with butter. Cut the phyllo into six 5 x 5-inch squares (13 x 13 cm). There will be scraps left over. Tuck each square into a prepared ramekin, butter side down, so that the excess phyllo sticks up over the edges of the ramekins in a kind of free-form basket shape. Set aside.

Preheat the oven to 375°F (190°C, or gas mark 5).

Melt the chocolate in a stainless steel bowl over simmering water until smooth. Set aside.

Separate the eggs and put the yolks in a mixing bowl fitted with the whisk attachment. Reserve the whites. Add 1 cup (200 g) of the sugar to the yolks and whip on high speed until ribboned, light colored, and doubled in volume— about 5 minutes. Fold in the flour, then the melted chocolate.

In another mixing bowl, whip the egg whites until they begin to froth, then add the remaining sugar in three additions as you whip the whites to firm peak. Fold the whites into the chocolate mixture thoroughly, but gently.

Spoon the batter into the phyllo nests, tapping the bottom of each ramekin on the counter to release any large air bubbles. Place the ramekins on a baking sheet.

Bake for 15 to 20 minutes, until the phyllo is golden brown and the cake is risen and set in the middle. Remove from the oven and allow to cool slightly. The cakes will fall.

To serve, remove the nests from the ramekins by lifting them out by the parchment strips. These can be made in advance and reheated in the oven or microwave prior to serving. They need to be warm to remove from the ramekins, as the butter on the phyllo must be melted or it will stick.

YIELD: Serves 6

ADD IT! A small spoonful of crushed strawberries over each basket would be lovely.

Mocha Refrigerator Cake

This is a riff off one of our all-time favorite recipes, the zebra cake. (Personal consumption record: Five slices in one sitting. We were young and foolish.)

- 3 cups (705 ml) **heavy cream**
- 1/4 cup (10 g) **instant coffee** powder or granules
- 1 cup (120 g) **confectioners' sugar**
- 2 packages (9 ounces, or 225 g, each) **Nabisco Famous Chocolate Wafer cookies**

Combine the cream, coffee powder, and sugar in a mixing bowl and whip with a mixer until stiff peaks form. With a wide spreading knife, spread a dollop of whipped cream on a wafer and top it with another cookie. Keep alternating whipped cream and cookies until you've created a stack of about five or six cookies. Then turn the stack on its side on a long plate. Repeat the process with another stack and add to the first. Keep doing with the entire first box of cookies; you should have a log about 14 to 18 inches (35 to 50 cm) long. Repeat with the second box of cookies and place the cookie stacks next to each other. Frost the cake with the remainder of the whipped cream and cover with plastic wrap. (We generally porcupine the cake with a few toothpicks to keep the wrap from sticking to the whipped cream.) Refrigerate overnight.

To serve, slice the cake at a 45-degree angle so that the cake comes out striped like a zebra.

YIELD: Serves 10 to 12

ADD IT! Top the cake with fresh raspberries or serve with fresh sliced strawberries. Heaven.

Amaretto Cake

Amaretto, an almond-flavored liqueur originally from Italy, imparts a nutty kick to this recipe. There are many knockoffs of the original liqueur available, and all will work just fine.

> 1 cup (90 g) sliced **almonds**
> 1 package (20 ounces, or 560 g) **yellow cake mix**
> 1 package (6 ounces, or 170 g) **vanilla pudding mix**
> 4 **eggs**
> 1 cup (235 ml) **amaretto liqueur**
> 1/2 cup (120 ml) vegetable oil
> 3/4 cup (175 ml) water
> 1/4 cup (1/2 stick, or 55 g) butter

Preheat the oven to 325°F (170°C, gas mark 3). Grease a 12-inch bundt pan.

Sprinkle the almonds around the bottom of the pan.

In a large mixing bowl, combine the cake mix and pudding mix.

In another bowl, whisk the eggs lightly and add 1/2 cup (120 ml) of the liqueur, the oil, and 1/2 cup of the water. Stir into the dry ingredients and mix for 3 to 4 minutes. Pour into the prepared pan.

Bake for 50 to 55 minutes, until a tester inserted into the center of the cake comes out clean. Invert the cake out of the pan onto a serving platter and allow to cool completely.

Combine the remaining 1/2 cup (120 ml) liqueur and the remaining 1/4 cup (60 ml) water and butter in a small saucepan. Bring to a boil and cook for 3 to 4 minutes at a gentle boil. Using a kebab skewer or long toothpick, poke 20 or so holes down through the cake, then spoon the hot liquid evenly over the top of the cake, allowing it to absorb in.

YIELD: Serves 12 to 15

Gingerbread

Here's a homey and comforting dessert that's great plain or a la mode.

$1/2$ cup (1 stick, or 112 g) butter

$1/2$ cup (100 g) **sugar**

1 **egg**

1 cup (340 g) **molasses**

2 $1/4$ cups (280 g) **self-rising flour**, sifted or stirred before measured

$1/2$ teaspoon salt

2 teaspoons **apple pie spice**

1 cup (235 ml) hot water

Preheat the oven to 350°F (180°C, gas mark 4). Grease and flour a 9-inch square baking pan.

Using a mixer on medium speed, cream the butter and sugar together until light; whisk the egg lightly and add; beat well. Stir the molasses into the creamed mixture.

In a separate bowl, sift together the flour, salt, and apple pie spice. Add gradually to the batter, stirring until just thoroughly blended.

Add the hot water gradually, stirring until the mixture is smooth. Pour into the prepared pan.

Bake for 30 to 35 minutes. Allow to cool for at least 10 minutes in the pan and cut into squares. Serve warm or at room temperature.

YIELD: Serves 10 to 12

Sour Cream Pound Cake

This cake has a tender mouthfeel and mild taste that makes it perfect with afternoon coffee.

> 1 cup (2 sticks, or 225 g) butter
>
> 1 1/2 cups (300 g) **sugar**
>
> 4 **eggs**
>
> 2 teaspoons **vanilla extract**
>
> 2 cups (250 g) **self-rising flour**
>
> 1/2 teaspoon salt
>
> 1/2 cup (120 ml) water
>
> 1 cup (230 g) **sour cream**

Preheat the oven to 350°F (180°C, gas mark 4). Grease and flour two 9 x 5-inch loaf pans.

Combine the butter and the sugar in a mixing bowl. Beat on high speed, using the paddle attachment of a stand mixer if you have one, until the mixture is fluffy—about 5 minutes. Add the eggs one at a time, beating well after each addition. Add the vanilla and beat until combined.

In another bowl, combine the flour and salt. Add half of the flour mixture to the butter mixture, then add the water, then the rest of the flour mixture, beating on low speed after each addition until just combined. Add the sour cream and beat to combine. After all the ingredients are added, continue beating on medium speed for 2 minutes. Spread the batter evenly in the prepared pan.

Bake for 50 to 55 minutes, until a tester inserted in the center of the cake comes out clean. Allow to cool in the pans for 5 minutes, then turn the cake out onto a rack to cool completely.

YIELD: Serves 12 to 16

ADD IT! Sprinkle a dusting of confectioners' sugar on top.

Buttermilk Crumb Cake

This is a really nice snacking cake, and it's also great with morning coffee or brunch.

2 1/2 cups (310 g) **all-purpose flour**

3/4 cup (1 1/2 sticks, or 170 g) butter, softened

1 cup (200 g) **cinnamon sugar** (See "Making Cinnamon Sugar" on page 12.)

1/2 teaspoon salt

1 **egg**, beaten slightly

1 cup (235 ml) **buttermilk**

1 teaspoon **baking soda**

Preheat the oven to 350°F (180°C, gas mark 4). Grease a 9-inch square baking pan.

Combine the flour, butter, sugar, and salt in a mixing bowl. Using a pastry cutter or your fingers, cut the butter into the dry ingredients until it resembles cornmeal in texture. Reserve 1 cup of this mixture and add the egg, buttermilk, and baking soda to the rest. Stir to combine thoroughly and pour into the prepared pan. Smooth out the top and sprinkle the reserved flour mixture over the top of the batter.

Bake for 35 to 40 minutes, until a tester inserted into the center of the cake comes out clean.

YIELD: Serves 9 to 12

ADD IT! Stir in 1 teaspoon nutmeg with the flour.

Cream Cheese Pound Cake

This is a classic pound cake; it's great with ice cream, fresh fruit, you name it.

1/2 cup (1 stick, or 112 g) butter

8 ounces (225 g) **cream cheese**

1 1/2 cups (300 g) **sugar**

4 **eggs**

2 teaspoons **vanilla extract**

2 cups (250 g) **self-rising flour**

1/2 cup (120 ml) water

Preheat the oven to 350°F (180°C, gas mark 4). Grease and flour two 9 x 5-inch loaf pans.

Combine the butter, cream cheese, and sugar in a mixing bowl. Using the paddle attachment of a stand mixer, beat on high speed until fluffy—about 5 minutes. Add the eggs, one at a time, beating well after each addition. Add the vanilla and beat until combined. Add half of the flour, then the water, then the rest of the flour, beating on low speed after each addition until just combined. After all the ingredients are added, continue beating on medium speed for 2 minutes. Spread the batter evenly in the prepared pans.

Bake for 50 to 55 minutes, until a tester inserted in the center of the cake comes out clean. Cool in the pan for 5 to 10 minutes, then turn the cakes out onto a rack to cool completely.

YIELD: Serves 12 to 16 (Makes two loaves.)

Almond Cake

This cake is a flavorful step away from the everyday trifecta of chocolate/vanilla/spice layer-cake choices.

> 1 1/2 cups (300 g) **sugar**
>
> 1 cup (200 g) shortening
>
> 3 **eggs**
>
> 3 teaspoons **almond extract**
>
> 1 1/2 cups (355 ml) **milk**
>
> 2 cups (250 g) **self-rising flour**
>
> 1/2 teaspoon salt

Preheat the oven to 350°F (180°C, gas mark 4). Grease and flour a 9 x 13-inch pan or two 9-inch round cake pans.

Using the paddle attachment of a stand mixer, cream together the sugar and shortening for 3 to 4 minutes, until light and fluffy. Add the eggs, one at a time, beating well after each addition.

In a separate bowl, mix together the almond extract and milk.

In a separate bowl, mix together the flour and salt. Alternate adding the almond extract mixture and the flour mixture to the butter mixture, each in thirds, beating just to mix after each addition. After all the ingredients are added, beat on medium speed for 5 minutes. Spread the batter into the pan(s).

Bake for 25 to 30 minutes, until a tester inserted into the center of the cake comes out clean. Cool the cakes in the pans for 10 minutes, then turn them out onto wire racks to cool completely.

YIELD: Serves 10 to 12

ADD IT! Sprinkle sugared sliced almonds over the top of the cake for garnish.

Almond Genoise

A genoise cake sounds more intimidating than it really is. It's named after its place of origin, Genoa, Italy, and it is a very versatile cake that's used as a base for many more elaborate desserts, such as petits fours. The basic cake is made up of flour, sugar, and eggs, but it adapts beautifully to many flavor adaptations, such as this one featuring almonds.

6 **eggs**, separated

1 1/4 cups (250 g) **sugar**

2 teaspoons **vanilla extract**

2 cups (190 g) finely ground blanched **almonds**

1/2 cup (60 g) **all-purpose flour**

1/2 teaspoon salt

Preheat the oven to 350°F (180°C, gas mark 4). Coat the inside of a 10-inch springform pan with nonstick cooking spray and cover the bottom of the pan with a round of parchment paper.

Put the egg yolks and 1 cup (200 g) of the sugar in the stand mixer bowl, and using the whisk attachment, mix on high speed until ribboned and light yellow. Add the vanilla and mix until incorporated into the yolk mixture. Fold in the almonds.

In a separate bowl, sift together the flour and salt and fold into the yolk mixture until just combined.

In another bowl, whip the egg whites with the remaining 1/4 cup (50 g) sugar to firm peaks. Fold the whites into the yolk mixture. Spread into the prepared pan.

Bake for 35 to 40 minutes, until a tester inserted into the center of the cake comes out clean. Cool completely in the pan, then remove the side of the pan and invert onto a rack. Remove the bottom of the pan and the parchment paper. Turn the cake right side up onto a serving plate.

YIELD: Serves 8 to 10

🍰 Hazelnut Genoise

Here the classic genoise cake gets a flavor twist from hazelnuts.

>   6 **eggs**, separated
>   1 1/4 cups (250 g) **sugar**
>   1 **orange**
>   2 cups (150 g) finely ground blanched **hazelnuts**
>   1/2 cup (60 g) **all-purpose flour**
>   1/2 teaspoon salt

Preheat the oven to 350°F (180°C, gas mark 4). Coat the inside of a 10-inch springform pan with nonstick cooking spray and cover the bottom of the pan with a round of parchment paper.

Put the egg yolks and 1 cup (200 g) of the sugar in the mixing bowl, and using the whisk attachment, mix on high speed until ribboned and light yellow. Zest the orange and add the finely minced zest. Squeeze the orange and add the juice, mixing well. Fold in the hazelnuts.

In a separate bowl, sift together the flour and salt and fold into the yolk mixture until just combined.

In another bowl whip the egg whites with the remaining 1/4 cup (50 g) sugar to firm peaks. Fold the whites into the yolk mixture. Spread into the prepared pan.

Bake for 35 to 40 minutes, until a tester inserted into the center of the cake comes out clean. Cool completely in the pan, then remove the side of the pan and invert onto a rack. Remove the bottom of the pan and the parchment paper. Turn right side up onto a serving plate.

YIELD: Serves 8 to 10

Coconut Layer Cake

This is a homey, June-Cleaver-type confection with the added benefit of being delicious!

1 package (20 ounces, or 560 g) **white cake mix**

4 **eggs**

Vegetable oil as directed in cake mix instructions

Water as directed in cake mix instructions

1/2 cup (1 stick, or 112 g) butter

2 pounds (about 5 cups, or 600 g) **confectioners' sugar**

1 teaspoon **vanilla extract**

2 cups (150 g) **sweetened shredded coconut**

Preheat the oven to 350°F (180°C, gas mark 4). Grease and flour two 9-inch round cake pans.

Prepare the cake mix according to the package directions, using 2 of the eggs as well as whatever oil and water are called for. Divide the batter between the cake pans.

Bake for 30 to 35 minutes, until a tester inserted into the center of the cakes comes out clean. Cool in the pans for 15 minutes, then turn the cakes out onto racks to cool completely.

Separate the remaining 2 eggs, discarding the yolks and putting the whites in a large mixing bowl. Add the butter, sugar, and vanilla and whip for 5 to 8 minutes, until fluffy and smooth. Stir in the coconut.

Put one cake layer on a serving platter. Spread some of the coconut frosting on top of the cake and top with the other cake layer. Frost the top and sides of the cake with the remaining frosting.

YIELD: Serves 12

ADD IT! Garnish with a handful of toasted coconut flakes.

Banana Cream Cake

2 envelopes ($1/4$ ounce, or 7.5 g, each) **unflavored gelatin**

$1/2$ cup (120 ml) water

6 **eggs**

2 cups (450 g) mashed **banana** (about 4 bananas)

1 container (16 ounces, or 455 g) **nondairy topping**

1 package (20 ounces, or 560 g) **yellow cake mix**

Vegetable oil as directed in cake mix instructions

Water as directed in cake mix instructions

Spray a 9-inch springform pan with nonstick cooking spray and line the bottom and sides with parchment paper.

Sprinkle the gelatin over the water in a small saucepan. Allow the gelatin to soften for 5 minutes, then heat over low heat, stirring, until the gelatin is dissolved, 3 to 4 minutes.

Put 4 of the eggs into a stainless steel mixing bowl and whisk. Add the gelatin mixture and place the bowl over a pan of simmering water, whisking constantly, until the mixture is light colored, doubled in volume, and you can see the bottom of the bowl as you whisk. Remove from the heat and stir in the banana. Allow to cool for 10 minutes, then fold in half the nondairy topping. Spoon the mixture into the prepared springform pan and refrigerate for at least 6 hours, preferably overnight.

Preheat the oven to 350°F (180°C, gas mark 4). Grease and flour two 9-inch round cake pans.

In a mixing bowl, prepare the cake mix, using the remaining 2 eggs and the oil and water according to package directions. Divide the cake batter between the prepared pans.

Bake for 25 to 30 minutes, until a tester inserted into the center of the cake comes out clean. Allow the cakes to cool in the pans for 15 to 20 minutes, then turn the cakes out onto a rack to cool completely.

Place one cake layer on a serving platter. Remove the side of the springform pan and the parchment paper surrounding the banana mousse and invert the mousse on top of the cake. Remove the bottom of the springform pan and the parchment paper. Carefully top with the remaining cake layer. Frost the top of the cake with the remaining nondairy topping.

YIELD: Serves 10 to 12

ADD IT! Garnish the top of the cake with sliced bananas and chocolate shavings.

Lemon Genoise

6 **eggs**, separated
1 cup (200 g) **sugar**
3 **lemons**
1 teaspoon **vanilla extract**
1 1/2 cups (180 g) **all-purpose flour**
1/2 teaspoon salt

Preheat the oven to 350°F (180°C, gas mark 4). Coat the inside of a 10-inch springform pan with nonstick cooking spray and cover the bottom of the pan with a round of parchment paper.

Put the egg yolks and sugar in the stand mixer bowl and using the whisk attachment, mix on high speed until the mixture is ribboned and light yellow. Grate the lemon to yield about 1 tablespoon zest and add the zest to the egg yolk mixture. Squeeze the lemons to yield about 1/2 cup (120 ml) juice and add the lemon juice to the egg yolk mixture, mixing well. Mix in the vanilla.

In a separate bowl, sift together the flour and salt and add to the mixing bowl. Mix until well combined.

In another bowl whip the egg whites to firm peaks. Fold the whites into the yolk mixture. Spread into the prepared pan.

Bake for 35 to 40 minutes, until a tester inserted into the center of the cake comes out clean. Cool completely in the pan, then remove the side of the pan and invert onto a rack. Remove the bottom of the pan and the parchment paper. Turn right side up onto a serving plate.

YIELD: Serves 8 to 10

Basic Vanilla Cake

If you don't have vanilla sugar on hand, add 3 teaspoons of vanilla extract to the mix.

1 1/2 cups (300 g) **vanilla sugar** (See "Making Vanilla Sugar" on page 12.)

1 cup (200 g) shortening

3 **eggs**

2 cups (250 g) **self-rising flour**

1/2 teaspoon salt

1 1/2 cups (355 ml) **milk**

Preheat the oven to 350° F (180°C, gas mark 4). Grease and flour a 9 x 13-inch pan or two 9-inch round cake pans.

Using the paddle attachment of a stand mixer, cream together the sugar and shortening for 3 to 4 minutes, until light and fluffy. Add the eggs, one at a time, beating well after each egg.

In a separate bowl, mix together the flour and salt. Add the dry ingredients to the sugar mixture in thirds, alternating with the milk, beating just to mix after each addition. After all the ingredients are added, beat on medium speed for 5 minutes. Spread the batter into the pan(s).

Bake for 30 to 35 minutes, until a tester inserted into the center of the cake comes out clean.

YIELD: Serves 10 to 12

ADD IT! This cake acts as a springboard to many possibilities. You can frost with Chocolate Butter Icing (page 494) or just cover the whole thing with your favorite jam or jelly, heated with a little butter.

Chocolate-Buttermilk Cake

We're suckers for this homey cake, and we like it best with Vanilla Buttercream Frosting (page 495).

1 1/2 cups (300 g) **sugar**

1 cup (200 g) shortening

3 **eggs**

3/4 cup (65 g) **cocoa powder**

2 cups (250 g) **self-rising flour**

1/2 teaspoon salt

1 1/2 cups (355 ml) **buttermilk**

Preheat the oven to 350° F (180°C, gas mark 4). Grease and flour a 9 x 13-inch pan or two 9-inch round cake pans.

Using the paddle attachment of a stand mixer, cream together the sugar and shortening for 3 to 4 minutes, until light and fluffy. Add the eggs, one at a time, beating well after each egg.

In a separate bowl, sift together the cocoa powder, flour, and salt and add in thirds, alternating with the buttermilk, beating just to mix after each addition. After all the ingredients are added, beat on medium speed for 5 minutes. Spread the batter into the pan(s).

Bake for 30 to35 minutes, until a tester inserted into the center of the cake comes out clean.

YIELD: Serves 10 to 12

Chocolate Genoise

This rich, light cake is both versatile and easy to make.

> 6 **eggs**, separated
>
> 1 cup (200 g) **sugar**
>
> 1 teaspoon **vanilla extract**
>
> 6 ounces (170 g) semisweet or **bittersweet chocolate**, melted
>
> 1/2 cup (60 g) **all-purpose flour**
>
> 1/4 teaspoon salt

Preheat the oven to 350°F (180°C, gas mark 4). Coat the inside of a 10-inch springform pan with nonstick cooking spray and cover the bottom of the pan with a round of parchment paper.

Put the egg yolks and the sugar in the stand mixer bowl and using the whisk attachment, mix on high speed until ribboned and light yellow. Add the vanilla and mix it in well. Add the chocolate and mix until fully incorporated into the yolk mixture.

In a separate bowl, sift together the flour and salt and fold into the yolk mixture until just combined.

In another bowl, whip the egg whites to firm peaks. Fold the whites into the yolk mixture. Spread into the prepared pan.

Bake for 35 to 40 minutes, until a tester inserted into the center of the cake comes out clean. Cool completely in the pan, then remove the side of the pan and invert onto a rack. Remove the bottom of the pan and the parchment paper. Turn right side up onto a serving plate.

YIELD: Serves 8 to 10

Chocolate-Chestnut Cake

Try this cake during the holidays, when chestnut products are plentiful. If you can't find chestnut puree, drain a bottle of peeled chestnuts and heat in a pan with 1 cup (235 ml) water and 2/3 cup (130 g) sugar. Heat for 15 to 20 minutes. Then puree the chestnuts and sugar syrup together.

1 package (20 ounces, or 560 g) **German chocolate cake mix**

4 **eggs**

Vegetable oil as directed in cake mix instructions

Water as directed in cake mix instructions

1 package (10 ounces, or 280 g) **sweetened chestnut puree**

2 cups (475 ml) **heavy cream**

8 ounces (225 g) **milk chocolate**

Preheat the oven to 350°F (180°C, gas mark 4). Grease and flour two 9-inch round cake pans.

Prepare the cake mix according to package directions, using 2 of the eggs and water and oil as directed on the package. Divide the batter between the cake pans.

Bake for 25 to 30 minutes, until a tester inserted into the center of the cakes comes out clean. Cool in the pan for 15 minutes, then turn the cakes out onto racks to cool completely.

In a stand mixer bowl, combine the chestnut puree and 1 cup (235 ml) of the cream. Mix on high speed for 8 to 10 minutes, until light and fluffy. Spread half of the mixture on the top of each of the cake layers.

Put the chocolate in a stainless steel mixing bowl and place the bowl over a saucepan of simmering water until the chocolate is melted. Set aside at room temperature.

In another stainless steel mixing bowl, whisk the remaining 2 eggs over the simmering water until light, thickened, and doubled in volume. Stir in the melted chocolate. Set aside to cool for 15 minutes (at room temperature).

Whip the remaining 1 cup (235 ml) cream to stiff peaks and fold into the chocolate. Spread the chocolate mousse on top of the chestnut puree on the cakes. Refrigerate both cakes for at least 2 hours, then carefully stack one on top of the other on a serving platter.

YIELD: Serves 12

ADD IT! You may garnish with additional whipped cream, chocolate shavings, and the delicious candied chestnuts known as *marrons glacés*, if desired.

Chocolate-Raspberry Layer Cake

Chocolate and raspberries are classic flavor buddies, and adding whipped cream for frosting is the pièce de résistance.

1 package (20 ounces, or 560 g) **devil's food cake mix**

2 **eggs**

Vegetable oil as directed in cake mix instructions

Water as directed in cake mix instructions

1 cup (320 g) **raspberry jam**

2 cups (475 ml) **heavy cream**

$1/2$ cup (100 g) **vanilla sugar** (See "Making Vanilla Sugar" on page 12.)

Preheat the oven to 350°F (180°C, gas mark 4). Grease and flour two 9-inch round cake pans.

Prepare the cake mix according to package directions, using the 2 eggs, as well as whatever oil and water is called for. Divide the batter between the cake pans.

Bake for 25 to 30 minutes, until a tester inserted into the center of the cakes comes out clean. Cool in the pan for 15 minutes, then turn the cakes out onto racks to cool completely.

Put one cake layer on a serving platter. Spread the jam on top of the cake and top with the other cake layer.

Combine the cream and sugar in a mixing bowl and whip to stiff peaks. Frost the top and sides of the cake with the whipped cream. Refrigerate until needed.

YIELD: Serves 12

ADD IT! Decorate with fresh raspberries and chocolate shavings.

🥞 Mocha Cake

Chocolate and coffee have packed an unbeatable one-two flavor punch for years, and with good reason—the coffee cuts the richness of the chocolate and the chocolate deepens the coffee flavor; a truly symbiotic relationship.

> 1 1/2 cups (300 g) **sugar**
>
> 1 cup (200 g) shortening
>
> 3 **eggs**
>
> 3/4 cup (65 g) **cocoa powder**
>
> 2 cups (250 g) **self-rising flour**
>
> 1/2 teaspoon salt
>
> 1 cup (235 ml) **black coffee**

Preheat the oven to 350°F (180°C, gas mark 4). Grease and flour a 9 x 13-inch pan or two 9-inch round cake pans.

Using the paddle attachment of a stand mixer, cream together the sugar and shortening for 3 to 4 minutes, until light and fluffy. Add the eggs, one at a time, beating well after each egg.

In a separate bowl, sift together the cocoa powder, flour, and salt and add in thirds, alternating with the coffee, beating just to mix after each addition. After all the ingredients are added, beat on medium speed for 5 minutes. Spread the batter into the pan(s).

Bake for 25 to 30 minutes, until a tester inserted into the center of the cake comes out clean. Cool in the pan for 10 minutes, then turn the cakes out onto wire racks to cool completely.

YIELD: Serves 10 to 12

ADD IT! Whip 2 cups (475 ml) heavy cream with 3 tablespoons (8 g) instant coffee powder and the same amount confectioners' sugar. Frost cake with this whipped cream and garnish with chocolate shavings.

Angel Food Cake

This light and airy cake owes its celestial texture to egg whites that have been beaten until they are stiff and hold their peaks, so don't skimp on the beating!

> 1 cup (135 g) **cake flour**
>
> 1/2 teaspoon salt
>
> 1 1/2 cups (300 g) **sugar**
>
> 12 **egg** whites
>
> 1 teaspoon **almond extract**
>
> 1 teaspoon **vanilla extract**

Preheat the oven to 375°F (190°C, gas mark 5). Grease and flour an angel food cake pan.

In a small bowl, sift together the flour, salt, and 3/4 cup (150 g) of the sugar.

In the bowl of a stand mixer, using the whisk attachment, whip the egg whites until they begin to froth. Add one-third of the remaining sugar and continue to whip the whites, adding the rest of the sugar in two additions. Whip the whites to stiff peaks.

Fold the flour mixture into the egg whites until just incorporated. Fold in the almond and vanilla. Fill the angel food pan with the batter and bump the pan against the counter a couple of times to remove any large air bubbles.

Bake for 40 to 45 minutes, until the cake is golden brown and a tester inserted into the center of the cake comes out clean. Invert the pan onto its feet, or on the neck of a bottle. Cool the cake completely in the pan before removing.

YIELD: Serves 10 to 12.

ADD IT! A classic combination is to frost the cake with whipped cream and serve with fresh berries.

Apple-Sour Cream Torte

Here's a torte that's almost a coffee cake.

> 12 ounces (340 g) **gingersnaps**
>
> 1/2 cup (1 stick, or 112 g) butter

3 pounds (1.5 kg) **Granny Smith apples** (about 6 apples)

4 **eggs**

1 1/2 cups (300 g) **vanilla sugar** (See "Making Vanilla Sugar" on page 12.)

1/2 teaspoon salt

2 cups (460 g) **sour cream**

Preheat the oven to 350° F (180°C, gas mark 4). Grease a 9-inch springform pan and line the bottom of the pan with parchment paper.

Put the gingersnaps in a large resealable plastic bag and crush them with a rolling pin or bottle. (A food processor also works quite well.) Put the cookie crumbs in a mixing bowl.

In a saucepan, melt the butter over low heat and combine with the cookie crumbs, mixing thoroughly. Press into the bottom of the prepared pan.

Bake for 12 to 15 minutes. Remove from oven and cool thoroughly.

Reduce the oven temperature to 325°F (170°C, gas mark 3).

Peel and core the apples and cut them into 1/4-inch slices. Separate the eggs and put the yolks into a mixing bowl, reserving the whites in another mixing bowl. Add 1 cup (200 g) of the sugar and the salt to the yolks and beat until pale yellow and doubled in volume—about 5 minutes. Fold in the sour cream, then fold in the apples.

Whip the egg whites until frothy, then add the remaining 1/2 cup (100 g) sugar and continue beating the whites to stiff peaks. Gently fold the whites into the other mixture. Spoon into the springform pan and smooth the top. Place the springform pan into a larger pan and fill with about 1 inch (2 1/2 cm) boiling water.

Bake in the water bath for 45 to 50 minutes, until the filling is set. Cool in the water bath.

Refrigerate for at least 6 hours, preferably overnight. Remove the sides of the springform pan and invert the torte onto a plate or cake round. Remove the bottom of the pan and the parchment and re-invert onto a serving platter or cake round.

YIELD: Serves 12

ADD IT! Add 2 teaspoons cinnamon and 1/2 teaspoon nutmeg to the batter yolk/sugar mixture.

Lemon Mousse Torte

1 cup (235 ml) frozen **lemonade concentrate**, thawed

2 envelopes ($^1/4$ ounce, 7.5 g, each) **unflavored gelatin**

6 **eggs**

2 cups (475 ml) **heavy cream**

1 package (16 ounces, or 455 g) **white cake mix**

Water as directed in cake mix instructions

Vegetable oil as directed in cake mix instructions

Prepare a 9-inch springform pan by lightly greasing and then lining the bottom with parchment paper.

In a stainless steel bowl, combine the lemonade concentrate, gelatin, and 4 of the eggs. Place the bowl over a saucepan with simmering water and whisk continually until the mixture has thickened, doubled in volume, and you can see streaks of the bowl as you whisk. Set the bowl aside to cool for 5 to 10 minutes.

In a separate bowl, whip the cream to stiff peaks and fold into the lemon mixture. Spoon the mousse into the prepared springform pan and refrigerate overnight.

Preheat the oven to 350°F (180°C, gas mark 4). Grease and flour a 9-inch springform pan and line the bottom of the pan with parchment paper.

Prepare the cake mix according to package directions, using the remaining 2 eggs, water, and oil as directed in the cake mix instructions. Spread the batter in the springform pan.

Bake for 25 to 30 minutes, until a tester inserted into the center of the cake comes out clean. Cool in the pan for 15 minutes, remove the sides of the pan, and invert the cake onto a rack. Remove the bottom of the pan and the parchment paper and allow the cake to cool completely. Carefully cut the cake in half horizontally, so that you have two layers. Place one layer on a serving platter.

Remove the lemon mousse from the springform pan by removing the pan sides. Invert the mousse onto the cake layer. Remove the bottom of the pan and the parchment paper and top the mousse with the remaining cake layer. Refrigerate for 2 to 3 hours.

YIELD: Serves 12

Raspberry Mousse Torte

A note on the raspberries: If you can't find raspberries in syrup, add a couple tablespoons of sugar to regular frozen berries.

> 1 package (10 ounces, or 280g) **frozen raspberries** in syrup, thawed
>
> 1 envelope ($^{1}/4$ ounce, or 7.5 g, each) **unflavored gelatin**
>
> 4 **eggs**
>
> 3 cups (705 ml) **heavy cream**
>
> 1 package (20 ounces, or 560 g) **white cake mix**
>
> Vegetable oil as directed in cake mix instructions
>
> Water as directed in cake mix instructions

Lightly grease the bottom and sides of a 9-inch springform pan and line with parchment paper.

Puree the raspberries and syrup in a blender. Force the mixture through a fine sieve and discard the seeds. Put the raspberry liquid into a small saucepan and sprinkle the gelatin over. Allow the gelatin to soften for 5 minutes, then heat over low heat for 4 to 5 minutes, until the gelatin has dissolved.

Place 2 of the eggs in a stainless steel mixing bowl and whisk in the raspberry mixture. Place the bowl over a pan of simmering water and, whisking constantly, cook until the mixture doubles in size and becomes frothy and light colored. Refrigerate, stirring every 15 minutes, until cooled and partially set—about 1 hour.

Whip 1 cup (235 ml) of the cream to stiff peaks and fold into the raspberry mixture. Spoon evenly into the prepared springform pan and refrigerate for at least 6 hours, preferably overnight.

Preheat the oven to 325°F (170°C, gas mark 3). Grease and flour two 9-inch round cake pans. Prepare the cake mix according to package instructions, using the 2 remaining eggs and oil and water as directed in the cake mix instructions. Divide the cake mix between the two pans.

Bake for 25 to 30 minutes, until a tester inserted into the center of the cakes comes out clean. Cool in the pan for 15 minutes, then turn the cakes onto cooling racks to cool completely.

Place one cake layer on a serving platter. Remove the sides of the springform pan and the parchment around the raspberry mousse, then invert the mousse onto the cake. Remove the pan bottom and parchment paper and gently top with the remaining cake layer.

In a bowl, whip the remaining 2 cups (475 ml) cream to stiff peaks and frost the top and sides of the cake.

YIELD: Serves 12

ADD IT! Circle the top of the cake with fresh raspberries.

Piña Colada Torte

This torte is a taste of the tropics.

> 1 sheet frozen **puff pastry dough** (6 x 9 inch, or 15 x 22 ^{1}/2 cm), thawed
>
> 15 ounces (440 ml) **piña colada mix**
>
> 2 envelopes (^{1}/4 ounce, or 7.5 g, each) **unflavored gelatin**
>
> 2 cups (475 ml) **heavy cream**
>
> 1 cup (75 g) sweetened **shredded coconut**

Preheat the oven to 400°F (200°C, gas mark 6).

On a floured surface roll out the dough to a 9-inch (22.5 cm) square. Using the bottom of a 9-inch springform pan as a template, cut out a circle of dough. Place the dough circle on a parchment-lined baking sheet. Place a baking rack upside down on top of the dough to prevent overexuberent puffing.

Bake for 15 to 20 minutes, until golden brown. Remove the rack and allow the pastry to cool on the pan.

Line the bottom of a 9-inch springform pan with parchment paper. When the pastry is cooled, place it in the bottom of the springform pan.

Mix together the piña colada mix and the gelatin in a small saucepan. Cook over medium heat until the gelatin is dissolved—about 5 minutes. Refrigerate until cold, but do not allow to set—about an hour.

When the mixture is cooled, in a separate bowl, whip the cream to stiff peaks and fold in the piña colada mixture. Fold in the coconut. Spoon into the springform pan on top of the pastry layer. Spread evenly. Refrigerate for at least 6 hours, preferably overnight.

Remove the side of the pan and invert the torte onto a plate. Remove the bottom of the pan and the parchment and invert onto another serving plate or cake round so that it is again right side up.

YIELD: Serves 12

ADD IT! Garnish with more whipped cream if desired.

Brownie Sundae Torte

This makes a terrific birthday cake for the brownie sundae lovers among us!

> 2 packages (13 ounces, or 370 g each) **brownie mix**
>
> 2 **eggs**
>
> 1 quart (570 g) **vanilla ice cream**
>
> 2 cups (475 ml) **Caramel Sauce** (page 486) or store-bought caramel sauce
>
> 2 cups (475 ml) **heavy cream**

Preheat the oven to 350°F (180°C, gas mark 4). Grease two 9-inch springform pans and line the bottoms with parchment paper.

Prepare the brownie mixes as directed on the package. Divide the batter between the two prepared pans.

Bake for 25 to 30 minutes. Allow the brownies to cool in the pan for 15 minutes, then remove the sides of the pans, invert the brownies onto racks, remove the bottoms of the pans and the parchment, and allow the brownies to cool completely.

When the brownies have cooled, soften the ice cream at room temperature until it is soft enough to spread—about 15 minutes, or 30 to 45 seconds in the microwave. Again, line a 9-inch springform pan with parchment, on the bottom and on the sides. Trim the edges of the brownie rounds, removing about 1/4 inch all around. Reserve the brownie trimmings. Place one brownie round in the springform pan. Spread with the ice cream, reserving 1 cup (140 g), and drizzle with 1 cup (235 ml) of the caramel sauce. Press the other brownie round gently on top of the ice cream and freeze for at least 2 hours. Allow the reserved ice cream to melt, then refrigerate.

Remove the cake from the freezer. Remove the sides of the springform pan and the parchment paper around the side of the torte. Invert the torte onto a plate, remove the pan bottom and parchment, and invert back onto a serving plate. Whip the cream together with the reserved melted ice cream to stiff peaks. Frost the sides and top of the torte with the whipped cream mixture. Chop up the reserved brownie trimmings and sprinkle over the cake. Drizzle with the remaining caramel sauce. Serve immediately, or refrigerate up to 1 hour before serving.

YIELD: Serves 12

Chocolate-Caramel Crepe Torte

This is an excellent dessert for a romantic dinner for two!

> 2 cups (400 g) **vanilla sugar** (See "Making Vanilla Sugar" on page 12.)
> About 4 tablespoons (60 ml) water
> 1 ¹/2 cups (355 ml) **heavy cream**
> 10 ounces (280 g) **semisweet chocolate**, cut into small pieces
> 3 **eggs**
> 1 package (10 ounces, or 280 g) 8-inch **crepes**

In a heavy bottomed 1-quart saucepan, mix 1 cup (200 g) of the sugar with enough water to make the sugar the texture of wet sand. Put the pan on medium-high heat and cook until the liquid turns a medium brown. (This will take a while as the water needs to cook out of the wet sand mixture.) Remove from the heat and immediately pour in ¹/2 cup (120 ml) of the cream. (Be careful as it will sputter.) Mix with a wooden spoon, on the heat if needed, until smooth. Set aside to cool.

In a stainless steel mixing bowl, melt the chocolate over a pan of simmering water. Stir until smooth and set aside.

In another stainless steel bowl, lightly whisk the eggs and combine with the remaining 1 cup (200 g) of sugar. Whisking constantly, cook over the simmering water until the mixture lightens in color, thickens, and roughly doubles in volume. (It should take 8 to 10 minutes.) Remove from the heat and fold in the melted chocolate thoroughly. Set aside to cool.

In a separate bowl, whip the remaining cream to stiff peaks and fold into the cooled chocolate mixture until fully combined and a smooth mousse.

Grease the bottom and sides of an 8-inch springform pan with nonstick cooking spray and cover the bottom and sides of the pan with parchment paper. Place a crepe in the bottom of the pan and spoon 1 cup (235 ml) of the chocolate mousse over. Smooth over the crepe evenly and drizzle with some of the caramel. Repeat until the pan is filled—5 to 6 layers. Refrigerate the torte for several hours, preferably overnight. Remove the sides of the pan and parchment and invert the torte into a cardboard cake round. (Cake rounds are used as a base when making filled cakes. They are sold at any kitchen/baking store. They are handy when you want to move the cake, which might be fragile.) Remove the bottom of the pan and the parchment and reinvert onto a serving platter or cake round.

YIELD: Serves 8

ADD IT! Decorate with additional whipped cream and chocolate shavings if desired.

Chocolate-Chai Latte Torte

Chai latte, that drink of the moment, is made up of tea spiced with flavors such as ginger, cardamom, cloves, and cinnamon that are brewed and mixed with milk for a sweet, creamy beverage. It adds a great spicy kick when you use powdered drink mix as a flavoring.

> 1 package (12 ounces, 340 g) **brownie mix**
> 1 **egg**
> 1 1/2 cups (355 ml) water
> 1/3 cup (75 ml) vegetable oil
> 1 cup (175 g) instant powdered **chai latte mix**
> 2 envelopes (1/4 ounce, or 7.5 g, each) **unflavored gelatin**
> 1 cup (235 ml) water
> 2 cups (475 ml) **heavy cream**

Preheat the oven to 350°F (180°C, gas mark 4). Grease the bottom of a 9-inch springform pan and line the bottom of the pan with a round of parchment paper.

In a mixing bowl, combine the brownie mix, egg, and 1/2 cup (120 ml) of the water and the oil. Spread into the pan.

Bake for 20 to 25 minutes. Allow to cool in the pan.

Mix the chai latte and the gelatin with the remaining 1 cup (235 ml) water in a small saucepan. Cook over medium heat until the gelatin is dissolved—about 5 minutes. Refrigerate until cold, but do not allow to set—about 1 hour. When the chai latte mixture is cooled, whip the cream to stiff peaks and fold in the chai latte mixture. Spoon into the springform pan on top of the baked brownie layer. Spread evenly and refrigerate for at least 6 hours, preferably overnight.

Remove the side of the pan and invert the torte onto a plate. Remove the bottom of the pan and the parchment and invert onto another serving plate or cake round so that the brownie layer is again on the bottom.

YIELD: Serves 12

ADD IT! You may garnish with more whipped cream and crumbled cooked brownies.

Chocolate Cookie Torte

This is like a giant double chocolate whoopie pie. What's not to like?

1 cup (200 g) **sugar**

$1/2$ cup (45 g) **cocoa powder**

2 ounces (55 g) **General Mills Café Vienna coffee mix**

$1/3$ cup (65 g) shortening

$1/2$ cup (120 ml) water

1 package (11 ounces, or 310 g) **pie crust mix**

$2^1/2$ cups (595 ml) **heavy cream**

Combine the sugar, cocoa powder, coffee mix, shortening, and water in a small saucepan. Cook over medium heat, stirring often, until the ingredients are all dissolved and the mixture is smooth.

In a mixing bowl, stir together the pie crust mix and $3/4$ cup (175 ml) of the chocolate mixture, reserving the remaining chocolate mixture. Blend until smooth and divide the dough into four pieces. Shape into patties and refrigerate the dough, wrapped in plastic wrap, for 15 to 20 minutes.

Preheat the oven to 350°F (180°C, gas mark 4). Line 2 cookie sheets with parchment paper and mark two 8-inch (20 cm) circles on each. Roll each of the four pieces of dough out into $1/2$-inch thick circles and place on the parchment. Using your fingertips, work the dough so that it just fills the marked circles. Bake for 10 to 12 minutes, until almost set. Cool completely on the cookie sheets.

Combine the remaining chocolate mixture and the cream in a mixing bowl and whip to stiff peaks. Place one cookie on a serving plate and layer with one-fourth of the cream. Repeat using the rest of the ingredients. Refrigerate for at least 6 hours, preferably overnight, to let the cookies soften.

YIELD: Serves 8 to 10

Chocolate-Eggnog Torte

This torte works well during the holidays, when grocery shelves overflow with ready-made eggnog.

> 2 cups (475 ml) prepared **eggnog**
> 2 envelopes (¹/4 ounce, or 7.5 g, each) **unflavored gelatin**
> 1 cup (235 ml) **heavy cream**
> 1 package (16 ounces, or 455 g) **chocolate cake mix**
> Vegetable oil as directed in cake mix instructions
> **Eggs** as directed in cake mix instructions

Grease a 9-inch springform pan and then line the bottom with a round of parchment paper.

Put the eggnog and the gelatin into a small saucepan and cook over low heat, stirring often, until the gelatin is dissolved—about 10 minutes. Put the mixture into a large mixing bowl and refrigerate, stirring every 10 minutes, until the gelatin is partially set and the mixture is beginning to thicken.

In a separate bowl, whip the cream to stiff peaks and fold into the eggnog. Spoon into the prepared springform pan and refrigerate overnight.

Preheat the oven to 350°F (180°C, gas mark 4). Grease and flour a 9-inch springform pan and line the bottom of the pan with parchment paper.

Prepare the chocolate cake mix according to package directions, using the amount of eggs and vegetable oil called for on the instructions, and spread the batter in the springform pan.

Bake for 25 to 30 minutes, until a tester inserted into the center of the cake comes out clean. Cool in the pan for 15 minutes, remove the sides of the pan, and invert the cake onto a rack. Remove the bottom of the pan and the parchment paper and allow the cake to cool completely. Carefully cut the cake in half horizontally, so that you have two rounds. Place one round on a serving platter.

Remove the eggnog mousse from the springform pan by removing the pan sides. Invert the eggnog layer onto the chocolate cake round. Remove the bottom of the pan and the parchment paper and top the eggnog with the remaining cake round. Refrigerate for 2 to 3 hours.

YIELD: Serves 12

Chocolate-Peanut Butter Cheesecake Torte

You got peanut butter on my chocolate! No, you got chocolate on my peanut butter!
It's a chicken or egg debate, but the end result is delicious.

> 1 pound (455 g) **cream cheese**
>
> 1/4 cup (30 g) **all-purpose flour**
>
> 8 **eggs**
>
> 1 1/2 cups (390 g) creamy **peanut butter**
>
> 1 package (16 ounces, or 455 g) **chocolate cake mix**
>
> Vegetable oil as directed in the cake mix instructions

Prepare a 9-inch springform pan by greasing the bottom and lining the bottom
with a round of parchment paper.

In a mixing bowl, using the paddle attachment of a stand mixer, mix the cream
cheese for 8 to 10 minutes on medium speed, scraping the bowl several times,
until the cream cheese is perfectly smooth. Add the flour and mix to blend. Add
6 of the eggs, one at a time, incorporating each fully as added. Add the peanut
butter and blend well. Spread the batter in the springform pan and place the pan
in a larger baking pan. Fill the larger container with 1 inch (2 1/2 cm) of very hot
water.

Bake for 45 to 50 minutes, until the cheesecake is set, but jiggles slightly.
Remove from the oven and cool in the water bath. Remove the springform pan
from the water bath and refrigerate the cheesecake for at least 6 hours, preferably
overnight.

Preheat the oven to 350°F (180°C, gas mark 4). Grease and flour a 9-inch
springform pan and line the bottom of the pan with parchment paper.

Prepare the chocolate cake batter according to package directions, using the
remaining 2 eggs and vegetable oil as directed in the cake mix instructions.
Spread the batter in the springform pan.

Bake for 25 to 30 minutes, until a tester inserted into the center of the cake
comes out clean. Cool in the pan for 15 minutes, remove the sides of the pan,
and invert the cake onto a rack. Remove the bottom of the pan and the parchment paper and allow the cake to cool completely. Carefully cut the cake in half
horizontally, so that you have two layers. Place one round on a serving platter.

Remove the cheesecake from the springform pan by removing the pan sides. Invert the cheesecake onto the chocolate cake layer. Remove the bottom of the pan and the parchment paper and top the cheesecake with the remaining chocolate cake layer. Refrigerate for 2 to 3 hours.

YIELD: Serves 12

ADD IT! Drizzle Chocolate Sauce (page 492) or store-bought chocolate sauce over each slice when serving.

Mexican Chocolate Trifle Torte

The botanical name for chocolate is *Theobroma*, meaning "food of the gods." Considering the historical importance of chocolate in the Mexican culture, where it was revered by the Aztecs, the name is most appropriate.

8 ounces (225 g) **semisweet chocolate**, cut into small chunks

1/2 teaspoon **cinnamon**

1/4 cup (1 stick, or 112 g) butter

1 can (8 ounces, or 235 ml) **sweetened condensed milk**

2 cups (475 ml) **heavy cream**

32 sponge **ladyfingers**

In a stainless steel bowl set over simmering water, combine the chocolate, cinnamon, butter, and condensed milk. Cook, stirring often, until the ingredients are melted together and smooth. Set aside to cool for 10 to 15 minutes at room temperature.

In a separate bowl, whip the cream to stiff peaks and fold into the cooled chocolate mixture. Refrigerate.

Line the bottom and sides of an 8-inch springform pan with parchment paper. Line the bottom and sides of the pan with the ladyfingers. Spoon in half of the chocolate mousse and smooth. Add a layer of ladyfingers and top with the rest of the mousse. Refrigerate for at least 4 hours, preferably overnight.

To serve, remove the sides of the pan and the parchment paper from the sides of the torte. Invert the torte onto a cake round and remove the pan bottom and the parchment. Reinvert onto a cake round or serving platter.

YIELD: Serves 8 to 10

No-Bake Chocolate Cappuccino Torte

This is fantastic. It's one of our favorite recipes in the whole book.

- 2 packages (9 ounces, or 255 g, each) **Nabisco Famous Chocolate Wafer cookies**
- 4 cups (950 ml) **heavy cream**
- 1 pound (455 g) **semisweet chocolate**, cut into small chunks
- 1/4 cup (10 g) plus 1 tablespoon (3 g) **instant coffee powder** or granules
- 1 cup (120 g) plus 2 tablespoons (16 g) **confectioners' sugar**

Spray a 9-inch springform pan with nonstick cooking spray and line the bottom and sides with parchment paper.

Line the bottom of the pan with a layer of cookies.

In a saucepan, heat 1 cup (235 ml) of the cream just to a boil. Put the chocolate in a mixing bowl and pour the hot cream over it. Allow to sit for 1 minute, then mix with a spoon until the chocolate is completely melted and the mixture is smooth. Spread one-third of the chocolate on the cookies.

In a separate bowl, mix the remaining 3 cups (705 ml) cream, the coffee powder or granules, and the sugar and whip until the cream is at stiff peaks. Spoon one-third of the whipped cream mixture into the pan and smooth out with a spatula. Repeat with another layer of cookies, chocolate, and whipped cream. Top with a third layer of cookies and a layer of whipped cream. Drizzle remaining chocolate over the top.

Refrigerate for at least 8 hours, preferably overnight. Remove the sides of the pan and the parchment paper lining the sides. Invert the torte onto a plate or cake round and remove the bottom of the pan and the parchment paper. Reinvert onto a serving platter or cake round.

YIELD: Serves 12

ADD IT! Circle the top of the cake with fresh raspberries.

Mocha-Hazelnut Torte

2 sheets frozen puff **pastry dough** (6 x 9 inch, or 15 x 22.5 cm), thawed

2 cups (590 g) **Nutella chocolate-hazelnut spread**

1 cup, or 5 ounces (140 g) dry **cappuccino mix**

2 envelopes (1/4 ounce, or 7.5 g, each) **unflavored gelatin**

1 cup (235 ml) water

2 cups (475 ml) **heavy cream**

Preheat the oven to 400°F (200°C, gas mark 6).

On a floured surface, roll out each sheet of the dough to a 9-inch (22.5 cm) square. Using the bottom of a 9-inch springform pan as a template, cut out two circles of dough. Place the dough circles on a parchment-lined baking sheet. Place a baking rack upside down on top of each piece of dough to keep them from overpuffing.

Bake for 15 to 20 minutes, until golden brown. Remove the racks and allow the pastry to cool on the pan.

Line the bottom of a 9-inch springform pan with parchment paper. When the pastry is cooled, spread each piece with 1 cup (295 g) of the Nutella. Place 1 layer in the bottom of the springform pan. Reserve the other layer of pastry.

Mix together the cappuccino mix, gelatin, and water in a small saucepan. Cook over medium heat until the gelatin is dissolved—about 5 minutes. Refrigerate until cold, but do not allow to set.

When the mixture is cooled, in a separate bowl, whip the cream to stiff peaks and fold into the cappuccino mixture. Spoon into the springform pan on top of the pastry layer. Spread evenly and top with the other pastry layer, finishing with the remaining 1 cup (295 g) Nutella on top and gently pressing the pastry into the cappuccino cream. Refrigerate for at least 6 hours, preferably overnight.

Remove the side of the pan and invert the torte onto a plate. Remove the bottom of the pan and the parchment and invert onto another serving plate or cake round so that it is again right side up.

YIELD: Serves 12

ADD IT! Garnish with more whipped cream if desired.

Ginger Amaretto Torte

Ginger is one of those foods that manages to be old-fashioned and trendy at the same time. Here, it pairs with amaretto for a lovely combination.

1 package (12 ounces, or 340 g) **Amoretti cookies**

1/2 cup (1 stick, or 112 g) butter

1 jar (12 ounces, or 340 g) **ginger preserves**

1 envelope (1/4 ounce, or 7.5 g) **unflavored gelatin**

1 container (16 ounces, or 455 g) **vanilla yogurt**

2 cups (475 ml) **heavy cream**

Preheat the oven to 350°F (180°C, gas mark 4). Grease a 9-inch springform pan and line the bottom of the pan with parchment paper.

Put the cookies in a large resealable plastic bag and crush using a rolling pin or bottle (You can opt for putting the cookies through the food processor, too.).

In a saucepan, melt the butter over low heat and mix in with the cookie crumbs. Press this mixture into the bottom of the prepared pan.

Bake for 12 to 15 minutes. Allow to cool completely. Line the sides of the pan with plastic wrap or parchment paper.

Put the ginger preserves into a small saucepan and sprinkle the gelatin over them. Let them sit for 5 to 6 minutes to soften the gelatin, then melt the preserves over low heat. Continue to cook on low heat for 4 to 5 minutes, until the gelatin has dissolved. Put this mixture into a large mixing bowl. Fold in the yogurt.

In a separate bowl, whip the cream to stiff peaks and fold into the yogurt mixture. Spoon into the prepared pan and smooth out. Refrigerate for at least 6 hours, preferably overnight.

Remove the sides of the pan and the plastic wrap or parchment paper. Invert the torte into a plate or cardboard cake round and remove the bottom of the pan and the parchment paper. Invert back onto a serving platter.

YIELD: Serves 12

ADD IT! Decorate with additional whipped cream and crystallized ginger if desired.

Gingerbread-Pumpkin Cheesecake Torte

This rich and delicious torte makes a fine harvest time alternative to the ubiquitous pie.

> 2 pounds (1 kg) **cream cheese**
> 1/4 cup (30 g) **all-purpose flour**
> 8 **eggs**
> 2 cups (540 g) canned spiced and sweetened **pumpkin**
> 1 package (16 ounces, or 455 g) **gingerbread mix**

Preheat the oven to 325°F (170°C, gas mark 3). Prepare a 9-inch springform pan by greasing the bottom and lining the bottom with a round of parchment paper.

In a mixing bowl, using the paddle attachment of a stand mixer, mix the cream cheese for 8 to 10 minutes on medium speed, scraping the bowl several times, until the cream cheese is perfectly smooth. Add the flour and mix to blend. Add 6 of the eggs, one at a time, incorporating each fully as added. Add the pumpkin and blend well. Spread the mixture in the springform pan and place the pan in a larger pan. Fill the larger pan with 1 inch (2 1/2 cm) of very hot water.

Bake for 45 to 50 minutes, until the cheesecake is set, but jiggles slightly. Remove from the oven and cool in the water bath. Remove the springform pan from the water bath and refrigerate the cheesecake for at least 6 hours, preferably overnight.

Preheat the oven to 350°F (180°C, gas mark 4). Grease and flour a 9-inch springform pan and line the bottom of the pan with parchment paper.

Prepare the gingerbread mix according to package directions, using the 2 remaining eggs, and spread the batter in the springform pan.

Bake for 25 to 30 minutes, until a tester inserted into the center of the cake comes out clean. Cool in the pan for 15 minutes, remove the sides of the pan, and invert the gingerbread onto a rack. Remove the bottom of the pan and the parchment paper and allow the gingerbread to cool completely. Carefully cut the gingerbread in half horizontally, so that you have two layers. Place one layer on a serving platter.

Remove the cheesecake from the springform pan by removing the pan sides. Invert the cheesecake onto the gingerbread. Remove the bottom of the pan and the parchment paper and top the cheesecake with the remaining gingerbread layer. Refrigerate for 2 to 3 hours.

YIELD: Serves 12.

Pumpkin Torte

If you cannot find prespiced and sweetened pumpkin, add $1/2$ teaspoon cinnamon, $1/2$ teaspoon ginger, $1/4$ teaspoon freshly grated nutmeg, and 2 additional tablespoons of dark brown sugar to the mix.

> 2 packages (9 ounces, or 255 g, each) **Nabisco Famous Chocolate Wafer cookies**
>
> $1/2$ cup (1 stick, or 112 g) butter, melted
>
> 1 can (15 ounces, or 430 g) spiced and sweetened **pumpkin**
>
> 2 tablespoons (15 g) **dark brown sugar**
>
> $3/4$ cup (180 g) **mascarpone cheese**
>
> $3/4$ cup (175 ml) **heavy cream**

Preheat the oven to 350°F (180°C, gas mark 4). Grease the bottom of a 10-inch springform pan and line the bottom of the pan with parchment paper.

In a food processor, grind up 1 package of the cookies until you have about 3 cups of cookie crumbs. Reserve the remaining cookies. Combine 2 cups of crumbs with the butter and stir until combined. Press the mixture evenly into the bottom of a 10-inch springform pan.

Bake for 12 to 15 minutes, until the crumbs are set and the crust is lightly browned. Cool completely in the pan.

In a large bowl, combine the pumpkin, sugar, mascarpone cheese, and cream. Beat on medium speed until well combined.

Spread half of the pumpkin mixture over the cookie crust and smooth out. Cover the pumpkin mixture with the remaining cookies, overlapping slightly. Spoon the remaining pumpkin mixture over and smooth. Sprinkle the top with the remaining 1 cup cookie crumbs. Cover with plastic wrap and refrigerate for at least 6 hours, preferably overnight.

Remove the pan sides and flip the torte onto a cake round. Remove the pan bottom and the parchment paper. Flip the cake right side up onto a serving platter or another cake round.

YIELD: Serves 10 to 12

Basic New York Style Cheesecake

Knowing how to make a basic cheesecake gives you an excellent framework for branching out in the cheesecake world. This cake is very amenable to being flavored any number of different ways, and it also takes kindly to sauces of almost any flavor being drizzled over.

For the crust:

> 2 cups (200 g) **graham cracker crumbs**
> 1/2 cup (100 g) **vanilla sugar** (See "Making Vanilla Sugar" on page 12.)
> 1/2 cup (1 stick, or 112 g) butter, melted

For the cheesecake:

> 3 pounds (1.5 kg) **cream cheese**
> 2 cups (400 g) **vanilla sugar** (See "Making Vanilla Sugar" on page 12.)
> 1/4 cup (60 g) all-purpose flour
> 7 eggs, plus 2 **egg** yolks

To make the crust:

Preheat the oven to 350°F (180°C, gas mark 4). Spray a 12-inch springform pan with nonstick cooking spray. Cut out a 12-inch circle of parchment paper and line the bottom of the pan. Line the outside bottom and sides of the pan with foil.

Mix the graham cracker crumbs and the sugar in a mixing bowl. Stir the butter thoroughly into the crumb mixture. Press the mixture into the bottom of the springform pan evenly.

Bake for 12 to 15 minutes, until the crumbs are set and the crust is lightly browned. Cool completely in the pan.

To make the filling:

Place the cream cheese in a mixing bowl and mix it on medium speed until perfectly smooth, 8 to 10 minutes. Add the sugar and flour and beat for another 4 to 5 minutes, scraping down the bowl and beater often. Add the eggs and yolks, one at a time, beating until incorporated after each egg. Pour the batter onto the prepared crust and place the springform pan into larger baking dish. Pour 1 to 2 inches (2^1/2 to 5 cm) of hot water into the baking pan.

Bake for 55 to 60 minutes, until set. (The center will jiggle slightly, be careful to not allow the cake to soufflé.) Allow to cool in the water bath, then refrigerate overnight. Remove the pan sides and flip the cake onto a cardboard cake round. Remove the bottom of the pan and the parchment, then flip again right side up onto another cake round or a serving platter. Cut with a thin knife run under hot water.

YIELD: Serves 16

ADD IT! ^{1}/4 cup (60 ml) lemon juice; ^{1}/2 cup (120 ml) Grand Marnier, Kahlúa, or Framboise; 1 cup (90 g) cocoa powder—there are many ways to flavor this cheesecake.

Almond Cheesecake

The mild flavor of almonds adds spice to this cheesecake without going over the top.

For the crust:

> 1 sheet frozen puff **pastry dough**, 9 x 13 inches (22 ^{1}/2 x 32 ^{1}/2 cm), thawed
> 2 cups (185 g) sliced blanched **almonds**

For the filling:

> 1 ^{1}/2 pounds (675 g) **cream cheese**
> 4 **eggs**
> 1 can (14 ounces, or 425 ml) **sweetened condensed milk**

To make the crust:

Preheat the oven to 350°F (180°C, gas mark 4). Spray a 10-inch springform pan with nonstick cooking spray. Cut out a 10-inch circle of parchment paper and line the bottom of the pan. Line the outside bottom and sides of the pan with foil.

Roll out the pastry dough until it is 10 inches (25 cm) square. Cut out a 10-inch circle and place in the bottom of the springform pan. Brush the top of the dough with water and sprinkle 1 cup (90 g) of the almonds on top.

Bake for 18 to 20 minutes, until golden brown. Cool completely in the pan.

To make the filling:

Place the cream cheese in a mixing bowl and mix it on medium speed until perfectly smooth, 8 to 10 minutes. Add the eggs, one at a time, beating until incorporated after each egg. Add the condensed milk and mix until well combined. Pour the batter onto the prepared crust and top with the remaining 1 cup (90 g) almonds. Place the springform pan into larger baking dish. Pour 1 to 2 inches (2 1/2 to 5 cm) of hot water into the baking pan.

Bake for 55 to 60 minutes, until set. (The center will jiggle slightly. Watch that the cake does not soufflé.) Allow to cool in the water bath, then refrigerate overnight. Remove the pan sides and flip the cake onto a cardboard cake round. Remove the bottom of the pan and the parchment, then flip again right side up onto another cake round or a serving platter. Cut with a thin knife run under hot water.

YIELD: Serves 12

Banana-Coconut Cheesecake

Banana-coconut, a classic flavor combination, translates beautifully to cheesecake.

For the crust:

>   2 cups crushed **vanilla wafer cookies** (about 30 cookies)
>   1/2 cup (1 stick, or 112g) butter, melted

For the filling:

> 1 1/2 pounds (675 g) **cream cheese**
>
> 3 **eggs**
>
> 1 cup (235 ml) **coconut milk**
>
> 1 cup (225 g) mashed **banana** (about 2 bananas)

To make the crust:

Preheat the oven to 350°F (180°C, gas mark 4). Spray a 10-inch springform pan with nonstick cooking spray. Cut out a 10-inch circle of parchment paper and line the bottom of the pan. Line the outside bottom and sides of the pan with foil.

In a bowl, mix together the cookie crumbs and butter. Press the mixture into the bottom of the springform pan evenly.

Bake for 12 to 15 minutes, until the crumbs are set. Cool completely in the pan.

To make the filling:

Place the cream cheese in a mixing bowl and mix it on medium speed until perfectly smooth, 8 to 10 minutes. Add the eggs, one at a time, beating until incorporated after each egg. Add the coconut milk and the banana and mix until well combined. Pour the batter onto the prepared crust and place the springform pan into larger baking dish. Pour 1 to 2 inches (2 1/2 to 5 cm) of hot water into the baking pan.

Bake for 55 to 60 minutes, until set. (The center will jiggle slightly. Watch that the cake does not soufflé.) Allow to cool in the water bath, then refrigerate overnight. Remove the pan sides and flip the cake onto a cardboard cake round. Remove the bottom of the pan and the parchment, then flip again right side up onto another cake round or a serving platter. Cut with a thin knife run under hot water.

YIELD: Serves 12

ADD IT! For a slightly sweeter cake, add 1/4 cup (35 g) light brown sugar to the mixture along with the coconut milk.

Key Lime Cheesecake

Here's a cheesecake take on key lime pie with a chocolate-crust twist. We find bottled key lime juice at our local supermarket.

For the crust:

 2 cups crushed **Nabisco Famous Chocolate Wafer cookies** (about 25 cookies)
 1/2 cup (1 stick, 112 g) butter, melted

For the filling:

 2 pounds (910 g) **cream cheese**
 3 **eggs**
 1 can (8 ounces, or 235 ml) **sweetened condensed milk**
 3/4 cup (175 ml) **key lime juice**

To make the crust:

Preheat the oven to 350°F (180°C, gas mark 4). Spray a 10-inch springform pan with nonstick cooking spray. Cut out a 10-inch circle of parchment paper and line the bottom of the pan. Line the outside bottom and sides of the pan with foil.

Mix together the cookie crumbs and the butter. Press the mixture into the bottom of the springform pan evenly.

Bake for 12 to 15 minutes, until the crumbs are set. Cool completely in the pan.

To make the filling:

Place the cream cheese in a mixing bowl and mix it on medium speed until perfectly smooth, 8 to 10 minutes. Add the eggs, one at a time, beating until incorporated after each egg. Add the condensed milk and lime juice and mix until well combined. Pour the batter onto the prepared crust and place the springform pan into a larger baking dish. Pour 1 to 2 (2 1/2 to 5 cm) inches of hot water into the baking pan.

Bake for 55 to 60 minutes, until set. (The center will jiggle slightly. Watch that the cake does not soufflé.) Allow to cool in the water bath, then refrigerate overnight. Remove the pan sides and flip the cake onto a cardboard cake round. Remove the bottom of the pan and the parchment, then flip again right side up onto another cake round or a serving platter. Cut with a thin knife run under hot water.

YIELD: Serves 12

🍰 Lemon Cheesecake

For the crust:

>   1 1/2 cups (180 g) **all-purpose flour**
>   1 cup (200 g) **sugar**
>   1/4 teaspoon salt
>   1 cup (2 sticks, or 225 g) butter

For the filling:

>   3 pounds (1.5 kg) **cream cheese**
>   2 cups (400 g) **sugar**
>   1/4 cup (30 g) **all-purpose flour**
>   7 eggs, plus 2 **egg yolks**
>   3 **lemons**

To make the crust:

Preheat the oven to 350°F (180°C, gas mark 4). Spray a 12-inch springform pan with nonstick cooking spray. Cut out a 12-inch circle of parchment paper and line the bottom of the pan. Line the outside bottom and sides of the pan with foil.

Mix the flour, salt, and the sugar in a mixing bowl. Cut the butter into the dry ingredients, until the mixture resembles coarse meal. Press the mixture into the bottom of the springform pan evenly.

Bake for 12 to 15 minutes, until the crust is set and is lightly browned. Cool completely in the pan.

To make the filling:

Place the cream cheese in a mixing bowl and mix it on medium speed until perfectly smooth, 8 to 10 minutes. Add the sugar and flour and beat for another 4 to 5 minutes, scraping down the bowl and beater often. Add the eggs and yolks, one at a time, beating until incorporated after each egg.

Zest and squeeze the lemons until you have 2 tablespoons (10 g) grated lemon zest and $^1/_2$ cup (120 ml) lemon juice. Add the lemon zest and juice to the filling and mix well. Pour the batter onto the prepared crust and place the springform pan into a larger baking dish. Pour 1 to 2 inches (2$^1/_2$ to 5 cm) of hot water into the baking pan.

Bake for 55 to 60 minutes, until set. (The center will jiggle slightly. Watch that the cake does not soufflé.) Allow to cool in the water bath, then refrigerate overnight. Remove the pan sides and flip the cake onto a cardboard cake round. Remove the bottom of the pan and the parchment, then flip again right side up onto another cake round or a serving platter. Cut with a thin knife run under hot water.

YIELD: Serves 16

ADD IT! Garnish with whipped cream and candied lemon zest.

Strawberry Cheesecake

For the crust:

> 2 cups crushed **Vanilla Wafer Cookies** (about 30 cookies)
> $^1/_2$ cup (1 stick, or 112 g) butter, melted

For the filling:

> 1 package (12 ounces, or 300 g) frozen **strawberries** in syrup, thawed
> 1 $^1/_2$ pounds (675 g) **cream cheese**
> 3 **eggs**
> 1 can (8 ounces, or 235 ml) **sweetened condensed milk**

To make the crust:

Preheat the oven to 350°F (180°C, gas mark 4). Spray a 10-inch springform pan with pan spray. Cut out a 10-inch circle of parchment paper and line the bottom of the pan. Line the outside bottom and sides of the pan with foil. Mix together the cookie crumbs and the butter. Press the mixture into the bottom of the pan evenly. Bake for 12 to 15 minutes, until the crumbs are set. Cool completely.

To make the filling:

Puree the strawberries and syrup in a food processor fitted with the metal blade. Set aside. Mix the cream cheese until perfectly smooth, about 8 to 10 minutes. Add the eggs, one at a time, beating until incorporated after each egg. Add the condensed milk and strawberry puree and mix until well combined. Pour the batter onto the prepared crust. Place the springform pan into a baking dish large enough to fit it. Pour 1 to 2 inches of hot water into the baking pan.

Bake for 55 to 60 minutes, until set. The center will jiggle slightly. Watch to not allow the cake to soufflé. Allow to cool in the water bath, then refrigerate overnight. Remove the pan sides and flip the cake onto a cake round. Remove the bottom of the pan and the parchment, then flip again right side up onto another cake round, or a serving platter. Cut with a thin knife run under hot water.

YIELD: Serves 12

ADD IT! Line the top of the cake with fresh strawberries for a pretty look. Ladle crushed fresh strawberries over each slice.

No Bake Raspberry Cheesecake

Well, you do have to briefly bake the crust, but the filling remains undefiled by the touch of an oven.

For the crust:

> 2 cups crushed **Vanilla Wafer Cookies** (about 30 cookies)
> 1/2 cup (1 stick, or 112 g) butter, melted

For the filling:

> 1 envelope **unflavored gelatin**
> 1 package (16 ounces) frozen **raspberries** in syrup
> 1 pound (450 g) **cream cheese**
> 2 cups (455 g) **vanilla yogurt**

To make the crust:

Preheat the oven to 350°F (180°C, gas mark 4). Spray a 10-inch springform pan with pan spray. Cut out a 10-inch circle of parchment paper and line the bottom of the pan. Line the outside bottom and sides of the pan with foil. Mix together the cookie crumbs and the butter. Press the mixture into the bottom of the springform pan evenly. Bake for 12 to 15 minutes, until the crumbs are set. Cool completely.

To make the filling:

Put the gelatin in a small saucepan. Drain the raspberries, reserving the syrup. Add the syrup to the gelatin and cook over low heat, stirring, until the gelatin is dissolved–about 5 minutes. Cool slightly. Mix the cream cheese until perfectly smooth, about 8 to 10 minutes. Add the vanilla yogurt and the raspberry-gelatin mixture and beat until fully incorporated and smooth. Stir in the raspberries. Pour the batter onto the prepared crust and refrigerate for at least 8 hours, preferably overnight.

To serve, remove the pan sides and flip the cake onto a cake round. Remove the bottom of the pan and the parchment, then flip again right side up onto another cake round, or a serving platter. Cut with a thin knife run under hot water.

YIELD: Serves 12

Orange Cream Cheesecake

For the crust:

> 2 cups crushed **vanilla wafer cookies** (about 30 cookies)
>
> $1/2$ cup (1 stick, 112 g) butter, melted

For the filling:

> 2 pounds (910 g) **cream cheese**
>
> 3 **eggs**
>
> 1 can (8 ounces, or 235 ml) **sweetened condensed milk**
>
> $1/2$ cup (120 ml) frozen **orange juice concentrate**, thawed

To make the crust:

Preheat the oven to 350°F (180°C, gas mark 4). Spray a 10-inch springform pan with nonstick cooking spray. Cut out a 10-inch circle of parchment paper and line the bottom of the pan. Line the outside bottom and sides of the pan with foil. Mix together the cookie crumbs and the butter. Press the mixture into the bottom of the springform pan evenly.

Bake for 12 to 15 minutes, until the crumbs are set. Cool completely.

To make the filling:

Place the cream cheese in a mixing bowl and mix it on medium speed until perfectly smooth, 8 to 10 minutes. Add the eggs, one at a time, beating until incorporated after each egg. Add the condensed milk and mix until well combined. Stir in the orange juice concentrate and beat until well combined. Pour the batter onto the prepared crust and place the springform pan into a larger baking dish. Pour 1 to 2 inches ($2^{1}/2$ to 5 cm) of hot water into the baking pan.

Bake for 55 to 60 minutes, until set. (The center will jiggle slightly. Watch to not allow the cake to soufflé.) Allow to cool in the water bath, then refrigerate overnight. Remove the pan sides and flip the cake onto a cardboard cake round. Remove the bottom of the pan and the parchment, then flip again right side up onto another cake round or a serving platter. Cut with a thin knife run under hot water.

YIELD: Serves 12

ADD IT! Drizzle thin hot chocolate sauce over each slice.

Super Chocolate Cheesecake

Here's a recipe for the loud and proud multitudes of chocolate fanatics out there.

For the crust:

> 2 cups crushed **Nabisco Famous Chocolate Wafer cookies** (about 25 cookies)
>
> 1/2 cup (1 stick, or 112 g) butter, melted

For the filling:

> 8 ounces (225 g) **milk chocolate**
>
> 2 pounds (910 g) **cream cheese**
>
> 3 **eggs**
>
> 1 can (14 ounces, or 425 ml) **chocolate sweetened condensed milk**

To make the crust:

Preheat the oven to 350°F (180°C, gas mark 4). Spray a 10-inch springform pan with nonstick cooking spray. Cut out a 10-inch circle of parchment paper and line the bottom of the pan. Line the outside bottom and sides of the pan with foil.

In a bowl, mix together the cookie crumbs and the butter. Press the mixture into the bottom of the springform pan evenly.

Bake for 12 to 15 minutes, until the crumbs are set. Cool completely in the pan.

To make the filling:

Melt half of the chocolate in a double boiler and set aside.

Place the cream cheese in a mixing bowl and mix it on medium speed until perfectly smooth, 8 to 10 minutes. Add the eggs, one at a time, beating until incorporated after each egg. Add the condensed milk and mix until well combined. Stir in the melted chocolate. Pour the batter onto the prepared crust and place the springform pan into a larger baking dish. Pour 1 to 2 inches (2½ to 5 cm) of hot water into the baking pan.

Bake for 55 to 60 minutes, until set. (The center will jiggle slightly. Watch that the cake does not soufflé.) Allow to cool in the water bath, then refrigerate overnight. Remove the pan sides and flip the cake onto a cardboard cake round. Remove the bottom of the pan and the parchment, then flip again right side up onto another cake round or a serving platter.

In a saucepan, melt the remaining chocolate and drizzle it decoratively over the top of the cake. Cut with a thin knife run under hot water.

YIELD: Serves 12

🍰 Chocolate-Cherry Cheesecake

If you can't find chocolate condensed milk, add 4 ounces (115 g) melted semisweet chocolate to the mixture.

For the crust:

> 2 cups (200 g) crushed **Nabisco Famous Chocolate Wafer cookies**
> 1/2 cup (1 stick, or 112 g) butter, melted

For the filling:

> 2 pounds (910 g) **cream cheese**
> 3 **eggs**
> 1 cup (235 ml) chocolate **sweetened condensed milk**
> 1 can (14 ounces, or 400 g) **cherry pie filling**

To make the crust:

Preheat the oven to 350°F (180°C, gas mark 4). Spray a 10-inch springform pan with nonstick cooking spray. Cut out a 10-inch circle of parchment paper and line the bottom of the pan. Line the outside bottom and sides of the pan with foil.

In a bowl, mix together the cookie crumbs and the butter. Press the mixture into the bottom of the springform pan evenly.

Bake for 12 to 15 minutes, until the crumbs are set. Cool completely in the pan.

To make the filling:

Place the cream cheese in a mixing bowl and mix it on medium speed until perfectly smooth, 8 to 10 minutes. Add the eggs, one at a time, beating until incorporated after each egg. Add the condensed milk and mix until well combined. Pour the batter onto the prepared crust and place the springform pan into a larger baking dish. Pour 1 to 2 inches (2 1/2 to 5 cm) of hot water into the baking pan.

Bake for 55 to 60 minutes, until set. (The center will jiggle slightly. Watch to not allow the cake to soufflé.) Allow to cool in the water bath, then refrigerate overnight. Remove the pan sides and flip the cake onto a cardboard cake round. Remove the bottom of the pan and the parchment, then flip again right side up onto another cake round or a serving platter. Top with the cherry pie filling. Cut with a thin knife run under hot water.

YIELD: Serves 12

Chocolate-Strawberry Swirl Cheesecake

If you can't find chocolate condensed milk, add 4 ounces (115 g) melted semisweet chocolate to the mixture.

For the crust:

> 2 cups **crushed vanilla wafer cookies** (about 30 cookies)
> 1/2 cup (1 stick, or 112g) butter, melted

For the filling:

> 2 pounds (910 g) **cream cheese**
> 3 **eggs**
> 14 ounces (425 ml) **chocolate sweetened condensed milk**
> 1 cup (320 g) **strawberry jam**

To make the crust:

Preheat the oven to 350°F (180°C, gas mark 4). Spray a 10-inch springform pan with nonstick cooking spray. Cut out a 10-inch circle of parchment paper and line the bottom of the pan. Line the outside bottom and sides of the pan with foil.

In a bowl, mix together the cookie crumbs and the butter. Press the mixture into the bottom of the springform pan evenly.

Bake for 12 to 15 minutes, until the crumbs are set. Cool completely in the pan.

To make the filling:

Place the cream cheese in a mixing bowl and mix it on medium speed until perfectly smooth, 8 to 10 minutes. Add the eggs, one at a time, beating until incorporated after each egg. Add the condensed milk and mix until well combined. Pour the batter onto the prepared crust. Spoon the jam around the top of the cake and swirl the jam into the filling using a spoon. Place the springform pan into a larger baking dish. Pour 1 to 2 inches (2 1/2 to 5 cm) of hot water into the baking pan.

Bake for 55 to 60 minutes, until set. (The center will jiggle slightly. Watch to not allow the cake to soufflé.) Allow to cool in the water bath, then refrigerate overnight. Remove the pan sides and flip the cake onto a cardboard cake round. Remove the bottom of the pan and the parchment, then flip again right side up onto another cake round or a serving platter. Cut with a thin knife run under hot water.

YIELD: Serves 12

ADD IT! Swirl some mini chocolate chips into the filling along with the jam.

🍰 Oreo Cheesecake

If you can't find chocolate condensed milk, stir 4 ounces (115 g) melted semisweet chocolate or 1/3 cup (30 g) cocoa powder into the mix.

For the crust:

> 2 cups crushed **Oreo cookies** (about 15 cookies)
> 1/2 cup (1 stick, or 112 g) butter, melted

For the filling:

> 2 pounds (910 g) **cream cheese**
> 3 **eggs**
> 1 can (14 ounces, or 425 ml) **chocolate sweetened condensed milk**
> 2 teaspoons **vanilla extract**
> 1 cup crushed **Oreo cookies**

To make the crust:

Preheat the oven to 350°F (180°C, gas mark 4). Spray a 10-inch springform pan with nonstick cooking spray. Cut out a 10-inch circle of parchment paper and line the bottom of the pan. Line the outside bottom and sides of the pan with foil.

In a bowl, mix together the cookie crumbs and butter. Press the mixture into the bottom of the springform pan evenly.

Bake for 12 to 15 minutes, until the crumbs are set. Cool completely in the pan.

To make the filling:

Place the cream cheese in a mixing bowl and mix it on medium speed until perfectly smooth, 8 to 10 minutes. Add the eggs, one at a time, beating until incorporated after each egg. Add the condensed milk and vanilla and mix until well combined. Stir in the crushed cookies. Pour the batter onto the prepared crust and place the springform pan into a larger baking dish. Pour 1 to 2 inches (2 1/2 to 5 cm) of hot water into the baking pan.

Bake for 55 to 60 minutes, until set. (The center will jiggle slightly. Watch that the cake does not soufflé.) Allow to cool in the water bath, then refrigerate overnight. Remove the pan sides and flip the cake onto a cardboard cake round.

Remove the bottom of the pan and the parchment, then flip again right side up onto another cake round or a serving platter. Cut with a thin knife run under hot water.

YIELD: Serves 12

Peanut Butter Chocolate Chip Cheesecake

Talk about over the top: rich dairy, peanut butter, and chocolate, all in one dessert. This is a dessert monger's idea of heaven.

For the crust:

> 2 cups crushed **peanut butter sandwich cookies**
>
> $1/2$ cup (1 stick, or 112 g) butter, melted

For the filling:

> $1 1/2$ pounds (675 g) **cream cheese**
>
> 3 **eggs**
>
> 1 cup creamy **peanut butter**
>
> 2 cups semisweet **chocolate chips**

To make the crust:

Preheat the oven to 350°F (180°C, gas mark 4). Spray a 10-inch springform pan with nonstick cooking spray. Cut out a 10-inch circle of parchment paper and line the bottom of the pan. Line the outside bottom and sides of the pan with foil. Mix together the cookie crumbs and the butter. Press the mixture into the bottom of the springform pan evenly. Bake for 12 to 15 minutes, until the crumbs are set. Cool completely.

To make the filling:

Mix the cream cheese until perfectly smooth, about 8 to 10 minutes. Add the eggs, one at a time, beating until incorporated after each egg. Add the peanut butter and mix for 3 to 4 minutes, until smooth. Stir in the chocolate chips. Pour the batter onto the prepared crust and place the springform pan into a baking dish large enough to fit it. Pour 1 to 2 inches ($2 1/2$ to 5 cm) of hot water into the baking pan.

Bake for 55 to 60 minutes, until set. The center will jiggle slightly. Watch that the cake does not soufflé. Allow to cool in the water bath, then refrigerate overnight. Remove the pan sides and flip the cake onto a cake round. Remove the bottom of the pan and the parchment, then flip again right side up onto another cake round, or a serving platter. Cut with a thin knife run under hot water.

YIELD: Serves 12

Girl Scout Cookie Cheesecake

Chocolate and mint—a heavenly combination! If you can't find chocolate condensed milk, mix 4 ounces (115 g) melted chocolate or cocoa powder into the mixture.

For the crust:

> 2 cups crushed **Nabisco Famous chocolate wafer cookies** (about 25 cookies)
> 1/2 cup (1 stick, or 112 g) butter, melted

For the filling:

> 1 1/2 pounds (675 g) **cream cheese**
> 3 **eggs**
> 1 can (14 ounces, or 425 ml) **chocolate sweetened condensed milk**
> 1/2 cup (120 ml) **peppermint schnapps**

To make the crust:

Preheat the oven to 350°F (180°C, gas mark 4). Spray a 10-inch springform pan with nonstick cooking spray. Cut out a 10-inch circle of parchment paper and line the bottom of the pan. Line the outside bottom and sides of the pan with foil.

In a bowl, mix together the cookie crumbs and the butter. Press the mixture into the bottom of the springform pan evenly.

Bake for 12 to 15 minutes, until the crumbs are set. Cool completely in the pan.

To make the filling:

Place the cream cheese in a mixing bowl and mix it on medium speed until perfectly smooth, 8 to 10 minutes. Add the eggs, one at a time, beating until incorporated after each egg. Add the condensed milk and the schnapps and mix until well combined and smooth. Pour the batter onto the prepared crust and place the springform pan into a larger baking dish. Pour 1 to 2 inches ($2^1/2$ to 5 cm) of hot water into the baking pan.

Bake for 55 to 60 minutes, until set. (The center will jiggle slightly. Be careful to not allow the cake to soufflé.) Allow to cool in the water bath, then refrigerate overnight. Remove the pan sides and flip the cake onto a cardboard cake round. Remove the bottom of the pan and the parchment, then flip again right side up onto another cake round or a serving platter. Cut with a thin knife run under hot water.

YIELD: Serves 12

Ginger Cheesecake

We have a small fetish for candied ginger, an old-fashioned candy that has a real afterburner bite. That spicy kick really brings this cheesecake to the next level.

For the crust:

> 2 cups crushed **gingersnap cookies**
>
> 1/2 cup (1 stick, or 112 g) butter, melted

For the filling:

> 2 pounds (910 g) **cream cheese**
>
> 3 **eggs**
>
> 1 can (14 ounces, or 425 ml) **sweetened condensed milk**
>
> 1 cup (220 g) **candied ginger**, finely minced, plus slices for garnish

To make the crust:

Preheat the oven to 350°F (180°C, gas mark 4). Spray a 10-inch springform pan with pan spray. Cut out a 10-inch circle of parchment paper and line the bottom of the pan. Line the outside bottom and sides of the pan with foil. Mix together the cookie crumbs and the butter. Press the mixture into the bottom of the springform pan evenly. Bake for 12 to 15 minutes, until the crumbs are set. Cool completely.

To make the filling:

Mix the cream cheese until perfectly smooth, about 8 to 10 minutes. Add the eggs, one at a time, beating until incorporated after each egg. Add the condensed milk and mix until well combined and smooth. Stir in the minced candied ginger. Pour the batter onto the prepared crust and place the springform pan into a baking dish large enough to fit it. Pour 1 to 2 inches of hot water into the baking pan.

Bake for 55 to 60 minutes, until set. The center will jiggle slightly. Allow to cool in the water bath, then remove and refrigerate overnight. Remove the pan sides and flip the cake onto a cake round. Remove the bottom of the pan and the parchment, then flip again right side up onto another cake round, or a serving platter. Garnish with candied ginger slices. Cut with a thin knife run under hot water.

YIELD: Serves 12

Irish Cream Cheesecake

For the crust:

> 2 cups crushed **vanilla wafer cookies** (about 30 cookies)
>
> 1/2 cup (1 stick, or 112 g) butter, melted

For the filling:

> 2 pounds (910 g) **cream cheese**
>
> 3 **eggs**
>
> 1 can (8 ounces, or 235 ml) **sweetened condensed milk**
>
> 1 cup (235 ml) **Irish cream liqueur**

To make the crust:

Preheat the oven to 350°F (180°C, gas mark 4). Spray a 10-inch springform pan with nonstick cooking spray. Cut out a 10-inch circle of parchment paper and line the bottom of the pan. Line the outside bottom and sides of the pan with foil.

In a bowl, mix together the cookie crumbs and butter. Press the mixture into the bottom of the springform pan evenly.

Bake for 12 to 15 minutes, until the crumbs are set. Cool completely in the pan.

To make the filling:

Place the cream cheese in a mixing bowl and mix it on medium speed until perfectly smooth, 8 to 10 minutes. Add the eggs, one at a time, beating until incorporated after each egg. Add the condensed milk and Irish cream. Mix until well combined. Stir in the Irish cream. Pour the batter onto the prepared crust and place the springform pan into a larger baking dish. Pour 1 to 2 inches (2 1/2 to 5 cm) of hot water into the baking pan.

Bake for 55 to 60 minutes, until set. (The center will jiggle slightly. Watch to not allow the cake to soufflé.) Allow to cool in the water bath, then refrigerate overnight. Remove the pan sides and flip the cake onto a cardboard cake round. Remove the bottom of the pan and the parchment, then flip again right side up onto another cake round or a serving platter. Cut with a thin knife run under hot water.

YIELD: Serves 12

ADD IT! Top this cheesecake with whipped cream that has a little Irish cream mixed into it.

Italian Cheesecake

This is a lighter version of cheesecake made with ricotta cheese instead of the more common cream cheese.

For the crust:

> 2 cups (200 g) **graham cracker crumbs**
>
> 1/2 cup (100 g) **vanilla sugar** (See "Making Vanilla Sugar" on page 12.)
>
> 1/2 cup (1 stick, or 112 g) butter, melted

For the filling:

> 1 container (15 ounces, or 430 g) **ricotta cheese**
>
> 2 cups (400 g) **vanilla sugar** (See "Making Vanilla Sugar" on page 12.)
>
> 1/4 cup (30 g) all-purpose flour
>
> 6 **eggs**

To make the crust:

Preheat the oven to 350°F (180°C, gas mark 4). Spray a 10-inch springform pan with nonstick cooking spray. Cut out a 10-inch circle of parchment paper and line the bottom of the pan. Line the outside bottom and sides of the pan with foil.

Mix the graham cracker crumbs and the sugar in a mixing bowl. Stir the butter into the crumb mixture. Press the mixture into the bottom of the springform pan evenly.

Bake for 12 to 15 minutes, until the crumbs are set and the crust is lightly browned. Cool completely in the pan.

To make the filling:

Beat the ricotta on medium speed until perfectly smooth, 4 to 5 minutes.

Add the sugar and flour and beat for another 4 to 5 minutes, scraping down the bowl and beater often. Add the eggs, one at a time, beating until incorporated after each egg. Pour the batter onto the prepared crust and place the springform pan into a larger baking dish. Pour 1 to 2 inches (2 1/2 to 5 cm) of hot water into the baking pan.

Bake for 55 to 60 minutes, until set. (The center will jiggle slightly. Watch that the cake does not soufflé.) Allow to cool in the water bath, then refrigerate overnight. Remove the pan sides and flip the cake onto a cardboard cake round. Remove the bottom of the pan and the parchment, then flip again right side up onto another cake round or a serving platter. Cut with a thin knife run under hot water.

YIELD: Serves 12

ADD IT! This would be delicious with Warm Lemon Sauce (page 485) poured over it.

Pumpkin Cheesecake

Pre-spiced and sweetened pumpkin puree is now widely available. (We found it in every major supermarket we looked in.) If you can't find sweetened spiced pumpkin, use regular canned pumpkin and add 2 teaspoons apple pie spice and 1 cup (225 g) packed light brown sugar to the batter.

For the crust:

> 2 cups **gingersnap crumbs** (about 20 cookies)
>
> 1/2 cup (1 stick, or 112g) butter, melted

For the filling:

> 2 pounds (910 g) **cream cheese**
>
> 1/4 cup (30 g) **all-purpose flour**
>
> 6 **eggs**
>
> 1 can (16 ounces, or 455 g) spiced and sweetened **pumpkin**

To make the crust:

Preheat the oven to 350°F (180°C, gas mark 4). Spray a 12-inch springform pan with nonstick cooking spray. Cut out a 12-inch circle of parchment paper and line the bottom of the pan. Line the outside bottom and sides of the pan with foil.

Put the gingersnap crumbs in a mixing bowl. Add the butter and stir it into the crumbs. Press the mixture into the bottom of the springform pan evenly.

Bake for 12 to 15 minutes, until the crumbs are set and the crust is lightly browned. Cool completely in the pan.

To make the filling:

Place the cream cheese in a mixing bowl and mix it on medium speed until perfectly smooth, 8 to 10 minutes. Add the flour and beat for another 4 to 5 minutes, scraping down the bowl and beater often. Add the eggs, one at a time, beating until incorporated after each egg. Add the pumpkin and mix until well combined. Pour the batter onto the prepared crust and place the springform pan into a larger baking dish. Pour 1 to 2 inches (2 1/2 to 5 cm) of hot water into the baking pan.

Bake for 55 to 60 minutes, until set. (The center will jiggle slightly. Watch to not allow the cake to soufflé.) Allow to cool in the water bath, then refrigerate overnight. Remove the pan sides and flip the cake onto a cardboard cake round. Remove the bottom of the pan and the parchment, then flip again right side up onto another cake round or a serving platter. Cut with a thin knife run under hot water.

YIELD: Serves 16

ADD IT! Drizzle maple syrup over each slice before serving.

Toffee Cheesecake

After a childhood spent nibbling Heath bars, this cheesecake is like a dream come true.

For the crust:

> 2 cups crushed **Nabisco Famous Chocolate Wafer cookies** (about 25 cookies)
> 1/2 cup (1 stick, or 112 g) butter, melted

For the filling:

> 2 pounds (910 g) **cream cheese**
> 3 **eggs**
> 1 can (14 ounces, or 425 ml) **sweetened condensed milk**
> 2 cups (350 g) **toffee bits**

To make the crust:

Preheat the oven to 350°F (180°C, gas mark 4). Spray a 10-inch springform pan with nonstick cooking spray. Cut out a 10-inch circle of parchment paper and line the bottom of the pan. Line the outside bottom and sides of the pan with foil.

In a bowl, mix together the cookie crumbs and butter. Press the mixture into the bottom of the springform pan evenly.

Bake for 12 to 15 minutes, until the crumbs are set. Cool completely in the pan.

To make the filling:

Place the cream cheese in a mixing bowl and mix it on medium speed until perfectly smooth, 8 to 10 minutes. Add the eggs, one at a time, beating until incorporated after each egg. Add the condensed milk and mix until well combined. Stir in the toffee bits. Pour the batter onto the prepared crust and place the springform pan into a larger baking dish. Pour 1 to 2 inches (2 1/2 to 5 cm) of hot water into the baking pan.

Bake for 55 to 60 minutes, until set. (The center will jiggle slightly. Watch that the cake does not soufflé.) Allow to cool in the water bath, then refrigerate overnight. Remove the pan sides and flip the cake onto a cardboard cake round. Remove the bottom of the pan and the parchment, then flip again right side up onto another cake round or a serving platter. Cut with a thin knife run under hot water.

YIELD: Serves 12

ADD IT! Hot chocolate sauce drizzled over each slice would make this irresistable.

CHAPTER FOUR

Pies and Tarts

According to an informal study we conducted, dessert favorites tend to split along gender lines: Women almost always go for cake, while men overwhelmingly vote for pie when given a choice. In fact, we know several people who insist on birthday pie instead of cake. And why not? Fruit pies, cream pies, custard pies, pies with some degree of chocolate in them—the choices are endless, and the preparation can be incredibly simple. If you want to dress things up a tad, try a tart, which has a slightly swankier reputation, but, again, doesn't have to be difficult to make. And the results, of course, will be delicious.

Basic Pie Crust

Making pie crust is as easy as falling off a log, although fewer and fewer people do it these days (make pie crust—we have no data on how many fall off a log.) We will be using this basic pie crust recipe in many of the following pie recipes, although we won't tell if you choose to use premade pie crust. In all good conscience, however, we have to say that while prepared crust has come a long way, a good homemade crust will always bake up flakier and more tender.

This is a recipe for a two-crust, 9-inch pie. For a one-crust pie, just cut the recipe in half. Even better, make two pies.

Now a word about the fat. You can choose from the delightful trio of lard, shortening, or butter. It is a matter of personal preference. They all work, although butter is a bit harder to work with than the other two. To our way of thinking, a pie crust should have a fresh and neutral flavor. There should be no off notes, nor should the crust be assertive in flavor. The crust should be tender and flaky—but not completely shatter. We find that shortening is the best choice, but we understand people who prefer lard. We think that butter is best left to tart shells, but hey, it's your pie.

> $1/2$ teaspoon salt
> $2^1/2$ cups (310 g) all-purpose flour
> $3/4$ cup (150 g) shortening
> $1/2$ cup (60 ml) cold water

Combine the salt and flour in a mixing bowl. Add the shortening and cut into the flour until the mixture resembles cornmeal. Stir in the water and bring the dough together in a ball. Knead on a floured surface a few times, cover with plastic wrap, and allow the dough to rest for 10 minutes. It is now ready to make into pie.

Divide the dough in half and roll out one-half into a circle 12 inches in diameter. Roll the dough around the rolling pin and transfer to the pie pan. Drape the dough over the pie pan and fit the dough into the pan. Fill the pie shell with your chosen filling. Roll out the other half of the dough and drape over the filling. Trim the edges of both crusts, leaving about $1/2$ inch of overhang all the way around. Pinch the two crusts together to seal and crimp decoratively. (See "Crimping Pie Dough" on page 19.)

◉ Pecan Pie

Our sainted mother once gave Carol's husband, Don, quite possibly the best birthday present ever: Pie of the Month Club, in which she baked the pie of his choice every month for a year. Pecan pie was his first choice (and second, and third.) With good reason—it's good stuff!

> 1/2 recipe **Basic Pie Crust** (page 94) or similar portion prepared crust
>
> 1 1/2 cups (150 g) **pecan halves** or pieces
>
> 4 **eggs**
>
> 3/4 cup (175 ml) **light corn syrup**
>
> 3/4 cup (150 g) **vanilla sugar** (See "Making Vanilla Sugar" on page 12.)
>
> 1/2 teaspoon salt
>
> 1/2 cup (1 stick, or 112 g) butter

Preheat the oven to 350°F (180°C, gas mark 4).

Prepare the pie crust per the recipe or package instructions.

Put the pecans in the unbaked pie crust.

In a mixing bowl lightly whisk the eggs and add the corn syrup, sugar, and salt. Mix thoroughly.

In a saucepan, melt the butter over low heat and stir into the egg mixture. Pour the mixture over the pecans.

Bake on a baking sheet for 40 to 45 minutes, until the crust is golden brown and the filling is set. Cool on a rack.

YIELD: Serves 6 to 8

ADD IT! For a slightly deeper, rawer taste, substitute molasses for the corn syrup.

Classic Apple Pie

All-American and always all right by us. We like it just as much at breakfast as we do for dessert. (P.S.: Our mother makes the best apple pie in the universe.) Cortland, Macintosh, or Granny Smith are good choices for this pie.

1 recipe **Basic Pie Crust** (page 94) or similar portion prepared crust

3 pounds (1.5 kg) **apples** (about 6 to 7)

1 cup (200 g) **sugar**

1/4 teaspoon salt

3 teaspoons **apple pie spice**

Juice of 1 **lemon**

2 tablespoons (28 g) butter, cut into small pieces

Preheat the oven to 350°F (180°C, gas mark 4).

Prepare the pie crust per the recipe or package instructions.

Peel and core the apples and cut them into 1/8-inch slices. In a large bowl, mix the apples, sugar, salt, and apple pie spice. Pile the mixture into the pie crust. Drizzle the lemon juice over and dot with the butter. Cover with the other crust and crimp the edges closed. Poke a few steam holes in the top of the pie.

Bake on a baking sheet for 45 to 50 minutes, until golden brown and the filling is bubbling out the seams just a bit. Cool before serving.

YIELD: Serves 6 to 8

ADD IT! If you can find cinnamon ice cream to serve on the side, you will be in heaven.

Dutch Apple Pie

The crunchy streusel topping makes this one a favorite, particularly for people with pie crimping anxiety. Cortland, Empire, Macintosh, or Granny Smith apples are good choices for this pie.

1/2 recipe **Basic Pie Crust** (page 94) or similar portion prepared crust

3 pounds (1.5 kg) **apples** (about 6 to 7)

1 cup (200 g) sugar

1/2 teaspoon salt

4 teaspoons **apple pie spice**

1 cup (120 g) **all-purpose flour**

1/2 cup (110 g) packed **light brown sugar**

1/2 cup (1 stick, or 112 g) butter

Preheat the oven to 350°F (180°C, gas mark 4).

Prepare the pie crust per the recipe or package instructions.

Peel and core the apples. Slice thin into 1/8-inch thick slices and put the apples into a large bowl. Add 1/2 cup (100 g) of the sugar, 1/4 teaspoon of the salt, and 2 teaspoons of the apple pie spice and mix well. Pile the apples into the pie crust.

Mix the remaining 1/2 cup (100 g) sugar, the remaining 1/4 teaspoon salt, and the remaining 2 teaspoons apple pie spice, the flour, and the brown sugar in a bowl. Cut in the butter until the mixture resembles peas and there are no more evident pieces of butter. Sprinkle the streusel evenly over the apples.

Bake for 45 to 50 minutes, until the streusel and crust are golden brown and the apples are bubbling. Cool.

YIELD: Serves 6 to 8

Sour Cream~Dutch Apple Pie

This pie is a variation on a delicious theme. We like Cortland, Empire, Macintosh, or Granny Smith apples for baking.

> 1/2 recipe **Basic Pie Crust** (page 94) or similar portion prepared crust
> 2 pounds (1 kg) **apples** (about 5 to 6)
> 1 1/2 cups (345 g) **sour cream**
> 1 cup (200 g) **sugar**
> 1/2 teaspoon salt
> 4 teaspoons **apple pie spice**
> 1 cup (120 g) **all-purpose flour**
> 1/2 cup (1 stick, or 112 g) butter

Preheat the oven to 350°F (180°C, gas mark 4).

Prepare the pie crust per the recipe or package instructions.

Peel and core the apples. Slice the apples into 1/8-inch thick slices and put them into a large bowl. Add the sour cream, 1/2 cup (100 g) of the sugar, 1/4 teaspoon of the salt, and 2 teaspoons of the apple pie spice and mix well. Pile the apples into the pie crust. (The apples should rise a little above the pie plate, but not hugely so.)

Mix the remaining 1/2 cup (100 g) sugar, the remaining 1/4 teaspoon salt, the remaining 2 teaspoons apple pie spice, and the flour in a bowl. Cut in the butter until the mixture resembles peas and there are no remaining large pieces. Sprinkle the streusel over the apples.

Bake on a baking sheet for 50 to 55 minutes, until the streusel and crust are golden brown and the apples are bubbling. Cool on a rack.

YIELD: Serves 6 to 8

Fresh Peach Pie

In New England, peach season is a compact and glorious highlight of late August. There's nothing better than taking a great big juicy bite of a perfect peach and feeling the juice dribble down your chin—unless it's the same peach in a pie. You can also use frozen sliced peaches to great success anytime.

> 1 recipe **Basic Pie Crust** (page 94) or similar portion prepared crust
>
> 3 pounds (1.5 kg) **peaches** (If using frozen, do not thaw.)
>
> 1 cup (200 g) **sugar**
>
> 1 teaspoon **cinnamon**
>
> 3 tablespoons (25 g) **cornstarch**
>
> 1/4 teaspoon salt
>
> 2 tablespoons (28 g) butter, cut into small pieces

Preheat the oven to 350°F (180°C, gas mark 4).

Prepare the pie crust per the recipe or package instructions.

Bring a large pot of water to a boil. Drop in the peaches for 15 to 20 seconds, then drain and run the peaches under cold water. Using a paring knife, remove the skins. Halve the peaches, remove the pits, and slice them up.

In a large bowl, mix together the peach slices, sugar, cinnamon, cornstarch, and salt. Pour into the pie crust. Dot with butter and top with the crust. Seal and crimp.

Bake on a baking sheet for 45 to 50 minutes, until the crust is golden brown and the filling is bubbling. Cool on a rack.

YIELD: Serves 6 to 8

Peach-Blueberry Pie

We think this might be the best summer fruit pie there is, but we need to conduct further exhaustive tasting research before we can state this conclusively. The sacrifices we make for science!

> 1 recipe **Basic Pie Crust** (page 94) or similar portion prepared crust
>
> 1 pound (455 g) **peaches**
>
> 2 cups (290 g) **blueberries**
>
> 1 cup (200 g) sugar
>
> 1 teaspoon **cinnamon**
>
> 2 tablespoons (15 g) **all-purpose flour**
>
> 1/4 teaspoon salt
>
> 2 tablespoons (28 g) butter, cut into small pieces

Preheat the oven to 350°F (180°C, gas mark 4).

Prepare the pie crust per the recipe or package instructions.

Bring a large pot of water to a boil. Drop in the peaches for 15 to 20 seconds, then drain and run the peaches under cold water. Using a paring knife, remove the skins. Halve the peaches, remove the pits, and slice up the fruit.

In a large bowl, mix together the blueberries and the peach slices, sugar, cinnamon, flour, and salt. Pour into the pie crust. Dot with butter and top with the crust. Seal and crimp the edges closed. Poke a few steam holes in the top crust.

Bake on a baking sheet for 45 to 50 minutes, until the crust is golden brown and the filling is bubbling. Cool on a rack.

YIELD: Serves 6 to 8

Blueberry Pie

Our folks use to drag us every summer up the slopes of Mt. Cranmore in New Hampshire to collect the tiny wild berries that clung to the rock ledges. To us, a handful of warm blueberries distills the taste of high summer to its essence. As such, it's not surprising that we consider wild blueberries the best for pies. Fresh or frozen both work fine, however.

- 1 recipe **Basic Pie Crust** (page 94) or similar portion prepared crust
- 3 cups (435 g) **blueberries** (If using frozen, do not thaw.)
- 1 cup (200 g) **sugar**
- 1 teaspoon **cinnamon**
- 3 tablespoons (25 g) **cornstarch**
- 1/4 teaspoon salt
- 2 tablespoons (28 g) butter, cut into small pieces

Preheat the oven to 350°F (180°C, gas mark 4). Prepare the pie crust per the recipe or package instructions. Line a 9-inch pie pan with one of the prepared crusts.

In a large bowl, mix together the blueberries, sugar, cinnamon, cornstarch, and salt. Pour into the pie crust. Dot with the butter and top with the remaining pie crust. Seal and crimp the edges shut.

Bake on a baking sheet for 45 to 50 minutes, until the crust is golden brown and the filling is bubbling. Cool on a rack.

YIELD: Serves 6 to 8

ADD IT! What else but vanilla ice cream alongside?

Mango Mousse Pie

This is a light pie for a warm evening.

- 1/2 cup (35 g) sweetened **shredded coconut**
- 6 ounces (175 ml) **sweetened condensed milk**
- 2 cups **fresh mango** pieces (about 2 mangos) or 1 jar (24 ounces, or 680 g) fresh-packed mango, drained
- 1 cup (235 ml) **heavy cream**
- 1 store-bought **graham cracker crumb pie crust**

To toast the coconut, spread the flakes out on the baking sheet of a toaster oven and toast until light brown.

Put the condensed milk and the mango in the bowl of a food processor fitted with the metal blade. Process until smooth and pour the puree into a mixing bowl.

In a separate bowl, whip the cream to stiff peaks. Gently fold the cream in thirds into the mango mixture. Pour the mousse into the pie crust and sprinkle the toasted coconut over. Refrigerate for at least 4 hours.

YIELD: Serves 6 to 8

Orange-Granola Crunch Pie

We know—anything with granola in it sounds suspiciously healthy, and why do we need that in a pie? But this pie is the bomb. It's light and tangy, and the added crunch is terrific.

- 1 container (8 ounces, or 225 g) **vanilla yogurt**
- 2 cans (8 ounces, or 225 g, each) **mandarin oranges**
- 1 cup (125 g) **granola**
- 1 cup (235 ml) **heavy cream**
- 1 store-bought **graham cracker crumb pie crust**

Put the yogurt in a mixing bowl. Drain the oranges and mix them in with the yogurt until well combined. Fold in the granola.

In a separate bowl, whip the cream to stiff peak and fold into the yogurt mixture. Pour into the crust. Refrigerate for 2 to 4 hours.

YIELD: Serves 6 to 8

ADD IT! Garnish with additional granola and whipped cream if desired.

Cherry Pie

Tart cherries like Montmorency cherries are the key to a great pie. Stay away from bings or other sweet varieties. If you can get fresh, great; otherwise frozen are just fine. Many people like a lattice crust on cherry pie.

1 recipe **Basic Pie Crust** (page 94) or similar portion prepared crust

3 cups (300 g) **tart cherries**, pitted (If using frozen, do not thaw.)

1 cup (200 g) **sugar**

1 teaspoon **cinnamon**

3 tablespoons (25 g) **cornstarch**

1/4 teaspoon salt

2 tablespoons (28 g) butter, cut into small pieces

Preheat the oven to 350°F (180°C, gas mark 4).

Prepare the pie crust per the recipe or package instructions.

In a large bowl, mix together the cherries, sugar, cinnamon, cornstarch, and salt. Pour into the pie crust. Dot with butter and top with the crust. Seal and crimp the edges together.

Bake on a baking sheet for 45 to 50 minutes, until the crust is golden brown and the filling is bubbling. Cool on a rack.

YIELD: Serves 6 to 8

Raspberry Pie

This is perfect for late summer when the raspberries are in season, although frozen berries also work. The filling in this one will be a jam-like consistency.

> 1 recipe **Basic Pie Crust** (page 94) or similar portion prepared crust
>
> 3 cups (370 g) **raspberries** (If using frozen, do not thaw.)
>
> 1 cup (200 g) **sugar**
>
> $1/2$ teaspoon **nutmeg**
>
> 3 tablespoons (25 g) **cornstarch**
>
> $1/4$ teaspoon salt
>
> 2 tablespoons ($1/4$ stick, or 28 g) **butter**, cut into small pieces

Preheat the oven to 350°F (180°C, gas mark 4).

Prepare the pie crust per the recipe or package instructions.

In a large bowl, mix together the raspberries, sugar, nutmeg, cornstarch, and salt. Pour into the pie crust. Dot with butter and top with the crust. Seal and crimp the edges closed.

Bake on a baking sheet for 45 to 50 minutes, until the crust is golden brown and the filling is bubbling. Cool on a rack.

YIELD: Serves 6 to 8

Strawberry Pie

> $1/2$ recipe **Basic Pie Crust** (page 94) or similar portion prepared crust
>
> 3 cups (500 g) **strawberries**, hulled and sliced, plus 10 to 12 whole strawberries for garnish
>
> $1 1/4$ cups (250 g) **sugar**
>
> 3 tablespoons (25 g) **cornstarch**
>
> $1/2$ cup (120 ml) water
>
> 1 cup (235 ml) **heavy cream**

Preheat the oven to 350°F (180°C, gas mark 4).

Prepare the pie crust per the recipe or package instructions.

Bake the crust for 15 to 20 minutes, until golden brown. Remove from oven and allow the crust to cool completely.

In a saucepan, mix together the strawberries, 1 cup (200 g) of the sugar, and the cornstarch. Add the water. Cook over medium heat, stirring, for 10 to 12 minutes, until the mixture thickens. Pour into the prepared pie crust and refrigerate for at least 2 hours.

Whip the cream with the remaining sugar. Cover the top of the pie with the whipped cream. Decorate with the whole strawberries.

YIELD: Serves 6 to 8

Strawberry-Cream Cheese Pie

Our friend Alice Kelly goes out one fine June morning every year and breaks her back picking strawberries. Then she comes home and has a strawberry mashing frenzy so that she can freeze enough to keep her rich in this pie for the entire year. We like to visit for pie in January, as we are not nearly so organized.

> 1/2 recipe **Basic Pie Crust** (page 94) or similar portion prepared crust
> 1 quart (16 ounces, or 455 g) **fresh strawberries**, hulled
> 1 cup (200 g) **sugar**
> 3 tablespoons (25 g) **cornstarch**
> 3 ounces (85 g) **cream cheese**

Preheat the oven to 350°F (180°C, gas mark 4).

Prepare the pie crust according to the recipe or package instructions.

Bake the crust for 20 to 25 minutes, until golden brown. Cool completely.

Mash the berries well. Stir in a saucepan with the sugar and cornstarch. Cook on low to medium heat, stirring constantly, until mixture thickens and boils. Once it starts to boil, stir and cook for 1 minute more. Cool for 15 to 20 minutes.

In a bowl, beat the cream cheese until smooth and spread on the bottom of the pie crust. Pour the strawberries onto the cream cheese and smooth out top. Refrigerate uncovered for several hours.

YIELD: Serves 6 to 8

ADD IT! This is great served with whipped cream.

Raisin~Sour Cream Pie

Here's an old-fashioned pie that is still found in northern New England diners. If you like mincemeat, we bet you'll like this one, too.

1/2 recipe **Basic Pie Crust** (page 94) or similar portion prepared crust

2 cups (290 g) **raisins**

1 cup (230 g) **sour cream**

4 **egg yolks**

1 cup (200 g) **cinnamon sugar** (See "Making Cinnamon Sugar" on page 12.)

Preheat the oven to 350°F (180°C, gas mark 4). Prepare the pie crust per the recipe or package instructions.

In a mixing bowl, combine the raisins, sour cream, egg yolks, and sugar. Stir until well combined. Pour into the pie crust.

Bake on a baking sheet for 45 to 50 minutes, until the filling is set. Cool to room temperature.

YIELD: Serves 6 to 8

ADD IT! Mix 1/4 cup (around 25 g) chopped nuts of your choice into the filling for some crunch.

Rhubarb Pie

Sweet and tart—a springtime favorite. This recipe is for the purist who wants no truck with new-fangled strawberry additions.

1 recipe **Basic Pie Crust** (page 94) or similar portion prepared crust

3 cups (365 g) diced **rhubarb**

1 cup (200 g) **sugar**

1 teaspoon **apple pie spice**

2 tablespoons (15 g) **cornstarch**

1/4 teaspoon salt

2 tablespoons (28 g) butter, cut into small pieces

Preheat the oven to 350°F (180°C, gas mark 4).

Prepare the pie crust per the recipe or package instructions.

In a large bowl, mix together the rhubarb, sugar, apple pie spice, cornstarch, and salt. Pour into the pie crust. Dot with butter and top with the crust. Seal and crimp the edges together.

Bake on a baking sheet for 45 to 50 minutes, until the crust is golden brown and the filling is bubbling. Cool on a rack.

YIELD: Serves 6 to 8

Key Lime Pie

Smaller, sweeter, and yellower than the garden variety limes you buy for gin and tonics, key limes are a seasonal pleasure. If you can't find the fresh fruit (and it is unlikely you will), bottled key lime juice is widely available.

> 1/2 cup (120 ml) **key lime juice**
> 12 ounces (355 ml) **evaporated milk**
> 4 **egg yolks**
> 1 cup (200 g) **sugar**
> 1 store-bought **graham cracker crumb pie crust**

Preheat the oven to 350°F (180°C, gas mark 4).

Put the lime juice and evaporated milk into a saucepan and bring to a simmer.

Put the yolks into a mixing bowl and whisk lightly. Add the sugar and whisk together. Whisk in the hot liquid in a thin stream and stir until the sugar is dissolved. Pour into the pie crust.

Bake on a baking sheet for 35 to 40 minutes, until the filling is set. Refrigerate for 4 to 6 hours.

YIELD: Serves 6 to 8

Brownie Pie

If you can't find chocolate condensed milk, add 2 tablespoons (10 g) cocoa powder to regular condensed milk.

1/2 recipe **Basic Pie Crust** (page 94) or similar portion prepared crust

1 cup (175 g) **semisweet chocolate chips**

1/4 cup (1/2 stick, or 55 g) butter

1 can (8 ounces, or 235 ml) **chocolate sweetened condensed milk**

1/2 cup (60 g) **biscuit baking mix**

2 **eggs**

Preheat the oven to 375°F (190°C, gas mark 5). Prepare the pie crust per the recipe or package directions and place in a 9-inch pie pan. Bake the pie crust for 10 minutes; remove from the oven. Reduce the oven temperature to 350°F (180°C, gas mark 4).

Combine the chocolate chips and butter in a saucepan and melt them over low heat. Put the chocolate mixture into a mixing bowl and add the condensed milk, biscuit mix, and eggs. Beat on medium speed until smooth.

Pour the chocolate mixture into the pie crust. Bake 35 to 40 minutes, or until center is set. Serve warm or at room temperature.

YIELD: Serves 6 to 8

ADD IT! For some crunch, add in 1 cup (125 g) chopped walnuts along with the biscuit mix.

Brownie-Cherry Cheesecake Pie

This makes for a rich and delicious dish that you can further gild with warm Chocolate Sauce (page 492) or store-bought chocolate sauce and whipped cream. If you wish for less of an individual cherry presence, send the cherry pie filling through a food processor to break the cherries up.

    1 package (16 ounces, or 455 g) **brownie mix**

    1 **egg**

    1/4 cup (60 ml) vegetable oil

    1/2 cup (120 ml) water

    1 **chocolate cookie pie crust**

    9 ounces (255 g) canned **cherry pie filling**

    1/2 cup (115 g) **cream cheese**, softened

Preheat the oven to 350°F (180°C, gas mark 4).

In a mixing bowl, stir together the brownie mix, egg, oil, and water. Put half of the brownie batter in the pie crust and spread the cherry pie filling on top. Dot with the cream cheese. Cover with the remaining brownie batter.

Bake for 55 to 60 minutes, until the brownie batter is set. Cool to room temperature.

YIELD: Serves 6 to 8

ADD IT! Beat 1 teaspoon milk into the cream cheese to make it easier to spread.

NOTE: If your market does not carry these crusts, you can make your own by grinding 12 to 15 Oreo cookies in a food processor, mixing them with 8 tablespoons (115 g) melted butter, and pressing the crumbs into an 8-inch pie pan. Bake for 8 to 10 minutes and cool.

Chocolate Chess Pie

Chess pie is a classic Southern pastry, although the origins of the name are unclear. We prefer the story about the southern cook, who when asked what kind of pie she was serving, answered, "Oh, jes' pie." Here, we add a flavor twist with chocolate.

1/2 recipe **Basic Pie Crust** (page 94) or similar portion prepared crust

1/2 cup (1 stick, or 112 g) butter

2 ounces (55 g) **bittersweet chocolate**

1 cup (200 g) **sugar**

1/8 teaspoon salt

3 **eggs**

1 teaspoon **vanilla extract**

Preheat the oven to 350°F (180°C, gas mark 4).

Prepare the pie crust per the recipe or package directions

In a heavy 1-quart saucepan, melt the butter and chocolate together over low heat. Mix well.

Combine the sugar and the salt in a mixing bowl. Add the eggs and vanilla and mix well. Stir in the chocolate mixture and mix until thoroughly combined. Pour the mixture into the pie crust.

Bake for 35 to 40 minutes, until the filling is just set. Cool.

YIELD: Serves 6 to 8

ADD IT! Vanilla ice cream or whipped cream add further riches to the plate.

Chocolate Silk Pie

This makes a light-textured but very rich pie.

   1/2 recipe **Basic Pie Crust** (page 94) or similar portion prepared crust

   3/4 cup (1 1/2 sticks, or 170 g) **butter**, softened

   1 cup (200 g) **sugar**

   2 ounces (55 g) **bittersweet chocolate**

   1/8 teaspoon salt

   4 **eggs**, you can use pasturized eggs

Preheat the oven to 350°F (180°C, gas mark 4).

Prepare the pie crust per the recipe or package directions and bake for 20 to 25 minutes, until golden brown. Cool completely.

Cream the butter and sugar together until fluffy—4 to 5 minutes—and set aside.

In a heavy 1-quart saucepan, melt the chocolate over low heat. Mix the melted chocolate and salt into the butter mixture until combined. Add the eggs, one at a time, beating for 5 minutes after each addition. Spoon mixture into the pie crust and refrigerate for at least 4 hours.

YIELD: Serves 6 to 8

ADD IT! Cut the richness of the pie with a scattering of fresh raspberries.

Chocolate-Hazelnut Cream Pie

This is a custardlike pie, with the added crunch of nuts.

$^1/_2$ recipe **Basic Pie Crust** (page 94) or similar portion prepared crust

4 ounces (115 g) **milk chocolate**

1 $^1/_2$ cups (355 ml) **chocolate milk**

$^1/_8$ teaspoon salt

3 **eggs**

1 cup (115 g) chopped **hazelnuts**

Preheat the oven to 350°F (180°C, gas mark 4).

Prepare the pie crust per the recipe or package directions.

In a heavy 1-quart saucepan, melt the chocolate over low heat. Stir in the milk and salt and bring the mixture to a simmer.

Whisk the eggs in a mixing bowl and add the hot liquid in a stream, whisking.

Put the hazelnuts into the pie crust and pour the chocolate mixture over them.

Bake for 35 to 40 minutes, until the filling is just set. Refrigerate for at least 2 hours.

YIELD: Serves 6 to 8

ADD IT! Toss a handful of chocolate chips into the bottom of the pie crust along with the hazelnuts for deeper chocolate flavor.

Chocolate-Peanut Butter Pie

This is the stuff—rich, multiflavored, possessed of the ability to lure the unsuspecting person from a sound sleep to a plateful of pie in a matter of minutes.

$1/2$ recipe **Basic Pie Crust** (page 94) or similar portion prepared pie crust

1 cup (175 g) semisweet **chocolate chips**

1 cup chunky (260 g) **peanut butter**

1 cup (235 ml) light **corn syrup**

$1/2$ cup (1 stick, or 112 g) butter

4 **eggs**

Preheat the oven to 350°F (180°C, gas mark 4).

Prepare the pie crust per the recipe or package directions.

Put the chocolate chips in the pie crust.

In a saucepan, mix together the peanut butter, corn syrup, and butter. Cook over medium heat until the butter and peanut butter have melted.

Whisk the eggs in a mixing bowl and whisk into the melted mixture. Pour into the pie crust.

Bake on a cookie sheet for 40 to 45 minutes, until the filling is set. Allow to cool on a rack, then refrigerate or serve at room temperature.

YIELD: Serves 6 to 8

☙ Chocolate-Toffee Pie

Our molars ache just thinking of the sweetness of this one. But while we fear retribution at the hands of a posse of indignant dentists, we have to say that testers large and small gave this one two thumbs up.

> 1 jar (10 ounces, or 280 g) **marshmallow fluff**
> 6 ounces (170 g) **milk chocolate**
> 1 cup (175 g) **toffee bits**
> 1 cup (235 ml) **heavy cream**
> 1 **chocolate cookie pie crust**

In a saucepan, melt the marshmallow and the chocolate over low heat, mixing thoroughly. Allow to cool for 10 minutes, then fold in the toffee.

In a bowl, whip the cream to stiff peaks and fold into the chocolate mixture. Pour into the pie crust and refrigerate for at least 2 hours.

YIELD: Serves 6 to 8

ADD IT! You can dial back the sweetness by substituting dark chocolate for milk chocolate.

☙ Kentucky Derby Pie

This is a traditional Derby Day treat. It is basically a chocolate chip cookie baked into a pie crust, and we're all for it.

> 1/2 recipe **Basic Pie Crust** (page 94) or similar portion prepared crust
> 1 package (16 ounces, or 455 g) **chocolate chip cookie mix**
> 2 **eggs**
> 1 cup (125 g) chopped **walnuts**
> 1/2 cup (120 ml) **chocolate syrup**

Preheat the oven to 350°F (180°C, gas mark 4).

Prepare the pie crust per the recipe or package instructions.

In a large bowl, mix together the cookie mix, eggs, and walnuts. Spoon into the pie crust.

Bake on a baking sheet for 30 to 35 minutes, until just set. Allow to cool, then drizzle the chocolate syrup over the top.

YIELD: Serves 6 to 8

ADD IT! Of course, a billowing drift of whipped cream would be delicious, as would a handful of whatever fresh berries might be in season.

Mocha Sundae Pie

Did you promise to bring dessert to the neighborhood barbeque and it's too hot to turn on the oven? Make this. The sweet tooth patrol will thank you.

      1 quart (570 g) **coffee ice cream**

      1 **chocolate cookie pie crust**

      1 cup (235 ml) store-bought **chocolate sauce**

      1 cup (235 ml) **Caramel Sauce** (page 486) or store-bought

      1/2 cup (60 g) chopped **walnuts**

Soften the ice cream at room temperature for 30 minutes or in the microwave for 45 seconds or so. Scoop half of the ice cream into the pie crust, then drizzle with some of the chocolate sauce and caramel sauce and sprinkle on some of the nuts. Repeat with the remaining ingredients. Freeze for at least 1 hour.

YIELD: Serves 6 to 8

ADD IT! Feel free to garnish each slice with a cherry and, of course, whipped cream.

Butterscotch Pie

> 1/2 recipe **Basic Pie Crust** (page 94) or similar portion prepared crust
>
> 1 cup (225 g) packed **light brown sugar**
>
> 4 **eggs**
>
> 2 cups (475 ml) **half and half**
>
> 2 teaspoons **vanilla extract**

Preheat the oven to 350°F (180°C, gas mark 4).

Prepare the pie crust per the recipe or package directions.

In a bowl, beat together the sugar, eggs, half and half, and vanilla. Pour into the pie crust.

Bake on a cookie sheet for 40 to 45 minutes, until the filling is set. Allow to cool on a rack, then refrigerate or serve at room temperature.

YIELD: Serves 6 to 8

ADD IT! Scatter a handful of toffee bits or chopped pecans across the top of the pie before serving.

Butterscotch Meringue Pie

Brown sugar produces a workable, if slightly less fluffy, meringue of a fashionably trendy pale taupe color.

> 1/2 recipe **Basic Pie Crust** (page 94) or similar portion prepared crust
>
> 3 tablespoons (45 g) butter
>
> 2 1/4 cups (325 g) **light brown sugar**
>
> 2 cups (475 ml) **milk**
>
> 3 **eggs**
>
> 3 tablespoons (25 g) **all-purpose flour**
>
> 1/2 teaspoon salt
>
> 1 1/2 teaspoons **vanilla extract**

Preheat the oven to 350°F (180°C, gas mark 4).

Prepare the pie crust per the recipe or package directions and bake it for 20 to 25 minutes, until golden brown. Allow to cool.

Melt the butter on low heat in a heavy bottomed 2-quart saucepan. Add 2 cups (290 g) of the sugar and ½ cup (120 ml) of the milk. Bring to a boil, reduce heat to medium, and cook for 4 to 5 minutes, stirring. Set aside.

Separate the eggs, reserving the whites. Put the yolks in a mixing bowl with the remaining 1½ cups (355 ml) milk, the flour, and the salt. Whisk until smooth. Add the hot sugar/butter mixture in a thin stream, whisking. Return all to the saucepan and cook over medium-high heat until it thickens to the consistency of thick gravy, about 5 minutes. Remove from heat and add 1 teaspoon of the vanilla. Pour into the baked pie crust.

In another mixing bowl whip the egg whites, adding the rest of the sugar in three additions, and the remaining vanilla with the last of the sugar, until the whites are at stiff peaks. Spread the meringue over the butterscotch filling, sealing the edges to the pie crust.

Reheat the oven to 350°F (180°C, gas mark 4).

Bake for 10 to 15 minutes until the meringue is lightly browned. Cool.

YIELD: Serves 6 to 8

ADD IT! You can substitute white sugar in the meringue if you want it to attain Himalayan heights and a bright white color.

✸ Creamsicle Pie

This would also work with lemon gelatin and lemonade, lime gelatin, and limeade, etc. It's a light pie for a hot day.

    1 package (3 ounces, or 85 g) **orange gelatin**
    1/2 cup (120 ml) boiling water
    1 cup (235 ml) **orange juice**
    1 cup (235 ml) **heavy cream**
    1 store-bought **graham cracker crumb pie crust**
    12 **fruit slice candies**

Put the gelatin in a bowl and add the water. Stir to dissolve the gelatin, then add the orange juice. Refrigerate until the gelatin begins to thicken, but not to fully set—about 1 hour.

Put the gelatin into a mixing bowl and mix on high speed with the whisk attachment until fluffy—about 5 minutes.

In another bowl, whip the cream to stiff peaks. Fold the whipped cream into the gelatin. Pour into the pie crust and refrigerate for 4 to 6 hours.

Decorate with the candy.

YIELD: Serves 4 to 6

✸ Custard Pie

This is a soothing and old-fashioned pie, but it has stood the test of time for good reasons. If you don't have vanilla sugar, add 1/2 teaspoon vanilla to the filling.

    1/2 recipe **Basic Pie Crust** (page 94) or similar portion prepared crust
    4 **eggs**
    1 cup (200 g) **vanilla sugar** (See "Making Vanilla Sugar" on page 12.)
    1 1/2 cups (355 ml) **half and half**
    1/2 teaspoon **nutmeg**

Preheat the oven to 350°F (180°C, gas mark 4).

Prepare the pie crust per the recipe or package instructions.

In a mixing bowl, whisk the eggs lightly. Add the sugar and combine well.

In a saucepan, heat the half and half to a simmer and whisk into the eggs. Stir in the nutmeg and pour the custard into the prepared pie crust.

Bake for 45 to 50 minutes, until the filling is set. Cool on a rack and then refrigerate for several hours.

YIELD: Serves 6 to 8

ADD IT! There are all sorts of possibilities to jazz up this basic custard. You can add flavored extracts or a handful of raisins or other chopped fruit, just for starters.

Daiquiri Pie

Why mess with a blender and ice cubes when you can make a daiquiri dessert instead?

> 2 pouches ($^1/_2$ ounce, or 15 g, each) **powdered daiquiri mix**
> $^1/_2$ cup (120 ml) water
> 1 envelope ($^1/_4$ ounce, or 7.5 g) **unflavored gelatin**
> 2 cups (455 g) **vanilla yogurt**
> 2 cups (150 g) **nondairy dessert topping**
> 1 store-bought **graham cracker crumb pie crust**

In a small saucepan, mix the daiquiri mix and water. Sprinkle the gelatin over and allow to soften for 5 minutes. Heat on low for 4 to 5 minutes, until the gelatin has dissolved.

Put the yogurt into a mixing bowl and whisk in the gelatin liquid. Fold in the nondairy topping and spoon the whole mixture into the pie crust. Refrigerate for at least 4 hours.

YIELD: Serves 6 to 8

Dulce de Leche Pie

Essentially, this is sweet cream pie.

> 3 **eggs**
> 1 cup (200 g) **sugar**
> 2 to 3 tablespoons (28 to 45 ml) water
> 2 cups (475 ml) **half and half**
> 1 tablespoon (14 ml) **rum extract**
> 1 store-bought **graham cracker crumb pie crust**

Preheat the oven to 350°F (180°C, gas mark 4).

Put the eggs into a large mixing bowl and whisk lightly.

Put the sugar into a heavy bottomed 2-quart saucepan. Add enough water so that the sugar is the consistency of wet sand. Put the pan on high heat and cook, not stirring, until the sugar is golden brown. Remove from the heat and add the half and half (be careful, the caramel will boil up). Stir until the caramel is dissolved and put back onto medium heat. Bring to a simmer and whisk the liquid into the eggs in a thin stream. Add the rum extract and pour into the pie crust.

Bake on a cookie sheet for 35 to 40 minutes, until the filling is set. Refrigerate for 4 to 6 hours.

YIELD: Serves 4 to 6

Irish Cream Pie

With very little baking time, this makes a cooling choice for a summer dinner party.

> 1/2 recipe **Basic Pie Crust** (page 94) or similar portion prepared crust
> 3 **eggs**
> 1/2 cup (120 ml) **Irish cream liqueur**
> 3/4 cup (175 ml) **heavy cream**
> 1/2 cup **chocolate shavings** (about 2 to 3 ounces, or 55 to 85 g)

Preheat the oven to 350°F (180°C, gas mark 4).

Prepare the pie crust per the recipe or package instructions and bake it empty for 20 to 25 minutes, until golden brown. Allow to cool.

Separate the eggs, reserving the whites. Put the yolks and the liqueur into a stainless steel bowl and set it over a pan of simmering water. Whisk until the mixture thickens, 2 to 3 minutes, and set aside to cool for 10 minutes.

In a separate bowl, whip the egg whites to stiff peak and fold into the yolk mixture.

In a separate bowl, whip the cream to stiff peaks and fold into the mixture yolk. Spoon the mixture into the pie crust and refrigerate for at least 2 hours. Decorate with the chocolate.

YIELD: Serves 6 to 8.

Maple Cream Pie

This custard pie brings the taste of Vermont to the dessert table.

> 1/2 recipe **Basic Pie Crust** (page 94) or similar portion prepared crust
> 3 tablespoons (25 g) **cornstarch**
> 2 cups (475 ml) **half and half**
> 1 cup (235 ml) **pure maple syrup**
> 4 **eggs**

Preheat the oven to 350°F (180°C, gas mark 4).

Prepare the pie crust per the recipe or package instructions.

Whisk together the cornstarch and 1 cup (235 ml) of the half and half until lumps dissolve. Mix the cornstarch mixture thoroughly with the remaining half and half and the maple syrup and eggs and pour into the pie crust.

Bake on a cookie sheet for 40 to 45 minutes, until the filling is set. Allow to cool on a rack, then refrigerate or serve at room temperature.

YIELD: Serves 6 to 8

ADD IT! Circle the top of the pie with candied pecan halves for a pretty look.

Sweet Potato Pie

1/2 recipe **Basic Pie Crust** (page 94) or similar portion prepared crust

3 medium **sweet potatoes**

1/4 cup (1/2 stick, or 55 g) butter

1/2 cup (100 g) **cinnamon sugar** (See "Making Cinnamon Sugar" on page 12.)

1/2 teaspoon salt

2 **eggs**, well beaten, plus 2 **egg** whites

1 can (14 ounces, or 425 ml) **sweetened condensed milk**

Preheat the oven to 350°F (180°C, gas mark 4).

Prepare the pie crust according to the recipe or package instructions.

Peel the sweet potatoes and put in a 2-quart saucepan. Boil until tender; drain, and mash.

Combine the butter, sugar, salt, and nutmeg in large bowl and beat at medium speed until creamy. Beat in the sweet potatoes until well mixed. Beat in the 2 eggs.

Whisk the egg whites in a separate bowl until frothy and add to batter. Beat in the condensed milk in increments until well combined. Spoon the mixture into the pie crust.

Bake for 50 to 60 minutes or until set. Cool to room temperature before serving. Refrigerate leftover pie.

YIELD: Serves 10 to 12

ADD IT! A sprinkle of nutmeg on top is the perfect finishing touch.

Basic Tart Shell

This is the basic butter tart shell recipe. It is quick and easy to make and results in a tender crust that doesn't melt away when baked. This recipe will fill one 12-inch tart pan.

1/4 cup (1/2 stick, or 55 g) **butter**

1/4 cup (50 g) **shortening**, chilled

1 1/2 (180 g) cups **all-purpose flour**

3 tablespoon (35 g) **sugar**

1/2 teaspoon **salt**

1/4 cup (60 ml) or so cold water

Put all of the ingredients except the water into a food processor fitted with the metal blade. Process until the mixture resembles a fine meal. With the motor running, add the water in a thin stream, adding only enough to just bring the dough together.

Place a piece of plastic wrap on the counter and put the dough in it, including any loose crumbs. Knead the dough a few times to bring the dough together in a ball, then flatten out into a 6-inch disk. Wrap up in the plastic and refrigerate for 1/2 hour.

Flour a work surface and roll the dough out into a circle 15 inches or so across. Roll the dough around the rolling pin and drape it over a 12-inch tart pan with a removable bottom. Tuck the dough into the bottom of the pan and onto the fluted sides. Using the heel of your hand and the top of the tart shell side, cut off any excess dough.

Freeze the tart shell until hard—about 1 hour. It is now ready to fill and bake or to blind bake unfilled.

If your recipe calls for blind baking the tart, line the inside of the tart shell, bottom and sides, with foil. Fill the center with 2 to 3 cups (for a large tart) of dried beans, uncooked rice, or metal pellets (pie weights), which are sold in cooking stores expressedly for this purpose. Bake to the desired degree of doneness, then remove the foil, with the weights still in it. You can save the whole set-up for the next tart.

To partially bake a shell, preheat the oven to 375°F (190°C, gas mark 5). Put the pie weights in the shell to keep the dough from bubbling and bake for 20 minutes. Let cool.

To fully bake a shell, preheat the oven to 375°F (190°C, gas mark 5). Put the pie weights in the shell to keep the dough from bubbling and bake for 20 minutes. Then remove the weights from the shell and bake the empty shell for an additional 10 minutes, until the shell is a pale golden brown. Let cool.

Almond Tart

Almonds and orange—it's a great flavor twist!

> 1 recipe **Basic Tart Shell**—unbaked (page 123)
>
> 2 cups (185 g) sliced **almonds**
>
> 1 cup (200 g) **sugar**
>
> 1 1/2 cups (355 ml) **heavy cream**
>
> 1 **orange**

Prepare the tart shell per the recipe.

Preheat the oven to 350°F (180°C, gas mark 4).

Put the almonds in a layer in the tart shell.

Mix together the sugar and cream in a 2-quart saucepan. Zest the orange and finely chop the zest. Add to the cream. Cook over high heat until the cream just boils and the sugar is dissolved and remove from the heat. Squeeze the orange and stir in the juice, then pour the liquid over the almonds.

Bake for 45 to 50 minutes, until the filling is just set. Cool completely then remove the sides of the tart pan.

YIELD: Serves 8 to 10

❧ Coconut Tart

1 recipe **Basic Tart Shell**—partially baked (page 123)

1 cup (200 g) **sugar**

2 **eggs**

1 1/2 cups (355 ml) **whole milk**

1 1/2 cups (110 g) **sweetened shredded coconut**

Preheat the oven to 375°F (190°C, gas mark 5).

Prepare the tart shell; add pie weights and partially bake, about 20 minutes. Remove from oven and cool; reduce oven heat to 350°F (180°C, gas mark 4).

Mix the sugar, eggs, and milk in a mixing bowl, beating them for 1 minute. Stir in 1 cup of the coconut flakes and pour the mixture into the tart shell.

Bake for 25 to 30 minutes, until the filling is just set. Cool completely, then refrigerate for at least 1 hour. Remove the sides of the tart pan.

Reduce the oven to 350°F (180°C, gas mark 4).

Bake the remaining coconut flakes on a cookie sheet for 10 to 12 minutes, until just toasted. Sprinkle over the tart as a garnish.

YIELD: Serves 8

ADD IT! Layer sliced bananas in the tart shell before adding the filling.

Coconut-Macadamia Nut Tart

1 recipe **Basic Tart Shell**—made by substituting brown sugar in the basic recipe and partially baked (page 123)

1 cup (135 g) **macadamia nuts**

1 can (14 ounces, or 425 ml) **coconut milk**

1 cup (225 g) **light brown sugar**, packed

3 **eggs**

Preheat the oven to 375°F (190°C, gas mark 5).

Prepare the tart shell per the recipe and partially bake, about 20 minutes. Remove from oven and cool; reduce oven heat to 350°F (180°C, gas mark 4).

Roughly chop the macadamia nuts (or whirl them through the food processor) and put them in the tart shell.

Mix the coconut milk, sugar, and eggs in a mixing bowl, beating for 1 to 2 minutes. Pour over the nuts in the tart shell.

Bake for 25 to 30 minutes, until the filling is just set. Cool completely. Remove the sides of the tart pan. Serve chilled or at room temperature.

YIELD: Serves 8

ADD IT! Sprinkle lightly toasted coconut flakes over the top of the tart.

Apple Custard Tart

Hey, with eggs and apples, you could serve this tart for breakfast! Cortland or Granny Smith are good apple choices for this tart.

    1 recipe **Basic Tart Shell**—unbaked (page 123)

    1 1/2 pounds (700 g) **apples** (about 4 apples)

    3/4 cup (150 g) **cinnamon sugar** (See "Making Cinnamon Sugar" on page 12.)

    4 **eggs**

    1 can (12 ounces, or 355 ml) **evaporated milk**

Prepare the tart shell per the recipe.

Preheat the oven to 350°F (180°C, gas mark 4).

Peel and core the apples and cut them into 1/2-inch wedges. Toss the wedges of apples with the sugar until the apples are coated. Arrange the apples in overlapping circles in the tart shell.

In a mixing bowl, whisk together the eggs and evaporated milk. Pour over the apples in the tart shell.

Bake for 55 to 60 minutes, until the apples are soft and golden brown, the custard is set, and the crust is golden. Cool to room temperature and remove the sides of the tart pan. Serve at room temperature or chilled.

YIELD: Serves 8

ADD IT! Drizzle with Caramel Sauce (page 486) before serving.

Gingersnap-Apple Tart

The spicy bite of ginger really plays to the sweet tartness of apples.

> 1 package (16 ounces, or 455 g) **gingersnaps**
> 1/2 cup (1 stick, or 112 g) butter
> 1 1/2 pounds (700 g) **apples** (Cortland or Granny Smith are good choices.)
> 3/4 cup (150 g) **vanilla sugar** (See "Making Vanilla Sugar" on page 12.)
> 3 **eggs**
> 1 cup (235 ml) **heavy cream**

Whirl the gingersnaps through a food processor until they are ground into fine crumbs.

Melt the butter over low heat and mix with they crumbs until thoroughly combined. Press the crumb mixture into the bottom and sides of a 12-inch tart pan and freeze until hard—at least 1 hour.

Preheat the oven to 350°F (180°C, gas mark 4).

Peel and core the apples and cut them into 1/2-inch wedges. In a bowl, toss the apples with the sugar until the apples are coated. Arrange the apples in overlapping circles in the tart shell.

In a mixing bowl, whisk together the eggs and the cream. Pour over the apples in the tart shell.

Bake for 40 to 45 minutes, until the apples are soft and golden brown, the custard is set, and the crust is baked through. Cool to room temperature and remove the sides of the tart pan. Serve at room temperature or chilled.

YIELD: Serves 8

ADD IT! Garnish with finely chopped candied ginger.

Cherry Custard Tart

We cannot tell a lie: This is delicious!

> 1 recipe **Basic Tart Shell**—fully baked (page 123)
> 1 pound (455 g) tart **cherries**, such as Montmorency

1/2 cup (100 g) **sugar**

1 package (8 ounces, or 225 g) **custard mix**

2 cups (475 ml) **milk**

Prepare the tart shell per the recipe and fully bake. Let it cool.

Pit the cherries. Put them into a saucepan over medium heat and stir in the sugar. Cook for 8 to 10 minutes, until the cherries are softened and the sugar is dissolved. Cool the cherries to room temperature.

Make the custard by mixing the custard mix and the milk in a mixing bowl. Pour the custard into the prepared tart shell and then spoon the cherries over the custard. Refrigerate for at least 4 hours. Remove the sides of the tart pan.

YIELD: Serves 8.

Easy Fresh Berry Tart

1 package (1 pound, or 455 g) **vanilla wafer cookies**

1/2 cup (1 stick, or 112 g) butter

1 container (12 ounces, or 340 g) **prepared custard**

1/2 pint (150 g) **raspberries**

1/2 pint (200 g) **blueberries**

1/2 pint (200 g) **blackberries**

Using a food processor, or bashing them with a rolling pin, crush enough of the cookies to make 2 cups of fine crumbs.

Melt the butter over low heat and mix with the crumbs thoroughly. Press the crumb mixture onto the bottom and sides of a 12-inch tart pan with removable side. Freeze for 1 hour.

Preheat the oven to 400°F (200°C, gas mark 6). Bake the tart shell for 15 minutes, until golden brown. Remove from the oven and cool completely.

Spread the custard on the bottom of the cooled tart shell. Arrange the berries on top. Refrigerate for at least 1 hour. Remove the side of the tart shell.

YIELD: Serves 8

Fresh Strawberry Tart

Picking strawberries during our summer jobs on the local farm taught us one lesson: Yes, it is possible to eat too many. We've recovered our taste for them and love the brief glorious season of native strawberries in New England.

> 1 recipe **Basic Tart Shell**—fully baked (page 123)
> 1 package (12 ounces, 300 g) **prepared custard**
> 1 quart (575 g) **strawberries**
> 1/2 cup (60 g) **confectioners' sugar**

Preheat the oven to 375°F (190°C, gas mark 5). Prepare the tart shell per the recipe and fully bake using the blind baking method (see page 19). Remove from oven and cool.

Spread the custard evenly on the bottom of the tart shell. Hull the berries and slice them in half lengthwise. Arrange the berry halves, cut side down, in concentric circles on top of the custard, lightly pressing them in. Put the confectioners' sugar in a sifter and sift over the tart. Remove the sides of the tart pan.

YIELD: Serves 8

Strawberry-Almond Meringue Tart

Adding almonds to the meringue cuts the sweetness and adds a flavor twist.

> 1 recipe **Basic Tart Shell**—fully baked (page 123)
> 2 cups (640 g) **strawberry jam**
> 1 cup (145 g) blanched **almonds**
> 4 **egg** whites
> 1/2 cup (100 g) **sugar**

Prepare the tart shell per the recipe and fully bake it. Remove from oven and cool.

Reduce the oven heat to 350°F (180°C, gas mark 4).

Spread the jam on the bottom of the tart shell.

In a food processor or blender, grind the almonds into a fine meal and set aside.

Whip the egg whites in a mixing bowl and add the sugar in three additions after the eggs whites start to froth. Whip to stiff peak, though still glossy. Fold in the almonds and spread this mixture on top of the jam, sealing to the edges.

Bake for 10 to 12 minutes, until the meringue is browned. Cool in the pan. Remove the sides of the tart pan.

YIELD: Serves 8

ADD IT! Sprinkle a handful of chocolate chips on top of the jam before adding the meringue layer.

❧ Strawberry~Rhubarb Crumble Tart

Spring means strawberry rhubarb pie to many people, but try that classic combination in a tart instead.

>   1 recipe **Basic Tart Shell**—unbaked (page 123)
>   2 cups (245 g) diced **rhubarb**
>   2 cups (330 g) sliced **strawberries**
>   2 cups (400 g) **cinnamon sugar** (See "Making Cinnamon Sugar" on page 12.)
>   1 cup (120 g) **all-purpose flour**
> $1/2$ cup (1 stick, or 112 g) butter

Prepare the tart shell per the recipe.

Preheat the oven to 350°F (180°C, gas mark 4).

Mix the rhubarb, strawberries, 1 cup (200 g) of the sugar, and 1 teaspoon of the cinnamon in a mixing bowl until the fruit is coated. Pour into the tart shell and level.

Mix the remaining cinnamon, the flour, and the remaining 1 cup (200 g) of sugar in a mixing bowl. Cut the butter into small pieces and add to the bowl. Work the butter into the dry ingredients until completely blended. Cover the fruit with the streusel.

Bake for 45 to 50 minutes, until the topping is golden brown. Cool, then remove the sides of the tart pan.

YIELD: Serves 8

Strawberry Tart in Almond Crust

For the crust:

> 1 cup (145 g) blanched **almonds**
>
> 1/2 cup (60 g) **all-purpose flour**
>
> 1/2 cup (100 g) **sugar**
>
> 1/2 teaspoon salt
>
> 1/2 cup (1 stick, or 112 g) butter, cut into small pieces
>
> 1/2 cup (120 ml) ice water

For the filling:

> 2 cups (640 g) **strawberry jam**
>
> 1 quart (575 g) **strawberries**, hulled and halved

To make the crust:

Put the almonds in a food processor fitted with the metal blade and process until very finely ground. Add the flour, sugar, and salt. Pulse to mix. Add the butter and process until the mixture resembles coarse meal. With the processor running, add the water slowly until a dough is formed. (You may not need all of the water.) Turn the dough and any dry crumbs out onto a floured surface and knead to bring together as a dough ball. Wrap in plastic wrap and refrigerate for at least 1 hour.

Flour a work surface and roll the dough out into a circle 15 inches or so across. Roll the dough around the rolling pin and drape it over a 12-inch tart pan with removable bottom. Tuck the dough into the bottom of the pan and onto the fluted sides. Using the heel of your hand and the top of the tart shell side, cut off any excess dough.

Freeze the tart shell until hard—about 1 hour.

Preheat the oven to 375°F (190°C, gas mark 5). Weight the tart shell with pie weights and bake for 20 minutes; remove pie weights and bake for 10 minutes more, until golden brown. Remove from oven and cool.

Put the jam in a food processor fitted with the metal blade. Process until smooth. Put the jam into a small saucepan and heat over low heat until melted—about 5 minutes. Spread on the bottom of the cooked tart shell.

Arrange the berries, cut sides down, on top of the jam. Refrigerate for at least 1 hour. Remove the sides of the tart pan.

YIELD: Serves 8

Raspberry Tart

When the Queen of Hearts stole those tarts, you *know* they were raspberry.

> 1 recipe **Basic Tart Shell**—fully baked (page 123)
> 1 cup (235 ml) **orange juice**
> 1/2 cup (100 g) **sugar**
> 2 tablespoons (15 g) **cornstarch**
> 4 cups (500 g) fresh **raspberries**

Prepare the tart shell per the recipe and fully bake it. Remove from oven and cool.

Combine the orange juice, sugar, and cornstarch in a saucepan. Heat over medium-high heat, stirring, until the mixture thickens and is no longer cloudy. Spread the mixture in the tart shell. Arrange the raspberries in concentric circles on top of the orange mixture, lightly pressing them in. Refrigerate for at least 1 hour. Remove the sides of the tart pan.

YIELD: Serves 8

🌀 Roasted Grape Tart

It may sound odd, but roasting grapes gives them a rich flavor that's delicious.

> 1 recipe **Basic Tart Shell**—fully baked (page 123)
>
> 3 cups (275 g) seedless green **grapes**
>
> 1 container (12 ounces, or 340 g) **store-bought custard**
>
> 1/2 cup (60 g) confectioners' **sugar**

Prepare the tart shell per the recipe and fully bake it using the blind baking method. Remove from oven and cool.

Reduce the oven temperature to 350°F (180°C, gas mark 4).

Stem the grapes and put them on a baking sheet. Roast in the oven for 20 to 25 minutes, until a bit browned, but not deflated. Cool on the pan.

Spread the custard on the bottom of the tart shell. Top with the grapes, gently pressing into the custard. Sift the confectioners' sugar over the grapes. Remove the sides of the tart pan.

YIELD: Serves 8

🌀 Key Lime Tart

If you can get your hands on fresh key limes, by all means use them! Otherwise, bottled juice will do. And be sure to have your Jimmy Buffet tunes playing while making this tart!

> 1 recipe **Basic Tart Shell**—partially baked (page 123)
>
> 6 ounces (175 ml) **key lime juice**
>
> 2 **egg yolks**
>
> 16 ounces (475 ml) **sweetened condensed milk**

Prepare the tart shell per the recipe instructions and partially bake it using the blind baking method. Remove from oven and cool.

Reduce the oven heat to 350°F (180°C, gas mark 4).

Mix the lime juice, egg yolks, and condensed milk in a mixing bowl, beating them for 1 minute. Pour into the tart shell.

Bake for 20 to 25 minutes, until the filling is just set. Cool completely, then refrigerate for at least 1 hour. Remove the sides of the tart pan.

YIELD: Serves 8

Lemon Tart

Somehow, the tart tang of a lemon dessert imparts the comforting illusion of health and ascetic forbearance. It's a mirage, but comforting nonetheless.

> 1 recipe **Basic Tart Shell**—partially baked (page 123)
> 3/4 cup (175 ml) fresh **lemon juice**
> 1 cup (200 g) sugar
> 2 tablespoons (15 g) **all-purpose flour**
> 3 **egg yolks**
> 1/2 cup **confectioners' sugar**

Prepare the tart shell per the recipe instructions and partially bake it using the blind baking method. Remove from oven and cool.

Reduce the oven heat to 350°F (180°C, gas mark 4).

Mix the lemon juice, sugar, flour, and eggs yolks in a mixing bowl, beating them for 1 minute. Pour into the tart shell.

Bake for 25 to 30 minutes, until the filling is just set. Cool completely, then refrigerate for at least 1 hour. Remove the sides of the tart pan. Sift the confectioners' sugar on top of the filling.

YIELD: Serves 8

ADD IT! Really, there's no excuse for not serving this with a dollop of fresh whipped cream alongside.

Lemon Tartlets

Quick, easy, and delicious—a perfect bring-along to a summer dinner party.

> 1 package (4 ounces, or 115 g) individual **graham cracker tartlet shells**
> 20 to 24 ounces (560 to 670 g) store-bought **lemon curd**
> 1 cup (235 ml) **heavy cream**
> 1/2 teaspoon **vanilla extract**
> 2 teaspoons **confectioners' sugar**

Fill each tartlet shell two-thirds full with lemon curd.

In a mixing bowl, combine the cream, vanilla, and sugar and beat on high speed until stiff peaks form. Spoon a dollop of whipped cream on top of each tart.

YIELD: Serves 6

Lemon~Blueberry Tart

Fresh lemons for juice are always preferable to the bottled variety, but either will work.

> 1 recipe **Basic Tart Shell**—partially baked (page 123)
> 2 cups (290 g) **blueberries**
> 1/4 cup (1/2 stick, or 55 g) butter
> 3 **egg yolks**
> 1 cup (200 g) **sugar**
> Pinch salt
> 1/2 cup (120 ml) **lemon juice**

Prepare the tart shell per the recipe and partially bake. Remove from oven and cool.

Reduce the oven heat to 350°F (180°C, gas mark 4).

Put the blueberries into the tart shell.

In a saucepan, melt the butter and combine with the egg yolks, sugar, and salt in a mixing bowl. Whisk vigorously for 1 minute, then add the lemon juice and whisk for another minute. (Don't worry if the mixture looks curdled.) Pour over the blueberries.

Bake for 25 to 30 minutes, until the filling is set. Cool completely. Remove the sides of the tart pan.

YIELD: Serves 8

ADD IT! Dust with confectioners' sugar before serving. And for some reason, we think that candied violets would look fetching on top of this tart.

❦ Lemon-Mascarpone Tart

This makes a light but rich tart that's good cool or room temperature.

    1 recipe **Basic Tart Shell**—partially baked (page 123)

    3/4 cup (175 ml) fresh **lemon juice**

    1 cup (200 g) **sugar**

    2 **eggs**

    1 cup (240 g) **mascarpone cheese**

Prepare the tart shell per the recipe instructions and partially bake. Remove and cool.

Mix the lemon juice, sugar, eggs, and mascarpone cheese in a mixing bowl, beating them for 1 minute. Pour into the tart shell.

Bake for 20 to 25 minutes, until the filling is just set. Cool completely, then refrigerate for at least 1 hour. Remove the sides of the tart pan.

YIELD: Serves 8

ADD IT! Toss 1 cup (125 g) fresh raspberries in a little sugar and sprinkle them around the top of the tart.

🍐 Pear Tart

This is the classic tart you drool over in French patisseries.

> 1 recipe **Basic Tart Shell**—unbaked (page 123)
>
> 4 **pears** (Bartlett or Anjou are good choices.)
>
> 2 cups (400 g) **vanilla sugar** (See "Making Vanilla Sugar" on page 12.)
>
> 4 cups (950 ml) water
>
> 3 **eggs**
>
> 1 cup (235 ml) **heavy cream**

Prepare the tart shell per the recipe.

Peel the pears, removing the stem. Halve the pears lengthwise and scoop out the cores. (A melon baller does a fine job of this.)

Mix 1 1/2 cups (300 g) of the sugar with the water in a saucepan or sauté pan just large enough to accommodate the pears. Heat over high heat until the sugar is dissolved, then reduce to low heat and add the pears. Poach the pears until they are easily pierced with a sharp knife—about 30 minutes. Refrigerate in the poaching liquid until chilled.

Preheat the oven to 375°F (190°C, gas mark 5).

In a mixing bowl whisk together the eggs, cream, and the remaining 1/2 cup (100 g) sugar. Arrange the pear halves, flat sides down, in the tart shell, then pour the custard mixture over.

Bake for 40 to 45 minutes, until the custard is set and the crust is golden brown. Allow to cool, then remove the sides of the tart pan.

YIELD: Serves 8

ADD IT! Try adding 1/2 cup (110 g) almond paste to the custard mixture.

Plum Streusel Tart

We have never quite been able to replicate the plum tart that we had as exchange students in Germany during high school; Frau Ganz's version remains the gold standard. After much experimentation, we have been able to come close though.

1 recipe **Basic Tart Shell**—unbaked (page 123)
2 pounds (1 kg) **plums** (Italian prune plums are good for this.)
1 container (8 ounces, or 225 g) **almond paste**
1/2 cup (100 g) **sugar**
1/2 cup (30 g) **all-purpose flour**
Pinch salt
1/4 cup (1/2 stick, or 55 g) butter

Prepare the tart shell per the recipe.

Preheat the oven heat to 350°F (180°C, gas mark 4).

Halve and pit the plums. Spread the almond paste on the frozen tart shell, then cover with the plum halves, arranging them in concentric circles slightly overlapping.

Mix together the sugar, flour, and salt. Cut in the butter until the mixture looks like coarse meal. Sprinkle the mixture over the plums.

Bake for 45 to 50 minutes, until the plums are soft and bubbling and the topping and crust are golden brown. Cool in the shell, then remove the sides of the tart pan.

YIELD: Serves 8

ADD IT! Add 1/2 teaspoon nutmeg into the topping mixture.

Date Crumble Tart

Dates, like prunes, have an unfair rap. In our never-ending quest to succor orphan foods, we've given dates a chance to shine in this recipe.

> 1 recipe **Basic Tart Shell**—unbaked (page 123)
> 2 cups (350 g) pitted and chopped dried **dates**
> 2 cups (475 ml) water
> 1 cup (2.75 ounces, or 75 g) **quick cook oats**
> 1 cup (120 g) **all-purpose flour**
> 1 cup (200 g) **cinnamon sugar** (See "Making Cinnamon Sugar" on page 12.)
> 1/2 cup (1 stick, or 112 g) butter

Prepare the tart shell per recipe instructions.

Put the dates in a 2-quart saucepan with the water. Cook over medium heat until the dates are soft—about 20 minutes. Drain the dates.

Mix the oats, flour, and cinnamon sugar in a mixing bowl. Cut the butter into small pieces and add to the bowl. With your fingers, work the butter into the dry ingredients until completely blended.

Preheat the oven to 350°F (180°C, gas mark 4).

Spread the dates in the tart shell and cover with the crumble topping.

Bake for 40 to 45 minutes, until the tart is golden brown. Cool, then remove the sides of the tart pan.

YIELD: Serves 8

ADD IT! Substitute a shot of brandy for 1/2 cup (120 ml) of the cooking water for the dates.

Free-Form Apple Tart

This rustic tart is fabulous for the next three-course picnic you plan. Cortland or Granny Smith are good apple choices for this tart.

For the pastry:

> 1 1/2 cups (180 g) **all-purpose flour**
>
> 1/2 teaspoon salt
>
> 1/4 cup (50 g) **cinnamon sugar** (See "Making Cinnamon Sugar" on page 12.)
>
> 1/4 cup (1/2 stick, or 55 g) butter
>
> 1/4 cup (50 g) **shortening**
>
> 1/2 cup (120 ml) ice water

For the filling:

> 2 pounds (1 kg) **apples** (about 5 to 6 apples)
>
> 1/2 cup (100 g) **cinnamon sugar** (See "Making Cinnamon Sugar" on page 12.)
>
> 1 **egg**
>
> 1 tablespoon (14 ml) water

To make the pastry:

Combine the flour, salt, and sugar in a food processor fitted with the metal blade. Cut the butter into chunks and add, along with the shortening. Process until the mixture resembles coarse meal, then add enough water, with the motor running, to just bring the dough together. (You may not need all the water.) Turn the dough and any loose crumbs out onto a floured surface and knead 4 to 5 times to bring everything together into a smooth dough. Wrap the dough in plastic wrap and refrigerate for at least 2 hours.

To make the filling:

Peel the apples, core them, and cut each half into 4 wedges. Mix the sugar with the apples until well coated.

Preheat the oven to 375°F (190°C, gas mark 5).

Flour a flat surface and roll the dough out to a 16-inch circle. (Don't worry if the edges are not even, or if the circle is not perfectly round—this is free form!) Transfer the dough to a baking sheet and pile the apples in the middle 10 inches of the circle. Fold the edges over, leaving some of the apples exposed in the middle. Whisk the egg with 1 tablespoon water and brush onto the dough.

Bake for 40 to 45 minutes, until the apples are soft and the crust golden brown. Cool.

YIELD: Serves 6 to 8

ADD IT! Mix $1/4$ teaspoon freshly grated nutmeg and a dash of ground ginger into the apple mixture.

Free~Form Peach Tart

We like to bake this one in August, when fresh native peaches are at their height. Add a scoop of vanilla ice cream to a slice warm from the oven—heaven.

For the pastry:

> 1$1/2$ cups (180 g) **all-purpose flour**
> $1/2$ teaspoon salt
> $1/4$ cup (50 g) **sugar**
> $1/2$ cup (1 stick, or 112 g) butter
> $1/2$ cup (120 ml) ice water

For the filling:

> 2 pounds (1 kg) **peaches**
> $1/2$ cup (100 g) **sugar**
> 2 tablespoons (15 g) **cornstarch**
> 1 **egg**
> 1 tablespoon (14 ml) water

To make the pastry:

Combine the flour, salt, and sugar in a food processor fitted with the metal blade. Cut the butter into chunks and add. Process until the mixture resembles coarse meal, then add enough water, with the motor running, to just bring the dough together. (You may not need all the water.) Turn the dough, along with any loose crumbs, out onto a floured surface and knead 4 to 5 times to bring everything together into a smooth dough. Wrap the dough in plastic wrap and refrigerate for at least 2 hours.

To make the filling:

Bring a large pot of water to a boil and drop in the peaches. Cook for 20 seconds then drain and shock in ice water. Peel, halve, and pit the peaches and cut each half into 4 wedges.

In a bowl, combine the sugar and cornstarch and mix with the peaches to coat them.

Preheat the oven to 375°F (190°C, gas mark 5).

Flour a flat surface and roll the dough out to a 16-inch circle. (Don't worry if the edges are not even, or if the circle is not perfectly round, as we are going for a rustic look.) Transfer the dough to a baking sheet and pile the peaches in the middle 10 inches of the circle. Fold the edges over, leaving some of the peaches exposed in the middle.

In a bowl, whisk the egg with the 1 tablespoon water and brush onto the dough.

Bake for 40 to 45 minutes, until the peaches are soft and the crust golden brown. Cool.

YIELD: Serves 6 to 8

Free-Form Plum Tart

We love plum tarts so much that we hide them from the kids. All that sugar will rot their teeth anyway.

For the pastry:

> 1 1/2 cups (180 g) **all-purpose flour**
> 1/2 teaspoon salt
> 1/4 cup (50 g) **sugar**
> 1/2 cup (1 stick, or 112 g) butter
> 1/2 cup (120 ml) ice water

For the filling:

> 2 pounds (1 kg) **plums**
> 1 cup (200 g) **sugar**
> 2 tablespoons (15 g) **cornstarch**
> 1 **egg**
> 1 tablespoon (14 ml) water

To make the pastry:

Combine the flour, salt, and sugar in a food processor fitted with the metal blade. Cut the butter into chunks and add. Process until the mixture resembles coarse meal, then add enough water, with the motor running, to just bring the dough together. (You may not need all the water.) Turn the dough and any loose crumbs out onto a floured surface and knead 4 to 5 times to bring everything together into a smooth dough. Wrap the dough in plastic wrap and refrigerate for at least 2 hours.

To make the filling:

Halve and pit the plums and cut each half into 4 wedges.

In a bowl, mix the sugar and cornstarch and mix with the plums to coat them.

Preheat the oven to 375°F (190°C, gas mark 5).

Flour a flat surface and roll the dough out to a 16-inch circle. (Don't worry if the edges are not even, or if the circle is not perfectly round.) Transfer the dough to a baking sheet. Pile the plums in the middle 10 inches of the circle. Fold the edges over, leaving some of the plums exposed in the middle.

In a bowl, whisk the egg with the 1 tablespoon water and brush onto the dough.

Bake for 40 to 45 minutes, until the plums are soft and the crust golden brown. Cool.

YIELD: Serves 6 to 8

ADD IT! For a cool visual effect, try mixing yellow, green, and purple plums together in this tart.

Rich Chocolate Tart

If you like chocolate pudding, you'll like this tart.

> 1 recipe **Basic Tart Shell**—partially baked (page 123)
> 6 ounces (170 g) **semisweet chocolate**
> **3 eggs**
> 1 1/2 cups (355 ml) **light cream**

Prepare the tart shell per the recipe and partially bake it.

Reduce the oven heat to 350°F (180°C, gas mark 4).

Chop the chocolate and put it in a stainless steel mixing bowl. Place the bowl over simmering water and melt the chocolate; remove from heat.

Whisk the eggs in a mixing bowl and whisk in the cream. Stir in the melted chocolate until thoroughly combined. Pour the mixture into the tart shell.

Bake for 25 to 30 minutes, until the filling is just set. Cool completely, then refrigerate for at least 1 hour. Remove the sides of the tart pan.

YIELD: Serves 8

ADD IT! Chocolate pairs beautifully with many berries, and a dollop of whipped cream wouldn't hurt, either.

Super Chocolate Tart

Next time you have your chocolate fiend friends for dinner, try this on for size.

> 2 cups **Oreo cookie crumbs** (about 15 cookies)
> 1/2 cup (1 stick, or 112 g) **butter**
> 8 ounces (225 g) **semisweet chocolate**
> 3/4 cup (175 ml) **heavy cream**
> 3 ounces (85 g) **white chocolate**

Grind up the cookies to crumbs in a food processor.

In a saucepan, melt the butter over low heat and combine with the crumbs in a mixing bowl, mixing thoroughly. Press the mixture into the bottom and sides of a 10-inch tart pan with removable side. Freeze for 1 hour.

Preheat the oven to 350°F (180°C, gas mark 4).

Bake the tart shell for 15 to 20 minutes. Cool completely.

Chop the semisweet chocolate and put it in a stainless steel mixing bowl. Add the cream and place the bowl over a pan of simmering water. Cook, stirring, until the chocolate is melted and the mixture is smooth. Pour into the tart shell. Refrigerate for at least 1 hour.

Chop the white chocolate and put it in a stainless steel mixing bowl. Place the bowl over a pan of simmering water. Cook, stirring until the white chocolate is melted and the mixture is smooth. Drizzle the white chocolate over the chocolate filling from a spoon. Refrigerate for another 30 minutes. Remove the tart pan side.

YIELD: Serves 8 to 10

ADD IT! Garnish with whipped cream if desired.

Turtle Tart

1 recipe **Basic Tart Shell**—fully baked (page 123)

1 cup (235 ml) **Caramel Sauce** (page 486) or store-bought caramel sauce

6 ounces (170 g) **milk chocolate**

1 cup (235 ml) **heavy cream**

Prepare the tart shell per the recipe and fully bake it. Remove from oven and cool.

Spread the caramel sauce in the tart shell.

Chop the chocolate and put it into a stainless steel mixing bowl. Heat the cream just to a boil and pour it over the chocolate. Let it sit for 2 minutes, then stir until smooth. If the chocolate is not melted, place the bowl over a pan of simmering water and stir until smooth. Pour over the caramel sauce. Refrigerate at least 4 hours. Remove the sides of the tart pan.

YIELD: Serves 8

ADD IT! Scatter some chopped pecans over the caramel sauce before adding the chocolate. Garnish with additional whipped cream, if desired.

Chocolate Chip Cookie~Chocolate Tart

2 tubes (12 ounces, or 340 g, each) refrigerated **chocolate chip cookie dough**

6 ounces (170 g) **milk chocolate**

2 **eggs**

1 1/2 cups (355 ml) **light cream**

1 cup (125 g) chopped **walnuts**

Mix all of the cookie dough together in a ball, then roll it out to a 15-inch circle. Roll the dough around the rolling pin and drape it over a 12-inch tart pan with removable bottom. Tuck the dough into the bottom of the pan and press into the fluted sides. Using the heel of your hand and the top of the tart shell side, cut off any excess dough. Freeze the tart shell until hard—about 1 hour.

Preheat the oven to 350°F (180°C, gas mark 4).

Blind bake the tart shell partially, 12 to 15 minutes. Remove the shell from the oven and let cool, but leave the oven on.

While the tart is cooling, chop the chocolate and put it in a stainless steel mixing bowl. Place the bowl over simmering water and melt the chocolate.

Whisk the eggs in a mixing bowl and whisk in the cream. Stir in the melted chocolate. Put the walnuts in the tart shell and pour in the chocolate mixture.

Bake for 25 to 30 minutes, until the filling is just set. Cool completely, then refrigerate for at least 1 hour. Remove the sides of the tart pan.

YIELD: Serves 8

ADD IT! Serve with ice cream for a decadent treat.

Chocolate-Cappuccino Tartlets

1 sheet frozen **puff pastry dough** (6 x 9 inch, or 15 x 22 $^1/_2$ cm), thawed

1 $^1/_2$ cups (355 ml) **heavy cream**

6 ounces (170 g) **semisweet chocolate chips**

3 teaspoons **instant coffee powder** or granules

3 teaspoons confectioners' **sugar**

Preheat the oven to 400°F (200°C, gas mark 6).

Thaw pastry at room temperature until soft, about 30 minutes. Lightly flour surface and unfold pastry sheet. Roll out to about 9 x 18 inches and cut into 3-inch squares. Press squares into cupcake tins and bake for about 12 minutes, until golden brown. Remove and cool.

Heat $^1/_2$ cup (120 ml) of the cream just until the boil.

Put the chocolate in a mixing bowl and pour the hot cream over it. Allow to sit for 1 minute, then mix with a spoon until the chocolate is completely melted and the mixture is smooth. Spoon a small portion into the bottom of each tartlet.

Mix the remaining cream, the coffee powder, and the sugar in a large mixing bowl and whip until the cream holds stiff peak. Spoon into each tartlet. Refrigerate until ready to serve.

YIELD: Makes 18 tartlets

Chocolate-Hazelnut Tart

We love chocolate and hazelnuts together—great flavor buddies with a sophisticated edge.

> 1 recipe **Basic Tart Shell**—partially baked (page 123)
>
> 1 cup (135 g) peeled **hazelnuts**
>
> 6 ounces (170 g) **semisweet chocolate**
>
> 3 **eggs**
>
> 1 cup (235 ml) **heavy cream**

Preheat the oven to 375°F (190°C, gas mark 5).

Prepare the tart shell per the recipe and partially bake, about 20 minutes. Remove from oven and cool; reduce oven heat to 350°F (180°C, gas mark 4).

Put the hazelnuts into the tart shell. Chop the chocolate and put it in a stainless steel mixing bowl. Place the bowl over simmering water and melt the chocolate. Whisk the eggs in a mixing bowl and whisk in the heavy cream. Stir in the melted chocolate. Pour over the hazelnuts in the tart shell.

Bake for 20 to 25 minutes, until the filling is just set. Cool completely, then refrigerate for at least 1 hour. Remove the sides of the tart pan.

YIELD: Serves 8

Chocolate-Mascarpone Tart

How to make chocolate a more luscious dessert? Why, by adding equally rich and luscious mascarpone cheese, of course. We find our mascarpone in tubs in the gourmet cheese section of the supermarket.

For the crust:

> 2 cups (200 g) **graham cracker crumbs**
>
> 1/2 cup (100 g) **vanilla sugar** (See "Making Vanilla Sugar" on page 12.)
>
> 1/2 cup (1 stick, or 112 g) butter, melted

For the filling:

  12 ounces (340 g) **bittersweet chocolate**

  1 cup (235 ml) **half and half**

  1/4 cup (1/2 stick, or 55 g) butter

For the topping:

  8 ounces (225 g) **mascarpone cheese**

  1/2 cup (120 ml) **half and half**

  1/2 cup (100 g) **vanilla sugar** (See "Making Vanilla Sugar" on page 12.)

Preheat the oven to 400°F (200°C, gas mark 6).

To make the crust:

Combine the graham cracker crumbs and the sugar in a mixing bowl. Stir the butter into the graham cracker crumb mixture until thoroughly combined. Press into the bottom and sides of a 10-inch fluted tart pan with removable bottom. Put the pan on a baking sheet. Freeze for 1 hour.

Bake for 15 to 18 minutes, until set and lightly browned. Cool completely.

To make the filling:

In a double boiler, melt the chocolate. Whisk in the half and half and the butter until the butter is melted. Pour into the prepared tart shell and refrigerate for at least 2 hours.

To make the topping:

Combine the mascarpone cheese, half and half, and sugar in a mixing bowl. Whip on high speed until light and fluffy—5 to 8 minutes. Spread over the chocolate mixture or put the topping in a piping bag fitted with a star tip and pipe onto the chocolate decoratively. Refrigerate for 1 hour. Remove the sides of the tart shell.

YIELD: Serves 10 to 12

ADD IT! Drizzle with Raspberry Sauce (page 484) before serving.

⚜ Cappuccino Tart

We find cappuccino powdered mix in with all the exotic powdered coffee drinks.

> 1 recipe **Basic Tart Shell**—fully baked (page 123)
>
> 6 ounces (170 g) powdered **cappuccino mix**
>
> 1 cup (235 ml) water
>
> 2 envelopes (^{1}/4 ounce, or 7.5 g) **unflavored gelatin**
>
> 1 cup (235 ml) **heavy cream**

Preheat the oven to 350°F (180°C, gas mark 4).

Prepare the tart shell per the recipe and fully bake. Cool completely.

Combine the cappuccino mix and water in a saucepan. Stir until partially dissolved. Sprinkle the gelatin over the liquid and let it sit for 5 minutes. Heat the pan over medium heat until the cappuccino mix and the gelatin are dissolved— 5 to 6 minutes. Put the mixture in a mixing bowl and refrigerate for about 1 hour, until the mixture is starting to set and thicken.

Put the cream into a mixing bowl and whip to stiff peak. Whisk one-third of the cream into the cappuccino mixture, then gently fold in the remainder. Pour the filling into the prepared tart shell and refrigerate for at least 4 hours. Remove the sides of the tart pan.

YIELD: Serves 8

ADD IT! Chocolate shavings on the top of this tart add richness. Garnish with additional whipped cream, if desired.

🦀 Chai Latte Tart

We find powdered chai latte mix in with all the exotic powdered coffee drinks.

> 1 recipe **Basic Tart Shell**—fully baked (page 123)
>
> 3/4 cup (130 g) **instant powdered chai latte mix**
>
> 1 cup (235 ml) water
>
> 1 envelope (1/4 ounce, or 7.5 g) **unflavored gelatin**
>
> 1 cup (235 ml) **heavy cream**

Preheat the oven to 350°F (180°C, gas mark 4).

Prepare the tart shell per the recipe and fully bake. Cool completely.

Combine the chai mix and water in a saucepan. Stir until the chai mix is mostly dissolved. Sprinkle the gelatin over the liquid and let it sit for 5 minutes. Heat the pan over medium heat until the chai mix and the gelatin are dissolved—5 to 6 minutes. Put the mixture in a mixing bowl and refrigerate for about 1 hour, until the mixture is starting to set and thicken.

Put the cream into a mixing bowl and whip to stiff peak. Whisk one-third of the cream into the chai mixture, then fold the remainder in gently. Pour the filling into the prepared tart shell and refrigerate for at least 4 hours. Remove the sides of the tart pan.

YIELD: Serves 8

ADD IT! Garnish with additional whipped cream, if desired.

◉ Deluxe S'Mores Tartlets

You can use crunchy or creamy peanut butter for this, but we prefer creamy.

> 2 packages (4 ounces, or 115 g, each) **individual graham cracker tartlet shells**
> 3/4 cup (195 g) creamy **peanut butter**
> 3/4 cup (130 g) **milk chocolate chips**
> 2/3 cup (33 g) **mini marshmallows**

Preheat the oven to 400°F (200°C, gas mark 6).

Put the tart shells on a cookie sheet. Spoon 1 tablespoon of peanut butter into each, followed by a handful of chocolate bits. Top with several mini marshmallows.

Bake for 10 to 12 minutes, until the filling is soft and bubbly. Remove and cool.

YIELD: Makes 12 tartlets

❦ Creamsicle Tart

Transforming an ice cream truck favorite into a more sophisticated tart pleases dessert lovers both large and small.

    1 recipe **Basic Tart Shell**—partially baked (page 123)

    4 ounces (120 ml) frozen **orange juice concentrate**, thawed

    1 cup (200 g) **sugar**

    3 **egg yolks**

    1 cup (235 ml) **light cream**

Prepare the tart shell per the recipe and partially bake, about 20 minutes. Remove from oven and cool; reduce oven heat to 350°F (180°C, gas mark 4).

Mix the orange juice concentrate, sugar, egg yolks, and cream in a mixing bowl, beating them for 1 minute. Pour into the tart shell.

Bake for 20 to 25 minutes, until the filling is just set. Cool completely, then refrigerate for at least 1 hour. Remove the sides of the tart pan.

YIELD: Serves 8

ADD IT! Decorate with white chocolate shavings and candied orange peel.

Piña Colada Tart

If you like the sweet tropical flavor of a piña colada, this will hit the spot.

> 1 recipe **Basic Tart Shell**—partially baked (page 123)
>
> 1 1/2 cups (355 ml) **piña colada mix**
>
> 2 **eggs**
>
> 1 cup (235 ml) **whole milk**

Prepare the tart shell per the recipe and partially bake it using the blind baking method.

Mix the piña colada mix, eggs, and milk in a mixing bowl and beat for 1 minute. Pour into the tart shell.

Bake for 30 to 35 minutes, until the filling is just set. Cool completely, then refrigerate for at least 1 hour. Remove the sides of the tart pan.

YIELD: Serves 8 to 10

CHAPTER FIVE

Cookies

Everybody has memories of the cookie jar full of homemade cookies (usually chocolate chip). Never mind that these memories are often more mirage than reality. The fact is, baking cookies evokes powerful imagery of home, pulling peace gently into our harried days and transforming the act of cooking from an exercise in efficient nutrition into something that's done for pleasure. Perhaps it's because we can choose to make cookies; they don't have to be on the dinner table at 6 p.m. every night. Perhaps it's because cookies are one of the few kitchen efforts not greeted with gagging noises and cries of "Yuck" and "Gross." Whatever the reason, we think that cookies, more than any other dessert, are served with love.

(And by the way—move beyond chocolate chip! We dare you!)

Classic Sugar Cookies

Sugar cookies are right up there with chocolate chip cookies as first-ballot inductees into the Childhood Dessert Hall of Fame.

> 1 cup (2 sticks, or 225 g) butter
>
> 1 cup (200 g) **sugar**, plus more for sprinkling
>
> 2 **eggs**
>
> 2 teaspoons **vanilla extract**
>
> 2 cups (250 g) **all-purpose flour**
>
> 1 teaspoon **baking powder**
>
> 1/4 teaspoon salt

Using a mixer on medium speed, cream together the butter and sugar until light and creamy—about 5 minutes. Add the eggs and the vanilla and beat for 3 to 4 minutes longer.

Sift together the flour, baking powder, and salt and add to the mixing bowl. Mix until thoroughly combined. Form the dough into a ball and wrap in plastic wrap. Refrigerate for at least 1 hour.

Preheat the oven to 350°F (180°C, gas mark 4). Line a cookie sheet with parchment paper.

Flour a flat surface and roll the dough out to about 1/4-inch thickness. Cut the dough out using cookie cutters or a juice glass. Place the pieces on the cookie sheet. Sprinkle with sugar.

Bake for 12 to 15 minutes, until golden at the edges. Cool for a couple of minutes on the cookie sheet, then transfer the cookies to a wire rack to cool completely.

YIELD: Makes about 36 cookies

ADD IT! Sprinkle with turbinado sugar before baking for a special sparkly effect.

Spritz Cookies

This is the rich butter cookie everyone loves.

> 1 cup (2 sticks, or 225 g) butter
>
> 4 ounces (115 g) **cream cheese**
>
> 3/4 cup (150 g) **sugar**
>
> 1/2 teaspoon **almond extract**
>
> 1 teaspoon **vanilla extract**
>
> 2 cups (250 g) **all-purpose flour**
>
> 1/4 teaspoon salt

Using a mixer on high speed, cream the butter, cream cheese, and sugar, scraping the bowl and beaters several times, until perfectly smooth, light, and fluffy—about 10 minutes. Add the almond and vanilla extracts and beat for 2 to 3 minutes more. Add the flour and salt and mix on low speed until smooth. Refrigerate the dough for about 1 hour.

Preheat the oven to 350°F (180°C, gas mark 4). Line a cookie sheet with parchment paper.

Flour a flat surface and roll the dough out to about 1/4-inch thickness. Cut the dough out using cookie cutters or a juice glass. Place the cut-out cookies 3 inches (7.5 cm) apart on the cookie sheet.

Bake for 10 to 12 minutes, until golden brown.

YIELD: Makes about 48 cookies

ADD IT! Try adding an egg to the recipe and piping the cookies with a piping bag fitted with a medium star tip for a fancy effect.

Southern Tea Cakes

The buttermilk gives these an extra tang.

- 1 cup (2 sticks, or 225 g) butter
- 3 cups (600 g) **vanilla sugar** (See "Making Vanilla Sugar" on page 12.)
- 2 **eggs**
- 4 cups (500 g) **all-purpose flour**
- 1 teaspoon **baking soda**
- 1 teaspoon salt
- 1/2 cup (120 ml) **buttermilk**

Using a mixer on medium speed, cream together the butter and sugar until light and creamy—about 5 minutes. Add the eggs and beat for 3 to 4 minutes longer.

Sift together the flour, baking soda, and salt. Add the buttermilk and the flour mixture alternately to the butter mixture, mixing until thoroughly combined. Form the dough into a ball and wrap in plastic wrap. Refrigerate for at least 1 hour.

Preheat the oven to 350°F (180°C, gas mark 4). Line a cookie sheet with parchment paper.

Flour a flat surface and roll the dough out to about 1/4-inch thickness. Cut the dough out using cookie cutters or a juice glass. Place the pieces onto the cookie sheet.

Bake for 10 to 12 minutes, until golden at the edges. Cool for a couple of minutes on the cookie sheet, then transfer the cookies to a wire rack to cool completely.

YIELD: Makes about 24 cookies.

Pudding Cookies

This is a very sweet cookie that's popular with children.

> 1/2 cup (1 stick, or 112 g) butter, melted
>
> 1/2 cup (100 g) **sugar**
>
> 2 **eggs**
>
> 1 package (3.4 ounces, or 100 g) **instant vanilla pudding mix**
>
> 2 teaspoons **baking powder**
>
> 1 cup (120 g) **all-purpose flour**

Preheat the oven to 350°F (180°C, gas mark 4). Lightly grease two cookie sheets.

Using a mixer on medium speed, cream the butter and the sugar together until fluffy—about 5 minutes. Add the eggs and beat for 3 minutes longer.

In another bowl, stir together the pudding mix, baking powder, and flour until combined. Add to the shortening mixture and mix until smooth. Drop by tablespoonfuls onto the cookie sheet.

Bake for 10 to 12 minutes, until just golden brown on the edges.

YIELD: Makes about 36 cookies

ADD IT! This cookie works with any flavor of pudding mix, so experiment!

Almond Butter Cookies

This is a simple classic that disappears with great rapidity.

    1 cup (2 sticks, or 225 g) butter
    1 cup (200 g) **sugar**, plus more for sprinkling
    2 **egg yolks**
    1 tablespoon (14 ml) **almond extract**
    2 cups (250 g) **all-purpose flour**
    1 teaspoon **baking powder**
    1/4 teaspoon salt

Using a mixer on medium speed, cream together the butter and sugar until light and creamy—3 to 4 minutes. Add the egg yolks and the almond extract and beat for 2 to 3 minutes longer.

Sift together the flour, baking powder, and salt and add to the mixing bowl. Mix until thoroughly combined. Form the dough into a ball and wrap in plastic wrap. Refrigerate for at least 1 hour.

Preheat the oven to 350°F (180°C, gas mark 4). Cover a baking sheet with parchment paper.

Flour a flat surface and roll the dough out to about 1/4-inch thickness. Cut the dough out using cookie cutters or a juice glass. Sprinkle the cookies with sugar and place on the baking sheet.

Bake for 10 to 12 minutes, until golden at the edges. Cool for a couple of minutes on the pan, then transfer the cookies to a wire rack to cool completely.

YIELD: Makes about 24 cookies

ADD IT! Brush the cookies with egg white and sprinkle with chopped almonds before baking.

☃ Amaretti

2 cups (290 g) **unblanched almonds**

1 1/2 (300 g) cups **sugar**

1/4 cup (30 g) **all-purpose flour**

1/4 teaspoon salt

4 **egg whites**

1 teaspoon **almond extract**

Preheat the oven to 325°F (170°C, gas mark 3). Lightly grease two cookie sheets.

Put the almonds in a food processor fitted with the metal blade and grind to a fine meal. Put the ground almonds in a mixing bowl and stir in the sugar, flour, and salt.

Combine the egg whites and almond extract in a mixing bowl and whip until opaque, just barely to soft peak. Fold the egg whites into the nut mixture. Drop onto the cookie sheets by teaspoonfuls, about 2 inches (5 cm) apart.

Bake for 20 minutes. Cool on wire racks.

YIELD: Makes about 48 cookies

ADD IT! Press a honey-frosted almond on top of each cookie before baking.

🦌 Zimtstern

Our father fondly recalls his grandmother making these cookies when he was a boy and getting to frost the cookies. A Christmas favorite in our family.

6 **egg whites**

1 pound (455 g) **confectioners' sugar**, plus more for rolling

Grated zest of 1 **lemon**

1 1/2 tablespoons **cinnamon**

1 1/4 pound (570 g) **unblanched almonds**, grated fine

Beat the egg whites, sugar, and lemon zest until very stiff. Add the cinnamon and mix. Set aside 1 cup of the mixture for frosting. Add the almonds to the remainder and combine until well mixed. Refrigerate overnight.

Preheat the oven to 325°F (170°C, gas mark 3).

Sprinkle a flat surface with confectioners' sugar and roll out the dough to about 3/8-inch thickness. Cut out with a 1-inch star-shaped cookie cutter. Ice each cookie with the mixture that was set aside. Place the cookies on parchment lined baking pans.

Bake for 12 to 15 minutes. Allow to cool for 3 to 4 minutes on the baking pans, then cool completely on wire racks.

YIELD: Makes about 48 cookies

Mandelgebackenes

One of the Hildebrand clan's traditional Christmas cookies, this translates roughly to baked almond. We're in favor.

- 1 pound (455 g) finely grated **almonds** (a scant 3 1/4 cups)
- 1 pound (455 g) **dark brown sugar**
- 3 tablespoons (20 g) **cinnamon**
- 2 **egg whites**
- 2 cups (240 g) **confectioners' sugar**
- 1 cup (235 ml) water

Using your hands, work the almonds, brown sugar, cinnamon, and egg whites together in a bowl. Cover and refrigerate overnight. (The dough will be very stiff and sticky.)

Preheat the oven to 325°F (170°C, gas mark 3). Cover two cookie sheets with parchment paper.

Sprinkle a working surface with some confectioners' sugar. Working in batches, roll out the dough until about 1/4-inch thick. Cut out with fancy cookie cutters and place on the cookie sheets.

Bake for 12 to 15 minutes. (The cookies will not look crisp when they come out.)

While the cookies are baking, cook the confectioners' sugar with the water over medium-low heat until the sugar is dissolved. While the cookies are still hot, brush with the thin sugar glaze.

YIELD: Makes about 48 cookies

Mandelkranze (Almond Rings)

A very rich and delicious butter cookie, this is another of the traditional German Christmas cookies.

1 1/2 cups (3 sticks, or 337 g) butter

1 1/4 cups (1/2 pound, or 225 g) **granulated sugar**

3 **eggs**, separated

4 cups (1 pound, or 455 g) **flour**

1/2 cup (100 g) **cinnamon sugar** (See "Making Cinnamon Sugar" on page 12.)

1/4 cup (25 g) coarsely chopped unblanched **almonds**

Using a mixer on medium speed, cream the butter and granulated sugar together until light and fluffy, about 5 minutes. Add the yolks, one at a time, incorporating well after each addition. Add the flour and mix thoroughly. Refrigerate overnight.

Preheat the oven to 325°F (170°C, gas mark 3). Cover two cookie sheets with parchment paper.

Sprinkle a flat surface with confectioners' sugar and roll out dough in small quantities, keeping the rest refrigerated. Cut out with a ring-shaped cookie cutter.

Lightly beat the egg whites.

Combine the cinnamon sugar and almonds in a wide, shallow bowl. Paint each ring with the egg whites and then flip the painted side into the sugar. Place on the cookie sheets, coated side up.

Bake for 10 to 12 minutes. Cool on the pan for 4 to 5 minutes, then transfer to wire racks to cool completely.

YIELD: Makes about 36 cookies

⚞ Florentines

These chewy candylike cookies are Austrian in origin, although the name certainly implies otherwise.

> 1/2 cup (1 stick, or 112 g) butter
>
> 1 cup (200 g) **sugar**
>
> 1/2 cup (120 ml) **heavy cream**
>
> 1 cup (235 ml) **dark corn syrup**
>
> 2 teaspoons **cinnamon**
>
> 1 1/2 teaspoons salt
>
> 3 cups (285 g) finely ground blanched **almonds**
>
> Shortening

Combine all ingredients except the almonds in a 2-quart saucepan. Cook over medium-high heat, stirring, until the butter is melted and the sugar is dissolved. Bring the mixture to a boil. Stir in the almonds and cook, stirring, for 1 to 2 minutes. Cool the batter.

Preheat the oven to 300°F (150°C, gas mark 2). Line a cookie sheet with a Silpat (French nonstick baking mat) or parchment paper.

When cool enough to handle, form the batter into 1-inch balls with hands coated with shortening to prevent sticking. Place the balls on the cookie sheet and flatten with the palm of your hand.

Bake until bubbled on top—10 to 12 minutes. Transfer to a cooling rack. Cool completely.

YIELD: Makes about 36 cookies

ADD IT! Melt 6 ounces (170 g) semisweet chocolate and drizzle it over the baked, cooled cookies.

🦎 Nut Crescents

For the dough:

> 1 cup (2 sticks, or 225 g) butter
> 1/2 cup (100 g) **sugar**
> 2 **egg yolks**
> 2 cups (250 g) **all-purpose flour**
> Pinch salt
> 1/2 cup (45 g) grated unblanched **almonds**

For the filling:

> 2 **egg whites**
> 1/2 cup (100 g) **sugar**
> 1 cup (90 g) grated unblanched **almonds**

To make the dough:

Cream together the butter and sugar until fluffy and light—about 5 minutes. Add the egg yolks and beat for 2 to 3 minutes. Stir in the flour, salt, and almonds until combined. Wrap the dough in plastic wrap and allow to rest for 10 minutes.

Preheat the oven to 325°F (170°C, gas mark 3). Line two cookie sheets with parchment paper.

To make the filling:

In a small mixing bowl, whisk the egg whites until they are frothy, then whisk in the sugar. Stir in the almonds.

Roll out the dough to 1/4-inch thick on a lightly floured surface. Cut the dough into triangles 3-inches tall and 3 inches on the base. Spoon the filling mixture over the triangles. Roll up the dough and curl the ends to form crescents. Put the crescents onto the cookie sheets.

Bake for 15 to 18 minutes, until lightly brown. Cool on the cookie sheets.

YIELD: Makes about 24 cookies

Almond and Apricot Purses

The slight tartness of the apricot plays nicely off the almonds' nuttiness.

> 1/2 cup (1 stick, or 112 g) butter
>
> 4 ounces (115 g) **cream cheese**
>
> 1/2 cup (60 g) **confectioners' sugar**, plus more for dusting
>
> 2 cups (250 g) **all-purpose flour**
>
> 1/2 teaspoon salt
>
> 2 cups (640 g) **apricot jam**
>
> 1 cup (110 g) slivered **almonds**

Cream the butter, cream cheese, and sugar until light, fluffy, and smooth. Add the flour and salt and mix on low speed until smooth. Form the dough into a ball and wrap in plastic. Refrigerate for 1 hour.

Preheat the oven to 350°F (180°C, gas mark 4). Cover a baking sheet with parchment paper.

Flour a flat surface and roll the dough out 1/8- to 1/4-inch thick. Cut the dough into 3-inch squares. Place 1 teaspoon apricot jam and a few almonds in the center of each square. Bring the four corners to the middle and pinch them together over the filling. (To make them more pliable and easier to form into purses, try warming them for a few seconds in the microwave before pinching.) Place the finished purses on the baking sheet.

Bake for 12 to 15 minutes, until golden brown. Cool on wire racks.

YIELD: Makes about 24 cookies

ADD IT! Add a bit of minced amaretto-soaked dried apricots to the filling for piquancy.

Almond-Coconut-Rum Macaroons

4 **egg whites**

1 cup (120 g) **confectioners' sugar**

2 cups (290 g) blanched **almonds**, finely ground

2 cups (150 g) sweetened **shredded coconut**

1/4 cup (60 ml) **golden rum**

Preheat the oven to 350°F (180°C, gas mark 4). Line a cookie sheet with parchment paper.

Using a mixer on medium speed, beat the egg whites until frothy, then slowly add the sugar until soft peaks form. Fold in the almonds, coconut, and rum and mix on high speed for 5 to 6 minutes, until the mixture is fluffy. Drop by table-spoonfuls onto the cookie sheet.

Bake for 12 to 15 minutes, until lightly browned. Cool on racks.

YIELD: Makes about 24 cookies

ADD IT! Try it with 1/4 cup (45 g) chopped dates or dried tropical fruit.

Almond Spice Biscotti

According to recipe tester Mary Harris, these cookies are so addictive they need a warning label.

> 1 cup (2 sticks, or 225 g) butter, softened
>
> 1 cup (200 g) **sugar**
>
> 2 **eggs**
>
> 2 cups (250 g) **self-rising flour**, plus more for forming
>
> 1 tablespoon **cinnamon**
>
> 1 cup (90 g) chopped blanched **almonds**

Preheat the oven to 350°F (180°C, gas mark 4).

Using a mixer on medium speed, cream together the butter and sugar until light and creamy—about 5 minutes. Add the eggs and beat for 3 to 4 minutes longer. Stir together the flour and cinnamon. Add this to the mixing bowl and mix until thoroughly combined. Stir in the almonds.

Lightly flour a flat surface. Transfer to lightly greased cookie sheet, form the dough into a log, about 12 inches long by 4 inches wide by 1 inch tall, adding flour as necessary for forming.

Bake for 22 to 25 minutes, until a tester inserted into the center comes out clean, but the cookie log is still soft. Cool on the pan completely.

Reheat the oven to 300°F (150°C, gas mark 2). Slice the cookie log into 1-inch slices and lay the cookies on their sides on an ungreased cookie sheet.

Bake for 20 to 25 minutes and remove from the oven. Let the biscotti cool and harden on cookie sheet and gently transfer to a wire rack.

YIELD: Makes about 12 cookies

Aniseed Cookies

These cookies have a delightful black licorice flavor.

    1 cup (2 sticks, or 225 g) butter

    1 cup (200 g) **sugar**

    2 **eggs**

    2 tablespoons (28 ml) **anisette liqueur**

    3 tablespoons (20 g) **anise seed**

    2 cups (250 g) **all-purpose flour**

    1/4 teaspoon salt

Using a mixer on medium speed, cream together the butter and sugar until light and creamy—about 5 minutes. Add the eggs and the anisette and beat for 3 to 4 minutes longer. Add the anise seed, flour, and salt and mix until thoroughly combined. Form the dough into a ball and wrap in plastic wrap. Refrigerate for at least 1 hour.

Preheat the oven to 350°F (180°C, gas mark 4). Cover two cookie sheets with parchment paper.

Flour a flat surface and roll the dough out to about 1/4-inch thickness. Cut the dough out using cookie cutters or a juice glass. Place the pieces on the cookie sheets.

Bake for 12 to 15 minutes, until lightly browned. Cool for a couple of minutes on the cookie sheets, then transfer the cookies to a wire rack to cool completely.

YIELD: Makes about 24 cookies

Cashew Butter Cookies

We find cashew butter at natural food and gourmet stores. It's great as a peanut butter alternative on sandwiches, too.

1/2 cup (100 g) shortening

1/2 cup (100 g) **sugar**

1/2 cup (170 g) **honey**

1 cup (250 g) **cashew butter**

2 **eggs**

2 cups (250 g) **all-purpose flour**

Preheat the oven to 350°F (180°C, gas mark 4). Lightly grease two cookie sheets.

Using a mixer on medium speed, cream together the shortening and sugar in a large mixing bowl until light and fluffy—about 5 minutes. Add the honey, cashew butter, and eggs and beat for 3 to 4 minutes. Add the flour and mix until fully incorporated. Drop by the tablespoonful onto the cookie sheets, leaving 3 inches (7.5 cm) or so between cookies.

Bake for 12 to 15 minutes, until lightly browned and set, but still soft. Cool on the cookie sheets for 2 to 3 minutes, then transfer to a wire rack to cool completely.

YIELD: Makes about 36 cookies

🧸 Coconut Macaroons

These cookies are very fast to make, and this recipe yields a very moist cookie rich in coconut flavor.

1/2 cup (100 g) shortening

1 cup (200 g) **sugar**

2 teaspoons **vanilla extract**

2 cups (150 g) sweetened **shredded coconut**

1 cup (120 g) **all-purpose flour**

1/2 teaspoon salt

2 **egg whites**

Preheat the oven to 325°F (170°C, gas mark 3). Cover two cookie sheets with parchment paper.

Using a mixer on medium speed, cream together the shortening and sugar until light and fluffy—about 5 minutes. Add the vanilla and beat for another minute. Stir in the coconut, flour, and salt until well combined. Add the egg whites and beat for 4 to 5 minutes. Drop by the tablespoonful onto the cookie sheets, leaving 2 inches (5 cm) between cookies. (If you want a more perfect looking cookie, roll them into rounds instead of dropping them by spoon.)

Bake for 15 to 18 minutes, until lightly browned. Move to a wire rack and cool completely.

YIELD: Makes about 24 cookies

Coconut Pecan Drops

These gooey drops are a pantry favorite.

2 cups (200 g) **pecan pieces**

1 cup (75 g) sweetened **shredded coconut**

1 cup (225 g) packed **light brown sugar**

4 **egg whites**

2 teaspoons **vanilla extract**

Preheat the oven to 350°F (180°C, gas mark 4). Lightly grease two cookie sheets.

Mix the pecans, coconut, and sugar in a large mixing bowl.

In another mixing bowl, whip the egg whites to soft peak. Fold into the nut mixture, then fold in the vanilla. Drop by the tablespoonful onto the cookie sheets, leaving 3 inches (7.5 cm) or so between cookies.

Bake for 10 to 12 minutes, until set, but still soft. Cool on the cookie sheets for 2 to 3 minutes, then transfer to a wire rack to cool completely.

YIELD: Makes about 30 cookies

♣ Mary Burke's Addictive Cookies

We've never met Mary Burke, but her daughter gave us this recipe, and she was right. They are addictive. You'd never believe it looking at the ingredients, but these cookies are wonderful.

 2 cups (350 g) **butterscotch chips**
 4 cups (144 g) **potato sticks**
 1 cup (145 g) unsalted **dry roasted peanuts**

Cover a cookie sheet with waxed paper.

Melt the butterscotch chips in the microwave or in a double boiler.

Put the potato sticks in a mixing bowl and pour the melted butterscotch over. Stir well, trying to not break the sticks too much. Stir in the peanuts. Using 2 spoons, drop spoonfuls of the mixture onto the cookie sheet. Allow to harden for 1 to 2 hours.

YIELD: Makes 30 to 40 cookies

🎄 Pecan Shortbread

We love cutting the richness of shortbreads with nut flavors.

> 1 cup (2 sticks, or 225 g) butter
>
> 1 cup (200 g) **vanilla sugar** (see "Making Vanilla Sugar" on page 12.), plus more for sprinkling
>
> 2 **eggs**
>
> 2 cups (250 g) **all-purpose flour**
>
> 1 teaspoon **baking powder**
>
> 1/4 teaspoon salt
>
> 1 cup (100 g) **chopped pecans**

Using a mixer on medium speed, cream together the butter and sugar until light and creamy—about 5 minutes. Add the eggs and beat for 3 to 4 minutes.

Sift together the flour, baking powder, and salt and add to the mixing bowl, along with the pecans. Mix until thoroughly combined. Form the dough into a ball and wrap in plastic wrap. Refrigerate for at least 1 hour.

Preheat the oven to 350°F (180°C, gas mark 4). Line two cookie sheets with parchment paper.

Flour a flat surface and roll the dough out to about 1/4-inch thickness. Cut the dough out using cookie cutters or a juice glass. Place the pieces on the cookie sheet. Sprinkle with sugar.

Bake for 12 to 15 minutes, until golden at the edges. Cool for a couple of minutes on the cookie sheets, then transfer to a wire rack to cool completely.

YIELD: Makes about 24 cookies

Mini Turtle Tarts

For the tart dough:

> 1/4 cup (1/2 stick, or 55 g) butter
>
> 1/4 cup (50 g) shortening
>
> 1 1/2 cups (180 g) **all-purpose flour**
>
> 1/2 cup (100 g) **sugar**
>
> 1/2 teaspoon salt
>
> 1/2 cup (120 ml) (approximately) cold water

For the filling:

> 24 **caramels**, unwrapped
>
> 1 cup (175 g) **semisweet chocolate chips**
>
> 1 cup (100 g) chopped **pecans**

To make the dough:

Put all of the ingredients except the water into a food processor fitted with the metal blade. Process until the mixture resembles a fine meal. With the motor running, add the water in a thin stream, adding only enough to just bring the dough together.

Place a piece of plastic wrap on the counter and put the dough in it, including any loose crumbs. Knead a few times to bring the dough together in a ball, then flatten out into a disk. Wrap up in the plastic and refrigerate for 1/2 hour.

Flour a work surface and roll the dough out to 1/4-inch thickness. Cut 2-inch circles and tuck them into the holes of a mini muffin pan that has been sprayed with nonstick cooking spray. Freeze the tart shells for 1 hour.

Preheat the oven to 350°F (180°C, gas mark 4).

To make the filling:

Cut the caramels into quarters. Fill the tart shells three-quarters of the way with the caramels, chocolate chips, and pecans.

Bake for 20 to 25 minutes, until the filling is melted and the tart shells are golden. Cool in the pans.

YIELD: Makes about 24 cookies

Maple-Walnut Cookies

These cookies are perfect for March in New England, when the sap is running.

1 cup (2 sticks, or 225 g) butter

1/2 cup (100 g) **sugar**

1/2 cup (120 ml) **maple syrup**

2 **eggs**

2 cups (250 g) **all-purpose flour**

1/4 teaspoon salt

1 cup (125 g) chopped **walnuts**

Preheat the oven to 350°F (180°C, gas mark 4). Lightly grease two cookie sheets.

Using a mixer on medium speed, cream together the butter and sugar in a large mixing bowl until light and fluffy—about 5 minutes. Add the syrup and eggs and beat for 3 to 4 minutes. Add the flour and salt and mix until fully incorporated. Stir in the walnuts. Drop by the tablespoonful onto the cookie sheets, leaving 3 inches (7.5 cm) or so between cookies.

Bake for 12 to 15 minutes, until lightly browned around edges and set, but still soft. Cool on the cookie sheets for 2 to 3 minutes, then transfer to a wire rack to cool completely.

YIELD: Makes about 36 cookies

Maple Frosted Shortbreads

Talk about gilding the lily—adding frosting to shortbread cookies lifts them to a whole new level of fabulousness.

1/2 cup (1 stick, or 112 g) butter

1/2 cup (100 g) **granulated sugar**

1 cup (120 g) **all-purpose flour**

Pinch salt

1 cup (125 g) chopped **walnuts**, divided

1 1/2 cups (180 g) **confectioners' sugar**

1/4 cup (60 ml) **maple syrup**

Using a mixer on medium speed, cream together the butter and granulated sugar until light and fluffy—about 5 minutes. Add the flour, salt, and 1/2 cup (60 g) of the walnuts. Beat on low speed until thoroughly combined. Wrap the dough in plastic wrap and refrigerate for 2 hours.

Preheat the oven to 350°F (180°C, gas mark 4). Line two baking sheets with parchment paper.

Roll the dough on a floured surface to 1/2 inch thick. Using cookie cutters, cut out 1-inch rounds. Place the rounds on the cookie sheet.

Bake for 15 to 20 minutes, until golden brown. Cool on racks.

When the cookies are cooled, whisk together the confectioners' sugar and maple syrup in a mixing bowl. Spoon the icing onto the cookies, then sprinkle the remaining 1/2 cup (60 g) walnuts over the icing. Allow to set.

YIELD: Makes about 18 cookies

Maple Sugar Cookies

You can often buy maple sugar at specialty stores and sugar houses (if you have these in your area). But you can substitute ^{1}/2 cup (100 g) white sugar mixed with ^{1}/2 cup (120 ml) maple syrup if finding maple sugar is a problem.

> ^{1}/2 cup (1 stick, or 112 g) butter
>
> 1 cup (200 g) **maple sugar**
>
> 2 **eggs**
>
> 2 cups (250 g) **all-purpose flour**
>
> 1 teaspoon **baking powder**
>
> ^{1}/4 teaspoon salt
>
> 1 cup (125 g) chopped **walnuts**

Using a mixer on medium speed, cream together the butter and maple sugar until light and creamy—about 5 minutes. Add the eggs and beat for 3 to 4 minutes longer.

Sift together the flour, baking powder, and salt and add to the mixing bowl. Mix until thoroughly combined. Stir in the walnuts. Form the dough into a ball and wrap in plastic wrap. Refrigerate for at least 1 hour.

Preheat the oven to 350°F (180°C, gas mark 4). Line two cookie sheets with parchment paper.

Flour a flat surface and roll the dough out to about 1/4-inch thickness. Cut the dough out using cookie cutters or a juice glass. Place the pieces on the cookie sheet.

Bake for 12 to 15 minutes, until golden at the edges. Cool for a couple of minutes on the cookie sheets, then transfer the cookies to a wire rack to cool completely.

YIELD: Makes about 24 cookies

Apple-Date Cookies

1/2 cup (1 stick, or 112 g) butter

1/2 cup (100 g) **sugar**

2 **eggs**

2 cups (250 g) **self-rising flour**

1 cup (125 g) peeled, diced **apples**

1 cup (175 g) diced **dates**

Preheat the oven to 350°F (180°C, gas mark 4). Lightly grease two cookie sheets.

Using a mixer on medium speed, cream together the butter and sugar in a large mixing bowl until light and fluffy—about 5 minutes. Add the eggs, one at a time, beating well after each addition. Add the flour and mix until fully incorporated. Stir in the apples and dates. Drop by the tablespoonful onto the cookie sheets, leaving 3 inches (7.5 cm) or so between cookies.

Bake for 12 to 15 minutes, until lightly browned and set, but still soft. Cool on the cookie sheets for 2 to 3 minutes, then transfer to a wire rack to cool completely.

YIELD: Makes about 36 cookies

Applesauce Spice Cookies

These cakey cookies fall under our pseudo-healthy cookie offerings.

- 1/2 cup (1 stick, or 112 g) butter, softened
- 1 cup (200 g) **sugar**
- 1 cup (255 g) **applesauce**
- 2 cups (250 g) **all-purpose flour**
- 1/2 teaspoon salt
- 1 teaspoon **baking powder**
- 3 teaspoons **apple pie spice**

Preheat the oven to 350°F (180°C, gas mark 4). Grease two cookie sheets.

Using a mixer on medium speed, cream together the butter and sugar in a large mixing bowl until light and fluffy—about 5 minutes. Add the applesauce and beat for 2 to 3 minutes.

Sift together the flour, salt, baking powder, and apple pie spice. Add this to the butter mixture and mix until fully incorporated. Drop by the tablespoonful on the cookie sheets, leaving 3 inches (7.5 cm) or so between cookies.

Bake for 12 to 15 minutes, until set but still soft. Cool on the cookie sheets for 2 to 3 minutes, then transfer to a wire rack to cool completely.

YIELD: Makes about 36 cookies

ADD IT! Toss in some diced tart apples for more apple flavor.

Apricot-Almond Cookies

Very tender, not too sweet, and slightly cakey—tester supreme Mary Harris loved these.

> 1 cup (2 sticks, or 225 g) butter
>
> 1 cup (200 g) **sugar**
>
> 3 **eggs**
>
> 2 cups (250 g) **self-rising flour**
>
> 1 cup (90 g) chopped **almonds**
>
> 1 cup (270 g) chopped dried **apricots**

Preheat the oven to 350°F (180°C, gas mark 4). Lightly grease two cookie sheets.

Using a mixer on medium speed, cream together the butter and sugar until light and creamy—about 5 minutes. Add the eggs and beat for 3 to 4 minutes longer. Add the flour and mix until thoroughly combined. Stir in the almonds and apricots. Drop by the tablespoonful onto the cookie sheets, leaving 3 inches (7.5 cm) or so between cookies.

Bake for 12 to 15 minutes, until lightly browned and set, but still soft. Cool on the cookie sheets for 2 to 3 minutes, then transfer to a wire rack to cool completely.

YIELD: Makes about 36 cookies

Phyllo Apricot Purses

Great coffee klatsch cookies—rich and delicious.

> 6 ounces (170 g) dried **apricots**
> 1/4 cup (60 ml) **Amaretto di Saronno**
> 6 ounces (170 g) **cream cheese**
> 1/2 cup (50 g) chopped **pecans**
> 12 sheets frozen **phyllo dough** (14 x 18 inch, or 35 x 45 cm), thawed
> 3/4 cup (1 1/2 sticks, or 170 g) butter, melted

Preheat the oven to 400°F (200°C, gas mark 6). Line a cookie sheet with parchment paper.

Soak the apricots in the amaretto for 15 to 20 minutes and drain. Whirl the apricots in a food processor until they are finely minced.

Place the cream cheese and pecans in a bowl and mix until thoroughly combined.

Place the phyllo dough on a clean, dry surface and cover—first with a sheet of plastic wrap, and then a damp towel.

Melt the butter over low heat. Lay out a phyllo sheet and, using a pastry brush, brush with melted butter. Lay another sheet on top of the first and repeat the buttering process. Repeat until there are six layers. Make four equidistant cuts crosswise on the phyllo and one lengthwise to divide the pastry into 8 pieces.

Put a scant spoonful of the filling on the middle of each square. Pull up the sides of each phyllo square and twist it into a small sack, like a paper bag with a twist at the top. Place the sacks on the cookie sheet. Brush with melted butter.

Bake for 10 to 15 minutes, or until phyllo is golden brown and somewhat crackly looking.

YIELD: Makes 16 purses

No Bake Apricot-Nut Drops

What's better than cookies that don't actually require an oven?

    1 cup (270 g) dried **apricots**
    1 cup (75 g) **sweetened shredded coconut**
    2 cups (55 g) **Corn Flakes**
    1 can (8 ounces, or 235 ml) **sweetened condensed milk**
    8 ounces (225 g) blanched **almonds**
    Butter, softened

Combine the apricots, coconut, and Corn Flakes in a food processor fitted with the metal blade. Process until the apricots are finely minced and the cereal is crumbs. Add the condensed milk and process until the mixture forms a ball. Scrape onto a sheet of plastic wrap, wrap up the dough, and refrigerate for 1 hour.

Clean the food processor bowl and dry it well. Add the almonds and process until they are finely ground. Put the ground almonds into a mixing bowl.

Line a cookie sheet with waxed paper.

Butter your hands and roll the dough into 1-inch balls. Roll the balls in the ground almonds. Place the cookies on the cookie sheet.

YIELD: Makes about 24 cookies

No Cook Fruit and Nut Balls

These cookies are a very quick and easy recipe for those 9 p.m. recollections of next-day bake-sale obligations.

> 1 cup (28 g) **Corn Flakes**, crushed into crumbs
>
> 1 cup (270 g) chopped dried **apricots**
>
> 1/2 cup (120 ml) **sweetened condensed milk**
>
> 1 cup (75 g) **sweetened shredded coconut**
>
> 1 cup (90 g) finely chopped **almonds**

Combine all of the ingredients except the almonds in a mixing bowl and mix until well combined.

Put the almonds in a pie plate. Roll the dough into 1-inch balls and then roll the balls in the almonds. Place on a cookie sheet covered with waxed paper and refrigerate for 1 hour.

YIELD: Makes about 36 balls

Banana-Chocolate Chip Drops

These cookies are very easy and fast to make. On top of that, they're tasty—a great way to fill the cookie jar.

1 cup (2 sticks, or 225 g) butter, softened

1 cup (200 g) **sugar**

1 cup (225 g) mashed ripe **banana**—about 2 bananas

2 cups (250 g) **all-purpose flour**

1/2 teaspoon salt

1 teaspoon **baking soda**

2 cups (350 g) **semisweet chocolate chips**

Preheat the oven to 350°F (180°C, gas mark 4). Lightly grease two cookie sheets.

Using a mixer on medium speed, cream together the butter and sugar in a large mixing bowl until light and fluffy—4 to 5 minutes. Add the banana and beat for 2 to 3 minutes.

Sift together the flour, salt, and baking soda. Add this to the butter mixture and mix until fully incorporated. Stir in the chocolate chips. Drop by the tablespoonful on the cookie sheets, leaving 3 inches (7.5 cm) or so between cookies.

Bake for 12 to 15 minutes, until lightly browned and set, but still soft. Cool on the cookie sheets for 2 to 3 minutes, then transfer to a wire rack to cool completely.

YIELD: Makes about 36 cookies

🦎 Cranberry-Oatmeal Cookies

This is a yummy twist on the traditional oatmeal raisin goodie.

> 1 cup (2 sticks, or 225 g) butter, softened
>
> 1 cup (225 g) packed **light brown sugar**
>
> 2 **eggs**
>
> 2 cups (250 g) **all-purpose flour**
>
> 1/4 teaspoon salt
>
> 1 cup (80 g) **rolled oats**
>
> 1 cup (120 g) **dried cranberries**

Preheat the oven to 350°F (180°C, gas mark 4). Lightly grease two cookie sheets.

Using a mixer on medium speed, cream together the butter and sugar in a large mixing bowl until light and fluffy—about 5 minutes. Add the eggs, one at a time, beating well after each addition. Add the flour and salt and mix until fully incorporated. Stir in the oats and cranberries. Drop by the tablespoonful onto the cookie sheets, leaving 3 inches (7.5 cm) or so between cookies.

Bake for 12 to 15 minutes, until lightly browned and set, but still soft. Cool on the cookie sheets for 2 to 3 minutes, then transfer to a wire rack to cool completely.

YIELD: Makes about 36 cookies

Iced Lemon Cookies

1 cup (2 sticks, or 225 g) butter

2 1/2 cups (300 g) **confectioners' sugar**, divided

2 **egg yolks**

Zest of two **lemons** and 1 tablespoon (14 ml) lemon juice

1 cup (145 g) blanched **almonds**, finely ground

1 cup (120 g) **self-rising flour**

1/4 teaspoon salt

Using a mixer on medium speed, cream together the butter and 1 1/2 cups (180 g) of the sugar until light and creamy—about 5 minutes. Add the egg yolks and the lemon zest and beat for 3 to 4 minutes longer. Add the almonds, flour, and salt and mix until thoroughly combined. Form the dough into a ball and wrap in plastic wrap. Refrigerate for at least 1 hour.

Preheat the oven to 300°F (150°C, gas mark 2). Line a cookie sheet with parchment paper.

Flour a flat surface and roll the dough out to about 1/4-inch thickness. Cut the dough out using cookie cutters or a juice glass. Place the pieces on the cookie sheet.

Bake for 16 to 18 minutes, until lightly browned. Cool for a couple of minutes on the cookie sheet, then transfer the cookies to a wire rack to cool.

Combine the remaining 1 cup sugar and the lemon juice in a small saucepan. Cook over low heat, stirring frequently, until the sugar is dissolved and the liquid clears. Bring to a boil, stirring constantly, and boil for 1 minute. Let cool for a minute and dip the cookies, top sides down, into the lemon glaze.

YIELD: Makes about 24 cookies.

ADD IT! Drop a thin curl of lemon zest on top of each glazed cookie before it sets.

Lemon Thins

1 1/2 to 2 **lemons**

1 cup (2 sticks, or 225 g) butter

3/4 cup (105 g) packed **light brown sugar**

2 **eggs**, separated, discarding the whites

2 teaspoons **vanilla extract**

2 cups (250 g) **all-purpose flour**

1/4 teaspoon salt

Preheat the oven to 350°F (180°C, gas mark 4). Cover two cookie sheets with parchment paper.

Zest the lemons finely to yield about 1 1/2 tablespoons zest. Squeeze the lemons to yield about 1/4 cup (60 ml) lemon juice.

Using a mixer on medium speed, cream together the butter and sugar in a large mixing bowl until light and fluffy—about 5 minutes. Add the lemon zest, egg yolks, lemon juice, and vanilla and beat for 3 to 4 minutes. Add the flour and salt and beat until smooth. Drop by the large tablespoonful on the cookie sheets, leaving 3 inches (7.5 cm) or so between cookies.

Bake for 12 to 14 minutes, until lightly browned at the edges. Cool on the cookie sheets for 2 to 3 minutes, then transfer to a wire rack to cool completely.

YIELD: Makes about 24 cookies.

🪆 Lemonade Cookies

These sunny yellow cookies are perfect for a spring tea.

> 1 cup (2 sticks, or 225 g) butter, softened
>
> 1/2 to 2/3 cup (110 to 145 g) **powdered lemonade mix**
> (depending on how tart you want the cookies)
>
> 2 **eggs**
>
> 2 cups (250 g) **all-purpose flour**
>
> 1/4 teaspoon salt
>
> 1 cup (120 g) **confectioners' sugar**

Preheat the oven to 350°F (180°C, gas mark 4). Lightly grease two cookie sheets.

Using a mixer on medium speed, cream together the butter and lemonade mix in a large mixing bowl until light and fluffy—about 5 minutes. Add the eggs, one at a time, beating well after each addition. Add the flour and salt and mix until fully incorporated. Drop by the tablespoonful onto the cookie sheets, leaving 3 inches (7.5 cm) or so between cookies.

Bake for 12 to 15 minutes, until lightly brown at edges and set but still soft. Cool on the cookie sheets for 2 to 3 minutes, then transfer to a wire rack to cool completely. Dust with the confectioners' sugar.

YIELD: Makes about 24 cookies

Lemon Lace Cookies

These cookies are delicate and delicious.

> 1 cup (2 sticks, or 225 g) butter
>
> 1/2 cup (60 g) **confectioners' sugar**, plus 1/4 cup (30 g) for the pressing
>
> 1 cup (120 g) **all-purpose flour**
>
> 1 cup (80 g) **rolled oats**
>
> 1 teaspoon grated **lemon zest**
>
> 1 teaspoon **vanilla extract**

Using a mixer on medium speed, cream together the butter and sugar until light and fluffy—about 5 minutes. Add the flour, oats, zest, and vanilla and beat on low speed until thoroughly combined. Wrap the dough in plastic wrap and refrigerate for 2 hours.

Preheat the oven to 350°F (180°C, gas mark 4).

On a lightly floured surface, roll out the dough into a log, about 1 inch thick. Cut off 1-inch pieces and roll them into balls. Place the balls on an ungreased cookie sheet. Dip the bottom of a juice glass into the sugar and flatten the dough balls.

Bake for 12 to 15 minutes, until lightly browned. Cool for 1 minute on the cookie sheet, then remove to a wire rack and cool completely.

YIELD: Makes about 24 cookies

🦁 Lemon~Coconut Chewies

1/2 cup (1 stick, or 112 g) butter, softened

1 cup (200 g) **sugar**

1 cup (225 g) **lemon yogurt**

2 cups (250 g) **all-purpose flour**

1/2 teaspoon salt

1 teaspoon **baking soda**

1 cup (75 g) **sweetened shredded coconut** (For smaller coconut bits, whirl the shredded coconuts in a food processor for a few seconds.)

Preheat the oven to 350°F (180°C, gas mark 4). Lightly grease two cookie sheets.

Using a mixer on medium speed, cream together the butter and sugar in a large mixing bowl until light and fluffy—about 5 minutes. Add the yogurt and beat for 2 to 3 minutes.

Sift together the flour, salt, and baking soda. Add this to the butter mixture and mix until fully incorporated. Stir in the coconut. Drop by the tablespoonful onto the cookie sheets, leaving 3 inches (7.5 cm) or so between cookies.

Bake for 12 to 15 minutes, until lightly browned and set, but still soft. Cool on the cookie sheets for 2 to 3 minutes, then transfer to a wire rack to cool completely.

YIELD: Makes about 36 cookies

ADD IT! Try adding 1 teaspoon of grated lemon zest to punch up the lemon kick.

Orange Drops

Orange marmalade was on our breakfast table every day when we were growing up, and these cookies reflect our reliance on having a jar on hand in the fridge.

> 1 cup (2 sticks, or 225 g) butter
>
> 1/2 cup (100 g) **sugar**
>
> 1 cup (320 g) **orange marmalade**
>
> 3 **eggs**
>
> 3 cups (360 g) **all-purpose flour**
>
> 1 teaspoon **baking powder**
>
> 1/4 teaspoon salt

Preheat the oven to 350°F (180°C, gas mark 4). Lightly grease two cookie sheets.

Using a mixer on medium speed, cream together the butter and sugar in a large mixing bowl until light and fluffy—about 5 minutes. Add the marmalade and eggs and beat for 3 to 4 minutes.

In another bowl, stir together the flour, baking powder, and salt. Add the flour mixture to the butter mixture and beat until fully incorporated. Drop by the tablespoonful onto the cookie sheets, leaving 3 inches (7.5 cm) or so between cookies.

Bake for 12 to 15 minutes, until lightly browned and set, but still soft. Cool on the cookie sheets for 2 to 3 minutes, then transfer to a wire rack to cool completely.

YIELD: Makes about 48 cookies

ADD IT! You could put mini chocolate chips in if you feel the need for chocolate in every dessert.

Orange-Coconut Drops

These are good sturdy cookies for the cookie jar.

    1 cup (2 sticks, or 225 g) butter, softened
    1 cup (200 g) **sugar**
    1/4 cup (70 g) frozen **orange juice concentrate**, thawed
    2 **eggs**
    2 cups (250 g) **self-rising flour**
    1/2 teaspoon salt
    1 cup (75 g) **sweetened shredded coconut**

Preheat the oven to 350°F (180°C, gas mark 4). Lightly grease two cookie sheets.

Using a mixer on medium speed, cream together the butter and sugar in a large mixing bowl until light and fluffy—about 5 minutes. Add the orange juice concentrate and the eggs and beat for 2 to 3 minutes.

Sift together the flour and salt. Add this to the butter mixture and mix until fully incorporated. Stir in the coconut. Drop by the tablespoonful onto the cookie sheets, leaving 3 inches (7.5 cm) or so between cookies.

Bake for 12 to 15 minutes, until lightly browned and set, but still soft. Cool on the cookie sheets for 2 to 3 minutes, then transfer to a wire rack to cool completely.

YIELD: Makes about 36 cookies

Orange-Hazelnut Biscotti

Mary Harris, cookie tester supreme, put these in her top five favorites.

> 1 **orange**
> 1 cup (2 sticks, or 225 g) butter, softened
> 1 cup (200 g) **sugar**
> 2 **eggs**
> 2 1/2 cups (310 g) **self-rising flour**, plus more for forming
> 1 cup (115 g) chopped skinned **hazelnuts**

Preheat the oven to 350°F (180°C, gas mark 4). Lightly grease a cookie sheet.

Grate the orange zest and squeeze the orange, reserving the juice. Set both aside.

Using a mixer on medium speed, cream together the butter and sugar until light and creamy—about 5 minutes. Add the eggs, orange zest, and orange juice and beat for 3 to 4 minutes longer. Add the flour and mix until thoroughly combined. Stir in the hazelnuts.

Lightly flour a flat surface. Form the dough into a log, about 12 inches long by 4 inches wide by 1 inch tall. Transfer the log of dough to the cookie sheet.

Bake for 22 to 25 minutes, until a tester inserted into the center comes out clean, but the cookie log is still soft. Cool on the cookie sheet completely.

Reheat the oven to 300°F (150°C, gas mark 2).

Slice the cookie log into 1-inch slices and place them on their sides on an ungreased cookie sheet. Bake for 20 to 25 minutes, until the slices are hardened. Remove from the oven, transfer to a wire rack, and cool completely.

YIELD: Makes about 12 cookies

Jam Cookies

We added a little raspberry pizzazz to a basic sugar cookie.

> 1 cup (2 sticks, or 225 g) butter
>
> 1 cup (200 g) **sugar**
>
> 2 **eggs**
>
> 2 1/4 cups (280 g) **all-purpose flour**
>
> 1 teaspoon **baking powder**
>
> 1/4 teaspoon salt
>
> 1 cup (320 g) **raspberry jam**

Using a mixer on medium speed, cream together the butter and sugar until light and creamy—4 to 5 minutes. Add the eggs and beat for 2 to 3 minutes longer.

Sift together the flour, baking powder, and salt and add to the mixing bowl. Mix until thoroughly combined. Form the dough into a ball and wrap in plastic wrap. Refrigerate for at least 1 hour.

Preheat the oven to 350°F (180°C, gas mark 4). Line a cookie sheet with parchment paper.

Flour a flat surface and roll the dough out to about 1/4-inch thickness. Cut the dough out using cookie cutters or a juice glass. Place the cookies 3 inches (7.5 cm) apart on the cookie sheet. Spoon 1/2 teaspoon jam onto the center of each cookie.

Bake for 12 to 15 minutes, until golden at the edges. Cool for a couple of minutes on the cookie sheet, then transfer the cookies to a wire rack to cool completely.

YIELD: Makes about 24 cookies

🏃 Kolaches

These cookies are of Czech origin and can be filled with a variety of things, fruit being one of the most popular items.

> 3 ounces (85 g) **cream cheese**
>
> 1/2 cup (1 stick, or 112 g) butter
>
> 1/2 cup (60 g) **confectioners' sugar**, plus more for dusting
>
> 1 cup (120 g) **all-purpose flour**
>
> Pinch salt
>
> 1 teaspoon **vanilla extract**
>
> 1/2 cup (160 g) **raspberry jam**

Using a mixer on medium speed, cream together the cream cheese, butter, and sugar until light and fluffy—about 5 minutes. Add the flour, salt, and vanilla and beat on low speed until thoroughly combined. Wrap the dough in plastic wrap and refrigerate for 2 hours.

Preheat the oven to 350°F (180°C, gas mark 4). Line a cookie sheet with parchment paper.

Roll the dough on a floured surface to 1/2-inch thickness. With a cookie cutter, cut out 2-inch rounds. Place the rounds on the cookie sheet. Using the back of a spoon, press an indentation in the center of each round. Spoon some jam into the indentation of each cookie.

Bake for 15 to 20 minutes, until golden brown. Cool on racks. Dust with additional confectioners' sugar.

YIELD: Makes about 12 to 14 cookies

🦎 Mini Jam Tarts

Don't be intimidated by the word tart; these are pretty easy to make!

For the tart dough:

> 1/4 cup (1/2 stick, or 55 g) butter
>
> 1/4 cup (50 g) shortening
>
> 1 1/2 cups (180 g) **all-purpose flour**
>
> 1/2 cup (100 g) **sugar**
>
> 1/2 teaspoon salt
>
> 1/2 cup (120 ml) or so cold water

For the filling:

> 3/4 cup (240 g) seedless **raspberry jam**
>
> 1/2 cup (50 g) **sugar**
>
> 2 **egg yolks**
>
> 2 tablespoons (15 g) **all-purpose flour**
>
> 1/4 cup (60 ml) **milk**

To make the tart dough:

Put all of the ingredients except the water into a food processor fitted with the metal blade. Process until the mixture resembles a fine meal. With the motor running, add the water in a thin stream, adding only enough to just bring the dough together.

Place a piece of plastic wrap on the counter and put the dough in it, including any loose crumbs. Knead a few times to bring the dough together in a ball, then flatten out into a disk. Wrap up in the plastic and refrigerate for 1/2 hour.

Flour a work surface and roll the dough out to 1/4-inch thickness. Cut 2-inch circles and tuck them into the holes of a mini muffin pan that has been sprayed with pan spray. Freeze the tart shells for 1 hour.

Preheat the oven to 350°F (180°C, gas mark 4).

To make the filling:

Combine all of the ingredients in a mixing bowl and stir until smooth. Half fill the tart shells with the filling.

Bake for 20 to 25 minutes, until the filling is set and the tart shells are golden. Cool in the pans.

YIELD: Makes about 24 cookies

Dessert Ravioli

These ravioli are novel and delicious. The filling melts in your mouth and plays beautifully with the crunchy coating.

>1 package (8 ounces, or 225 g) **cream cheese**
>
>2 tablespoons (15 g) **confectioners' sugar**
>
>1/2 bag (10 ounces, or 280 g) frozen dry (no syrup) **raspberries**
>
>16 **wonton wrappers**
>
>1/4 cup (1/2 stick, or 55 g) butter, melted
>
>Oil for frying
>
>1 1/2 cups (355 ml) **Hot Fudge Sauce** (page 487) or store-bought hot fudge sauce

Using a mixer on medium speed, beat the cream cheese together with the sugar until smooth, about 4 minutes. Add the raspberries and mix until well combined.

Place a wonton wrapper on a flat surface and put a spoonful of the cream cheese/raspberry filling in the center. Brush the edges of the wonton wrapper with melted butter and fold in half on the diagonal, making a triangular pasta. Pinch sides together firmly and repeat with each wonton.

In a large saucepan, heat the oil on medium heat and gently sauté the wontons a few at a time, turning occasionally, until they are golden brown on all sides. (Be sure to do this a few at a time; you don't want to crowd the pan or they won't brown properly.) Place the ravioli on a plate with a couple layers of paper towels to help drain the oil. Drizzle the hot fudge sauce over the raviolis. Serve warm.

YIELD: Serves 4

Mini Date-Nut Tarts

For the tart dough:

> 1/4 cup (1/2 stick, or 55 g) butter
>
> 1/4 cup (50 g) shortening
>
> 1 1/2 cups (180 g) **all-purpose flour**
>
> 1/2 cup (100 g) **sugar**
>
> 1/2 teaspoon salt
>
> 1/2 cup (120 ml) (approximately) cold water

For the filling:

> 1 1/2 cups (260 g) pitted **dates**, chopped
>
> 1/2 cup (100 g) **sugar**
>
> 1 1/2 cups (150 g) chopped **pecans**
>
> 1/2 cup (120 ml) **orange juice**

To make the dough:

Put all of the tart dough ingredients except the water into a food processor fitted with the metal blade. Process until the mixture resembles a fine meal. With the motor running, add the water in a thin stream, adding only enough to just bring the dough together.

Place a piece of plastic wrap on the counter and put the dough in it, including any loose crumbs. Knead a few times to bring the dough together in a ball, then flatten out into a disk. Wrap up in the plastic and refrigerate for 1/2 hour.

Flour a flat surface and roll the dough out to 1/4-inch thickness. Cut 2-inch circles and tuck them into the holes of a mini muffin pan that has been sprayed with nonstick cooking spray. Freeze the tart shells for 1 hour.

Preheat the oven to 350°F (180°C, gas mark 4).

To make the filling:

Combine all of the filling ingredients in a mixing bowl and stir until combined. Fill the tart shells with the filling.

Bake for 20 to 25 minutes, until the filling is set and the tart shells are golden. Cool in the pans.

YIELD: Makes about 24 cookies

Raisin Spice Cookies

1/2 cup (1 stick, or 112 g) butter, softened

1 cup (200 g) **sugar**

1 **egg**

3 teaspoons **pumpkin pie spice**

1 1/2 cups (180 g) **self-rising flour**

1 cup (145 g) **raisins**

Preheat the oven to 350°F (180°C, gas mark 4). Lightly grease two cookie sheets.

Using a mixer on medium speed, cream together the butter and sugar until light and fluffy—about 5 minutes. Add the egg and beat for another 2 to 3 minutes on high speed. Add the pumpkin pie spice and flour and beat on low speed until thoroughly combined. Add the raisins and stir until combined. Drop by teaspoonfuls onto the cookie sheets.

Bake for 12 to 15 minutes, until lightly browned. Cool on wire racks.

YIELD: Makes about 24 cookies

Cardamom Butter Cookies

Originally from India, cardamom has somehow become a favorite flavoring in Scandinavian desserts. Also known as grains of paradise, this fragrant spice is under-utilized in our opinion.

> 1 cup (2 sticks, or 225g) butter
>
> 1 cup (200 g) **sugar**, plus more for sprinkling
>
> 2 **eggs**
>
> 3 teaspoons ground **cardamom**
>
> 2 cups (250 g) **all-purpose flour**
>
> 1 teaspoon **baking powder**
>
> 1/4 teaspoon salt

Using a mixer on medium speed, cream together the butter and sugar until light and creamy—about 5 minutes. Add the eggs and beat for 3 to 4 minutes longer.

Sift together the cardamom, flour, baking powder, and salt and add to the mixing bowl. Mix until thoroughly combined. Form the dough into a ball and wrap in plastic wrap. Refrigerate for at least 1 hour.

Preheat the oven to 350°F (180°C, gas mark 4). Line a cookie sheet with parchment paper.

Flour a flat surface and roll the dough out to about 1/4 to 1/2-inch thickness. Cut the dough out using cookie cutters or a juice glass. Place the pieces on the cookie sheet. Sprinkle with sugar.

Bake for 12 to 15 minutes, or until golden at the edges. Cool for a couple of minutes on the cookie sheet, then transfer the cookies to a wire rack to cool completely.

YIELD: Makes about 24 cookies

ADD IT! Spice up these cookies with a scant sprinkling of white pepper along with the sugar on top of each cookie.

Chocolate Butter Cookies

It's the cooking version of the transitive property: If butter is good, and chocolate is good, then mixing them together must be great!

1 cup (2 sticks, or 225 g) butter

1 cup (200 g) **sugar**

2 **egg yolks**

1/2 cup (45 g) **cocoa powder**

2 cups (250 g) **all-purpose flour**

1 teaspoon **baking powder**

1/4 teaspoon salt

Using a mixer on medium speed, cream together the butter and sugar until light and creamy—3 to 5 minutes. Add the egg yolks and beat for 2 to 3 minutes longer.

Sift together the cocoa powder, flour, baking powder, and salt and add to the mixing bowl. Mix until thoroughly combined. Form the dough into a ball and wrap in plastic wrap. Refrigerate for at least 1 hour.

Preheat the oven to 350°F (180°C, gas mark 4). Line a cookie sheet with parchment paper.

Flour a flat surface and roll the dough out to about 1/4-inch thickness. Cut the dough out using cookie cutters or a juice glass. Place the pieces on the cookie sheet.

Bake for 10 to 12 minutes, until set looking. Cool for a couple of minutes on the cookie sheet, then transfer the cookies to a wire rack to cool completely.

YIELD: Makes about 24 cookies

ADD IT! Melt 2 ounces (55 g) semisweet chocolate and dip half of each cookie in the chocolate. Set on waxed paper to dry.

Mocha Drops

This is definitely a cookie that goes well with a tall glass of cold milk.

> 1 cup (2 sticks, or 225 g) butter, softened
>
> 1 cup (200 g) **sugar**
>
> 1/2 cup (120 ml) **coffee syrup**
>
> 2 **eggs**
>
> 2 cups (250 g) **all-purpose flour**
>
> 1/4 teaspoon salt
>
> 1/2 cup (45 g) **cocoa powder**

Preheat the oven to 350°F (180°C, gas mark 4). Lightly grease two cookie sheets.

Using a mixer on medium speed, cream together the butter and sugar in a large mixing bowl until light and fluffy—about 5 minutes. Add the coffee syrup and the eggs, beating well.

Sift together the flour, salt, and cocoa powder. Add to the mixing bowl and stir until fully incorporated. Drop by the tablespoonful on the cookie sheets, leaving 3 inches (7.5 cm) or so between cookies.

Bake for 12 to 15 minutes, until set, but still soft. Cool on the cookie sheet for 2 to 3 minutes, then transfer to a wire rack to cool completely.

YIELD: Makes about 36 cookies

Rich Fudge Cookies

   1/2 cup (1 stick, or 112 g) butter

   1 cup (175 g) **semisweet chocolate chips**

   1 can (14 ounces, or 425 ml) **sweetened condensed milk**

   1 teaspoon **vanilla extract**

   2 cups (250 g) **all-purpose flour**

   1/2 teaspoon salt

   1/2 cup (65 g) **cornstarch**

Melt the butter and chocolate chips together in a double boiler, stirring until smooth.

Combine the condensed milk and vanilla in a large mixing bowl and add the melted chocolate mixture.

Sift together the flour, salt, and cornstarch. Stir the dry ingredients into the wet, until completely combined. Refrigerate for at least 2 hours.

Preheat the oven to 350°F (180°C, gas mark 4). Line two cookie sheets with parchment paper.

Roll the dough out to 1/4-inch thickness and cut with cookie cutters. Place the cookies on the cookie sheets, leaving 2 to 3 inches (5 to 7.5 cm) between cookies.

Bake for 10 to 12 minutes, until set, but still soft. Cool on wire racks.

YIELD: Makes about 36 cookies

Chocolate Half Dips

1 cup (2 sticks, or 225 g) butter

3/4 cup (90 g) **confectioners' sugar**, plus more for rolling

1 teaspoon **vanilla extract**

2 cups (250 g) **all-purpose flour**

1/2 teaspoon salt

1 1/3 cups chopped **semisweet chocolate**

1 tablespoon (12 g) shortening

1/2 cup (3 1/4 ounces, or 96 g) **colored sprinkles**

Using a mixer on medium speed, cream together the butter and sugar until light and creamy—about 5 minutes. Add the vanilla and beat for 3 to 4 minutes longer.

Sift together the flour and salt and add to the mixing bowl. Mix on low speed until thoroughly combined. Form the dough into a ball and wrap in plastic wrap. Refrigerate for at least 1 hour.

Preheat the oven to 350°F (180°C, gas mark 4). Line a cookie sheet with parchment paper.

Dust a flat surface with sugar and roll the dough out to about 1/4-inch thickness. Cut the dough out using 2-inch cookie cutters or a juice glass. Place the pieces on the cookie sheet.

Bake for 12 to 15 minutes, until golden at the edges. Cool for a couple of minutes on the cookie sheet, then transfer the cookies to a wire rack to cool completely.

Melt the chocolate and shortening in a double boiler, stirring. Dip half of each cookie into the chocolate. Place the cookies on a cookie sheet covered with waxed paper. Sprinkle the sprinkles on the chocolate and allow to cool until the chocolate hardens.

YIELD: Makes about 24 cookies

Really Good Chocolate Chip Cookies

We think you'll find this to be a basic recipe that always pleases.

> 1 cup (2 sticks, or 225 g) butter, softened
>
> 1 cup (225 g) packed **light brown sugar**
>
> 2 **eggs**
>
> 1 tablespoon (14 ml) **vanilla extract**
>
> 2 cups (250 g) **self-rising flour**
>
> 2 cups (350 g) **semisweet chocolate chips**

Preheat the oven to 350°F (180°C, gas mark 4). Lightly grease two cookie sheets.

Using a mixer on medium speed, cream together the butter and sugar in a large mixing bowl until light and fluffy—about 5 minutes. Add the eggs and vanilla and beat for 2 to 3 minutes. Stir the flour in until fully incorporated. Stir in the chocolate chips. Drop by the tablespoonful onto the cookie sheets, leaving 3 inches (7.5 cm) or so between cookies.

Bake for 12 to 15 minutes, until lightly browned and set, but still soft. Cool on the cookie sheets for 2 to 3 minutes, then transfer to a wire rack to cool completely.

YIELD: Makes about 36 cookies

Chocolate-Chocolate Chip Cookies

3 cups (525 g) **semisweet chocolate chips**, divided

1 cup (2 sticks, or 225 g) butter

1 cup (225 g) packed **light brown sugar**

2 **eggs**

2 cups (250 g) **all-purpose flour**

1 teaspoon **baking powder**

1/2 teaspoon salt

Preheat the oven to 350°F (180°C, gas mark 4). Lightly grease two cookie sheets.

Melt 1 cup (175 g) of the chocolate chips in a double boiler. Set aside.

Using a mixer on medium speed, cream together the butter and sugar until light and creamy—about 5 minutes. Add the eggs and melted chocolate and beat for 3 to 4 minutes longer.

Sift together the flour, baking powder, and salt. Add to the mixing bowl and mix until thoroughly combined. Stir in the remaining chocolate chips. Drop by the tablespoonful onto the cookie sheets, leaving 3 inches (7.5 cm) or so between cookies.

Bake for 12 to 15 minutes, until lightly brown and set, but still soft. Cool on the cookie sheets for 2 to 3 minutes, then transfer to a wire rack to cool completely.

YIELD: Makes about 36 cookies

ADD IT! Add 1 tablespoon (5 g) cocoa powder to the dry ingredients for even more potent chocolate punch.

Chocolate Crisps

Here's further proof that many breakfast cereals are really dessert in disguise.

> 6 ounces (170 g) **milk chocolate**
>
> 1 cup (2 sticks, or 225 g) butter, softened
>
> 1 cup (200 g) **sugar**
>
> 2 **eggs**
>
> 2 cups (250 g) **self-rising flour**
>
> 2 cups (100 g) **Cocoa Crisp or Cocoa Puffs Cereal**

Preheat the oven to 350°F (180°C, gas mark 4). Lightly grease two cookie sheets.

Melt the chocolate in a double boiler and set aside.

Using a mixer on medium speed, cream together the butter and sugar in a large mixing bowl until light and fluffy—about 5 minutes. Add the eggs and beat for 2 to 3 minutes. Add the flour and mix until fully incorporated. Stir in the melted chocolate. Stir in the cereal. Drop by the tablespoonful onto the cookie sheets, leaving 3 inches (7.5 cm) or so between cookies.

Bake for 12 to 15 minutes, until lightly brown and set, but still soft. Cool on the cookie sheets for 2 to 3 minutes, then transfer to a wire rack to cool completely.

YIELD: Makes about 36 cookies

Chocolate-Marshmallow Drops

These are like s'mores, but without the graham cracker.

> 1/4 cup (1/2 stick, or 55 g) butter
>
> 2/3 cup (150 g) packed **light brown sugar**
>
> 2 **eggs**
>
> 1 1/2 cups (180 g) **self-rising flour**
>
> 2 cups (100 g) **mini marshmallows**
>
> 2 cups (350 g) **semisweet chocolate chips**

Preheat the oven to 350°F (180°C, gas mark 4). Lightly grease two cookie sheets.

Using a mixer on medium speed, cream together the butter and brown sugar in a large mixing bowl until light and fluffy—4 to 5 minutes. Add the eggs and beat for 2 to 3 minutes. Add the flour to the butter mixture and mix until fully incorporated. Stir in the marshmallows and chocolate chips. Drop by the tablespoonful on the cookie sheets, leaving 3 inches (7.5 cm) or so between cookies.

Bake for 12 to 15 minutes, until lightly brown and set, but still soft. Cool on the cookie sheets for 2 to 3 minutes, then transfer to a wire rack to cool completely.

YIELD: Makes about 36 cookies

♣ Chocolate Macaroons

1 1/2 cups (110 g) **sweetened shredded coconut**

1/2 cup (100 g) **sugar**

1/4 cup (45 g) **cocoa powder**

2 tablespoons (15 g) **all-purpose flour**

Pinch salt

2 **egg whites**

Preheat the oven to 325°F (170°C, gas mark 3). Lightly grease two cookie sheets.

Put the coconut into a mixing bowl. Sift the sugar, cocoa powder, flour, and salt together and stir them into the coconut.

In another bowl, whip the egg whites to stiff peak. Fold into the coconut mixture. Drop by tablespoonfuls onto the cookie sheet.

Bake for 20 to 25 minutes, until the cookies are puffed up and solid, but still soft. Cool on wire racks.

YIELD: Makes about 24 cookies

Chocolate-Almond Macaroons

Almond paste is commonly found in the baking section of the grocery store.

   1/2 cup (100 g) shortening

   3/4 cup (150 g) **sugar**

   8 ounces (225 g) **almond paste**

   3 **egg whites**

   1 teaspoon **vanilla extract**

   1/4 teaspoon salt

   6 ounces (170 g) **semisweet chocolate**

Preheat the oven to 350°F (180°C, gas mark 4). Line two cookie sheets with parchment paper.

Using a mixer on medium speed, cream together the shortening, sugar, and almond paste until light and fluffy—8 to 10 minutes. Add the egg whites, vanilla, and salt and beat for another 5 minutes. Drop by the tablespoon onto the cookie sheets, leaving 2 inches (5 cm) between cookies.

Bake for 15 to 18 minutes, until lightly browned. Move to a wire rack and cool completely.

Melt the chocolate in a double boiler. Dip the bottom halves of the cookies in the chocolate and set on a waxed paper covered cookie sheet. Cool to set the chocolate.

YIELD: Makes about 36 cookies

Chocolate-Coconut Chewies

  3 ounces (85 g) **semisweet chocolate**

  1 can (8 ounces, or 235 ml) **sweetened condensed milk**

  1 teaspoon **rum extract**

  1 bag (12 ounces, or 340 g) **sliced almonds**

  3 cups (225 g) **sweetened shredded coconut**

Preheat the oven to 350°F (180°C, gas mark 4). Lightly grease two cookie sheets.

Melt the chocolate and condensed milk together in a double boiler, stirring until smooth. Stir in the rum extract.

Mix together the almonds and the coconut in a mixing bowl. Pour the chocolate mixture over them and stir until the nuts and coconut are coated. Drop by the tablespoonful onto the cookie sheets, leaving 3 inches (7.5 cm) or so between cookies.

Bake for 12 to 15 minutes, until set, but still soft. Cool on the cookie sheets for 2 to 3 minutes, then transfer to a wire rack to cool completely.

YIELD: Makes about 48 cookies

Thin Mint-Macadamia Nut Cookies

8 ounces (225 g) thin **chocolate mint candies** (such as After Eight)

1/4 cup (1/2 stick, or 55g) butter, softened

1/2 cup (100 g) **sugar**

1 **egg**

Pinch salt

2 cups (250 g) **all-purpose flour**

1 cup (135 g) grated **macadamia nuts**

Melt the mints in a double boiler. Set aside.

Using a mixer on medium speed, cream the butter and the sugar together. Add the egg and beat for another minute. Stir in the melted mints. Stir in the salt and flour. Refrigerate the dough for 1 to 2 hours.

Preheat the oven to 350°F (180°C, gas mark 4). Lightly grease two cookie sheets.

Roll the dough into 1-inch balls. Roll the balls in the macadamia nuts. Place on the cookie sheets.

Bake for 10 to 12 minutes. Allow to cool on the cookie sheets for 1 minute, then transfer to wire racks to cool.

YIELD: Makes about 30 cookies.

Zebra Stripe Cookies

Another favorite cookie-jar cookie.

>1 cup (2 sticks, or 225 g) butter, softened
>
>2 cups (400 g) **sugar**
>
>2 **eggs**
>
>2 cups (250 g) **all-purpose flour**
>
>1/2 teaspoon salt
>
>2 teaspoons **vanilla extract**
>
>1/4 cup (25 g) **cocoa powder**

Using a mixer on medium speed, cream together the butter and sugar until light and fluffy—about 5 minutes. Add the eggs and beat for another 2 to 3 minutes on high speed. Add the flour, salt, and vanilla and beat on low speed until thoroughly combined. Remove half of the dough from the bowl and wrap it in plastic wrap. Add the cocoa powder to the bowl and beat until combined.

Roll out the two doughs into 1/2-inch thick sheets about 12 inches long by 6 inches wide. Cut each sheet in half lengthwise and stack them on top of each other, alternating white and chocolate and brushing the surface of the dough with a little water before topping with more dough. Refrigerate for 2 hours.

Preheat the oven to 350°F (180°C, gas mark 4). Line two cookie sheets with parchment paper.

With a sharp knife, cut 1/2-inch pieces from the dough log, so that you have cookies roughly 3 inches by 2 inches. Place the cookies on the cookie sheets.

Bake for 12 to 15 minutes, until golden brown. Cool on wire racks.

YIELD: Makes about 24 cookies.

Easy Cake Mix Cookies

No time for fancy cooking, but want some fresh cookies? Try this easy fix; kids love them!

  1 package (16 ounces, or 455 g) **chocolate cake mix**
  1/2 cup (1 stick, or 112 g) butter, melted
  1/3 cup (75 ml) water
  1 **egg**
  1 cup (125 g) chopped **walnuts**
  2 cups (350 g) **toffee chips**

Preheat the oven to 350°F (180°C, gas mark 4). Lightly grease two cookie sheets.

Combine the cake mix, butter, water, and egg in a mixing bowl and beat on medium speed until smooth. Stir in the walnuts and toffee chips. Drop by the tablespoonful onto the cookie sheets, leaving 3 inches (7.5 cm) or so between cookies.

Bake for 12 to 15 minutes, until set, but still soft. Cool on the cookie sheets for 2 to 3 minutes, then transfer to a wire rack to cool completely.

YIELD: Makes about 36 cookies

Super Meringues

4 **egg whites**

Pinch salt

1/4 teaspoon **cream of tartar**

1 1/2 cups (300 g) **sugar**

1 cup (175 g) **semisweet chocolate chips**

1 cup (100 g) **chopped pecans**

Preheat the oven to 250°F (120°C, gas mark 1/2). Line two cookie sheets with parchment paper.

Combine the egg whites, salt, and cream of tartar in a mixing bowl and beat on high speed until frothy. Add one-third of the sugar, beat until starting to set, add another one-third cup of the sugar, and continue beating until soft peak. Add the remaining one-third of the sugar and beat to glossy stiff peaks. (Do not over beat.) Fold in the chocolate chips and the pecans. Drop by tablespoonfuls onto the cookie sheets.

Bake for 25 to 30 minutes, until set and lightly browned. Cool completely on the cookie sheets.

YIELD: Makes about 24 cookies

❦ Reverse Chocolate-Peanut Butter Cookies

1 cup (2 sticks, or 225 g) butter, softened

1 cup (200 g) **vanilla sugar** (See "Making Vanilla Sugar" on page 12.)

2 **eggs**

2 cups (250 g) **self-rising flour**

1/2 cup (45 g) **cocoa powder**

1 to 2 cups (175 to 350 g) **peanut butter chips**

Preheat the oven to 350°F (180°C, gas mark 4). Lightly grease two cookie sheets.

Using a mixer on medium speed, cream together the butter and sugar in a large mixing bowl until light and fluffy—about 5 minutes. Add the eggs and beat for 2 to 3 minutes.

Sift together the flour and the cocoa powder. Add to the butter mixture and mix until fully incorporated. Stir in the peanut butter chips. Drop by the tablespoonful onto the cookie sheets, leaving 3 inches (7.5 cm) or so between cookies.

Bake for 12 to 15 minutes, until lightly brown and set, but still soft. Cool on the cookie sheets for 2 to 3 minutes, then transfer to a wire rack to cool completely.

YIELD: Makes about 36 cookies

Chocolate~Peanut Butter Kisses

1/2 cup (100 g) shortening

1 cup (200 g) **sugar**

1 cup (260 g) **peanut butter**, creamy or chunky

2 **eggs**

2 cups (250 g) **all-purpose flour**

36 **Hershey's Kisses**, unwrapped

Preheat the oven to 350°F (180°C, gas mark 4). Lightly grease two cookie sheets.

Using a mixer on medium speed, cream together the shortening and sugar in a large mixing bowl until light and fluffy—about 5 minutes. Add the peanut butter and eggs and beat for 3 to 4 minutes. Add the flour and mix until fully incorporated. Drop by the tablespoonful onto the cookie sheets, leaving 3 inches (7.5 cm) or so between cookies. Press a Hershey's Kiss lightly into the top of each cookie.

Bake for 12 to 15 minutes, until lightly browned and set, but still soft. Cool on the cookie sheets for 2 to 3 minutes, then transfer to a wire rack to cool completely.

YIELD: Makes about 36 cookies

Chocolate-Hazelnut Sandwich Cookies

These are pretty cookies that taste terrific with a big glass of cold milk; we had to hold people off from the plate.

> 1/2 cup (100 g) shortening
>
> 1 cup (200 g) **sugar**
>
> 2 **eggs**, separated
>
> 1 cup (120 g) **all-purpose flour**
>
> 1/2 teaspoon salt
>
> 2 cups (270 g) blanched **hazelnuts**, finely ground
>
> 1 container (8 ounces, or 225 g) **Nutella chocolate-hazelnut spread**

Preheat the oven to 325°F (170°C, gas mark 3). Cover two cookie sheets with parchment paper.

Using a mixer on medium speed, cream the shortening and the sugar until light and fluffy—about 5 minutes. Add the egg yolks and beat for 5 minutes on high speed. Add the flour and salt and mix on low speed until combined and the batter is smooth.

In a separate bowl, beat the egg whites into soft peaks and stir in the hazelnuts. Add the egg white mixture to the batter and mix to combine. Drop by teaspoonful on the cookie sheets, leaving room for the cookies to spread.

Bake for 18 to 20 minutes, until set and golden brown. Cool on wire racks.

When the cookies are cool, spread the Nutella on the flat sides of half the cookies and top with the remaining cookies to make sandwiches. (The Nutella takes a while to stiffen up.)

YIELD: Makes about 20 cookies

Mocha Biscotti

1 cup (2 sticks, or 225 g) butter, softened

1 cup (200 g) **sugar**

2 **eggs**

1/4 cup (60 ml) **coffee syrup**

2 1/4 cups (280 g) **self-rising flour**, plus more for forming

1/2 cup (45 g) **cocoa powder**

Preheat the oven to 350°F (180°C, gas mark 4). Lightly grease a cookie sheet.

Using a mixer on medium speed, cream together the butter and sugar until light and creamy—about 5 minutes. Add the eggs and coffee syrup and beat for 3 to 4 minutes longer.

Sift together the flour and cocoa powder, then add to the mixing bowl and mix until thoroughly combined.

Lightly flour a flat surface. Form the dough into a log, about 12 inches long by 4 inches wide by 1 inch tall. Transfer the log of dough to the cookie sheet.

Bake for 22 to 25 minutes, until a tester inserted into the center comes out clean, but the cookie log is still soft. Cool on the cookie sheet completely.

Reheat the oven to 300°F (150°C, gas mark 2).

Slice the cookie log into 1-inch slices and place them on their sides on an ungreased cookie sheet. Bake for 20 to 25 minutes, until the slices are hardened. Remove from the oven, transfer to a wire rack, and cool completely.

YIELD: Makes about 12 cookies

Chocolate-Dipped Biscotti

Here's a great fancy cookie for relatively little effort.

   1 cup (2 sticks, or 225 g) butter, softened

   1 cup (200 g) **sugar**

   2 **eggs**

   2 teaspoons **vanilla extract**

   2 1/2 cups (310 g) **self-rising flour**, plus more for forming

   6 ounces (170 g) **semisweet chocolate**

Preheat the oven to 350°F (180°C, gas mark 4). Lightly grease a cookie sheet.

Using a mixer on medium speed, cream together the butter and sugar until light and creamy—about 5 minutes. Add the eggs and the vanilla and beat for 3 to 4 minutes longer. Add the flour to the mixing bowl and mix until thoroughly combined.

Lightly flour a flat surface. Form the dough into a log about 12 inches long by 4 inches wide by 1 inch tall. Transfer to the cookie sheet.

Bake for 22 to 25 minutes, until a tester inserted into the center comes out clean, but the cookie log is still soft. Cool on the cookie sheet completely.

Reheat the oven to 300°F (150°C, gas mark 2). Line a cookie sheet with waxed paper.

Slice the cookie log into 1-inch slices and place the slices on their sides on an ungreased cookie sheet. Bake for 20 to 25 minutes and remove from the oven. Let biscotti cool and harden on cookie sheet and gently transfer to a wire rack.

Over low heat, melt the chocolate in a double boiler. Dip each cookie in halfway. Place the cookies on a wax-paper lined cookie sheet until the chocolate hardens.

YIELD: Makes about 12 cookies

ADD IT! Roll the chocolate-dipped end of the biscotti in the crushed nuts of your choice.

Chocolate-Dipped Sambuca Biscotti

Sambuca is an Italian liqueur flavored with anise that is found in most liquor stores.

1 cup (2 sticks, or 225 g) butter, softened

1 cup (200 g) **sugar**

2 **eggs**

1/4 cup (60 ml) **sambuca**

2 cups (250 g) **self-rising flour**, plus more for forming

6 ounces (170 g) **semisweet chocolate**

Preheat the oven to 350°F (180°C, gas mark 4). Lightly grease a cookie sheet.

Using a mixer on medium speed, cream together the butter and sugar until light and creamy—about 5 minutes. Add the eggs and the sambuca and beat for 3 to 4 minutes longer. Add the flour and mix until thoroughly combined.

Lightly flour a flat surface. Form the dough into a log, about 12 inches long by 4 inches wide by 1 inch tall. Transfer the log of dough to the cookie sheet.

Bake for 22 to 25 minutes, until a tester inserted into the center comes out clean, but the cookie log is still soft. Cool on the cookie sheet completely.

Reheat the oven to 300°F (150°C, gas mark 2).

Slice the cookie log into 1-inch slices and place them on their sides on an ungreased cookie sheet. Bake for 20 to 25 minutes. Remove from the oven, transfer to a wire rack, and cool completely.

Melt the chocolate in a double boiler. Dip each cookie in halfway. Place the cookies on a cookie sheet covered with waxed paper.

YIELD: Makes about 12 cookies

🦎 Trail Mix Drops

Use your favorite trail mix. We like one with dried fruits, nuts, and chocolate chips.

- 1 cup (2 sticks, or 225 g) butter, softened
- 1 cup (200 g) **sugar**
- 2 **eggs**
- 2 cups (250 g) **all-purpose flour**
- 1/2 teaspoon salt
- 1 teaspoon **baking powder**
- 2 cups (300 g) **trail mix**

Preheat the oven to 350°F (180°C, gas mark 4). Lightly grease two cookie sheets.

Using a mixer on medium speed, cream together the butter and sugar in a large mixing bowl until light and fluffy—about 5 minutes. Add the eggs and beat for 2 to 3 minutes.

Sift together the flour, salt, and baking powder. Add this to the butter mixture and mix until fully incorporated. Stir in the trail mix. Drop by the tablespoonful onto the cookie sheets, leaving 3 inches (7.5 cm)or so between cookies.

Bake for 12 to 15 minutes, until lightly browned and set, but still soft. Cool on the cookie sheets for 2 to 3 minutes, then transfer to a wire rack to cool completely.

YIELD: Makes about 36 cookies

Ginger Drops

These are a nice afternoon snack cookie, and they are a delicious twist on the basic sugar cookie.

1 cup (2 sticks, or 225 g) butter

1/2 cup (100 g) **sugar**

1 cup (320 g) **ginger preserves**

2 **eggs**

3 cups (360 g) **all-purpose flour**

1 teaspoon **baking powder**

1/4 teaspoon salt

Preheat the oven to 350°F (180°C, gas mark 4). Lightly grease two cookie sheets.

Using a mixer on medium speed, cream together the butter and sugar in a large mixing bowl until light and fluffy—about 5 minutes. Add the ginger preserves and eggs and beat for 3 to 4 minutes.

In another bowl stir together the flour, baking powder, and salt. Add the flour mixture to the butter mixture and beat until fully incorporated. Drop by the tablespoonful onto the cookie sheets, leaving 3 inches (7.5 cm) or so between cookies.

Bake for 12 to 15 minutes, until lightly browned and set, but still soft. Cool on the cookie sheets for 2 to 3 minutes, then transfer to a wire rack to cool completely.

YIELD: Makes about 48 cookies

🐾 Granola Cookies

You'll love this fast and easy way to make oatmeal cookies.

1 cup (2 sticks, or 225 g) butter, softened

1 cup (225 g) packed **light brown sugar**

2 **eggs**

1 cup (120 g) **all-purpose flour**

1 teaspoon **baking powder**

2 cups (250 g) **granola with raisins**

Preheat the oven to 350°F (180°C, gas mark 4). Lightly grease two cookie sheets.

Using a mixer on medium speed, cream together the butter and sugar in a large mixing bowl until light and fluffy—about 5 minutes. Add the eggs and beat for 2 to 3 minutes.

Stir the flour and baking powder together then add to the mixing bowl and beat until fully incorporated. Stir in the granola. Drop by the tablespoonful onto the cookie sheets, leaving 3 inches (7.5 cm) or so between cookies.

Bake for 12 to 15 minutes, until lightly browned and set, but still soft. Cool on the cookie sheets for 2 to 3 minutes, then transfer to a wire rack to cool completely.

YIELD: Makes about 36 cookies

Oatmeal Shortbread

We can just picture sitting by a cozy fire, eating these with a nice cup of tea.

- 1 cup (2 sticks, or 225 g) butter
- 1 cup (225 g) packed **light brown sugar**
- 2 **eggs**
- 1 teaspoon **vanilla extract**
- 1 cup (120 g) **all-purpose flour**
- 1/4 teaspoon salt
- 1 cup (80 g) **rolled oats**

Using a mixer on medium speed, cream together the butter and sugar until light and creamy—about 5 minutes. Add the eggs and vanilla and beat for 3 to 4 minutes. Add the flour and the salt and mix until thoroughly combined. Stir in the oats. Form the dough into a ball and wrap in plastic wrap. Refrigerate for at least 1 hour.

Preheat the oven to 350°F (180°C, gas mark 4). Line two cookie sheets with parchment paper.

Flour a flat surface and roll the dough out to about 1-inch thickness by 2 inches across. Cut the dough into 1/2-inch slices with a sharp knife. Place the pieces on the cookie sheet.

Bake for 12 to 15 minutes, until lightly browned. Cool for a couple of minutes on the cookie sheets, then transfer the cookies to a wire rack to cool completely.

YIELD: Makes about 24 cookies

🐸 Joe Froggers

Joe Froggers are big, soft molasses cookies made in the environs of Marblehead, Massachusetts, ever since colonial times. Seamen took them with them on long voyages because they kept so well.

> 1 cup (2 sticks, or 225 g) butter, softened
>
> 1 cup (200 g) **sugar**, plus 1/2 cup (100 g) for sprinkling
>
> 1 cup (235 ml) **dark molasses**
>
> 1 teaspoon **baking soda**
>
> 3 teaspoons **pumpkin pie spice**
>
> 4 cups (480 g) **all-purpose flour**, plus more for rolling

Using a mixer on medium speed, cream together the butter and sugar in a large mixing bowl until light and fluffy—about 3 to 5 minutes.

In a small bowl, stir together the molasses and baking soda.

In a separate bowl, sift together the pumpkin pie spice and flour. Add the molasses and the flour to the mixing bowl alternately until the flour is all incorporated and the dough is soft. Wrap in plastic and refrigerate for at least 1 hour.

Preheat the oven to 350°F (180°C, gas mark 4). Line two cookie sheets with parchment paper.

Flour a flat surface and roll out the dough to 1/4-inch thickness. Using a round cutter or a coffee can, cut out 3-inch rounds. Place the rounds on the cookie sheet and sprinkle sugar on top of each cookie.

Bake for 12 to 15 minutes, until set, but still soft. Cool on the cookie sheets for 2 to 3 minutes, then transfer to a wire rack to cool completely.

YIELD: Makes about 24 cookies

Yogurt~Oatmeal Chewies

This is a very quick recipe, perfect for when your kids tell you that they've signed you up for the school bake sale tomorrow.

$1/2$ cup (1 stick, or 112 g) butter, softened

1 cup (200 g) **sugar**

1 cup (225 g) **vanilla yogurt**

1 cup (120 g) **all-purpose flour**

$1/2$ teaspoon salt

1 teaspoon **baking soda**

2 cups (160 g) **rolled oats**

Preheat the oven to 350°F (180°C, gas mark 4). Lightly grease two cookie sheets.

Using a mixer on medium speed, cream together the butter and sugar in a large mixing bowl until light and fluffy—about 5 minutes. Add the yogurt and beat for 2 to 3 minutes.

Sift together the flour, salt, and baking soda. Add this to the butter mixture and mix until fully incorporated. Stir in the oats. Drop by the tablespoonful onto the cookie sheets, leaving 3 inches (7.5 cm) or so between cookies.

Bake for 12 to 15 minutes, until lightly browned and set, but still soft. Cool on the cookie sheets for 2 to 3 minutes, then transfer to a wire rack to cool.

YIELD: Makes about 36 cookies

ADD IT! Toss in 1 cup (145 g) raisins with the oats.

Jelly Bean Drops

This is a good way to get rid of all the leftover Easter jelly beans. These are very colorful in the cookie jar!

   1 cup (2 sticks, or 225 g) butter, softened
   1 cup (200 g) **sugar**
   1 teaspoon **vanilla extract**
   2 **eggs**
   2 cups (250 g) **all-purpose flour**
   1/4 teaspoon salt
   2 cups (7 ounces, or 200 g) **jelly beans**

Preheat the oven to 350°F (180°C, gas mark 4). Lightly grease two cookie sheets.

Using a mixer on medium speed, cream together the butter and sugar in a large mixing bowl until light and fluffy—about 5 minutes. Add the vanilla and eggs. Add the flour and salt and mix until fully incorporated. Stir in the jelly beans. Drop by the tablespoonful onto the cookie sheets, leaving 3 inches (7.5 cm) or so between cookies.

Bake for 12 to 15 minutes, until lightly browned and set, but still soft. Cool on the cookie sheets for 2 to 3 minutes, then transfer to a wire rack to cool completely.

YIELD: Makes about 36 cookies.

CHAPTER SIX

Brownies and Bars

Stalwarts of the bake sale table and the church coffee hour, brownies and bars stand tall as authentic Americana, beloved by children and parents alike. They are like the vigorous middle class of the dessert world, whose popularity and simplicity power many a community outing. Nobody is going to go wrong serving Congo Bars, after all. As long as there are glasses of milk and afternoon snacks to serve, we'll be making desserts like these.

Classic Fudge Brownies

If you don't have vanilla sugar, add 2 teaspoons of vanilla extract.

> 6 ounces (170 g) **bittersweet chocolate**
> 1/2 cup (1 stick, or 112 g) butter, softened
> 1/2 cup (100 g) shortening
> 1 cup (200 g) **vanilla sugar** (See "Making Vanilla Sugar" on page 12.)
> 3 **eggs**
> 1 cup (120 g) **self-rising flour**
> 1/2 teaspoon salt

Preheat the oven to 325°F (170°C, gas mark 3). Butter a 9 x 13-inch baking pan.

Chop the chocolate into small pieces and melt in a double boiler. Remove from the heat and set aside.

Using a mixer on medium speed, cream together the butter, shortening, and sugar until fluffy—about 5 minutes. Add the eggs, one at a time, mixing well after each addition.

In a separate bowl, mix the flour and salt and add to the mixing bowl, then mix to incorporate. Add the melted chocolate and mix until well incorporated. Pour into the prepared baking pan and spread evenly.

Bake for 30 to 35 minutes, until a tester inserted into the center comes out clean. Cool and cut into squares.

YIELD: Makes about 20 brownies

ADD IT! Sprinkle about 1 cup (125 g) chopped walnuts on top before baking.

Truffle Brownies

These are so decadent that they probably should be banned from polite society. This simple recipe yields rich brownies with a crusty outside and a dense, gooey inside, and these taste great straight from the fridge.

> 1 cup (2 sticks, or 225 g) butter
> 8 ounces (225 g) **bittersweet chocolate**
> 1 cup (200 g) **sugar**
> 1/4 cup (30 g) **all-purpose flour**
> 2 teaspoons **vanilla extract**
> 4 **eggs**, separated

Preheat the oven to 400°F (200°C, gas mark 6). Grease a 9-inch square baking pan.

In a stainless steel mixing bowl set over a saucepan of simmering water, melt together the butter, chocolate, and 1/2 cup (100 g) of the sugar, stirring, until the mixture is smooth and the sugar is dissolved. Remove from the heat and stir in the flour and vanilla. Add the egg yolks, one at a time, beating well on medium speed after each addition.

In another bowl, whip the egg whites until they begin to fluff, then add the remaining 1/2 cup (100 g) sugar and continue beating to stiff peaks. Fold the whites into the chocolate mixture and spread the batter in the prepared pan.

Bake for 20 minutes, cool to room temperature, then refrigerate for at least 4 hours. Cut into small squares.

YIELD: Makes 16 brownies

Mocha Brownies

If you want to send these into over-the-top territory, frost with Mocha Buttercream frosting (page 497).

6 ounces (170 g) **bittersweet chocolate**

1/2 cup (1 stick, or 112 g) butter, softened

1/2 cup (100 g) shortening

1 cup (200 g) **vanilla sugar** (See "Making Vanilla Sugar" on page 12.)

3 **eggs**

1 cup (120 g) **self-rising flour**

1/2 teaspoon salt

2 tablespoons (5 g) **instant coffee powder** dissolved with 2 tablespoons (28 ml) water

Preheat the oven to 325°F (170°C, gas mark 3). Butter a 9 x 13-inch baking pan.

Chop the chocolate into small pieces and melt in a double boiler. Remove from the heat and set aside.

Using a mixer on medium speed, cream together the butter, shortening, and sugar until fluffy—about 5 minutes. Add the eggs, one at a time, mixing well after each addition.

In a separate bowl, mix the flour and salt and add to the mixing bowl, then mix until well combined. Add the melted chocolate and mix until well incorporated, then stir in the coffee. Pour into the prepared baking pan and spread evenly.

Bake for 30 to 35 minutes, until a tester inserted into the center comes out clean. Cool and cut into squares.

YIELD: Makes about 20 brownies

Cheesecake Swirl Brownies

This is brownie tester Erin Mohica's all-time favorite recipe. "These were really pretty and really yummy. I didn't share these!" she said.

For the brownie batter:

> 7 ounces (200 g) **bittersweet chocolate**
> 1/2 cup (1 stick, or 112 g) butter, softened
> 1 cup (200 g) **vanilla sugar** (See "Making Vanilla Sugar" on page 12.)
> 3 **eggs**
> 3/4 cup (90 g) **all-purpose flour**
> Pinch salt

For the cheesecake batter:

> 1 pound (455 g) **cream cheese**
> 1 cup (200 g) **vanilla sugar** (See "Making Vanilla Sugar" on page 12.)
> 2 **eggs**
> 2 tablespoons (15 g) **flour**

To make the brownie batter:

Preheat the oven to 325°F (170°C, gas mark 3). Butter a 9 x 13-inch baking pan.

Chop the chocolate into small pieces and melt it in a double boiler. Using a mixer on medium speed, cream the butter and the sugar together until fluffy and light. Add the eggs, one at a time, beating well after each addition. Add the chocolate and mix until smooth. Stir in the flour and salt until just combined. Spread the batter in the prepared pan, reserving 1 cup.

To make the cheesecake batter:

Using a mixer on medium speed, cream the cream cheese and sugar together in a mixing bowl until smooth and fluffy. Add the eggs, one at a time, beating well after each addition. Add the flour and beat on medium speed for 2 minutes.

Spread the cheesecake batter on top of the brownie batter. Drop the reserved brownie batter on top by spoonfuls. Using a butter knife, swirl the batters together.

Bake for 45 to 50 minutes, until the middle is set and a tester inserted into the center comes out clean. Cool in the pan and cut into squares.

YIELD: Makes 24 brownies

Chocolate-Caramel Brownies

These are gooey and delicious taste treats.

> 6 ounces (170 g) **bittersweet chocolate**
> 1/2 cup (1 stick, 112 g) butter, softened
> 1/2 cup (100 g) shortening
> 1 cup (200 g) **vanilla sugar** (See "Making Vanilla Sugar" on page 12.)
> 3 **eggs**
> 1 cup (120 g) **self-rising flour**
> 1/2 teaspoon salt
> 1 cup **caramels** (about 15), unwrapped and cut into small pieces

Preheat the oven to 350°F (180°C, gas mark 4). Grease a 9 x 13-inch baking pan.

Chop the chocolate into small pieces and melt in a double boiler. Remove from the heat and set aside.

Using a mixer on medium speed, cream together the butter, shortening, and the sugar until fluffy—about 5 minutes. Add the eggs, one at a time, mixing well after each addition.

In a separate bowl, mix the flour and salt and add to the mixing bowl, then beat until all the ingredients are well combined. Add the melted chocolate and mix until well incorporated. Stir in the caramels. Pour into the prepared baking pan and spread evenly.

Bake for 30 to 35 minutes, until a tester inserted into the center comes out clean. Cool and cut into squares.

YIELD: Makes about 20 brownies

Chocolate-Mint Brownies

If you like Thin Mint Girl Scout Cookies, you'll love these.

> 6 ounces (170 g) **bittersweet chocolate**
>
> 1/2 cup (1 stick, or 112 g) butter, softened
>
> 1/2 cup (100 g) shortening
>
> 1 cup (200 g) **vanilla sugar** (See "Making Vanilla Sugar" on page 12.)
>
> 3 **eggs**
>
> 1 cup (120 g) **self-rising flour**
>
> 1/2 teaspoon salt
>
> 1 cup **Andes Mint candies**, unwrapped and coarsely chopped
> (about 20 candies)

Preheat the oven to 325°F (170°C, gas mark 3). Grease a 9 x 13-inch baking pan.

Chop the chocolate into small pieces and melt in a double boiler. Remove from the heat and set aside.

Using a mixer on medium speed, cream together the butter, shortening, and sugar until fluffy—about 5 minutes. Add the eggs, one at a time, mixing well after each egg.

In a separate bowl, mix the flour and salt. Add the dry ingredients to the mixing bowl and then mix to incorporate. Add the melted chocolate and mix until well incorporated. Stir in the mints. Pour into the prepared baking pan and spread evenly.

Bake for 30 to 35 minutes, until a tester inserted into the center comes out clean. Cool and cut into squares.

YIELD: Makes about 20 brownies

Chocolate-Orange Brownies

If you like those chocolate oranges they sell at Christmas, you'll love this recipe.

> 1 1/2 cups (5.5 ounces, or 155 g) **graham cracker crumbs**
>
> 1/2 cup (45 g) **cocoa powder**
>
> 1 **orange**
>
> 1 can (12 ounces, or 355 ml) **sweetened condensed milk**
>
> 1 cup (175 g) **semisweet chocolate chips**

Preheat the oven to 350°F (180°C, gas mark 4). Grease a 9-inch square baking pan.

Combine the cracker crumbs and the cocoa powder in a mixing bowl. Stir well. Grate the orange to yield about 1/3 cup zest and stir in the zest. Squeeze the orange and stir in the juice, along with the condensed milk. Stir in the chocolate chips. Spread in the prepared pan.

Bake for 25 to 30 minutes. Cool, then cut into squares.

YIELD: Makes 9 brownies

Raspberry Brownies

These cakelike—as opposed to fudgey—brownies have just enough raspberry flavor to balance the chocolate.

6 ounces (170 g) **bittersweet chocolate**

1/2 cup (1 stick, or 112 g) butter, softened

1/2 cup (100 g) shortening

1 cup (200 g) **sugar**

3 **eggs**

1 cup (320 g) seedless **raspberry jam**

1 1/2 cups (180 g) **self-rising flour**

1/2 teaspoon salt

Preheat the oven to 325°F (170°C, gas mark 3). Grease a 9 x 13-inch baking pan.

Chop the chocolate into small pieces and melt in a double boiler. Stir until smooth and remove from the heat; set aside.

Using a mixer on medium speed, cream together the butter, shortening, and sugar until fluffy—about 5 minutes. Add the eggs, one at a time, mixing well after each addition. Add the jam and beat for 1 minute.

In a separate bowl, mix the flour and salt and add to the mixing bowl, then mix to incorporate. Add the melted chocolate and mix until well incorporated. Pour into the prepared baking pan and spread evenly.

Bake for 30 to 35 minutes, until a tester inserted into the center comes out clean. Cool and cut into squares.

YIELD: Makes about 20 brownies

Double Peanut Brownies

This one's for the peanut devotee.

> 1/2 cup (1 stick, or 112 g) butter
> 1/2 cup (130 g) **chunky peanut butter**
> 1 cup (200 g) **sugar**
> 2 **eggs**
> 1 1/2 cups (180 g) **self-rising flour**
> 1 cup (175 g) **peanut butter chips**

Preheat the oven to 325°F (170°C, gas mark 3). Butter a 9 x 13-inch baking pan.

Using a mixer on medium speed, cream together the butter, peanut butter, and sugar until fluffy—about 5 minutes. Add the eggs, one at a time, mixing well after each addition. Mix in the flour until it is thoroughly combined. Stir in the peanut butter chips. Pour into the prepared baking pan and spread evenly.

Bake for 30 to 35 minutes, until a tester inserted into the center comes out clean. Cool and cut into squares.

YIELD: Makes about 20 brownies

Peanut Butter Cup Brownies

6 ounces (170 g) **bittersweet chocolate**

1/2 cup (1 stick, or 112 g) butter, softened

1/2 cup (100 g) shortening

1 cup (200 g) **vanilla sugar** (See "Making Vanilla Sugar" on page 12.)

3 **eggs**

1 cup (120 g) **self-rising flour**

1/2 teaspoon salt

2 cups mini **Reese's Peanut Butter Cups**, unwrapped (about 20 pieces)

Preheat the oven to 325°F (170°C, gas mark 3). Grease a 9 x 13-inch baking pan.

Chop the chocolate into small pieces and melt in a double boiler. Remove from the heat and set aside.

Using a mixer on medium speed, cream together the butter, shortening, and sugar until fluffy—about 5 minutes. Add the eggs, one at a time, mixing well after each addition.

In a separate bowl, mix the flour and salt and add to the mixing bowl, then mix to incorporate. Add the melted chocolate and mix until thoroughly combined. Stir in the candy. Pour into the prepared baking pan and spread evenly.

Bake for 30 to 35 minutes, until a tester inserted into the center comes out clean. Cool and cut into squares.

YIELD: Makes about 20 brownies

Peanut Butter Chip Brownies

6 ounces (170 g) **bittersweet chocolate**

1/2 cup (1 stick, or 112 g) butter, softened

1/2 cup (100 g) shortening

1 cup (200 g) **vanilla sugar** (See "Making Vanilla Sugar" on page 12.)

3 **eggs**

1 cup (120 g) **self-rising flour**

1/2 teaspoon salt

1 cup (175 g) **peanut butter chips**

Preheat the oven to 325°F (170°C, gas mark 3). Butter a 9 x 13-inch baking pan.

Chop the chocolate into small pieces and melt in a double boiler. Remove from the heat and set aside.

Using a mixer on medium speed, cream together the butter, shortening, and sugar until fluffy—about 5 minutes. Add the eggs, one at a time, mixing well after each addition.

In a separate bowl, mix the flour and salt and add to the mixing bowl, then mix to incorporate. Add the melted chocolate and mix until well combined. Stir in the peanut butter chips. Pour into the prepared baking pan and spread evenly.

Bake for 30 to 35 minutes, until a tester inserted into the center comes out clean. Cool and cut into squares.

YIELD: Makes about 20 brownies

Peanut Butter-Chocolate Marble Brownies

1/2 cup (1 stick, or 112 g) butter

1/4 cup (50 g) shortening

1 cup (200 g) **sugar**

2 **eggs**

2 cups (250 g) **self-rising flour**

1/2 cup (130 g) **creamy peanut butter**

8 ounces (225 g) **semisweet chocolate chips**

Preheat the oven to 325°F (170°C, gas mark 3). Grease a 9 x 13-inch baking pan.

Using a mixer on medium speed, cream together the butter, shortening, and sugar in a mixing bowl until light and fluffy—about 5 minutes. Add the eggs, one at a time, beating well after each addition. Add the flour and mix until incorporated.

Divide the batter into two mixing bowls. Add the peanut butter to the first bowl and mix until well combined. Set aside.

Melt the chocolate chips in a double boiler. Stir the melted chocolate into the other bowl of the batter.

Spread the chocolate batter in the prepared pan. Drop the peanut butter batter on top of the chocolate batter with a spoon and swirl them together using a knife.

Bake for 40 to 45 minutes, until a tester inserted into the center comes out clean. Allow to cool. Cut into squares.

YIELD: Makes 24 brownies

ADD IT! Put a layer of chocolate chips on top as soon as the brownies come out of oven. Let them melt and smooth out with a knife for a quick frosting.

Blondies

Also known as Congo Bars, these are basically chocolate chip cookies in bar form.

1/2 cup (1 stick, or 112 g) butter, softened

1/2 cup (100 g) shortening

1 cup (225 g) packed **light brown sugar**

3 **eggs**

2 teaspoons **vanilla extract**

1 cup (120 g) **self-rising flour**

1/2 teaspoon salt

1 cup (175 g) **semisweet chocolate chips**

Preheat the oven to 325°F (170°C, gas mark 3). Grease a 9 x 13-inch baking pan.

Using a mixer on medium speed, cream the butter, shortening, and sugar until fluffy—about 5 minutes. Add the eggs, one at a time, mixing well after each addition. Add the vanilla and beat until incorporated.

In a separate bowl, mix the flour and salt and add to the mixing bowl, then mix to incorporate. Stir in the chocolate chips. Pour into the prepared baking dish and spread evenly.

Bake for 30 to 35 minutes, until a tester inserted into the center comes out clean. Cool and cut into squares.

YIELD: Makes about 20 bars

ADD IT! Toss in 1/2 cup (60 g) chopped walnuts with the chocolate chips.

Butternut Bars

Chewy butterscotch and walnut bars—what else could you want?

> 1/2 cup (1 stick, or 112 g) butter
>
> 2 cups (290 g) **dark brown sugar**
>
> 2 **eggs**
>
> 1 teaspoon **vanilla extract**
>
> 1 1/2 cups (180 g) **self-rising flour**
>
> 1 cup (125 g) **chopped walnuts**

Preheat the oven to 350°F (180°C, gas mark 4). Grease a 9 x 13-inch baking pan.

Using a mixer on medium speed, cream the butter and sugar together for 5 minutes. Add the eggs, mixing well after each addition. Add the vanilla and mix it in. Stir in the flour until well combined. Stir in the walnuts. Spread in the prepared pan.

Bake for 35 to 40 minutes, until golden brown and a tester inserted into the center comes out clean. Cool in the pan. Cut into squares.

YIELD: Makes about 24 bars

ADD IT! Stir in 1 cup (100 g) of toffee bits with the walnuts.

Butter Pecan Bars

We love the buttery, rich taste of this bar.

For the crust:

> 1/2 cup (1 stick, or 112 g) butter, softened and cut into small pieces
>
> 1/2 cup (110 g) packed **light brown sugar**
>
> 1 teaspoon **vanilla extract**
>
> 2 cups (250 g) **all-purpose flour**
>
> 1/2 teaspoon salt

For the filling:

> 2/3 cup (150 g) butter
>
> 1/2 cup (110 g) **packed light brown sugar**
>
> 1 cup (100 g) **pecan pieces**
>
> 1 cup (175 g) **semisweet chocolate chips**

Preheat the oven to 350°F (180°C, gas mark 4).

To make the crust:

Combine all of the crust ingredients in the bowl of a food processor fitted with the metal blade. Process until the butter is fully incorporated and the mixture resembles a coarse meal. Press the dough evenly into the bottom of a 9 x 13-inch baking pan. Refrigerate while you make the filling.

To make the filling:

Combine the butter and sugar in a small saucepan and cook to a boil over medium-high heat. Boil, stirring, for 1 minute. Scatter the pecans over the crust and pour the sugar mixture over the pecans.

Bake for 20 to 25 minutes. Remove from the oven and immediately scatter the chocolate chips on top of the pecans. Let the chips melt for 1 minute, then swirl them around with a spoon. Cool to room temperature.

YIELD: Makes about 30 bars

Cashew Squares

Cashews introduce a wonderful, unique flavor to a classic butterscotch bar recipe.

$1/2$ cup (1 stick, or 112 g) butter

1 cup (225 g) packed **light brown sugar**

2 **eggs**

2 teaspoons **vanilla extract**

$1/4$ teaspoon salt

1 cup (120 g) **self-rising flour**

1 cup (140 g) unsalted **cashews**, whole

Preheat the oven to 325°F (170°C, gas mark 3). Grease a 9-inch square baking pan.

Using a mixer on medium speed, cream together the butter and sugar in a mixing bowl until light and fluffy—about 5 minutes. Add the eggs, one at a time, beating well after each addition. Add the vanilla and beat until incorporated. Add the salt and flour and beat until incorporated. Stir in the cashews. Spread in the prepared pan.

Bake for 40 to 45 minutes, until a tester inserted in the center comes out clean. Allow to cool.

YIELD: Makes 9 bars

ADD IT! Substitute $1/2$ cup (60 g) walnuts or pecans for $1/2$ cup (70 g) of the cashews for a mixed-nut bar

Coconut Tart Bars

For the crust:

> 1/2 cup (1 stick, or 112 g) butter
>
> 1/4 cup (50 g) shortening
>
> 1/2 cup (110 g) packed **light brown sugar**
>
> 1 cup (120 g) **all-purpose flour**
>
> 1/2 teaspoon salt
>
> 2 to 3 tablespoons (28 to 45 ml) cold water

For the filling:

> 1 cup (225 g) packed **light brown sugar**
>
> 3 **eggs**
>
> 1/2 cup (35 g) **sweetened shredded coconut**
>
> 3/4 cup (75 g) chopped **pecans**
>
> 1/4 cup (30 g) **all-purpose flour**

To make the crust:

Preheat the oven to 350°F (180°C, gas mark 4).

Combine all of the crust ingredients except the water in the bowl of a food processor fitted with the metal blade. Process until the butter is fully incorporated and the mixture resembles a coarse meal. Add the water, while the machine is running, just enough to bring the dough together (You may not need to use all of the water). Press the dough evenly into the bottom of a 9-inch square baking pan. Refrigerate while you make the filling.

To make the filling:

Combine the sugar and the egg and mix for 2 to 3 minutes. Stir in the coconut, pecans, and flour until well mixed. Pour into the baking pan.

Bake for 35 to 40 minutes, until the filling is set. Cool and cut into bars.

YIELD: Makes about 20 bars

ADD IT! Stir 1 teaspoon vanilla extract into the filling.

Pecan Cheesecake Squares

These bars are easy to make and perfect for holiday get-togethers.

> 1 box (16 ounces, or 455 g) **yellow cake mix**
>
> 4 **eggs**
>
> 1/2 cup (1 stick, or 112 g) butter, melted
>
> 2 cups (200 g) **pecan pieces**
>
> 1 package (8 ounces, or 225 g) **cream cheese**
>
> 1 pound (455 g) **confectioners' sugar**

Preheat the oven to 350°F (180°C, gas mark 4). Grease a 9 x 13-inch baking pan.

In a bowl, combine the cake mix, one egg, butter, and pecans and stir until well combined. Spoon the mixture into the bottom of the prepared baking pan.

In another mixing bowl, using a mixer on medium speed, beat the cream cheese with the sugar until smooth and fluffy. Add the remaining three eggs, one at a time, beating well after each addition. Pour over cake mixture.

Bake for 35 to 40 minutes, until the cheese filling is set. Cool, then refrigerate for at least 4 hours. Cut into squares.

YIELD: Makes 24 bars

ADD IT! Sprinkle candied pecan pieces into the filling before baking.

Maple-Walnut Bars

Maple and walnut are flavors made for each other.

> 1/2 cup (1 stick, or 112 g) butter
>
> 1/2 cup (100 g) **sugar**
>
> 1/2 cup (120 ml) **maple syrup**
>
> 2 **eggs**
>
> 1 1/2 cups (180 g) **self-rising flour**
>
> 1/4 teaspoon salt
>
> 1 cup (125 g) chopped **walnuts**

Preheat the oven to 350°F (180°C, gas mark 4). Grease a 9-inch square baking pan.

Using a mixer on high speed, cream together the butter and sugar until light and fluffy. Add the syrup and eggs and beat for 2 minutes. Stir in the flour and salt until fully incorporated, then add the walnuts. Spread in the prepared pan.

Bake for 35 to 40 minutes, until golden brown and a tester inserted into the center comes out clean. Cool in the pan and cut into bars.

YIELD: Makes 18 bars

ADD IT! Frost these with Maple Buttercream Frosting (page 497)

Apple Squares

Our mother has made these for years, and they are incredibly moist and yummy. Cortland, Macintosh, or Granny Smith are good apple choices for these bars.

> 1 pound (455 g) **apples** (about 3 apples)
> 1 3/4 cups (350 g) **vanilla sugar** (See "Making Vanilla Sugar" on page 12.)
> 3 **eggs**
> 2 cups (250 g) **self-rising flour**
> 2 teaspoons **apple pie spice**
> 1/2 teaspoon salt
> 1 cup (235 ml) vegetable oil

Preheat the oven to 350°F (180°C, gas mark 4). Grease a 9 x 13-inch baking pan.

Peel and core the apples and cut them into thin slices.

Combine the sugar and eggs in a mixing bowl and beat them on high speed until light colored and fluffy.

In a separate bowl, sift together the flour, apple pie spice, and salt. Stir into the sugar mixture. Stir in the oil until thoroughly blended. Fold in the apples. Spoon into the prepared pan and smooth off the top.

Bake for 40 to 45 minutes, until a tester inserted into the center comes out clean. Cool in the pan. Cut into squares.

YIELD: Makes about 32 bars

Apple Cinnamon Bars

If you can't find cinnamon chips, butterscotch chips are also yummy in this recipe.

1/2 cup (1 stick, or 112 g) butter
1/2 cup (100 g) shortening
1 cup (225 g) packed **dark brown sugar**
3 **eggs**
1 cup (255 g) **applesauce**
2 cups (250 g) **self-rising flour**   *Reg Flour   1 T bak pwd*
1/4 teaspoon salt
2 cups (350 g) **cinnamon chips**

Preheat the oven to 325°F (170°C, gas mark 3). Grease a 9 x 13-inch pan.

Using a mixer on medium speed, cream together the butter, shortening, and sugar on high speed until light and fluffy. Add the eggs, one at a time, beating well after each addition. Add the applesauce and beat until incorporated. Stir in the flour and salt until fully incorporated. Stir in the cinnamon chips. Spread in the prepared pan.

Bake for 45 to 50 minutes, until golden brown and a tester inserted into the center comes out clean. Cool in the pan and cut into bars.

YIELD: Makes 18 bars

ADD IT! Stir 1 cup (125 g) peeled diced apple into the mix.

Apple Pecan Squares

Fluffy and cakey, these make a great coffee klatsch snack.

    1/4 cup (1/2 stick, or 55 g) butter, softened
    1/4 cup (50 g) shortening
    3/4 cup (150 g) **sugar**
    2 cups (510 g) **applesauce with cinnamon**
    2 cups (250 g) **self-rising flour**
    1/4 teaspoon salt
    1 cup (80 g) **quick cooking oats**
    1/2 cup (50 g) **pecan pieces**

Preheat the oven to 350°F (180°C, gas mark 4). Grease a 9 x 13-inch baking pan.

Combine the butter, shortening, and sugar in a mixing bowl and beat on high speed until light and fluffy. Add the applesauce and beat for 3 minutes. Stir in the flour and salt until just combined, then fold in the oats and pecans. Spread in the prepared pan.

Bake for 40 to 45 minutes, until a tester inserted into the center comes out clean. Cool in the pan. Cut into squares.

YIELD: Makes 24 to 30 squares

ADD IT! Toss in 1/2 teaspoon cinnamon into the mix.

Apricot-Oat Bars

Apricots are another underappreciated fruit in the United States. Take a step toward apricot love with these bars.

For the crust:

> 1/4 cup (1/2 stick, or 55 g) butter, softened
>
> 1/4 cup (50 g) shortening
>
> 1/2 cup (100 g) **sugar**
>
> 1 **egg**
>
> 1 cup (120 g) **all-purpose flour**
>
> 1/2 teaspoon salt

For the filling:

> 2 cups (640 g) **apricot preserves**
>
> 1 cup (80 g) **quick cooking oats**
>
> 1/4 cup (1/2 stick, or 55 g) butter, cut into small pieces
>
> 1/4 cup (30 g) **all-purpose flour**
>
> 1/2 cup (100 g) **sugar**

To make the crust:

Preheat the oven to 350°F (180°C, gas mark 4).

Combine the butter, the shortening, and the sugar in a mixing bowl and beat on high speed until light and fluffy. Add the egg and beat for 2 minutes.

In a separate bowl, combine the flour and salt and stir into the batter until they are just incorporated. Press the dough evenly into the bottom of a 9-inch square baking pan. Refrigerate while you make the filling.

To make the filling:

Spread the apricot preserves evenly over the crust dough. In a mixing bowl, combine the oats, butter, flour, and sugar. Using your fingers, work the mixture until the butter is incorporated. Sprinkle evenly over the apricot preserves.

Bake for 35 to 40 minutes, until the filling is set. Cool and cut into bars.

YIELD: Makes about 20 bars

Banana-Chocolate Chip Bars

A light banana taste balances the rich chocolate beautifully in this bar. If you like chocolate chips in your banana bread, you'll like these.

> 1/2 cup (1 stick, or 112 g) butter
>
> 1 cup (225 g) packed **light brown sugar**
>
> 1 **egg**
>
> 1 cup (225 g) mashed **banana** (about 2 bananas)
>
> 1 1/2 cups (180 g) **self-rising flour**
>
> 1 cup (175 g) **semisweet chocolate chips**

Preheat the oven to 350°F (180°C, gas mark 4). Grease a 9-inch square baking pan.

Using a mixer on medium speed, cream the butter and sugar until fluffy. Add the egg and beat well. Add the banana and beat for 2 minutes. Stir in the flour until incorporated and then stir in the chocolate chips. Spread into the baking pan.

Bake for 30 to 35 minutes, until a tester inserted into the center comes out clean. Cool completely in the pan.

YIELD: Makes 9 bars

Cherry-Cheese Layer Bars

This bar offers a very creamy filling for the cheesecake lovers out there.

2 cups (200 g) **graham cracker crumbs**

1/2 cup (1 stick, or 112 g) butter, melted

1 package (8 ounces, or 225 g) **cream cheese**

1 cup (120 g) **confectioners' sugar**

2 **eggs**

1 can (14 ounces, or 400 g) **cherry pie filling**

Preheat the oven to 350°F (180°C, gas mark 4).

Combine the cracker crumbs and butter and mix together until the butter is evenly distributed. Press into a 9-inch square baking pan.

Bake for 10 to 12 minutes.

Using a mixer on high speed, cream together the cream cheese and sugar in a mixing bowl for 5 to 8 minutes, until the mixture is smooth and fluffy. Add the eggs, one at a time, beating well after each addition. Spread the cheese over the baked crust.

Bake for 25 to 30 minutes. Allow to cool to room temperature. Spread the pie filling on top. Refrigerate for at least 6 hours, preferably overnight. Cut into bars.

YIELD: Makes 24 bars

Lemon Squares

Everyone in our family loves these, even those who frown upon desserts containing the slightest taint of fruit.

For the crust:

> 1 1/2 cups (180 g) **all-purpose flour**
>
> 1 1/2 cups (180 g) **confectioners' sugar**
>
> Pinch salt
>
> 1/2 cup (1 stick, or 112 g) butter, cut into small pieces
>
> 1 **egg**
>
> 1/4 cup (60 ml) cold water

For the filling:

> 4 **lemons**
>
> 3 **eggs**
>
> 2 cups (240 g) **confectioners' sugar**, plus more for dusting
>
> 2 tablespoons (15 g) **all-purpose flour**
>
> 1/2 teaspoon **baking powder**

Preheat the oven to 350°F (180°C, gas mark 4). Grease a 9 x 13-inch baking pan.

To make the crust:

Combine the flour, sugar, and salt in a mixing bowl. Add the butter and cut into the dry ingredients until the mixture resembles coarse meal. Stir in the egg and slowly add the water to form a crumbly dough. (You may not need all the water, just enough to form a crumbly dough. A food processor works well for this procedure, too.) Lightly press the dough into the prepared pan.

To make the filling:

Squeeze the lemons to yield 2/3 cup (150 ml) lemon juice. Combine the lemon juice, eggs, sugar, flour, and baking powder in a mixing bowl and beat on medium speed for 2 to 3 minutes. Pour over the crust.

Bake for 35 to 40 minutes, until the filling is set. Cool, then sift more confectioners' sugar on top of the filling. Cut into squares.

YIELD: Makes about 32 bars

Lemon Pound Cake Squares

These are moist and light tasting bars.

> 1/2 cup (1 stick, or 112 g) butter
>
> 1 1/2 (300 g) cups **sugar**
>
> 2 **eggs**
>
> 1 cup (120 g) **self-rising flour**
>
> Zest and juice from 3 **lemons**
>
> 1/2 cup (120 ml) water

Preheat the oven to 350°F (180°C, gas mark 4). Grease a 9-inch square baking pan.

Using a mixer on medium speed, cream together the butter and 1 cup (200 g) of the sugar until light and fluffy. Add the eggs, one at a time, beating well after each addition. Add the flour and 1 tablespoon of the lemon zest. Beat until well incorporated. Add 1/4 cup (60 ml) lemon juice. Beat until combined. Pour into the prepared pan.

Bake for 35 to 40 minutes, until a tester inserted into the center comes out clean.

While the cake is baking, combine the other 1/2 cup (100 g) of sugar, 2 tablespoons (28 ml) lemon juice, and the water in a small saucepan. Bring to a boil and cook for 5 minutes at a low boil. Remove from the heat.

When the cake is done, stick it all over with a long toothpick or a metal skewer and pour the lemon syrup over. Allow to cool completely. Cut into squares.

YIELD: Makes 9 bars

Lemon Meringue Squares

Lemon meringue pie in a bar; what a concept.

> 2 1/2 cups (500 g) **sugar**
>
> 1/2 cup (1 stick, or 112 g), plus 2 tablespoons butter
>
> 6 **eggs**
>
> 1 cup (120 g) **all-purpose flour**
>
> 1/4 teaspoon salt
>
> 1/2 cup (120 ml) **lemon juice** (about 6 lemons)
>
> 2 tablespoons (15 g) **cornstarch**

Preheat the oven to 350°F (180°C, gas mark 4). Grease a 9 x 13-inch baking pan.

In a mixing bowl, combine 1 cup (200 g) of the sugar with 1/2 cup (112 g) of the butter. Cream until light and fluffy. Add 2 of the eggs and beat for 2 to 3 minutes. Stir in the flour and salt until thoroughly combined. Press the dough into the baking pan.

Bake for 20 to 25 minutes, until golden brown. Cool.

Separate the remaining 4 eggs and set aside the whites. Combine the yolks, lemon juice, cornstarch, and 1 cup (200 g) of the remaining sugar in a 1-quart saucepan. Whisk together and cook over medium heat, stirring, until the mixture thickens. (Do not boil.) Stir in the remaining 2 tablespoons butter until melted and spread the mixture over the baked crust. Refrigerate until set, about 1 hour.

Heat the oven to 400°F (200°C, gas mark 6). Whip the egg whites with the remaining 1/2 cup (100 g) sugar until stiff peaks form. Spread over the lemon filling and bake for 10 minutes, until the meringue is browned on top. Cool. Cut into squares.

YIELD: Makes 24 bars

Lime~Raspberry Bars

These are particularly refreshing when served refrigerated on a hot summer day.

1/2 cup (1 stick, or 112 g) butter

1/2 cup (100 g) shortening

1 cup (200 g) **sugar**

2 **eggs**

2 medium **limes**

1 cup (120 g) **self-rising flour**

1 1/2 cups (190 g) **raspberries** (If frozen, do not thaw.)

Preheat the oven to 350°F (180°C, gas mark 4). Grease a 9-inch square baking pan.

Using a mixer on medium speed, cream together the butter, shortening, and sugar until light and fluffy—about 5 minutes. Add the eggs, one at a time, beating well after each addition. Zest one lime and add the zest to the batter. Squeeze both limes and add the lime juice to the batter. Add the flour and mix until thoroughly combined. Stir in the raspberries. Spread the batter in the prepared pan.

Bake for 35 to 40 minutes, until a tester inserted into the center comes out clean. Cool in the pan.

YIELD: Makes 12 bars

Orange Cream Bars

It's the Creamsicle taste in a non-melting format—what's not to like?

> 1/2 cup (1 stick, or 112 g) butter
>
> 2 cups (400 g) **sugar**, divided
>
> 1 **egg**
>
> 1/2 cup (140 g) frozen **orange juice concentrate**, thawed, plus 2 tablespoons for the frosting
>
> 1 1/2 cups (180 g) **self-rising flour**
>
> 1/4 teaspoon salt
>
> 8 ounces (225 g) **cream cheese**

Preheat the oven to 350°F (180°C, gas mark 4). Grease a 9-inch square baking pan.

Using a mixer on medium speed, cream the butter and 1 cup (200 g) of the sugar together until smooth and fluffy—about 5 minutes. Add the egg and the orange juice concentrate and beat for 4 minutes. Stir in the flour and salt until thoroughly combined. Spread the batter in the prepared pan.

Bake for 30 to 35 minutes, until a tester inserted into the center comes out clean. Cool completely in the pan.

Combine the remaining orange juice, 1/4 cup (60 ml) water, and the remaining 1 cup (200 g) sugar in a small saucepan and heat over medium heat until the sugar is dissolved. Remove from heat and cool.

Put the cream cheese in a mixing bowl and add the orange juice mixture. Beat for 8 to 10 minutes, until smooth and fluffy. Spread over the bars and refrigerate for at least 1 hour. Cut into bars.

YIELD: Makes about 18 bars

Jam Bars

These are great with afternoon tea (or with a midnight glass of milk, too).

1 cup (200 g) **sugar**

1/2 cup (1 stick, or 112 g) butter

1 **egg,** plus 2 egg yolks

2 cups (250 g) **all-purpose flour**

1/4 teaspoon salt

2 cups (640 g) raspberry, strawberry, or other favorite **jam**

Preheat the oven to 350°F (180°C, gas mark 4). Grease a 9-inch square baking pan.

Using a mixer on medium speed, cream together the sugar and butter until light and fluffy—about 5 minutes. Add the egg and yolks and beat for another 2 minutes.

In a separate bowl, sift the flour and salt together and add to the sugar mixture. Stir until well combined. Spoon half of the batter into the prepared pan and press into the pan.

Bake for 10 minutes. Remove from the oven and spread with the jam. Top the jam with the remaining batter.

Bake for 30 to 35 minutes, until the dough is golden brown. Cool to room temperature. Cut into bars.

YIELD: Makes about 24 bars

Linzer Squares

A take on the famous Linzer torte—reduced to a bite-sized morsel.

> 1 cup (135 g) peeled **hazelnuts**
>
> 1/2 cup (1 stick, or 112 g) butter
>
> 1 cup (200 g) **sugar**
>
> 1/2 cup (60 g) **self-rising flour**
>
> 1/2 teaspoon salt
>
> 3 teaspoons **cinnamon**
>
> 1 1/2 cups (480 g) seedless **raspberry jam**

Preheat the oven to 325°F (170°C, gas mark 3). Butter a 9-inch square baking pan.

Put the hazelnuts in a food processor fitted with the metal blade and grind to a fine meal.

Using a mixer on medium speed, cream together the butter and sugar in a mixing bowl until fluffy—about 5 minutes.

Mix the flour, salt, and cinnamon together in a bowl and add to the creamed mixture. Mix to combine well. Stir in the ground hazelnuts. Spread half of the batter in the prepared baking pan. Carefully spread the jam on top and then top with the rest of the batter.

Bake for 25 to 30 minutes, until a tester inserted into the center comes out clean. Allow to cool fully, then cut into bars.

YIELD: Makes about 24 bars

Blueberry Crumble Bars

1/2 cup (1 stick, or 112 g) butter

1/4 cup (50 g) shortening

2 cups (400 g) **sugar**

2 cups (250 g) **all-purpose flour**

1 tablespoon (15 g) **baking powder**

1/4 teaspoon salt

1 cup (80 g) **quick cooking oats**

3 cups (435 g) **wild blueberries** (If using frozen, do not thaw.)

Preheat the oven to 350°F (180°C, gas mark 4). Grease a 9 x 13-inch baking pan.

Using a mixer on medium speed, cream together the butter, shortening, and 1 cup (200 g) of the sugar until light and fluffy—about 5 minutes.

In a separate bowl, sift the flour, baking powder, and salt together and add to the creamed mixture. Beat until well combined and then stir in the oats. Spoon half of the batter into the prepared pan and press into the pan.

In a bowl, mix the blueberries with the remaining 1 cup (200 g) sugar and top the batter with the berries. Scatter the remaining batter over the berries, pressing lightly.

Bake for 40 to 45 minutes, until the berries are bubbling and the cake is golden brown. Cool to room temperature and cut into bars.

YIELD: Makes about 24 bars

Cranberry Bars

This strikes us as a great dessert to make around Thanksgiving, to balance the overwhelming pie presence in most households.

1 cup (200 g) **vanilla sugar** (See "Making Vanilla Sugar" on page 12.)

2 **eggs**

1 cup (230 g) **sour cream**

1/4 cup (60 ml) vegetable oil

1 1/2 cups (180 g) **self-rising flour**

1/4 teaspoon salt

1 cup (120 g) dried **cranberries**

Preheat the oven to 350°F (180°C, gas mark 4). Grease a 9-inch square baking pan.

Using a mixer on medium speed, cream together the sugar and eggs in a mixing bowl until light and fluffy—4 to 5 minutes. Add the sour cream and oil and beat until smooth. Add the flour and the salt and beat until just incorporated into the batter. Stir in the cranberries. Pour into the prepared pan.

Bake for 30 to 35 minutes, until a tester inserted into the center comes out clean. Cut into squares.

YIELD: Makes 12 bars

ADD IT! Toss in 1/4 cup (25 g) grated orange zest.

Rhubarb Squares

Rhubarb is another misfit food. It seems that everybody or their neighbor has a big bushy plant full of the stuff in the yard, but nobody cooks with it, except for the obligatory strawberry-rhubarb pie. We recommend that you decimate the nearest plant. Rhubarb is good stuff!

1/2 cup (1 stick, or 112 g) butter

1/4 cup (50 g) shortening

2 cups (400 g) **sugar**

2 cups (250 g) **all-purpose flour**

1 tablespoon (15 g) **baking powder**

1/4 teaspoon salt

3 cups (365 g) diced fresh **rhubarb**, (1/2 inch long)

3 teaspoons **cinnamon**

Preheat the oven to 350°F (180°C, gas mark 4). Grease a 9 x 13-inch baking pan.

Using a mixer on medium speed, cream together the butter, shortening, and 1 cup (200 g) of the sugar until light and fluffy—about 5 minutes.

In a separate bowl, sift the flour, baking powder, and salt together and add to the creamed mixture. Stir until well combined. (This will be a very stiff and thick batter.) Spoon half of the batter into the prepared pan and press into the pan.

In a bowl, mix the rhubarb with the cinnamon and the remaining 1 cup (200 g) sugar and top the batter with the rhubarb. Scatter the remaining batter over the rhubarb, pressing lightly.

Bake for 40 to 45 minutes, until the rhubarb is bubbling and the cake is golden brown. Cool to room temperature. Cut into bars.

YIELD: Makes about 24 bars

Fig Bars

Before you gloss right over this recipe as containing neither peanut butter or chocolate, we beg you to reconsider: Figs are a succulent and sweet fruit, rich in vitamins A and C, as well as being a great source of B vitamins and calcium.

1 cup (200 g) **sugar**

1/2 cup (1 stick, or 112 g) butter

1 **egg**, plus 2 egg yolks

2 cups (250 g) **all-purpose flour**

1/4 teaspoon salt

1 can (12 ounces, or 340 g) **fig pastry filling**

Preheat the oven to 350°F (180°C, gas mark 4). Grease a 9-inch square baking pan.

Using a mixer on medium speed, cream together the sugar and butter until light and fluffy—about 5 minutes. Add the egg and yolks and beat for another 2 minutes.

In a separate bowl, sift the flour and the salt together and add to the creamed mixture. Stir until well combined. Spoon half of the batter into the prepared pan and press into the pan.

Bake for 10 minutes. Remove from the oven and spread with the fig filling. Top with the remaining batter.

Bake for 30 to 35 minutes, until the dough is golden brown. Cool to room temperature. Cut into bars.

YIELD: Makes about 24 bars

Pumpkin Bars

This is a delicious and mildly spicy frosted bar.

> 1/2 cup (100 g) shortening
>
> 1 cup (270 g) **canned spiced and sweetened pumpkin**
>
> 2 **eggs**
>
> 2 cups (475 ml) **sweetened condensed milk**
>
> 2 cups (250 g) **self-rising flour**
>
> 8 ounces (225 g) **cream cheese**

Preheat the oven to 350°F (180°C, gas mark 4). Grease a 9 x 13-inch baking pan.

Combine the shortening, pumpkin, eggs, and 1 cup (235 ml) of the condensed milk in a mixing bowl. Beat for 5 minutes. Stir in the flour until combined. Pour into the prepared pan.

Bake for 45 to 50 minutes, until a tester inserted into the center comes out clean. Cool completely in the pan.

Whip together the cream cheese and the remaining 1 cup (235 ml) condensed milk until smooth and creamy. Spread over the cooled cake. Refrigerate for at least 2 hours. Cut into bars.

YIELD: Makes 48 bars

Fudge-Shortbread Squares

You will want to cut these into fairly small squares—quite rich, but oh so good.

For the shortbread:

> 1 cup (200 g) **vanilla sugar** (See "Making Vanilla Sugar" on page 12.)
> 1/2 cup (1 stick, or 112 g) butter
> 1 cup (120 g) **all-purpose flour**
> 1/2 teaspoon salt

For the topping:

> 1 cup (175 g) **semisweet chocolate chips**
> 1 cup (235 ml) **sweetened condensed milk**
> 1 cup (90 g) sliced **almonds**

To make the shortbread:

Preheat the oven to 350°F (180°C, gas mark 4). Grease a 9-inch square baking pan.

Using a mixer on medium speed, cream the sugar and butter together until light and fluffy. Add the flour and salt and mix on low speed until combined. Press the dough into the prepared pan.

Bake for 25 to 30 minutes, until golden. Cool completely.

To make the topping:

Melt the chocolate chips in a saucepan; add the condensed milk and bring to a boil, stirring. Remove from the heat and beat with a mixer on high speed for 8 to 10 minutes, until the chocolate mixture thickens. Spread over the shortbread. Sprinkle the almonds on top. Refrigerate for 1 to 2 hours. Cut into bars.

YIELD: Makes 24 bars

Cookies and Cream Bars

Very easy, very yummy.

> 8 ounces (225 g) **cream cheese**
>
> 1 cup (200 g) **sugar**
>
> 1/4 cup (30 g) **all-purpose flour**
>
> 2 **eggs**
>
> 2 cups crushed **Oreo cookies** (about 15 cookies)

Preheat the oven to 350°F (180°C, gas mark 4). Grease a 9-inch square baking pan.

Using a mixer on medium speed, beat the cream cheese with the sugar and flour until smooth and creamy—about 10 minutes. Beat in the eggs for 2 minutes. Stir in the crushed cookies. Spread in the prepared pan.

Bake for 25 to 30 minutes, until set. Cool, then refrigerate for at least 2 hours.

Cut into bars. Store in Fridge.

YIELD: Makes 24 bars

Trail Mix Bars

You don't even have to turn on the oven for these, and they make for a great energy burst for hikers. You can get all sorts of extra flavors in by varying the type of granola you choose.

1/2 cup (1 stick, or 112 g) butter

1 cup (235 ml) **light corn syrup**

2 cups (250 g) **granola**

1/2 cup (70 g) **raisins**

1/2 cup (45 g) **sliced almonds**

1 cup (175 g) **semisweet chocolate chips**

Grease a 9-inch square baking pan.

Combine the butter and corn syrup in a 1-quart saucepan. Cook over medium-high heat until the butter melts and stir until the mixture boils. Remove from the heat.

In a large mixing bowl, combine the granola, raisins, almonds, and chocolate chips and pour the syrup over. Stir to fully coat everything. Press into the pan evenly and allow to cool. Cut into squares.

YIELD: Makes 9 bars

Goober Squares

Similar to the classic Rice Krispies treats, but with lots more flavor, this is a great project to make with small children.

> 1/2 cup (1 stick, or 112 g) butter
>
> 1/2 cup (120 ml) **corn syrup**
>
> 2 cups (100 g) **mini marshmallows**
>
> 3 cups (85 g) **Corn Flakes**
>
> 1 cup (145 g) dry roasted **peanuts**
>
> 1 cup (6 ounces, or 170 g) **M&M's**

Grease a 9-inch square baking pan.

In a 2-quart saucepan, combine the butter and the corn syrup. Melt them together over medium-high heat, stirring, and bring the mixture to a boil. Boil gently, stirring, for 5 minutes. Remove from the heat, add the marshmallows, and stir them in until they are melted.

In a large mixing bowl, combine the Corn Flakes, peanuts, and M&M's. Pour into the marshmallow mixture and stir until everything is coated. Spread in the prepared pan and allow to cool fully. Cut into squares.

YIELD: Makes 16 bars

Oat Bars

Think of it: High fiber, cholesterol-lowering properties, and chocolate—all in one bar!

1/2 cup (1 stick, or 112 g) butter

1 cup (225 g) packed **light brown sugar**

2 **eggs**

1/4 teaspoon salt

1 cup (120 g) **all-purpose flour**

1 1/2 cup (120 g) **quick-rolled oates**

8 ounces (225 g) **semisweet chocolate chips**

2 tablespoons (28 ml) water

Preheat the oven to 325°F (170°C, gas mark 3). Grease a 9-inch square baking pan.

Using a mixer on medium speed, cream together the butter and sugar in a mixing bowl until light and fluffy—about 5 minutes. Add the eggs, one at a time, beating well after each addition. Add the salt and flour. Mix until incorporated. Stir in the oats. Spread in the prepared pan.

Bake for 25 to 30 minutes, until a tester inserted into the center comes out clean. Allow to cool.

Melt the chocolate chips in a double boiler with the water. Spread the melted chocolate on top of the baked bars. Refrigerate for 1 hour. Cut into bars.

YIELD: Makes 12 bars

Wheat Bars

They made these at our high school back in the olden days when we were young, and we loved them so much that Bob weaseled the recipe out of one of the cafeteria ladies. Our guess is that the school got rolled wheat from the government, but you can find it at some supermarkets and at health food stores in the bulk department.

1 cup (2 sticks, or 225 g) butter, softened, plus 2 tablespoons
   (1/4 stick, or 28 g) butter

1 cup (225 g) **light brown sugar**, packed

1 **egg**

1 1/4 cups (150 g) **all-purpose flour**

1 1/4 cups (4 ounces, or 115 g) **rolled wheat**

6 ounces (170 g) **semisweet chocolate chips**

Preheat the oven to 350°F (180°C, gas mark 4). Grease a 9 x 13-inch baking pan.

Using a mixer on medium speed, cream together 1 cup of the butter and the sugar until light and fluffy—about 5 minutes. Add the egg and beat for another minute. Add the flour and rolled wheat and mix until blended. Spread the batter in the baking pan.

Bake for about 25 minutes, until golden brown and a tester inserted into the center comes out clean.

Meanwhile, melt the chocolate chips and the remaining 2 tablespoons butter together in a double boiler, or in the microwave. Spread on top of the bars while they are still warm. Cool completely. Cut into squares.

YIELD: Makes 18 bars

Three-Layer Bars

This is a bake-sale classic, and with good reason.

1/4 cup (1/2 stick, or 55 g) butter, melted

2 cups (7.2 ounces) **graham cracker crumbs**

1 cup (75 g) **sweetened shredded coconut**

1 can (12 ounces, or 355 ml) **sweetened condensed milk**

12 ounces (340 g) **semisweet chocolate chips**

1/2 cup (130 g) **creamy peanut butter**

Preheat the oven to 350°F (180°C, gas mark 4). Grease a 9-inch square baking pan.

Combine the butter and the cracker crumbs in a mixing bowl and stir until well combined. Press into the baking pan.

In another bowl, mix the coconut and condensed milk. Pour over the crumbs.

Bake for 15 to 20 minutes. Cool.

Melt the chocolate chips in a double boiler and add the peanut butter, stirring until the mixture is smooth. Spread this on top of the coconut. Refrigerate for at least 1 hour. Cut into bars.

YIELD: Makes 18 bars

Chocolate-Coconut Bars

This recipe is for the Mounds candy bar devotees out there.

For the crust:

> 1 package (16 ounces, or 455 g) **Nabisco Famous Chocolate Wafer Cookies**
> 1/2 cup (1 stick, or 112 g) butter

For the filling:

> 1 can (12 ounces, or 355 ml) **sweetened condensed milk**
> 1 egg
> 1 cup (75 g) **sweetened shredded coconut**

For the topping:

> 1 cup (175 g) **semisweet chocolate chips**
> 1 cup (235 ml) **sweetened condensed milk**

To make the crust:

Preheat the oven to 350°F (180°C, gas mark 4). Grease a 9-inch square baking pan.

Put the cookies in a food processor and grind them into fine crumbs; put the crumbs in a mixing bowl.

In a saucepan, melt the butter over low heat and stir into the cookie crumbs until thoroughly combined. Press the crumbs into the bottom of the prepared pan.

To make the filling:

In a mixing bowl, beat the condensed milk and the egg together for 2 to 3 minutes, then stir in the coconut. Spread over the cookie crust.

Bake for 20 to 25 minutes. Cool completely.

To make the topping:

Melt the chocolate chips in a saucepan. Add the condensed milk and bring to a boil, stirring. Remove from the heat and beat with a mixer on high speed for 8 to 10 minutes, until the chocolate mixture thickens. Spread over the coconut layer. Refrigerate for at least 4 hours. Cut into bars.

YIELD: Makes 18 bars

Chocolate-Hazelnut Bars

We find chocolate and hazelnuts to be one of the best flavor combinations around. You will too.

1/4 cup (1/2 stick, or 55 g) butter, softened

1 cup (300 g) **Nutella chocolate-hazelnut spread**

1 cup (200 g) **sugar**

3 **eggs**

1 cup (120 g) **self-rising flour**

1 cup (115 g) peeled, chopped **hazelnuts**

Preheat the oven to 325°F (170°C, gas mark 3). Grease a 9 x 13-inch baking pan.

Using a mixer on medium speed, cream together the butter, Nutella, and sugar until fluffy—about 5 minutes. Add the eggs, one at a time, mixing well after each addition.

Add the flour to the mixing bowl, then mix to incorporate. Stir in the hazelnuts. Pour into the prepared baking pan and spread evenly.

Bake for 30 to 35 minutes, until a tester inserted into the center comes out clean. Cool and cut into squares.

YIELD: Makes about 20 bars

ADD IT! Melt 1 cup (175 g) semisweet chocolate chips over low heat; add 1 cup (235 ml) sweetened condensed milk and bring to a boil. Beat with a mixer on high speed for 8 to 10 minutes, until the chocolate mixture thickens and frost the bars.

Peanut Butter Bars

Tester Alice Kelly's family followed her around with their tongues hanging out when she made these.

    1/4 cup (50 g) shortening
    2/3 cup (170 g) chunky **peanut butter**
    1 cup (200 g) **sugar**
    2 **eggs**
    1 cup (120 g) **all-purpose flour**
    1 cup (175 g) **semisweet chocolate chips**
    2 tablespoons (28 ml) water

Preheat the oven to 325°F (170°C, gas mark 3). Grease a 9-inch square baking pan.

Combine the shortening, peanut butter, and sugar in a mixing bowl. Beat until light and fluffy—about 5 minutes. Add the eggs, one at a time, beating well after each addition. Add flour and mix until incorporated. Spread in the prepared pan.

Bake for 40 to 45 minutes, until a tester inserted into the center comes out clean. Allow to cool.

Melt the chocolate chips in a double boiler with the water. Spread the melted chocolate on top of the baked bars. Refrigerate for 1 hour. Cut into bars.

YIELD: Makes 12 bars

Peanut Butter and Jelly Bars

If you've got kids who are PBJ hounds, they'll love these bars.

1/2 cup (1 stick, or 112 g) butter, softened

1/2 cup (130 g) creamy **peanut butter**

1 cup (225 g) **light brown sugar**, packed

2 eggs

1 1/2 cups (180 g) **self-rising flour**

2 cups (640 g) **grape jelly**

Preheat the oven to 350°F (180°C, gas mark 4). Grease a 9-inch square baking pan.

Using a mixer on medium speed, cream together the butter, peanut butter, and sugar in a mixing bowl for 5 minutes. Add the eggs, one at a time, beating well after each addition. Add the flour and beat to incorporate. Spread half of the batter in the prepared pan.

Bake for 15 minutes. Cool for 10 minutes, then spread the jelly on top and cover with the rest of the batter.

Bake for another 25 to 30 minutes. Cool in the pan and cut into bars.

YIELD: Makes 18 bars

Malted Milk Rice Treats

Carol's husband, Don, who has an unseemly affection for malted milk balls, thinks these are the Best. Things. Ever.

> 2 cups (7 ounces, or 200 g) **malted milk balls**
> 1/2 cup (1 stick, or 112 g) butter
> 2 cups (100 g) **mini marshmallows**
> 4 cups (55 g) **puffed rice cereal**
> 1 cup (145 g) **dry roasted peanuts**
> 1 cup (145 g) **raisins**

Grease a 9 x 13-inch baking pan.

Put the malted milk balls in a resealable plastic bag and crush them with a rolling pin.

In a 2-quart saucepan, melt the butter, malted milk balls, and marshmallows, stirring, until smooth.

Mix the puffed rice cereal, peanuts, and raisins in a mixing bowl. Stir in the melted mixture until all is well coated. Spoon into the prepared pan and press into the pan. Cool to room temperature. Cut into bars.

YIELD: Makes 24 bars

Frosted Flakes Bars

These bars are very sweet. If you want to tone down the sugar, try Corn Flakes instead of the Tony the Tiger variety. Regardless, however: They're Grrrreat!

2 cups (55 g) **Frosted Flakes** or Corn Flakes

1/2 cup (1 stick, or 112 g) butter

1/2 cup (35 g) **sweetened shredded coconut**

1/2 cup (60 g) chopped **walnuts**

1 cup (175 g) **semisweet chocolate chips**

1 can (12 ounces, or 355 ml) **sweetened condensed milk**

Preheat the oven to 350°F (180°C, gas mark 4). Grease a 9-inch square baking pan.

Put the cereal in a mixing bowl. Melt the butter over low heat, add to the cereal, and stir until thoroughly coated. Stir in the coconut and spread the mixture in the prepared pan. Scatter the walnuts and chocolate chips over the top and pour the condensed milk evenly over all.

Bake for 20 to 25 minutes, until the milk is absorbed, then cool to room temperature. Cut into bars.

YIELD: Makes 18 bars

CHAPTER SEVEN

Ice Cream and Frozen Desserts

Ice cream is a regional obsession in New England, which consumes more ice cream per person than any other part of the United States. Oddly enough, our family made ice cream every year in the dead of winter, because our frugal father couldn't bear to pay for ice cubes in the summer when we could chop all the ice we needed for free in January! We used a hand crank ice cream maker, which certainly made it more of a family event as we all took turns cranking the handle.

Now that we're older, our culinary horizons have expanded beyond ice cream when it comes to frozen delights. From bombes to glaces to granitas, it's clear that when it comes to desserts, cold can be very hot indeed.

Apricot Soufflé Glace

Cold soufflés are just as airy as their baked brethren, but they get their lightness from whisked egg whites and whipped cream. This is a delicate and dressy dessert.

> 2 **egg yolks**
> 1 cup (200 g) **sugar**
> 1 cup (235 ml) **milk**
> 1 can (12 ounces, or 340 g) **apricots** in syrup
> 2 cup (120 g) **whipped heavy cream**

Whisk the egg yolks and ½ cup (100 g) of the sugar in a mixing bowl until fluffy.

Heat the remaining ½ cup (100 g) sugar and the milk in a small saucepan until the sugar is dissolved and the milk is scalded. While whisking, pour the hot milk into the egg yolks in a thin stream. Return this mixture to the saucepan and cook over medium heat, stirring constantly, until the custard is thick enough to coat the back of a spoon. Pour the custard through a fine mesh strainer into a stainless steel bowl set in another container of ice water. Cool the custard completely.

Puree the apricots and syrup in a food processor or blender. Fold the apricot puree into the custard.

Whip the cream to soft peaks and whisk one-third of the whipped cream into the custard mixture. Gently, but thoroughly, fold the rest of the whipped cream in. Spoon into six 8-ounce soufflé cups fitted with parchment paper collars and freeze for at least 4 hours.

To serve, soften slightly at room temperature. Remove the paper collars.

YIELD: Makes 6 servings

❡ Banana Rum Soufflé Glace

These would taste terrific with Chocolate-Dipped Biscotti (page 224).

> 1 cup (200 g) **sugar**
> About 4 tablespoons (60 ml) water
> 3 **eggs whites**
> 1/4 cup (60 ml) **dark rum**
> 1 cup (225 g) pureed very ripe **banana** (about 2 bananas)
> 2 cups (475 ml) **heavy cream**

Combine the sugar with enough water to form "wet sand." Cook over medium-high heat, not stirring, until the syrup is golden brown and reaches 238 to 240°F (114° to 116°C) on a candy thermometer.

While the syrup is cooking, whip the egg whites to soft peak. With the mixer running, pour the hot syrup into the egg whites in a thin stream. Add the rum and continue to whip until the meringue is cool. Fold in the bananas.

Whip the cream to soft peaks and whisk one-third of the whipped cream into the egg mixture. Gently, but thoroughly, fold the rest of the whipped cream in. Spoon into six 8-ounce soufflé cups fitted with parchment paper collars and freeze for at least 4 hours.

To serve, soften slightly at room temperature. Remove the paper collars.

YIELD: Makes 6 servings

❦ Raspberry-Lime Soufflé Glace

Could we be trying to transfer our affection for raspberry-lime rickeys to frozen form? You be the judge.

> 2 **limes**
>
> 1 package (12 ounces, or 340 g) frozen unsweetened **raspberries**, thawed
>
> 1 cup (200 g) **sugar**
>
> About 4 tablespoons (60 ml) water
>
> 3 **egg whites**
>
> 2 cups (475 ml) **heavy cream**

Grate the zest from the limes and set aside. Halve and squeeze the limes and set the juice aside. Puree the raspberries in a food processor or blender. Force the raspberries through a fine meshed sieve and discard the seeds. Set aside.

Combine the sugar with enough water to form "wet sand." Cook over medium-high heat until the syrup reaches 238 to 240°F (114° to 116°C) on a candy thermometer.

While the syrup is cooking, whip the egg whites to soft peak. With the mixer running, pour the hot syrup into the egg whites in a thin stream. Add the lime zest and continue to whip until the mixture is cool. Fold in the lime juice and the raspberry puree.

Whip the cream to soft peaks and whisk one-third of the whipped cream into the egg mixture. Gently, but thoroughly, fold the rest of the whipped cream in. Spoon into six 8-ounce soufflé cups fitted with parchment paper collars and freeze for at least 4 hours.

To serve, soften slightly at room temperature. Remove the paper collars.

YIELD: Serves 6

Strawberry Soufflé Glace

1 package (12 ounces, or 340 g) frozen unsweetened **strawberries**, thawed

2 **egg yolks**

1 cup (200 g) **sugar**

1 cup (235 ml) whole **milk**

2 cups (475 ml) **heavy cream**

Puree the strawberries and syrup in a food processor or blender. Force the puree through a fine mesh sieve. Set aside.

Whisk the egg yolks and 1/2 cup (100 g) of the sugar in a mixing bowl until fluffy. Heat the remaining sugar and the milk in a small saucepan until the sugar is dissolved and the milk is scalded. While whisking, pour the hot milk into the egg yolks in a thin stream. Return this mixture to the saucepan and cook over medium heat, stirring constantly, until the custard is thick enough to coat the back of a spoon. Pour the custard through a fine mesh strainer into a stainless steel bowl set in another container of ice water. Cool the custard completely.

Fold the strawberry puree into the custard.

Whip the cream to soft peaks and whisk one-third of the whipped cream into the custard mixture. Gently, but thoroughly, fold the rest of the whipped cream in. Spoon into six 8-ounce soufflé cups fitted with parchment paper collars and freeze for at least 4 hours.

To serve, soften slightly at room temperature. Remove the paper collars.

YIELD: Makes 6 servings

❦ Plum Soufflé Glace

Most of the bigger liquor stores will have plum wine; if not, they can order it for you.

Canned plums are in the canned fruit section of almost any supermarket.

> 1 can (14 ounces, or 400 g) **plums**
> 1 cup (200 g) **sugar**
> About 4 tablespoons (60 ml) water
> 3 **egg whites**
> 1/4 cup (60 ml) **Japanese plum wine**
> 2 cups (475 ml) **heavy cream**

Drain the plums, reserving 1/2 cup (120 ml) of the syrup. Puree the plums and reserved syrup in a blender or food processor and force the puree through a fine mesh strainer. Set aside.

Combine the sugar with enough water to form "wet sand." Cook over medium-high heat until the syrup reaches 238 to 240°F (114° to 116°C) on a candy thermometer.

While the syrup is cooking, whip the egg whites to soft peaks. With the mixer running, pour the hot syrup into the egg whites in a thin stream. Add the plum wine and continue to whip until the meringue is cool. Fold in the plum puree.

Whip the cream to stiff peaks and whisk one-third of the whipped cream into the egg mixture. Gently, but thoroughly, fold the rest of the whipped cream in. Spoon into six 8-ounce soufflé cups fitted with parchment paper collars and freeze for at least 4 hours.

To serve, soften slightly at room temperature. Remove the paper collars.

YIELD: Makes 6 servings

Chestnut Soufflé Glace

1 cup (200 g) **sugar**

About 4 tablespoons (60 ml) water

3 **egg whites**

1/4 cup (60 ml) **dark rum**

6 ounces (170 g) sweetened **chestnut paste**

2 cups (475 ml) **heavy cream**

Combine the sugar with enough water to form "wet sand." Cook over medium-high heat, not stirring, until the syrup reaches 238 to 240°F (114° to 116°C) on a candy thermometer.

While the syrup is cooking, whip the egg whites to soft peaks. With the mixer running, pour the hot syrup into the egg whites in a thin stream.

In a separate bowl, mix together the rum and chestnut paste until the chestnut paste is softened. Add to the egg mixture and whip until the mixture is cool.

Whip the cream to soft peaks and whisk 1/3 of the whipped cream into the egg mixture. Gently, but thoroughly, fold the rest of the whipped cream in. Spoon into six 8-ounce soufflé cups fitted with parchment paper collars and freeze for at least 4 hours.

To serve, soften slightly at room temperature. Remove the paper collars.

YIELD: Makes 6 servings

ADD IT! Drizzle melted semisweet chocolate over the soufflés just before serving.

Chocolate Soufflé Glace

Cold soufflés are light and airy, thanks to whisked egg whites and whipped cream. These make a dressy dessert with relatively low effort.

1 cup (200 g) **sugar**

About 4 tablespoons (60 ml) water

3 **egg whites**

1/4 cup (60 ml) **crème de cacao**

4 ounces (115 g) **semisweet chocolate**

2 cups (475 ml) **heavy cream**

Combine the sugar with enough water to form "wet sand." Cook over medium-high heat until the syrup reaches 238 to 240°F (114° to 116°C) on a candy thermometer.

While the syrup is cooking, whip the egg whites to soft peaks. With the mixer running, pour the hot syrup into the egg whites in a thin stream. Add the liqueur and continue to whip until the meringue is cool.

Melt the chocolate in a double boiler. Fold into the egg mixture.

Whip the cream to stiff peaks and whisk one-third of the whipped cream into the egg mixture. Gently, but thoroughly, fold the rest of the whipped cream in. Spoon into six 8-ounce soufflé cups fitted with parchment paper collars and freeze for at least 4 hours.

To serve, soften slightly at room temperature. Remove the paper collars.

YIELD: Makes 6 servings

ADD IT! Dust cocoa powder across the top of each soufflé.

Mocha Soufflé Glace

1 cup (200 g) **sugar**

About 4 tablespoons (120 ml) water

3 **egg whites**

1/4 cup (60 ml) **coffee brandy**

4 ounces (115 g) **semisweet chocolate**

2 cups (475 ml) **heavy cream**

Combine the sugar with enough water to form "wet sand." Cook over medium-high heat until the syrup reaches 238 to 240°F (114° to 116°) on a candy thermometer.

While the syrup is cooking, whip the egg whites to soft peaks. With the mixer running, pour the hot syrup into the egg whites in a thin stream. Add the brandy and continue to whip until the mixture is cool.

Melt the chocolate in a double boiler and fold the chocolate into the egg mixture.

Whip the cream to soft peaks and whisk one-third of the whipped cream into the egg mixture. Gently, but thoroughly, fold the rest of the whipped cream in. Spoon into six 8-ounce soufflé cups fitted with parchment paper collars and freeze for at least 4 hours.

To serve, soften slightly at room temperature. Remove the paper collars.

YIELD: Makes 6 servings

Chocolate-Hazelnut Soufflé Glace

1 cup (200 g) **sugar**

About 4 tablespoons (60 ml) water

3 **egg whites**

1/4 cup (60 ml) **Frangelica**

4 ounces (115 g) **semisweet chocolate**

2 cups (475 ml) **heavy cream**

Combine the sugar with enough water to form "wet sand." Cook over medium-high heat until the syrup reaches 238 to 240°F (114° to 116°C) on a candy thermometer.

While the syrup is cooking, whip the egg whites to soft peaks. With the mixer running, pour the hot syrup into the egg whites in a thin stream. Add the liqueur and continue to whip until the meringue is cool.

Melt the chocolate in a double boiler. Fold the chocolate into the egg mixture. Whip the cream to soft peaks and whisk one-third of the whipped cream into the egg mixture. Gently, but thoroughly, fold the rest of the whipped cream in. Spoon into six 8-ounce soufflé cups fitted with parchment paper collars and freeze for at least 4 hours.

To serve, soften slightly at room temperature. Remove the paper collars.

YIELD: Makes 6 servings

Grand Marnier Soufflé Glace

Another of the airy cold soufflés, this one has the sophisticated taste of bitter orange.

> 1 cup (200 g) **sugar**
>
> About 4 tablespoons (60 ml) water
>
> 3 **egg whites**
>
> 1/4 cup (60 ml) **Grand Marnier**
>
> 1/2 cup (160 g) **orange marmalade**
>
> 2 cups (475 ml) **heavy cream**

Combine the sugar with enough water to form "wet sand." Cook over medium-high heat until the syrup reaches 238 to 240°F (114° to 116°C) on a candy thermometer.

While the syrup is cooking, whip the egg whites to soft peaks. With the mixer running, pour the hot syrup into the egg whites in a thin stream. Add the Grand Marnier and continue to whip until the mixture is cool. Fold in the marmalade.

Whip the cream to stiff peaks and whisk one-third of the whipped cream into the egg mixture. Gently, but thoroughly, fold the rest of the whipped cream in. Spoon into six 8-ounce soufflé cups fitted with parchment paper collars and freeze for at least 4 hours.

To serve, soften slightly at room temperature. Remove the paper collars.

YIELD: Serves 6

Bombe Syrup

This is a syrup recipe that we will use as a base in our bombe recipes.

> 1 cup (200 g) sugar
>
> 1/3 cup (75 ml) water

Combine the sugar and water in a small saucepan and heat over high heat until the mixture boils and the sugar is dissolved. Cool and store in the refrigerator, covered.

YIELD: Makes about 1/2 cup (120 ml)

Bombe Noisette

A bombe is a classic French dessert in which ice cream or sherbet is layered around a custard center. This one is built around hazelnut ice cream.

1 pint (285 g) **hazelnut ice cream**

3 **egg yolks**

3 ounces (90 ml) **Bombe Syrup** (page 296)

2 ounces (55 g) **bittersweet chocolate**, melted

1/2 cup (120 ml) **heavy cream**

Freeze a 1-quart bombe mold. (If you don't have a bombe mold, any shape mold, or a small stainless steel mixing bowl will do.)

Slightly soften the ice cream and spread a layer about 3/4-inch thick all around the inside of the mold. Freeze for at least 1 hour.

Put the egg yolks in a stainless steel mixing bowl and whisk them. Slowly whisk in the bombe syrup. Place the bowl over a pan of simmering water and whisk until the mixture becomes thick and creamy, the texture of a hollandaise sauce. Remove from the heat. Set the bowl in an ice water bath and whisk until the mixture is cold. Whisk in the melted chocolate.

In a separate bowl, whip the cream to soft peaks and fold into the egg mixture. Spoon into the center of the bombe mold and freeze for at least 4 hours.

To serve, briefly dip the bombe mold in hot water and then flip the bombe out of the mold onto a serving platter. Slice.

YIELD: Serves 6 to 8

❦ Bombe Tropical

A bombe is a classic French dessert in which ice cream or sherbet is layered around a custard center. This one is built around tropical flavors.

1 package (12 ounces, or 340 g) **coconut macaroons**

1 pint (285 g) **pineapple sherbet**

3 **egg yolks**

3 ounces (90 ml) **Bombe Syrup** (page 296)

1/2 cup (120 ml) **heavy cream**

Spray a 1-quart bombe mold (or other mold of your choice) with pan coating. Crumble the macaroons and thinly coat the inside of the mold with half of them, reserving the rest. Freeze the mold for 1 hour. Slightly soften the sherbet and spread it about 3/4-inch thick all around the inside of the mold, covering the cookie crumbs. Freeze for at least 1 hour.

Put the egg yolks in a stainless steel mixing bowl and whisk them. Slowly whisk in the bombe syrup. Place the bowl over a pan of simmering water and whisk until the mixture becomes thick and creamy, the texture of a hollandaise sauce. Remove from the heat. Set the bowl in an ice water bath and whisk until the mixture is cold. Whisk in the remaining macaroon crumbles.

In a separate bowl, whip the cream to soft peaks and fold into the egg mixture. Spoon into the center of the bombe mold and freeze for at least 4 hours.

To serve, briefly dip the bombe mold in hot water and then flip the bombe out of the mold onto a serving platter. Slice.

YIELD: Serves 6 to 8

Orange-Pineapple Bombe

We know there has to be a joke about Bombes Away! in here someplace...

> 1 pint (285 g) **orange sherbet**
>
> 3 **egg yolks**
>
> 3 ounces (90 ml) **Bombe Syrup** (page 296)
>
> 1 can (10 ounces, or 280 g) chopped **pineapple** in juice
>
> 1/2 cup (120 ml) **heavy cream**

Freeze a 1-quart bombe mold or other mold of your choice. Slightly soften the sherbet and line the bombe mold about 3/4-inch thick all around. Freeze for at least 1 hour.

Put the egg yolks in a stainless steel mixing bowl and whisk them. Slowly whisk in the bombe syrup. Place the bowl over a pan of simmering water and whisk until the mixture becomes thick and creamy, the texture of a hollandaise sauce. Remove from the heat. Set the bowl in an ice water bath and whisk until the mixture is cold. Drain the pineapple, reserving the juice. Whisk the juice into the bombe mixture.

Whip the cream to soft peaks and fold into the egg mixture. Fold in the pineapple tidbits. Spoon into the center of the bombe mold and freeze for at least 4 hours.

To serve, briefly dip the bombe mold in hot water and then flip the bombe out of the mold onto a serving platter. Slice.

YIELD: Serves 6 to 8

☙ Strawberry-Lemon Bombe

Try this for a light finish to an early summer meal.

> 1 pint (285 g) **lemon sorbet**
>
> 3 **egg yolks**
>
> 3 ounces (90 ml) **Bombe Syrup** (page 296)
>
> 1 pint (350 g) **strawberries**, hulled and pureed, reserving 3 to 4 berries
>
> 1/2 cup (120 ml) **heavy cream**

Freeze a 1-quart bombe mold or other mold of your choice. Slightly soften the sorbet and line the bombe mold about 3/4-inch thick all around. Freeze for at least 1 hour.

Whisk the egg yolks in a stainless steel mixing bowl. Slowly whisk in the bombe syrup. Place the bowl over a pan of simmering water and whisk until the mixture becomes thick and creamy, the texture of a hollandaise sauce. Remove from the heat. Set the bowl in an ice water bath and whisk until the mixture is cold. Whisk in the strawberry puree.

Whip the cream to soft peaks and fold into the egg mixture. Slice the reserved strawberries and fold them in. Spoon into the center of the bombe mold and freeze for at least 4 hours.

To serve, briefly dip the bombe mold in hot water and then flip the bombe out of the mold onto a serving platter. Slice.

YIELD: Serves 6 to 8

Chocolate Malted Bombe

This is a classy dessert with the flavor of a chocolate malted.

> 1 pint (285 g) **vanilla ice cream**
>
> 2 cups (7 ounces, or 200 g) **malted milk balls**
>
> 3 **egg yolks**
>
> 3 ounces (90 ml) **Bombe Syrup** (page 296)
>
> 1/2 cup (120 ml) **heavy cream**

Freeze a 1-quart bombe mold, or whatever mold you choose to use. Slightly soften the ice cream and line the bombe mold about 3/4-inch thick all around. Freeze for at least 1 hour.

Grind 1 cup of the malted milk balls in a food processor. Put the ground malted milk balls in a small saucepan and add 2 tablespoons (28 ml) water. Cook over low heat until the mixture is melted and smooth. Set aside in a warm place. Coarsely chop the remaining malted milk balls and set them aside.

Put the egg yolks in a stainless steel mixing bowl and whisk them. Slowly whisk in the bombe syrup. Place the bowl over a pan of simmering water and whisk until the mixture becomes thick and creamy, the texture of a hollandaise sauce. Remove from the heat. Set the bowl in an ice water bath and whisk until the mixture is cold. Whisk in the melted milk ball mixture.

Whip the cream to soft peaks and fold into the egg mixture. Fold in the chopped candy. Spoon into the center of the bombe mold and freeze for at least 4 hours.

To serve, briefly dip the bombe mold in hot water and then flip the bombe out of the mold onto a serving platter. Slice.

YIELD: Serves 6 to 8

❦ Mocha Bombe

This bombe is built around the timeless mix of chocolate and coffee.

> 1 pint (285 g) **chocolate ice cream**
>
> 3 **egg yolks**
>
> 3 ounces (90 ml) **Bombe Syrup** (page 296)
>
> 1 ounce (14 ml) **coffee brandy**
>
> 1/2 cup (120 ml) **heavy cream**

Freeze a 1-quart bombe mold. Slightly soften the ice cream and line the bombe mold about 3/4-inch thick all around. Freeze for at least 1 hour.

Put the egg yolks in a stainless steel mixing bowl and whisk them. Slowly whisk in the bombe syrup. Place the bowl over a pan of simmering water and whisk until the mixture becomes thick and creamy, the texture of a hollandaise sauce. Remove from the heat. Whisk in the coffee brandy. Set the bowl in an ice water bath and whisk until the mixture is cold.

Whip the cream to soft peaks and fold into the egg mixture. Spoon into the center of the bombe mold and freeze for at least 4 hours.

To serve, briefly dip the bombe mold in hot water and then flip the bombe out of the mold onto a serving platter. Slice.

YIELD: Serves 6 to 8

French Vanilla Ice Cream

Despite all the fancy mix-ins out there, vanilla ice cream will never go out of style. In fact, it remains the most popular flavor out there.

1 cup (235 ml) whole **milk**

3 cups (705 ml) **heavy cream**

3/4 cup (150 g) **sugar**

4 **egg yolks**

2 teaspoons **vanilla extract**

In a heavy bottomed 2-quart saucepan, heat the milk, cream, and sugar over medium-high heat, stirring occasionally, until the sugar is dissolved and the mixture is scalded.

Whisk the egg yolks in a mixing bowl. Pour the hot milk mixture into the egg yolks in a thin stream while whisking. Return the mixture to the saucepan and reduce the heat to medium. Cook, stirring constantly, until the mixture thickens enough to coat the back of a spoon. Do not allow it to boil. Remove from the heat and stir in the vanilla. Pass the mixture through a fine strainer into the ice cream freezer. Freeze in an ice cream maker according to the manufacturer's instructions.

YIELD: Makes 1 quart

Italian Almond Ice Cream

You can make this suitable for kids by substituting 1 teaspoon of almond extract for the amaretto.

3 cups (475 ml) **heavy cream**

3/4 cup (150 g) **sugar**

4 **egg yolks**

1/4 cup (60 ml) **amaretto**

1 cup (90 g) **almond slices**, toasted

In a heavy bottomed 2-quart saucepan, heat the cream and sugar over medium-high heat, stirring occasionally, until the sugar is dissolved and the mixture is scalded.

Whisk the egg yolks in a mixing bowl. Pour the hot milk mixture into the egg yolks in a thin stream while whisking. Return the mixture to the saucepan and reduce the heat to medium. Cook, stirring constantly, until the mixture thickens enough to coat the back of a spoon. Do not allow it to boil. Remove from the heat and stir in the amaretto. Pass the mixture through a fine strainer into the ice cream freezer. Freeze in an ice cream maker according to the manufacturer's instructions. Add the almonds when the ice cream is partially frozen.

YIELD: Makes 1 quart

Fresh Peach Ice Cream

We grew up a 2-minute walk from Benson's Ice Cream in West Boxford, Massachusetts, which we can objectively state has the best ice cream in the universe. They make seasonal fruit ice creams, and we've always loved their fresh peach ice cream. The fresher and juicier the peaches, the better the ice cream.

1 pound (455 g) **peaches**

1/2 cup (100 g) **sugar**

1 cup (235 ml) whole **milk**

2 cups (475 ml) **heavy cream**

1 teaspoon **vanilla extract**

Bring a pot of water to a boil. Drop the peaches in for 30 seconds, then drain and run them under cold water. Peel the peaches, remove the stones, and cut into thin slices. Reserve half the slices and put the rest into a food processor and process to a puree.

Combine the sugar and milk in a 1-quart saucepan. Cook over medium heat until the sugar is dissolved. Remove from the heat and stir in the cream and vanilla.

Stir the peach puree and the slices into the ice cream base and put it into the ice cream maker. Freeze in an ice cream maker according to the manufacturer's instructions.

YIELD: Makes 1 quart

Strawberry Ice Cream

Fresh strawberry ice cream is a real springtime treat.

> 1/2 cup (100 g) **sugar**
> 1 cup (235 ml) whole **milk**
> 2 cups (475 ml) **heavy cream**
> 1 teaspoon **vanilla extract**
> 1 pint (350 g) **strawberries**, hulled and thinly sliced

Combine the sugar and the milk in a 1-quart saucepan. Cook over medium heat until the sugar is dissolved. Remove from the heat and stir in the cream and vanilla.

Reserve half of the strawberries and put the rest into a food processor and process to a puree. Stir the strawberry puree and the slices into the ice cream base and put it into the ice cream maker. Freeze in an ice cream maker according to the manufacturer's instructions.

YIELD: Makes 1 quart

Black Raspberry Ice Cream

> 1/2 cup (100 g) **sugar**
>
> 1 cup (235 ml) **whole milk**
>
> 2 cups (475 ml) **heavy cream**
>
> 1 teaspoon **vanilla extract**
>
> 1 pint (300 g) **black raspberries**

Combine the sugar and milk in a 1-quart saucepan. Cook over medium heat until the sugar is dissolved. Remove from the heat and stir in the cream and vanilla.

Put half the raspberries into a food processor and process to a puree. Stir the raspberry puree and the whole raspberries into the ice cream base and put it into the ice cream maker. Freeze in an ice cream maker according to manufacturer's instructions.

YIELD: Makes 1 quart

Chai Tea Ice Cream

Chai's gently spicy taste is very trendy these days, and it translates beautifully to ice cream.

> 1 cup (235 ml) whole **milk**
>
> 2 cups (475 ml) **heavy cream**
>
> 1/2 cup (100 g) **sugar**
>
> 1 cup (235 ml) liquid **chai tea concentrate**
>
> 1 teaspoon **vanilla extract**

In a heavy bottomed 2-quart saucepan, heat the milk, cream, and sugar over medium-high heat, stirring occasionally, until the sugar is dissolved and the mixture is scalded. Stir in the chai concentrate and vanilla. Freeze in an ice cream maker according to the manufacturer's instructions.

YIELD: Makes 1 quart

Butter Pecan Ice Cream

Butter pecan is a gentle, old-fashioned flavor that is one of our favorites.

  1 cup (200 g) **sugar**

  1 cup (235 ml) whole **milk**

  1/4 cup (1/2 stick, or 44 g) butter

  2 cups (475 ml) **heavy cream**

  1 teaspoon **vanilla extract**

  1 cup (100 g) **pecan pieces**

Combine the sugar and the milk in a 1-quart saucepan. Cook over medium heat until the sugar is dissolved. Add the butter and stir until just melted. Remove from the heat and stir in the cream and vanilla.

Freeze in an ice cream maker according to the manufacturer's instructions, stirring in the pecans when the ice cream is partially frozen.

YIELD: Makes 1 quart

Toffee Crunch Ice Cream

  1/2 cup (100 g) **sugar**

  1 cup (235 ml) whole **milk**

  2 cups (475 ml) **heavy cream**

  1 teaspoon **vanilla extract**

  1 package (12 ounces, or 340 g) **toffee bits**

Combine the sugar and milk in a 1-quart saucepan. Cook over medium heat until the sugar is dissolved. Remove from the heat and stir in the cream and vanilla. Freeze in an ice cream maker according to the manufacturer's instructions, adding the toffee bits when the ice cream is partially frozen.

YIELD: Makes 1 quart

Coconut Ice Cream

1 cup (235 ml) **whole milk**

1 cup (235 ml) **heavy cream**

3/4 cup (150 g) **sugar**

1 cup (235 ml) **coconut milk**

1 cup (175 g) **sweetened shredded coconut**

In a heavy bottomed 2-quart saucepan, heat the milk, cream, and sugar over medium-high heat, stirring occasionally, until the sugar is dissolved and the mixture is scalded. Stir in the coconut milk and coconut. Freeze in an ice cream maker according to the manufacturer's instructions.

YIELD: Makes 1 quart

ADD IT! Pour some pureed mango over the top of each dish when serving.

Cinnamon Ice Cream

This is the best on an apple crisp or pie.

> 1 cup (235 ml) whole **milk**
>
> 3 cups (705 ml) **heavy cream**
>
> 3/4 cup (150 g) **sugar**
>
> 4 **egg yolks**
>
> 2 teaspoons **cinnamon**

In a heavy bottomed 2-quart saucepan, heat the milk, cream, and sugar over medium-high heat, stirring occasionally, until the sugar is dissolved and the mixture is scalded.

Whisk the egg yolks in a mixing bowl. Pour the hot milk mixture into the egg yolks in a thin stream while whisking. Return the mixture to the saucepan and reduce the heat to medium. Cook, stirring constantly, until the mixture thickens enough to coat the back of a spoon. Do not allow it to boil. Remove from the heat and stir in the cinnamon. Pass the mixture through a fine strainer into the ice cream freezer. Freeze in an ice cream maker according to the manufacturer's instructions.

YIELD: Makes 1 quart

Rich Chocolate Ice Cream

This one is for the serious chocolate lover.

- 8 ounces (225 g) **semisweet chocolate**, chopped into small pieces
- 1 cup (235 ml) whole **milk**
- 3 cups (705 ml) **heavy cream**
- 1/2 cup (100 g) **sugar**
- 4 **egg yolks**

Melt the chocolate in a double boiler. Set aside.

In a heavy bottomed 2-quart saucepan, heat the milk, cream, and sugar over medium-high heat, stirring occasionally, until the sugar is dissolved and the mixture is scalded.

Whisk the egg yolks in a mixing bowl. Pour the hot milk mixture into the egg yolks in a thin stream while whisking. Return the mixture to the saucepan and reduce the heat to medium. Cook, stirring constantly, until the mixture thickens enough to coat the back of a spoon. Do not allow it to boil. Remove from the heat and stir in the melted chocolate. Pass the mixture through a fine strainer into the ice cream freezer. Freeze in an ice cream maker according to the manufacturer's instructions.

YIELD: Makes 1 quart

Chocolate-Chocolate Chip Ice Cream

12 ounces (340 g) **semisweet chocolate chips**

1 cup (235 ml) whole **milk**

3 cups (705 ml) **heavy cream**

1/2 cup (100 g) **sugar**

4 **egg yolks**

Melt 8 ounces (225 g) of the chocolate in a double boiler. Set aside.

In a heavy bottomed 2-quart saucepan, heat the milk, cream, and sugar over medium-high heat, stirring occasionally, until the sugar is dissolved and the mixture is scalded.

Whisk the egg yolks together in a mixing bowl. Whisking constantly, pour the hot milk mixture into the egg yolks in a thin stream. Return the mixture to the pot and reduce the heat to medium. Cook, stirring constantly, until the mixture thickens enough to coat the back of a spoon. Do not allow it to boil. Remove from the heat and stir in the melted chocolate. Pass the mixture through a fine strainer into the ice cream freezer. Freeze in an ice cream maker according to the manufacturer's instructions, adding the reserved chocolate chips when the ice cream is partially frozen.

YIELD: Makes 1 quart

Mocha Chip Ice Cream

This is Carol's personal favorite ice cream flavor ever, and not an easy one to find, might we add.

> 1/2 cup (100 g) **sugar**
>
> 1 cup (235 ml) **whole milk**
>
> 2 cups (475 ml) **heavy cream**
>
> 1 cup (235 ml) **coffee syrup**
>
> 1 package (12 ounces, or 340 g) **semisweet chocolate chips**

Combine the sugar and milk in a 1-quart saucepan. Cook over medium heat until the sugar is dissolved. Remove from the heat and stir in the cream and coffee syrup. Freeze in an ice cream maker according to the manufacturer's instructions, adding the chocolate chips when the ice cream is partially frozen.

YIELD: Makes 1 quart

Cookies and Cream Ice Cream

We remember when a crumbled cookie mix-in was a novelty; now it's a classic.

1/2 cup (100 g) **sugar**

1 cup (235 ml) whole **milk**

2 cups (475 ml) **heavy cream**

1 teaspoon **vanilla extract**

8 ounces (225 g) **chocolate sandwich cookies**, crushed

Combine the sugar and the milk in a 1-quart saucepan. Cook over medium heat until the sugar is dissolved. Remove from the heat and stir in the cream and the vanilla.

Freeze in an ice cream maker according to the manufacturer's instructions, stirring in the cookie pieces when the ice cream is partially frozen.

YIELD: Makes 1 quart

Chocolate–Grand Marnier Ice Cream

Deep chocolate and flavorful orange make for a classy frozen treat.

> 8 ounces (225 g) **semisweet chocolate**
> 1 cup (235 ml) whole **milk**
> 3 cups (705 ml) **heavy cream**
> 1/2 cup (120 ml) **Grand Marnier** or other orange liqueur
> 4 **egg yolks**

Melt the chocolate in a double boiler. Set aside.

In a heavy bottomed 2-quart saucepan, heat the milk, cream, and liqueur over medium-high heat, stirring occasionally, until the mixture is scalded.

Whisk the egg yolks together in a mixing bowl. Pour the hot milk mixture into the egg yolks in a thin stream while whisking. Return the mixture to the pot and reduce the heat to medium. Cook, stirring constantly, until the mixture thickens enough to coat the back of a spoon. Do not allow it to boil. Remove from the heat and stir in the melted chocolate. Pass the mixture through a fine strainer into the ice cream freezer. Freeze in an ice cream maker according to the manufacturer's instructions.

YIELD: Makes 1 1/2 quarts

Rum~Raisin Ice Cream

Here's another classic old-fashioned flavor.

> 3 cups (705 ml) **heavy cream**
> 3/4 cup (150 g) **sugar**
> 4 **egg yolks**
> 2 tablespoons (28 ml) **rum extract**
> 1 cup (145 g) **raisins**

In a heavy bottomed 2-quart saucepan, heat the cream and sugar over medium-high heat, stirring occasionally, until the sugar is dissolved and the mixture is scalded.

Whisk the egg yolks in a mixing bowl. Pour the hot cream mixture into the egg yolks in a thin stream while whisking. Return the mixture to the saucepan and reduce the heat to medium. Cook, stirring constantly, until the mixture thickens enough to coat the back of a spoon. Do not allow it to boil. Remove from the heat and stir in the rum extract. Pass the mixture through a fine strainer into the ice cream freezer. Freeze in an ice cream maker according to the manufacturer's instructions. Add the raisins when the ice cream is partially frozen.

YIELD: Makes 1 quart

Lavender Ice Cream

A bit unusual, but it's great on a peach cobbler. Besides, who can resist purple ice cream?

We buy lavender in the spice section of the local food co-op, and we've also used fresh-from-the garden lavender.

- 1 cup (200 g) **sugar**
- 1 ounce (28 g) dried **lavender flowers**
- 1 cup (235 ml) water
- 1 cup (235 ml) whole **milk**
- 2 cups (475 ml) **heavy cream**
- 2 teaspoons **vanilla extract**

Combine the sugar, lavender flowers, and water in a 1-quart saucepan. Cook over medium heat until the sugar is dissolved and the mixture is syrupy and lightly purple. Remove from the heat and allow to sit for 1 hour. Strain the flowers out and discard them. Add the milk, cream, and vanilla. Freeze in an ice cream maker according to the manufacturer's instructions.

YIELD: Makes 1 quart

Maple Ice Cream

Up in Vermont there is this cult about Maple Creamees. We like this homemade, hard ice cream version better.

> 1 cup (235 ml) whole **milk**
>
> 3 cups (705 ml) **heavy cream**
>
> 3/4 cup (150 ml) **sugar**
>
> 4 **egg yolks**
>
> 1/2 cup (120 ml) **maple syrup**

In a heavy bottomed 2-quart saucepan, heat the milk, cream, and sugar over medium-high heat, stirring occasionally, until the sugar is dissolved and the mixture is scalded.

Whisk the egg yolks and maple syrup together in a mixing bowl. Pour the hot milk mixture into the egg yolks in a thin stream while whisking. Return the mixture to the saucepan and reduce the heat to medium. Cook, stirring constantly, until the mixture thickens enough to coat the back of a spoon. Do not allow it to boil. Pass the mixture through a fine strainer into the ice cream freezer. Freeze in an ice cream maker according to the manufacturer's instructions.

YIELD: Makes 1 1/2 quarts

Pumpkin-Marshmallow Ice Cream

1 cup (235 ml) whole **milk**

3 cups (705 ml) **heavy cream**

4 **egg yolks**

1 cup (270 g) canned **sweetened and spiced pumpkin**

1 cup (100 g) **mini marshmallows**

In a heavy bottomed 2-quart saucepan, heat the milk and the cream over medium-high heat until the mixture is scalded.

Whisk the egg yolks in a mixing bowl. Pour the hot milk mixture into the egg yolks in a thin stream while whisking. Return the mixture to the saucepan and reduce the heat to medium. Cook, stirring constantly, until the mixture thickens enough to coat the back of a spoon. Do not allow it to boil. Remove from the heat and stir in the pumpkin. Freeze in an ice cream maker according to the manufacturer's instructions, adding the marshmallows when the ice cream is partially frozen.

YIELD: Makes 1^1/2 quarts

Frozen Pudding

A taste of old-fashioned ice cream—this flavor is one of our dad's favorites.

> 3 cups (705 ml) **heavy cream**
> 3/4 cup (150 g) **sugar**
> 4 **egg yolks**
> 2 tablespoons (28 ml) **rum extract**
> 1 cup (220 g) chopped fruit cake **candied fruit mix**

In a heavy bottomed 2-quart saucepan, heat the cream and sugar over medium-high heat, stirring occasionally, until the sugar is dissolved and the mixture is scalded.

Whisk the egg yolks in a mixing bowl. Whisking constantly, pour the hot cream mixture into the egg yolks in a thin stream. Return the mixture to the saucepan and reduce the heat to medium. Cook, stirring constantly, until the mixture thickens enough to coat the back of a spoon. Do not allow it to boil. Remove from the heat and stir in the rum extract. Pass the mixture through a fine strainer into the ice cream freezer. Freeze in an ice cream maker according to the manufacturer's instructions. Add the dried fruit when the ice cream is partially frozen.

YIELD: Makes 1 quart

Orange-Spice Ice Cream Sandwiches

Since we are using sherbet, this is not technically an ice cream sandwich, but sherbet sandwich just doesn't have the same ring to it. No matter the name, the result is fabulous. We find that these are better made 2 to 3 days ahead of time, so that the cookies soften.

1/2 cup (1 stick, or 112 g) butter

3/4 cup (170 g) packed **light brown sugar**

1 cup (120 g) **all-purpose flour**

2 tablespoons **cornstarch**

3 teaspoons **pumpkin pie spice**

1/4 teaspoon salt

1 pint (285 g) **orange sherbet**

Using a mixer on medium speed, cream together the butter and sugar for 8 to 10 minutes, until smooth and fluffy.

Sift together the flour, cornstarch, pumpkin pie spice, and salt. Stir this into the butter mixture until thoroughly combined. Wrap the dough in plastic and refrigerate for 1 hour.

Preheat the oven to 350°F (180°C, gas mark 4). Cover a baking sheet with parchment paper.

Lightly flour a flat surface and roll out the dough 1/8-inch thick. Cut out 10 rounds 3 inches across each. Put the rounds on the baking sheet.

Bake for 20 to 25 minutes, until golden brown. Cool completely.

Lay out five of the cookies, with the sides that were down during baking now up. Divide the sherbet among the cookies, then press the other five cookies on top of the sherbet. Freeze for at least 3 hours.

YIELD: Serves 5

Butter Pecan Ice Cream Sandwiches

We find that these are better made 2 to 3 days ahead of time, so that the cookie softens.

1/2 cup (1 stick, or 112 g) butter
3/4 cup (170 g) packed **light brown sugar**
1 cup (120 g) **all-purpose flour**
2 tablespoons **cornstarch**
1/4 teaspoon salt
2 teaspoons **vanilla extract**
1 pint (285 g) **Butter Pecan Ice Cream** (page 308), slightly softened

Using a mixer on medium speed, cream together the butter and sugar for 5 to 6 minutes, until smooth and fluffy.

In a separate bowl, sift together the flour, cornstarch, and salt. Stir this into the butter mixture until thoroughly combined. Add the vanilla and mix for another minute. Wrap the dough in plastic and refrigerate for 1 hour.

Preheat the oven to 350°F (180°C, gas mark 4). Line a cookie sheet with parchment paper.

Lightly flour a flat surface and roll out the dough 1/8-inch thick. Cut out 10 rounds 3 inches across each. Put the rounds on the cookie sheet.

Bake for 20 to 25 minutes. Cool completely.

Lay out five of the cookies, with the sides that were down during baking now up. Divide the ice cream among the cookies, then press the other five cookies on top of the ice cream. Freeze for at least 3 hours.

YIELD: Serves 5

Chocolate-Hazelnut Gelato Sandwiches

We find that these are better made 2 to 3 days ahead of time, so that the cookie softens.

> 1/2 cup (1 stick, or 112 g) butter
>
> 3/4 cup (150 g) **sugar**
>
> 3/4 cup (90 g) **all-purpose flour**
>
> 2 tablespoons (15 g) **cornstarch**
>
> 1/4 cup (45 g) **cocoa powder**
>
> 1/4 teaspoon salt
>
> 1 pint (285 g) **hazelnut gelato**

Using a mixer on medium speed, cream together the butter and sugar for 5 to 6 minutes, until smooth and fluffy.

In a separate bowl, sift together the flour, cornstarch, cocoa powder, and salt. Stir this into the butter mixture until thoroughly combined. Wrap the dough in plastic and refrigerate for 1 hour.

Preheat the oven to 350°F (180°C, gas mark 4). Line a baking sheet with parchment paper.

Lightly flour a flat surface and roll out the dough 1/8-inch thick. Cut out 10 rounds 3 inches across each. Put the rounds on the baking sheet.

Bake for 20 to 25 minutes. Cool completely.

Lay out five of the cookies, with the sides that were down during baking now up. Divide the gelato among the cookies, then press the other five cookies on top of the gelato. Freeze for at least 3 hours.

YIELD: Serves 5

Waffle Ice Cream Sandwiches

8 frozen **waffles**, thawed

1 pint (285 g) **vanilla ice cream**

1/2 cup (120 ml) **chocolate syrup**

1/2 cup (60 g) chopped **walnuts**

Lay out four of the waffles and divide the ice cream among them, spreading it out. Pour the syrup over the ice cream and sprinkle with the nuts. Top with the other four waffles and press onto the ice cream. Freeze for 2 to 3 hours.

YIELD: Serves 4

Dessert Tacos

With the bright green ice cream and vibrant red sauce, these are a visual as well as taste treat.

4 **taco shells**

1/2 cup (100 g) **cinnamon sugar** (See "Making Cinnamon Sugar" on page 12.)

1 pint (285 g) **pistachio ice cream**

1 cup (235 ml) **Strawberry Sauce** (page 485) or store-bought strawberry sauce

1/2 cup **sweetened shredded coconut**

Brush the taco shells lightly with water and sprinkle with the sugar. Allow to dry. Fill the taco shells with the ice cream and top with the strawberry sauce and coconut.

YIELD: Serves 4

Ice Cream Truffles

This is a novelty that the whole family will enjoy.

> 1 pint (285 g) **chocolate ice cream**
> 1/4 cup (25 g) **candied orange peel**, finely minced
> 4 ounces (115 g) **Nabisco Famous Chocolate Wafer Cookies**
> 2 ounces (55 g) **paraffin**
> 6 ounces (170 g) **semisweet chocolate**

Soften the ice cream in the refrigerator for 1 hour. In a mixing bowl, combine the ice cream and the orange peel, mixing until well combined. Cover a baking sheet with waxed paper and, using a small ice cream scoop, make small balls of the ice cream, dropping them onto the waxed paper. You should have about 16 balls. Freeze for 1 hour.

Put the chocolate wafers in a food processor fit with the metal blade and process until there are fine crumbs. Put the crumbs into a pie pan. Roll the ice cream balls in your hands to round them smoothly and roll them in the cookie crumbs. Replace the balls on the waxed paper and freeze for 2 hours.

Melt the paraffin and the chocolate together in a double boiler and stir until smooth. Remove from the heat and allow to cool, but not to solidify. Dip the ice cream balls into the chocolate using 2 forks or spoons. Replace on the waxed paper and freeze for 2 to 3 hours.

YIELD: Makes 16 pieces

Ice Cream and Strawberry Crepes

We generally run into crepes in the produce aisle of the grocery store, particularly during berry season.

    1 quart (570 g) **vanilla ice cream**

    12 store-bought **crepes**

    1 package (16 ounces, or 455 g) frozen **strawberries** in syrup, thawed

    1 cup (235 ml) **heavy cream**

    2 tablespoons (25 g) **vanilla sugar** (See "Making Vanilla Sugar" on page 12.)

Soften the ice cream in the refrigerator for 1 hour. Lay out the crepes on a flat surface and spread 1/3 cup or so of ice cream on the center of each. Roll up the crepes and put them on a baking sheet lined with waxed paper. Freeze for at least 1 hour.

Puree the strawberries and syrup in a food processor. Divide the puree among 6 plates, reserving 1/2 cup.

Whip the cream with the sugar to soft peaks. Put 2 rolled crepes on top of the puree on each plate. Spoon the reserved puree over and top with whipped cream. Serve immediately.

YIELD: Serves 6

Mocha Crunch Crepes

1 quart (570 g) **coffee ice cream**

2 cups (350 g) **semisweet chocolate chips**

12 store-bought **crepes**

1 1/2 cups (355 ml) **heavy cream**

2 tablespoons (25 g) **vanilla sugar** (See "Making Vanilla Sugar" on page 12.)

Soften the ice cream in the refrigerator for 1 hour.

In a mixing bowl, combine the ice cream and 1 cup (175 g) of the chocolate chips, stirring until the chips are evenly distributed in the ice cream. Lay out the crepes on a flat surface and spread 1/3 cup or so of ice cream on the center of each. Roll up the crepes and put them on a baking sheet lined with waxed paper. Freeze for at least 1 hour.

In a double boiler, combine the rest of the chocolate chips and 1/2 cup (120 ml) of the cream. Stir occasionally until melted and smooth.

In a separate bowl, whip the remaining 1 cup (235 ml) cream with the sugar to soft peaks. Divide the chocolate sauce among 6 plates, reserving 1/2 cup. Put 2 rolled crepes on top of the chocolate on each plate. Spoon the reserved chocolate over and top with whipped cream. Serve immediately.

YIELD: Serves 6

Chocolate Toffee Cigars

We generally find crepes in the produce aisle of the grocery store, particularly during berry season.

> 1 quart (570 g) **vanilla ice cream**
>
> 12 store-bought **crepes**
>
> 2 cups (350 g) **semisweet chocolate chips**
>
> 2 tablespoons (1/4 stick, or 28 g) butter
>
> 2 cups (350 g) **toffee bits**

Soften the ice cream in the refrigerator for 1 hour. Lay out the crepes on a flat surface and spread 1/3 cup or so of ice cream on the center of each. Roll up the crepes and put them on a baking sheet lined with waxed paper. Freeze for at least 1 hour.

In a stainless steel pan set over boiling water, melt the chocolate chips. Stir in the butter until melted. Put the toffee bits into a wide shallow bowl. Using two forks, carefully and quickly dip each crepe into the chocolate and then roll in the toffee bits. Put back on baking sheet and refreeze for several hours.

YIELD: Serves 6

Profiteroles

Like éclairs, except filled with ice cream. Pâte choux is really easy to make. Once you get the hang of it, you will find lots of reasons to whip up a batch.

> 1 (235 ml) cup **milk**
> 1/2 cup (1 stick, or 112 g) butter
> 1/2 teaspoon salt
> 1 cup (120 g) **all-purpose flour**
> 4 **eggs**
> 1 pint (285 g) **vanilla ice cream**, or other favorite ice cream flavor
> 1 cup (235 ml) **Chocolate Sauce** (page 492), or store-bought chocolate sauce

Preheat the oven to 350°F (180°C, gas mark 4). Line a baking sheet with parchment paper.

Combine the milk, butter, and salt in a 2-quart saucepan and place over medium heat. Cook until the butter is melted and the liquid is at a simmer. Stir in the flour all at once with a wooden spoon until the dough forms a ball and pulls away from the sides of the pan. Remove from the heat and put it into a mixing bowl. Beat in the eggs, one at a time, using the paddle attachment of a stand mixer if you have one. Beat until each egg is fully incorporated and the dough is no longer "wet" before adding another.

Put the dough into a pastry bag fitted with a 1/2-inch round tip and pipe out about twenty 1-inch round mounds on the baking sheet.

Bake for 15 to 20 minutes, until puffed and golden brown. Cool completely.

To finish the dish, remove the bottoms from the baked cream puffs and fill with the ice cream. Place on individual dishes or a larger serving platter and drizzle with the chocolate sauce.

YIELD: Serves 4 to 6

Black and White Ice Cream Cake

This cake is great for a summer birthday celebration.

1/4 cup (1/2 stick, or 55 g) butter

1 package (1 pound, or 455 g) **chocolate sandwich cookies**

1 quart (570 g) **vanilla ice cream**

2 cups (475 ml) **chocolate sauce**

1 cup (235 ml) **heavy cream**

Preheat the oven to 350°F (180°C, gas mark 4). Spray an 8-inch springform pan with nonstick cooking spray and line the bottom with parchment paper.

Melt the butter over low heat.

Crush the cookies into coarse crumbs and mix one-third of the cookies (about 2 cups) with the butter in a mixing bowl. Press this mixture into the bottom of the prepared pan.

Bake for 12 to 15 minutes. Cool completely. Line the side of the pan with parchment paper.

Soften the ice cream until soft enough to work with but not melted. Spread half the ice cream on top of the cookie crust. Sprinkle half the remaining cookie crumbs over the ice cream and drizzle 1 cup (235 ml) of the chocolate sauce over. Top with the remaining ice cream, the rest of the cookies, and the remaining 1 cup (235 ml) of chocolate sauce. Freeze for at least 6 hours.

To serve, remove the side from the pan and invert the cake onto a plate. Re-invert onto a serving platter. Allow to soften at room temperature for 8 to 10 minutes.

Whip the cream to stiff peaks and pipe it onto the top of the cake to decorate.

YIELD: Serves 6 to 8

Frozen Plum Torte

Known as Umeshu, Japanese plum wine has been consumed for more than 1000 years in Japan. Many local liquor stores carry it or can procure it for you.

> 8 ounces (225 g) **gingersnaps**
> 1/2 cup (1 stick, or 112 g) butter
> 1 can (14 ounces, or 400 g) **plums** in syrup
> 4 **eggs**
> 1/2 cup (120 ml) **Japanese plum wine**
> 1 1/2 cups (355 ml) **heavy cream**

Preheat the oven to 350°F (180°C, gas mark 4). Line the bottom of a 9-inch springform pan with parchment paper.

Grind the cookies to fine crumbs. Melt the butter over low heat and stir in the crumbs until they are coated with the butter. Press into the bottom of the prepared pan.

Bake for 12 to 15 minutes. Cool completely.

Drain the plums, reserving the syrup. Put the plums into a food processor fitted with the metal blade and process until smooth.

Whisk the eggs, reserved plum syrup, and plum wine in a stainless steel mixing bowl set over simmering water until the mixture thickens and doubles in volume—5 to 8 minutes. Fold in the pureed plum. Allow to cool for 10 minutes.

Whip the cream to soft peaks and fold into the plum mixture. Spread over the ginger crust and freeze for at least 6 hours. Remove the pan and parchment paper. Allow to soften for about 10 minutes at room temperature.

YIELD: Serves 8 to 10

Frozen Bananas Foster Torte

1 quart (570 g) **vanilla ice cream**

32 sponge-type **ladyfingers**

4 **bananas**

1/2 cup (1 stick, or 112 g) butter

1 cup (225 g) packed **light brown sugar**

1/2 cup (120 ml) **dark rum**

Soften the ice cream in the refrigerator for 1 hour, until spreadable. Line the bottom of a 9-inch square baking pan with 16 of the ladyfingers.

Peel the bananas and cut them in half across, then cut each half into 3 to 4 slices lengthwise.

Heat a 12-inch sauté pan over high heat and add the butter. When the butter melts, add the bananas, sprinkle the sugar over, and toss lightly. Add the rum and allow it to flame. Remove from the heat and allow the mixture to cool for 2 to 3 minutes.

Spread half of the bananas and the sauce over the ladyfingers in the baking pan. Top with half the ice cream, spreading evenly. Repeat with another layer of ladyfingers, bananas, and ice cream. Freeze for at least 4 hours. Cut into 9 squares.

YIELD: Serves 9

Frozen Lemon Meringue Torte

2 dozen cake-type **ladyfingers**

6 **eggs**, separated

4 to 6 **lemons,** squeezed to yield 1/2 cup (120 ml) lemon juice

2 cups (400 g) **sugar**

1 cup (235 ml) **heavy cream**

Spray a 9-inch springform pan with nonstick cooking spray, then line the bottom with parchment paper. Spray the parchment paper with nonstick cooking spray and line the bottom, then the sides of the pan with the ladyfingers. Set aside.

Prepare a large mixing bowl of ice water. Combine the egg yolks, lemon juice, and 1 cup (200 g) of the sugar in a 1-quart saucepan. Place over medium-low heat and cook, stirring constantly, until the mixture thickens. Be careful not to allow the yolks to scramble. Plunge the pan into the ice water and stir the lemon curd until cooled.

Whip the cream and fold into the lemon curd. Fill the prepared springform pan evenly. Freeze for at least 6 hours.

When ready to serve, preheat the oven broiler. Whip the egg whites, adding the remaining 1 cup (200 g) sugar in 3 batches, starting when the whites start to froth. Whip to stiff, glossy peaks. Spread the meringue over the lemon filling and set under the broiler for 3 to 4 minutes, just until the meringue is toasted on the top. Remove from the oven and carefully remove the sides of the pan; they will be hot. Serve immediately.

YIELD: Serves 8 to 10

Frozen Orange Cream Torte

We loved the flavor of Creamsicles as kids; now here is a great summer dessert with the same tastes.

> 1/2 cup (1 stick, or 112 g) butter
>
> 1 cup (200 g) **sugar**
>
> 1 1/2 cups (5.4 ounces) **graham cracker crumbs**
>
> 12 ounces (355 ml) **evaporated milk**
>
> 1 cup (280 g) frozen **orange juice concentrate**, thawed
>
> 1 cup (235 ml) **heavy cream**

Preheat the oven to 350°F (180°C, gas mark 4). Line the bottom of a 10-inch springform pan with parchment paper.

Melt the butter over low heat. Mix 1/2 cup (100 g) of the sugar and the cracker crumbs in a mixing bowl and add the butter. Stir until well mixed. Press the crumb mixture into the bottom of the prepared pan.

Bake for 10 to 12 minutes. Cool completely. Line the side of the pan with parchment paper.

Put the evaporated milk in a mixing bowl with the orange juice and beat on high speed until thick—about 10 minutes.

Whip the cream to stiff peaks and fold into the orange mixture. Spread in the pan over the crust. Freeze for at least 6 hours.

To serve, remove the sides of the pan and the parchment paper. Flip the cake onto a plate and remove the bottom of the pan and the parchment. Flip back onto a serving platter.

YIELD: Serves 10 to 12

ADD IT! Decorate with additional whipped cream if desired.

Mandarin~Mocha Torte

1 quart (570 g) **coffee ice cream**

1 10-inch round store-bought **sponge cake**

2 cups (475 ml) **chocolate syrup**

2 cans (12 ounces, or 340 g, each) **mandarin orange segments**, drained

1 container (16 ounces, or 455 g) **nondairy topping**

Soften the ice cream in the refrigerator until spreadable—about 2 hours. Spray a 10-inch springform pan with nonstick cooking spray and line the bottom and sides with parchment paper.

Cut the cake horizontally so you have 2 thin 10-inch layers. Place 1 layer in the prepared pan and drizzle with 1 cup (235 ml) of the chocolate syrup. Spread half of the ice cream over the cake. Arrange half of the oranges over the ice cream. Spread half of the nondairy topping over the oranges. Repeat with another layer of cake, syrup, ice cream, oranges, and nondairy topping. Freeze for at least 4 hours.

To serve, leave at room temperature for 10 minutes. Remove the sides and the bottom of the pan and the parchment paper. Cut into serving pieces.

YIELD: Serves 10 to 12

Frozen Strawberry-Rhubarb Parfait Torte

It's a perfect springtime treat for strawberry season.

> 1/2 cup (1 stick, or 112 g) butter
>
> 1 1/2 cups (5.4 ounces) **graham cracker crumbs**
>
> 1 1/2 cups (300 g) **sugar**
>
> 1 quart (570 g) **cinnamon ice cream**
>
> 2 cups (245 g) diced **rhubarb**
>
> 2 cups (250 g) **strawberries**, sliced

Preheat the oven to 350°F (180°C, gas mark 4). Spray an 8-inch springform pan with nonstick cooking spray and line the bottom with parchment paper.

Melt the butter over low heat.

Mix the cracker crumbs and 1/2 cup (100 g) of the sugar in a mixing bowl. Stir in the butter until fully incorporated. Press this mixture into the bottom of the prepared pan.

Bake for 12 to 15 minutes. Cool completely. Line the sides of the pan with parchment paper.

Soften the ice cream until not melted, but soft enough to work with. Spread the ice cream on top of the crust. Put the pan in the freezer.

Combine the remaining 1 cup (200 g) of sugar and the rhubarb in a 2-quart saucepan and cook over medium heat until the sugar dissolves and the rhubarb is breaking down—12 to 15 minutes. Stir in the strawberries and allow to cool completely. When the fruit mixture is cooled, spread it over the ice cream in the springform pan. Freeze for at least 6 hours.

To serve, remove the side from the pan and invert the cake onto a cardboard cake round. Re-invert onto a serving platter. Allow to soften at room temperature for 8 to 10 minutes and slice.

YIELD: Serves 6 to 8

ADD IT! Serve with crushed strawberries over each slice.

♥ Frozen Hazelnut-Praline Torte

For the layers:

> 6 **egg whites**
>
> 1 cup (200 g) **sugar**
>
> 1 cup (125 g) ground **hazelnuts**

For the filling:

> 2 cups (400 g) **sugar**
>
> 1/2 cup (120 ml) water
>
> 1 cup (125 g) ground **hazelnuts**
>
> 4 **egg yolks**
>
> 1/4 cup (60 ml) **Frangelica**
>
> 1 1/2 cups (355 ml) **heavy cream**

To make the meringue layers:

Preheat the oven to 200°F (warm). Line a sheet pan with parchment paper and draw three 9-inch circles on the paper.

Whip the egg whites until they are foamy and add one-third of the sugar. Continue whipping, adding the sugar in two more batches, until the whites hold stiff peaks and are glossy. Fold in the hazelnuts. Put the whites into a piping bag fitted with a plain tip and pipe out disks filling the three circles.

Bake for 2 to 3 hours, until fully dry. Remove from the oven.

To make the filling:

Line the bottom and sides of a 9-inch springform pan with parchment paper.

Heat 1 1/2 cups of the sugar with the water over high heat, not stirring, until the syrup becomes a golden brown. Stir in the hazelnuts and pour onto a baking sheet covered with parchment paper. Allow to harden and fully cool. Break the candy into small pieces and grind to a powder in a food processor fitted with the metal blade.

Whisk the egg yolks, the remaining 1/2 cup sugar, and the liqueur in a stainless steel bowl set over simmering water until the eggs are thick and doubled in volume with a consistency of a hollandaise sauce. Allow to cool for 8 to 10 minutes. Fold in the candy powder.

Whip the cream to soft peaks and fold it in.

Place 1 meringue disk on the bottom of the pan and spread one-third of the filling on it. Top with another meringue disk and spread with more filling. Finish with the remaining disk and top with the remaining filling.

Freeze for at least 6 hours. Remove the pan and the parchment paper. Allow to soften for a few minutes at room temperature and cut.

YIELD: Serves 8-10

Frozen Peanut Butter Torte

8 ounces (225 g) **chocolate sandwich cookies**

1/2 cup (1 stick, or 112 g) butter

2 cups (520 g) creamy **peanut butter**

8 ounces (225 g) **cream cheese**

2 teaspoons **vanilla extract**

1 1/2 cups (355 ml) **heavy cream**

Preheat the oven to 350°F (180°C, gas mark 4). Line the bottom of a 9-inch springform pan with parchment paper.

Crush the cookies into crumbs and small chunks. Melt the butter over low heat and mix with the cookie crumbs in a mixing bowl. Press into the bottom of the prepared pan.

Bake for 10 to 12 minutes. Cool completely.

Using a mixer on medium speed, in a mixing bowl, whip together the peanut butter and cream cheese until smooth and fluffy. Add the vanilla and beat for another 2 minutes.

In another bowl, whip the cream to stiff peaks. Fold into the peanut butter mixture. Line the sides of the pan with parchment paper and spoon in the peanut butter mixture, spreading it evenly in the pan over the cookie crust. Freeze for at least 6 hours.

Remove the sides of the pan and the parchment paper and allow the torte to soften for 10 to 15 minutes at room temperature.

YIELD: Serves 10 to 12

ADD IT! Of course, you could drizzle hot fudge sauce over each slice.

Frozen Pumpkin Chiffon Torte

Instead of facing the inevitable battery of pumpkin pies at Thanksgiving, pull the rug out from underneath your relatives' palates and give them this instead. You'll be a bigger hero than the pilgrims.

1 pint (285 g) **vanilla ice cream**

1/2 cup (1 stick, or 112 g) butter

1/2 cup (100 g) **sugar**

1 1/2 cups (5.4 ounces) **graham cracker crumbs**

2 cups (540 g) canned spiced and sweetened **pumpkin**

1 cup (235 ml) **heavy cream**

Soften the ice cream at room temperature until almost melting.

While the ice cream is softening, preheat the oven to 350°F (180°C, gas mark 4). Line the bottom of a 10-inch springform pan with parchment paper.

Melt the butter over low heat. Mix the sugar and cracker crumbs in a mixing bowl and add the butter. Stir until well mixed. Press the crumb mixture into the bottom of the prepared pan.

Bake for 10 to 12 minutes. Cool completely. Line the side of the pan with parchment paper.

Put the ice cream in a mixing bowl and add the pumpkin. Beat on high speed until smoothly mixed—1 to 2 minutes.

Whip the cream to stiff peaks and fold into the pumpkin mixture. Spread in the pan over the crust. Freeze for at least 6 hours.

To serve, remove the sides of the pan and the parchment paper. Flip the cake onto a plate and remove the bottom of the pan and the parchment. Flip back onto a serving platter.

YIELD: Serves 10 to 12

ADD IT! Press a circle of candied pecan halves around the top of the torte before serving. Decorate with additional whipped cream if desired.

Individual Lemon Ices

We love that this is refreshing, delicious, and a novel serving bowl.

> 6 **lemons**
> 2 cups (475 ml) **lemon juice**
> 2 teaspoons ground **cardamom**
> 4 cups (800 g) **sugar**
> 2 cups (475 ml) water

Cut the top third off each lemon; carefully squeeze the lemons, being careful not to split the skins. Scrape the pith from each lemon and cut a small slice from the bottom of each lemon "bowl" so it sits flat. Put the bowls on a tray and freeze.

Put the lemon juice, cardamom, sugar, and water in a 2-quart saucepan. Heat over medium heat, stirring occasionally, until the mixture simmers and the sugar has dissolved. Pour into each lemon bowl and return to freezer until frozen through. Note: The ice will be crystalline, not smooth.

YIELD: Serves 6

Lemon-Rosemary Granita

Refreshing on a hot summer's evening, this icy treat is like nothing else.

> 6 **lemons**
>
> 1 teaspoon chopped fresh **rosemary**
>
> 2 cups (400 g) **sugar**
>
> 1 cup (235 ml) water

Halve and squeeze the lemons to yield 1 cup (235 ml) lemon juice. Put the lemon juice, rosemary, sugar, and water in a 1-quart saucepan and heat over medium heat to a simmer until the sugar has dissolved. Strain through a strainer and pour into a loaf pan and freeze for at least 6 hours. Scrape up with a spoon and serve. The ice will be crystalline, not smooth.

YIELD: Serves 4

CHAPTER EIGHT

Puddings and Custards

Puddings are one of those places where theory diverges widely from practice. In theory, we think of puddings in terms of English nursery tales full of comforting rice puddings cooked with love by matronly nannies. In practice, we tend to pull one of those little cardboard boxes off the shelf and follow the directions. (Still made with love, but in a lot less time.)

That's a bit of a shame, because puddings are pretty darn easy to make, and the pay-off is enormous in terms of delighted reception by fellow dinner table inhabitants. Try a chocolate bread pudding out on the kids someday, just for kicks. We're betting that they'll gobble it up faster than you can say "Christopher Robin."

Apple Tapioca

A starchy substance extracted from the root of the cassava plant, tapioca has long been a popular base for making pudding. Here, we juice up the basic pudding with apples.

- 1 teaspoon **lemon juice**
- 1/2 cup (90 g) quick cooking **tapioca**
- 1/2 teaspoon salt
- 1/2 cup (100 g) **sugar**
- 1 tablespoon (14 g) butter
- 2 cups (475 ml) water
- 2 **apples**, such as Granny Smith or Macintosh, peeled and cut into 1/2-inch chunks
- 1 teaspoon **vanilla extract**

Combine the lemon juice, tapioca, salt, sugar, and butter in a 2-quart saucepan. Add the water. Cook the tapioca until the butter is melted, then add the apples and cook until the tapioca is transparent—about 10 minutes. Stir in the vanilla. Spoon into a bowl and refrigerate for at least 1 hour.

YIELD: Serves 4 to 6

Apricot Mousse

Mousses are popular both hot and cold, sweet and savory, although they are probably best known as a dessert. Mousse is French for foam, and the term fits this airy dish perfectly.

> 1 jar (16 ounces, or 455 g) **apricot halves** in light syrup
>
> 1/4 cup (60 ml) **apricot brandy**
>
> 2 teaspoons **unflavored gelatin**
>
> 2 **eggs**
>
> 2 cups (475 ml) **heavy cream**

Puree the apricots and 1 cup (235 ml) of the syrup in a blender or food processor.

Put the brandy in a small saucepan and sprinkle the gelatin over. Allow to soften for 5 minutes, then heat over low heat, stirring, until the gelatin is melted. Set aside.

Combine the eggs, apricot puree, and brandy-gelatin mixture in a medium-size stainless steel mixing bowl. Whisking constantly, put the bowl over a pan of simmering water until the eggs are frothy, light colored, doubled in volume, and you can see streaks of the bottom of the bowl as you whisk. Remove from the heat and set aside to cool for 15 minutes.

Whip the cream to stiff peaks. Whisk one-third of the cream into the egg mixture, then gently fold the rest thoroughly into the mixture. Put the mousse in a piping bag and pipe into 8 serving cups or wine glasses. Refrigerate for at least 2 hours.

YIELD: Serves 8

ADD IT! Garnish with additional whipped cream.

Lemon Mousse

This dessert is light in taste and texture. Try using sweeter, distinctive Meyer lemons if you can find them.

> ¹/4 cup (60 ml) water
>
> 2 teaspoons **unflavored gelatin**
>
> 2 **lemons**
>
> 1 cup (200 g) **sugar**
>
> 2 **eggs**
>
> 2 cups (475 ml) **heavy cream**

Put the water in a small saucepan and sprinkle the gelatin over. Allow to soften for 5 minutes, then heat over low heat, stirring, until the gelatin is melted. Set aside.

Grate the zest from the lemons and squeeze them. Set the juice aside. Combine the sugar, lemon zest, eggs, and the gelatin in a medium-size stainless steel mixing bowl. Put the bowl over a saucepan of simmering water and whisk until the eggs are frothy, light colored, doubled in volume, and you can see streaks of the bottom of the bowl as you whisk. Remove from the heat and set aside. Whisk the lemon juice into the bowl and allow to cool for 15 minutes.

Whip the cream to stiff peaks. Whisk one-third of the cream into the egg mixture, then gently fold the rest in thoroughly. Put the mousse in a piping bag and pipe into 8 serving cups or wine glasses. Refrigerate for at least 4 hours.

YIELD: Serves 8

ADD IT! Garnish with additional whipped cream.

🥄 Raspberry Mousse

Try making lemon mousse too, and then layering with this one in a tall glass for a dramatic effect.

> 1 package (10 ounces, or 280 g) frozen **raspberries** in syrup, thawed
>
> ¼ cup (60 ml) **Framboise** or other raspberry liqueur
>
> 2 teaspoons **unflavored gelatin**
>
> 2 **eggs**
>
> 2 cups (475 ml) **heavy cream**

Puree the raspberries and syrup in a blender or food processor. Push the puree through a fine mesh strainer and discard the seeds.

Put the Framboise in a small saucepan and sprinkle the gelatin over. Allow to soften for 5 minutes, then heat over low heat, stirring, until the gelatin is melted. Set aside.

Combine the eggs, raspberry puree, and framboise-gelatin mixture in a medium-size stainless steel mixing bowl. Put the bowl over a pan of simmering water and whisk constantly until the eggs are frothy, light colored, doubled in volume, and you can see streaks of the bottom of the bowl as you whisk. Remove from the heat and set aside to cool for 15 minutes.

Whip the cream to stiff peaks. Whisk one-third of the cream into the egg mixture, then gently fold the rest in thoroughly. Put the mousse in a piping bag and pipe into 8 serving cups or wine glasses. Refrigerate for at least 2 hours.

YIELD: Serves 8

ADD IT! Garnish with additional whipped cream.

Chocolate Mousse

When people think mousse, nine out of ten mentally insert the word chocolate in front and get a goofy, dreamy look on their faces. There's a simple reason: It's fabulous stuff.

> 4 ounces (115 g) **bittersweet chocolate**
>
> 2 **eggs**
>
> 1/2 cup (100 g) **sugar**
>
> 1/4 cup (60 ml) **crème de cacao** (optional)
>
> 2 cups (475 ml) **heavy cream**

Chop the chocolate into small pieces. Put the chocolate in a small stainless steel mixing bowl and place the bowl over a pan of simmering water. Melt the chocolate, stir until smooth, and set aside.

Combine the eggs, sugar, and crème de cacao (if using) in a medium-size stainless steel mixing bowl. Whisking constantly, put the bowl over the simmering water until the eggs are frothy, light colored, doubled in volume, and you can see streaks of the bottom of the bowl as you whisk. Remove from the heat and fold in the chocolate. Set aside to cool for 15 minutes.

Whip the cream to stiff peaks. Whisk one-third of the cream into the chocolate mixture, then gently fold the rest thoroughly. Put the mousse in a piping bag and pipe into 8 serving cups or wine glasses. Refrigerate for at least 2 hours.

YIELD: Serves 8

ADD IT! Garnish with additional whipped cream and chocolate shavings if desired.

Mocha Mousse

4 ounces (115 g) **bittersweet chocolate**

2 **eggs**

1/2 cup (100 g) **sugar**

1/4 cup (60 ml) **coffee brandy**

2 cups (475 ml) **heavy cream**

Chop the chocolate into small pieces. Put the chocolate in a small stainless steel mixing bowl and place the bowl over a pan of simmering water. Melt the chocolate, stir until smooth, and set aside.

Combine the eggs, sugar, and brandy in a medium-size stainless steel mixing bowl. Whisking constantly, put the bowl over the simmering water until the eggs are frothy, light colored, doubled in volume, and you can see streaks of the bottom of the bowl as you whisk. Remove from the heat and fold in the chocolate. Set aside to cool for 15 minutes.

Whip the cream to stiff peaks. Whisk one-third of the cream into the chocolate mixture, then gently fold the rest in thoroughly. Put the mousse in a piping bag and pipe into 8 serving cups or wine glasses. Refrigerate for at least 2 hours.

YIELD: Serves 8

ADD IT! Garnish with additional whipped cream and chocolate shavings if desired.

Coffee Mousse

You could layer this mousse with the chocolate version in tall glasses to make a delicious striped mocha dessert. Of course, it's also scrumptious on its own. A note on the coffee syrup: We find ours next to the bottled chocolate syrups in the store.

1/4 cup (60 ml) **coffee brandy**

2 teaspoons **unflavored gelatin**

4 ounces (120 ml) **coffee syrup**

2 **eggs**

2 cups (475 ml) **heavy cream**

Put the brandy in a small saucepan and sprinkle the gelatin over. Heat over low heat, stirring, until the gelatin is melted. Set aside.

Combine the coffee syrup, eggs, and the coffee brandy-gelatin mixture in a medium-size stainless steel mixing bowl. Whisking constantly, put the bowl over a pan of simmering water until the eggs are frothy, light colored, doubled in volume, and you can see streaks of the bottom of the bowl as you whisk. Remove from the heat and set aside to cool for 15 minutes.

Whip the cream to stiff peaks. Whisk one-third of the cream into the egg mixture, then gently fold the rest thoroughly in. Put the mousse in a piping bag and pipe into 8 serving cups or wine glasses. Refrigerate for at least 2 hours.

YIELD: Serves 8

ADD IT! Garnish with additional whipped cream.

Green Tea Mousse

Green tea has all sorts of healthy properties, which might counteract the cream.

1 cup (235 ml) very strong brewed **green tea**

1 tablespoon (7 g) **unflavored gelatin**

1 cup (200 g) **sugar**

1/2 teaspoon ground **cardamom**

1 cup (235 ml) **heavy cream**

Place the tea in a small saucepan. Sprinkle the gelatin over the tea. Allow the gelatin to soften for 5 minutes, then stir in the sugar and cardamom. Heat over medium heat, stirring, until the sugar and the gelatin are dissolved. Refrigerate in a mixing bowl for 1 to 2 hours—until the gelatin has begun to set up but is not fully set.

Whip the cream to soft peaks and fold it into the tea mixture. Whip further, until the mixture is fluffy. Refrigerate for 4 to 6 hours.

YIELD: Serves 6

Baked Custard

Basic and simple, custard has a soul-satisfying goodness about it.

2 **eggs**

1/2 cup (100 g) **sugar**

Pinch salt

2 cups (475 ml) whole **milk**

2 teaspoons **vanilla extract**

1/2 teaspoon **nutmeg**

Preheat the oven to 325°F (170°C, gas mark 3).

Whisk the eggs in a mixing bowl. Stir in the sugar and salt.

Put the milk in a saucepan and bring almost to a boil over medium-high heat. Whisk into the eggs in a thin stream. Stir in the vanilla. Pour the liquid into a 1-quart deep baking dish. Put this dish into a larger heatproof pan. Fill the larger pan with boiling water about 1 to 2 inches up the side of the custard pan. Sprinkle the nutmeg on top of the custard.

Bake in the center of the oven for 35 to 40 minutes, until the custard is just set. Allow to cool in the water bath for about 30 minutes. Refrigerate for at least 2 hours.

YIELD: Serves 6 to 8

Vanilla Panna Cotta

Italian for "cooked cream," panna cotta is a popular dessert in restaurants.

 2 tablespoons (28 ml) water
 1 3/4 teaspoons **unflavored gelatin**
 1 1/2 cups (355 ml) **heavy cream**
 1/2 cup (120 ml) **crème fraîche**
 6 tablespoons (70 g) **sugar**
 Pinch salt
 2 teaspoons **vanilla extract**

Place the water in a small bowl. Sprinkle the gelatin over the water and set aside until softened, about 5 minutes.

Place the cream, crème fraîche, 3 tablespoons (35 g) of the sugar, and the salt in a saucepan. Bring to a boil over high heat, reduce to medium heat, and boil for 1 minute, stirring constantly. Watch closely to be sure that it doesn't boil over.

Remove the pan from the heat and whisk in the remaining 3 tablespoons (35 g) sugar and the gelatin mixture until dissolved. Stir in the vanilla.

Chill in the refrigerator or over an ice bath just until cool and slightly thicker than heavy cream, but not set. Pour into six 5-ounce ramekins. Refrigerate for 3 hours.

To serve, dip the ramekins into hot water for 30 seconds and then flip each panna cotta onto a serving plate.

ADD IT! Serve these with Chocolate-Dipped Biscotti (page 224) or some other crunchy chocolate cookie.

Chai Panna Cotta

Panna Cotta is Italian comfort food, a light, cold custard that can be flavored with any number of things, although the traditional taste is caramel. Here we update the dessert with chai tea.

2 tablespoons (28 ml) water

1 3/4 teaspoons **unflavored gelatin**

1 1/2 cups (355 ml) **heavy cream**

1/4 cup (60 ml) **crème fraîche**

1/2 cup (120 ml) liquid **chai tea** concentrate

6 tablespoons (70 g) **sugar**

Pinch salt

Place the water in a small bowl. Sprinkle the gelatin over the water and set aside until softened, about 5 minutes.

Place the cream, the crème fraîche, the chai tea, 3 tablespoons (35 g) of the sugar, and the salt in a saucepan. Bring to a boil over high heat, reduce to medium heat, and boil for 1 minute, stirring constantly. Watch closely so it doesn't boil over.

Remove the pan from the heat and whisk in the remaining 3 tablespoons sugar (35 g) and the gelatin mixture until dissolved

Chill in the refrigerator or over an ice bath just until cool and slightly thicker than heavy cream, but not set. Pour into six 5-ounce ramekins. Refrigerate for 3 hours.

To serve dip the ramekins into hot water for 30 seconds and then flip each panna cotta onto a serving plate.

YIELD: Serves 6

Coffee Panna Cotta

We think this is perfect for a summer's dinner on the patio. Next to a lake. With a full moon. And lots of candles. Okay, we'll just come out and say it: It would make a lovely romantic dinner dessert!

2 tablespoons (28 ml) water

1 3/4 teaspoons **unflavored gelatin**

1 1/2 cups (355 ml) **heavy cream**

1/2 cup (120 ml) **crème fraîche**

3 tablespoons (35 g) **sugar**

Pinch salt

1/4 cup (60 ml) **coffee syrup**

Place the water in a small bowl. Sprinkle the gelatin over the water and set aside until softened, about 5 minutes.

Place the cream, crème fraîche, 2 tablespoons (25 g) of the sugar, the salt, and the coffee syrup in a saucepan. Bring to a boil over high heat, reduce to medium heat, and boil for 1 minute, stirring constantly. Watch closely so it doesn't boil over.

Remove the pan from the heat and whisk in the remaining 1 tablespoon (10 g) sugar and the gelatin mixture until dissolved.

Chill in the refrigerator or over an ice bath just until cool and slightly thicker than heavy cream, but not set. Pour into six 5-ounce ramekins. Refrigerate for 3 hours.

To serve, dip the ramekins into hot water for 30 seconds and then flip each panna cotta onto a serving plate.

YIELD: Serves 6

Chocolate Panna Cotta

Panna cotta is Italian comfort food, a light, cold custard that can be flavored with any number of things, such as this chocolate version.

> 2 tablespoons (28 ml) water
> 1 3/4 teaspoons **unflavored gelatin**
> 1 1/2 cups (355 ml) **heavy cream**
> 1/2 cup (120 ml) **crème fraîche**
> 1/4 cup (50 g) **sugar**
> Pinch salt
> 3 ounces (85 g) **semisweet chocolate**

Place the water in a small bowl. Sprinkle the gelatin over the water and set aside until softened, about 5 minutes.

Place the cream, crème fraîche, 3 tablespoons (35 g) of the sugar, and the salt in a saucepan. Bring to a boil over high heat, reduce to medium heat, and boil for 1 minute, stirring constantly. Watch closely so it doesn't boil over.

Remove the pan from the heat and whisk in the remaining 1 tablespoon of sugar and the gelatin mixture until dissolved.

Melt the chocolate in a metal bowl set over simmering water and stir into the mixture.

Chill in the refrigerator or over an ice bath just until cool and slightly thicker than heavy cream, but not set. Pour into six 5-ounce ramekins. Refrigerate for at least 3 hours.

To serve, dip the ramekins into hot water for 30 seconds and then flip each panna cotta onto a serving plate.

YIELD: Serves 6

Maple Panna Cotta

It's New England flavor, Italian style.

> 2 tablespoons (28 ml) water
> 1 3/4 teaspoons **unflavored gelatin**
> 1 1/2 cups (355 ml) **heavy cream**
> 1/2 cup (120 ml) **crème fraîche**
> 3 tablespoons (35 g) **sugar**
> Pinch salt
> 1/4 cup (60 ml) **maple syrup**

Place the water in a small bowl. Sprinkle the gelatin over the water and set aside until softened, about 5 minutes.

Place the cream, crème fraîche, 2 tablespoons (25 g) of the sugar, the salt, and the maple syrup in a saucepan. Bring to a boil over high heat, reduce to medium heat, and boil for 1 minute, stirring constantly. Watch closely so that it doesn't boil over.

Remove the pan from the heat and whisk in the remaining 1 tablespoon (10 g) sugar and the gelatin mixture until dissolved.

Chill in the refrigerator or over an ice bath just until cool and slightly thicker than heavy cream, but not set. Pour into six 5-ounce ramekins. Refrigerate for 3 hours.

To serve, dip the ramekins into hot water for 30 seconds and then flip each panna cotta onto a serving plate.

YIELD: Serves 6

Rum Panna Cotta

2 tablespoons (28 ml) water

1 3/4 teaspoons **unflavored gelatin**

1 1/2 cups (355 ml) **heavy cream**

1/2 cup (120 ml) **crème fraîche**

6 tablespoons (70 g) **sugar**

Pinch salt

2 tablespoons (28 ml) **dark rum**

Place the water in a small bowl. Sprinkle the gelatin over the water and set aside until softened, about 5 minutes.

Place the cream, crème fraîche, 3 tablespoons (35 g) of the sugar, and the salt in a saucepan. Bring to a boil over high heat, reduce to medium heat, and boil for 1 minute, stirring constantly. Watch closely so it doesn't boil over.

Remove the pan from the heat and whisk in the remaining 3 tablespoons (35 g) sugar and the gelatin mixture until dissolved. Stir in the rum.

Chill in the refrigerator or over an ice bath just until cool and slightly thicker than heavy cream, but not set. Pour into six 5-ounce ramekins. Refrigerate for 3 hours.

To serve, dip the ramekins into hot water for 30 seconds and then flip each panna cotta onto a serving plate.

YIELD: Serves 6

ADD IT! A drizzle of caramel sauce over each panna cotta would complement the rum taste.

◖ Old-Fashioned Vanilla Pudding

This is basic and homey, and, boy, is it ever delicious.

> 2 cups (475 ml) whole **milk**
>
> 1 cup (200 g) **sugar**
>
> 1/4 cup (30 g) **cornstarch**
>
> Pinch salt
>
> 3 **eggs**
>
> 1 tablespoon (14 ml) **vanilla extract**
>
> 2 tablespoons (1/4 stick, or 28 g) butter

Put the milk in a 2-quart saucepan and put it on medium-high heat. Bring the milk up to a simmer.

While the milk is heating, mix the sugar, cornstarch, and salt in a mixing bowl. Add the eggs and whisk together. Pour the hot milk into the bowl in a thin stream while whisking. Return the liquid to the saucepan and heat, stirring constantly, until it thickens. Remove from the heat and whisk in the vanilla and butter until the butter is melted and the pudding is smooth. Pour into a serving bowl and refrigerate for at least 2 hours.

YIELD: Serves 4 to 6

Lemon Pudding

This pudding is great on its own or as a pie filling.

2 cups (475 ml) whole **milk**

1 cup (200 g) **sugar**

1/4 cup (30 g) **cornstarch**

Pinch salt

3 **lemons**

3 **eggs**

2 tablespoons (1/4 stick, or 28 g) butter

Put the milk in a 2-quart saucepan and put it on medium-high heat. Bring the milk up to a simmer.

While the milk is heating, mix the sugar, cornstarch, and salt in a mixing bowl. Grate the lemons and add 2 teaspoons of zest. Add the eggs and whisk together. Pour the hot milk into the bowl in a thin stream while whisking. Return the liquid to the saucepan and heat, stirring constantly, until it thickens. Remove from the heat and whisk in the butter until the butter is melted and the pudding is smooth. Squeeze the lemons and whisk in the lemon juice. Pour into a serving bowl and refrigerate for at least 2 hours.

YIELD: Serves 4 to 6

Steamed Persimmon Pudding

You want ripe, delicious persimmons to make this work. (Unripe persimmons, on the other hand, will make you pucker.)

    1 pound (455 g) ripe **persimmons** (about 3 or 4)
    1 cup (200 g) **cinnamon sugar** (See "Making Cinnamon Sugar" on page 12.)
    1 cup (120 g) **all-purpose flour**
    1 teaspoon **baking soda**
    1/2 cup (120 ml) whole or 2% **milk**
    2 tablespoons (1/4 stick, or 28 g) butter

Preheat the oven to 325°F (170°C, gas mark 3). Grease a 1-quart pudding mold.

Remove the tops from the persimmons and cut them into quarters. Put them in a food processor fitted with the metal blade and process until smooth. You should have about 1 cup (320 g) of fruit puree.

In a mixing bowl, combine the sugar, flour, and baking soda. Mix well.

In another bowl, mix together the milk and the persimmon puree. Melt the butter and mix it in. Stir this into the dry ingredients until well combined. Spoon the batter into the pudding mold. Cover tightly with foil and place the mold in a baking pan. Add 1 to 2 inches of boiling water to the pan.

Bake for 45 to 50 minutes. Allow to cool standing in the water bath. Remove the pudding from the mold.

YIELD: Serves 6 to 8

ADD IT! Chopped nuts, such as pecans or walnuts, or raisins are all good additions.

Butterscotch Pudding

    2 cups (475 ml) whole **milk**
    1 cup (225 g) packed **light brown sugar**
    1/4 cup (30 g) **cornstarch**
    Pinch salt

3 **eggs**

1 tablespoon (14 ml) **vanilla extract**

2 tablespoons (28 g) butter

Put the milk in a 2-quart saucepan and heat on medium-high heat until the milk simmers.

While the milk is heating, mix the sugar, cornstarch, and salt in a mixing bowl. Add the eggs and whisk together. Pour the hot milk into the bowl in a thin stream while whisking. Return the liquid to the saucepan and heat, stirring constantly, until it thickens. Remove from the heat and whisk in the vanilla and butter until the butter is melted and the pudding is smooth. Pour into a serving bowl and refrigerate for at least 2 hours.

YIELD: Serves 4 to 6

Coconut Pudding

2 cups (475 ml) whole **milk**

1 cup (200 g) **sugar**

¼ cup (30 g) **cornstarch**

Pinch salt

3 **eggs**

1 cup (75 g) **sweetened shredded coconut**

2 tablespoons (28 g) butter

Put the milk in a 2-quart saucepan and heat on medium-high heat until the milk simmers.

While the milk is heating, mix the sugar, cornstarch, and salt in a mixing bowl. Add the eggs and whisk together. Whisking constantly, pour the hot milk in a thin stream into the mixture. Stir in the coconut. Return the mixture to the saucepan and heat, stirring constantly, until it thickens. Remove from the heat and whisk in the butter until the butter is melted and the pudding is smooth. Pour into a serving bowl and refrigerate for at least 2 hours.

YIELD: Serves 4 to 6

Chocolate Pudding

Still an enduring family favorite, you'll eschew the boxed kind forever.

    2 cups (475 ml) whole **milk**
    1 cup (200 g) **vanilla sugar** (See "Making Vanilla Sugar" on page 12.)
    1/4 cup (30 g) **cornstarch**
    1/2 cup (45 g) **cocoa powder**
    Pinch salt
    3 **eggs**
    2 tablespoons (28 g) butter

Put 1 1/2 cups (355 ml) of the milk in a 2-quart saucepan and put it on medium-high heat. Bring the milk up to a simmer.

While the milk is heating, mix the sugar, cornstarch, cocoa powder, and salt in a mixing bowl. Add the eggs and the remaining 1/2 cup (120 ml) milk and whisk together. Pour the hot milk into the bowl in a thin stream while whisking. Return the liquid to the saucepan and heat, stirring constantly, until it thickens. Remove from the heat and whisk in the butter until the butter is melted and the pudding is smooth. Pour into a serving bowl and refrigerate for at least 2 hours.

YIELD: Serves 4 to 6

Grapenut Pudding

Here's an old diner favorite.

    4 **eggs**
    1 cup (200 g) **sugar**
    3 cups (705 ml) whole **milk**
    2 teaspoons **vanilla extract**
    1 cup (2 ounces, or 55 g) **Grapenuts cereal**

Preheat the oven to 300°F (150°C, gas mark 2).

Mix the eggs and sugar in a mixing bowl and whisk well.

Heat the milk in a 1-quart saucepan until scalded and pour the milk in a thin stream into the egg mixture, whisking constantly. Stir in the vanilla and cereal. Pour into a deep 2-quart baking dish and set the dish into a larger baking pan. Pour boiling water into the larger pan until it reaches halfway up the side of the smaller pan. Cover the smaller pan with foil.

Bake for 40 to 45 minutes, until the custard is set. Cool in the water bath for 20 minutes, then remove the custard from the water bath and refrigerate for at least 2 hours.

YIELD: Serves 6 to 8

Mary Kelly's Molasses Pudding

This recipe comes from writer extraordinaire Alice Kelly. This is a staple on her holiday table. It's generally served warm, but nobody turns their noses up at leftovers, either. It is traditionally served with Flora Dora Sauce (page 488).

    1 cup (200 g) **sugar**
    1 cup (120 g) **self-rising flour**
    1 cup (235 ml) **molasses**
    1/2 cup (120 ml) lukewarm whole **milk**
    1/2 cup (1 stick, or 112 g) butter, melted
    4 **eggs**, well beaten

Preheat the oven to 350°F (180°C, gas mark 4). Grease a 9-inch square baking pan.

Mix the sugar and flour until combined. Add the molasses, milk, and butter. Beat thoroughly and add the eggs. Mix until well combined and pour into the prepared pan.

Bake for 45 minutes.

YIELD: Serves 8

Snow Pudding

This is a traditional Christmas dinner dessert for the Hildebrand clan, served with a pitcher of crème anglaise and accompanied by a tray of German Christmas cookies. There are some rebels amongst us who suggest that it's too austere (translation: lacks chocolate), but we like the cool citrus bite after a lavish feast.

3/4 cup (150 g) **sugar**

1 envelope (1/4 ounce, or 7.5 g) **unflavored gelatin**

1/4 teaspoon salt

1 1/4 cups (295 ml) cold water

1 teaspoon grated **lemon zest**

1/4 cup (60 ml) **lemon juice**

 2 **egg whites**

In a saucepan, combine the sugar, gelatin, and salt. Add 1/2 cup (120 ml) of the water and stir over low heat until everything is dissolved. Remove from the heat and add the remaining 3/4 cup (175 ml) water, the lemon zest, and lemon juice. Refrigerate until partially but not completely set—about 45 minutes to an hour. Turn the mixture into a large chilled bowl and add the egg whites. Beat with an electric mixer until the mixture is quite stiff and holds its shape. Pour into a serving dish. Refrigerate until firm, at least 6 hours.

YIELD: Serves 10 to 12

Baked Lemon Pudding

Homemade puddings are a completely different beast than the instant boxed type (although those have their place, too). Try one and see! Any type of milk is fine for this recipe.

> ³⁄₄ cup (150 g) **sugar**
>
> 3 tablespoons (25 g) **all-purpose flour**
>
> Pinch salt
>
> 3 tablespoons (45 g) butter
>
> 2 **eggs**, separated
>
> 1 **lemon**
>
> 1 cup (235 ml) **milk**

Preheat the oven to 325°F (170°C, gas mark 3).

In a mixing bowl, combine the sugar, flour, and salt. Cut in the butter until the mixture resembles cornmeal. Stir the egg yolks into the bowl. Grate the lemon zest and halve and squeeze the lemon. Add the grated zest and the juice to the bowl and stir well. Add the milk and stir in until combined.

Whisk the egg whites to stiff peaks and fold into the mixture. Spoon into a deep 1-quart baking dish. Put the dish into another, larger dish. Add boiling water to the larger dish until it is halfway up the pudding dish.

Bake for 40 to 45 minutes. Cool in the water bath. You may serve either warm or chilled.

YIELD: Serves 4

ꙮ Baked Rice Pudding

Homey and nourishing, rice pudding is redolent of childhood comforts. It's delicious served either warm or cold.

> 1 1/2 cups (260 g) **cooked white rice**
>
> 2 cups (475 ml) **whole milk**
>
> 1 cup (200 g) **sugar**
>
> 2 **eggs**
>
> 1/4 teaspoon salt
>
> 2 teaspoons **vanilla extract**

Preheat the oven to 300°F (150°C, gas mark 2).

Put the rice in a 1-quart baking dish. Whisk together the remaining ingredients in a mixing bowl until well combined and pour over the rice. Stir the rice into the custard. Cover the dish with foil and put the dish in a larger baking dish. Pour boiling water into the larger dish until it comes halfway up the level of the custard.

Bake for 40 to 45 minutes, until the custard is set. Cool in the water bath for 20 minutes, then serve warm or refrigerate until cold. Be sure to refrigerate leftovers.

YIELD: Serves 6

ADD IT! Add 1/2 teaspoon nutmeg to the custard. Stir in 1 cup (145 g) raisins before baking.

Banana Bread Pudding

We think that a good bread pudding is one of life's great things.

> 1 loaf (1 pound, or 455 g) home-style white **bread**
>
> 3 **eggs**
>
> 2 cups (475 ml) **half and half**
>
> 1 cup (200 g) **vanilla sugar** (See "Making Vanilla Sugar" on page 12.)
>
> 2 cups (450 g) mashed **banana** (about 4 bananas)

Preheat the oven to 325°F (170°C, gas mark 3). Grease the bottom and sides of a 9 x 12-inch baking pan.

Remove the crusts from the bread and cut it into ³⁄4-inch cubes. Spread the bread cubes evenly in the pan.

Whisk the eggs, half and half, sugar, and banana together in a mixing bowl until thoroughly combined.

Pour the cream mixture over the bread cubes and press down with your hands to be sure all the bread is soaked with the custard. Cover with foil. Put the pan on a baking sheet with sides at least ¹⁄2 inch tall or in another, larger baking pan. Put into the oven and add ¹⁄2 inch of boiling water to the larger pan.

Bake for 40 to 45 minutes, adding more water if needed to the water bath. The pudding should be set, but still soft. Remove from the oven and remove the foil. Serve hot or cold. Refrigerate leftovers.

YIELD: Serves 10 to 12

ADD IT! Stir ¹⁄2 cup (85 g) chocolate chips into the pudding before baking.

Blueberry Bread Pudding

You can add spice to this by substituting cinnamon bread for white bread.

    1 loaf (1 pound, 455 g) home-style white **bread**

    2 cups (290 g) fresh or frozen wild **blueberries** (If using frozen, do not thaw.)

    3 **eggs**

    2 cups (475 ml) **half and half**

    1 cup (200 g) **vanilla sugar** (See "Making Vanilla Sugar" on page 12.)

Preheat the oven to 325°F (170°C, gas mark 3). Grease the bottom and sides of a 9 x 12-inch baking pan.

Remove the crusts from the bread and cut it into 3/4-inch cubes. Mix the bread with the blueberries and evenly distribute them across the bottom of the pan.

Whisk the eggs, half and half, and sugar together in a mixing bowl until thoroughly combined. Pour the cream mixture over the bread and press down with your hands to be sure all the bread is soaked with the custard. Cover with foil. Put the pan on a baking sheet with sides at least 1/2-inch tall or in another, larger baking pan. Put into the oven and add 1/2 inch of boiling water to the larger pan.

Bake for 40 to 45 minutes, adding more water if needed to the water bath. The pudding should be set, but still soft. Remove from the oven and remove the foil. Serve hot or cold. Refrigerate leftovers.

YIELD: Serves 10 to 12

Mango Bread Pudding

1 loaf (1 pound, or 455 g) home-style white **bread**

3 **eggs**

2 cups (475 ml) **half and half**

1 cup (200 g) **vanilla sugar** (See "Making Vanilla Sugar" on page 12.)

1 jar (16 ounces, or 455 g) fresh-packed **mango**

Preheat the oven to 325°F (170°C, gas mark 3). Grease the bottom and sides of a 9 x 12-inch baking pan.

Remove the crusts from the bread and cut it into 3/4-inch cubes. Spread the bread cubes evenly across the bottom of the pan.

Whisk eggs, half and half, and sugar together in a mixing bowl until thoroughly combined.

Drain the mango, reserving 1/2 cup (120 ml) of the juice. Cut up the mango into 1/2-inch pieces and mix them into the bread cubes. Add the reserved 1/2 cup juice to the custard mixture and pour the mixture over the bread. Press down with your hands to be sure all the bread is soaked with the custard. Cover with foil and put the pan on a baking sheet with sides at least 1/2-inch tall or in another, larger baking pan. Put into the oven and add 1/2 inch of boiling water to the larger pan.

Bake for 40 to 45 minutes, adding more water if needed to the water bath. The pudding should be set, but still soft. Remove from the oven and remove the foil. Serve hot or cold. Refrigerate leftovers.

YIELD: Serves 10 to 12

Raspberry Bread Pudding

    1 loaf (1 pound, or 455 g) home-style white **bread**

    3 **eggs**

    2 cups (475 ml) **half and half**

    1 cup (200 g) **vanilla sugar** (See "Making Vanilla Sugar" on page 12.)

    2 cups (250 g) fresh or frozen **raspberries** (If using frozen, do not thaw.)

Preheat the oven to 325°F (170°C, gas mark 3). Grease the bottom and sides of a 9 x 12-inch baking pan.

Remove the crusts from the bread and cut it into 3/4-inch cubes. Evenly spread the bread cubes across the bottom of the prepared pan.

Whisk the eggs, half and half, and sugar together in a mixing bowl until thoroughly combined.

Mix the raspberries with the bread cubes. Pour the cream mixture over and press down with your hands to be sure all the bread is soaked with the custard. Cover with foil. Put the pan on a baking sheet with sides at least 1/2-inch tall or in another, larger baking pan. Put into the oven and add 1/2 inch of boiling water to the larger pan.

Bake for 40 to 45 minutes, adding more water if needed to the water bath. The pudding should be set, but still soft. Remove from the oven and remove the foil. Serve hot or cold. Refrigerate leftovers.

YIELD: Serves 10 to 12

ADD IT! A drizzle of hot fudge sauce over each serving would be delightful.

Butterscotch Bread Pudding

1 loaf (1 pound, 455 g) home-style white **bread**

1 cup (175 g) **butterscotch chips**

3 **eggs**

2 cups (475 ml) **half and half**

1 cup (200 g) **vanilla sugar** (See "Making Vanilla Sugar" on page 000.)

Preheat the oven to 325°F (170°C, gas mark 3). Grease the bottom and sides of a 9 x 12-inch baking pan.

Remove the crusts from the bread and cut it into $3/4$-inch cubes. Mix the butterscotch chips with the bread cubes and spread the mixture evenly across the bottom of the pan.

Whisk the eggs, half and half, and sugar together in a mixing bowl until thoroughly combined. Pour the cream mixture over the bread and press down with your hands to be sure all the bread is soaked with the custard. Cover with foil. Put the pan on a baking sheet with sides at least $1/2$ inch tall or in another, larger baking pan. Put into the oven and add $1/2$ inch of boiling water to the larger pan.

Bake for 40 to 45 minutes, adding more water if needed to the water bath. The pudding should be set, but still soft. Remove from the oven and remove the foil. Serve hot or cold. Refrigerate leftovers.

YIELD: Serves 10 to 12

Chocolate Bread Pudding

This is a tremendously delicious and homey dessert for a cold winter's day, particularly when served with whipped cream on top.

    1 loaf (1 pound, 455 g) home-style white **bread**
    3 **eggs**
    2 cups (475 ml) **half and half**
    1 cup (200 g) **sugar**
    2 cups (350 g) **semisweet chocolate chips**

Preheat the oven to 325°F (170°C, gas mark 3). Grease the bottom and sides of a 9 x 12-inch baking pan.

Remove the crusts from the bread and cut it into ¾-inch cubes. Evenly spread the bread cubes across the bottom of the pan.

Whisk the eggs, half and half, and sugar together in a mixing bowl until thoroughly combined.

Melt 1 cup (175 g) of the chocolate chips in a stainless steel bowl set over simmering water, then whisk the melted chocolate into the cream mixture.

Sprinkle the remaining 1 cup (175 g) chocolate chips among the bread cubes. Pour the cream mixture over and press down with your hands to be sure all the bread is soaked with the custard. Cover with foil. Put the pan on a baking sheet with sides at least ½-inch tall or in another, larger baking pan. Put into the oven and add ½ inch of boiling water to the larger pan.

Bake for 40 to 45 minutes, adding more water if needed to the water bath. The pudding should be set, but still soft. Remove from the oven and remove the foil. Serve hot or cold. Refrigerate leftovers.

YIELD: Serves 10 to 12

Individual Dried Cherry Brioche Bread Puddings

  1 loaf (1 pound, or 455 g) brioche **bread** or challah bread

  2 cups (475 ml) **half and half**

  1 cup (200 g) **vanilla sugar** (See "Making Vanilla Sugar" on page 12.)

  4 **eggs**

  2 cups (6 ounces, or 170 g) dried tart **cherries**

Slice the bread into 1/4-inch slices. Butter six 6-ounce ramekins. Cut the bread into rounds the size of the inside diameter of the ramekins.

Combine the half and half and sugar in a saucepan and heat to a simmer, stirring until the sugar is dissolved.

Whisk the eggs together in a mixing bowl and add the hot half and half in a thin stream, whisking.

Place 1 round of bread in the bottom of each ramekin. Top with some dried cherries, then repeat with the remaining bread and cherries until the ramekins are filled almost to the top. Pour the custard over the bread in each ramekin. Allow to sit for 15 minutes.

Preheat the oven to 325°F (170°C, gas mark 3). Put the ramekins into a larger baking pan and fill the pan with boiling water about halfway up the ramekins. Cover with foil.

Bake for 35 to 40 minutes, until the custard is set. Remove from the oven, remove the foil, and allow the puddings to cool in the water bath for 15 minutes. Remove the puddings from the ramekins by freeing the sides with a knife and shaking them out onto plates.

YIELD: Serves 6

ADD IT! Decorate the plates with caramel sauce and top with whipped cream.

Coffee Gelatin

If you prefer desserts that err more towards spare and understated than loaded with baroque curls of all things sugar, this recipe is for you.

> 2 cups (475 ml) strong black **coffee** (regular or decaf)
> 1 cup (200 g) **sugar**, plus 2 tablespoons (25 g)
> ¼ cup (60 ml) coffee **brandy**
> 2 envelopes (¼ ounce, or 7.5 g, each) **unflavored gelatin**
> 1 cup (235 ml) **heavy cream**

Mix the coffee and 1 cup (200 g) of the sugar in a 1-quart saucepan.

Put the brandy in a bowl and sprinkle the gelatin over. Allow it to sit for 5 minutes to soften the gelatin, then add the gelatin-brandy mixture to the saucepan. Cook over medium heat until the gelatin and sugar are completely dissolved—8 to 10 minutes. Pour into a gelatin mold or a bowl. Refrigerate for at least 6 hours.

Whip the cream with the remaining 2 tablespoons (25 g) sugar to soft peaks. Unmold onto a platter, or dish the gelatin into serving bowls and top with the cream.

YIELD: Serves 6

Café au Lait Gelatin

This is an elegant gelatin that dresses up nicely if molded or chilled in individual bowls.

> 2 cups (475 ml) strong **coffee** (regular or decaf)
> 1 cup (235 ml) whole **milk**
> 1 cup (200 g) **sugar**
> 2 envelopes (¼ ounce, or 7.5 g, each) **unflavored gelatin**
> ¼ cup (60 ml) **coffee liqueur**

Combine the coffee, milk, and sugar in a 2-quart saucepan. Bring to a simmer over medium heat, stirring every minute or so.

While the coffee is heating, sprinkle the gelatin over the coffee liqueur in a small saucepan. When the gelatin has softened, about 5 minutes, heat the pan over medium-low heat until the gelatin is dissolved. Stir the gelatin into the coffee-milk mixture. Cook for 4 to 5 minutes longer, until all the sugar is dissolved. Pour into a mold or bowl and refrigerate for at least 6 hours, until set.

YIELD: Serves 6 to 8

ADD IT! Garnish with dollops of whipped cream.

🥄 Cappuccino Parfait

In French, parfait translates to perfect, and these cool concoctions certainly do slip down the throat perfectly easily. Serve parfaits in the most elegant glassware you have; you don't have to use the traditional footed parfait glasses.

> 4 cups (950 ml) strong black **coffee** (regular or decaf)
> 1 cup (200 g) **sugar**, plus 2 tablespoons (25 g)
> 1/4 cup (60 ml) **coffee brandy**
> 2 envelopes (1/4 ounce, or 7.5 g, each) **unflavored gelatin**
> 1 cup (235 ml) **heavy cream**

Mix the coffee and 1 cup (200 g) of the sugar in a 1-quart saucepan.

Put the brandy in a bowl and sprinkle the gelatin over. Allow it to sit for 5 minutes to soften the gelatin, then add the gelatin-brandy mixture to the saucepan. Cook over medium heat until the gelatin and sugar are completely dissolved—8 to 10 minutes.

Reserve and refrigerate 3/4 cup (175 ml) of the mixture. With the rest of the mixture, fill 6 parfait, Irish coffee, or other tall, footed glasses two-thirds of the way. Refrigerate.

After an hour or so, combine the reserved gelatin, now partially set, with the remaining 2 tablespoons (25 g) sugar and the cream in a mixing bowl. Whip this mixture to soft peaks. Top the gelatin in the glasses with this mousse. Refrigerate another 4 to 6 hours.

YIELD: Serves 6

Sicilian Trifle Parfait

Blood orange juice is dramatically red, and surprisingly available. If you can't find it, ordinary orange juice will work, too. It just won't be as swanky.

> 6 ounces (170 g) **bittersweet chocolate**
>
> 1 quart (30 ounces, or 850 g) part skim **ricotta**
>
> 1 cup (235 ml) blood **orange juice**
>
> 1 1/2 cups (180 g) **confectioners' sugar**
>
> 1 package (1 pound, or 455 g) **vanilla wafer cookies**

Chop the chocolate into small pieces and place it in a stainless steel mixing bowl. Place the bowl over a pan of simmering water and melt the chocolate, stirring until smooth. Set aside.

Combine the ricotta, blood orange juice, and sugar in a mixing bowl. Using an electric mixer with the whisk attachment, beat the mixture for 4 to 5 minutes, until fluffy. Put half the mixture in a mixing bowl and fold in the chocolate thoroughly.

Break the cookies into small pieces.

Using 8 parfait glasses, or tall wine glasses, spoon in a couple of tablespoons of the melted chocolate, some cookie pieces, then some of the orange mixture, then more cookies. Repeat until the glasses are full. Refrigerate at least 2 hours.

YIELD: Serves 8.

🥄 Vanilla Pots de Crème

The name is French for "pot of cream," and really, what could be more inviting than that? Like panna cotta, this custard dessert is served in small individual servings. You can buy pot de crème cups, or you can just use whatever tiny vessels you might have handy. It'll taste good either way!

> 1 cup (200 g) **sugar**
> 3 **eggs**
> 2 cups (475 ml) **heavy cream**
> 1/2 cup (120 ml) whole **milk**
> 2 **vanilla beans**

Preheat the oven to 300°F (150°C, gas mark 2).

Mix the sugar and eggs in a mixing bowl and whisk them well.

Put the cream and milk into a 1-quart saucepan. Cut the vanilla beans in half lengthwise. Scrape the seeds out with a sharp knife and add to the saucepan. Add the bean pods as well. Heat the mixture over high heat until it just boils. Remove from the heat and pour through a fine mesh sieve into the mixing bowl with the sugar and eggs while whisking. Pour the liquid into six 6-ounce ramekins and put the ramekins into a shallow baking pan. Fill the baking pan with boiling water halfway up the sides of the ramekins and cover the whole thing with foil, sealing the edges of the baking pan.

Bake for 30 to 35 minutes, until the custard is just set and still wiggles a bit in the middle. Cool for 15 to 20 minutes in the water bath and then refrigerate for at least 2 hours.

YIELD: Serves 6

ADD IT! Serve garnished with additional whipped cream, if desired.

Chocolate Pots de Crème

This may be the world's most sinful chocolate pudding, and here's the good thing: It is really simple to make.

> 6 ounces (170 g) **bittersweet chocolate**
>
> $1/2$ cup (100 g) **sugar**
>
> 3 **eggs**
>
> 2 teaspoons **brandy** or **vanilla extract**
>
> 2 cups (475 ml) **heavy cream**

Preheat the oven to 300°F (150°C, gas mark 2).

Chop the chocolate into small pieces. Put the chocolate into a food processor fitted with the steel blade. Add the sugar, eggs, and brandy.

Put the cream into a 1-quart saucepan and heat over high heat until it just boils. Remove from the heat and pour into the food processor with the motor running. Process until the chocolate is melted. Pour into six 6-ounce ramekins and put the ramekins into a shallow baking pan. Fill the baking pan with boiling water halfway up the sides of the ramekins and cover the whole thing with foil, sealing the edges of the baking pan.

Bake for 30 to 35 minutes, until the custard is just set and still wiggles a bit in the middle. Cool for 15 to 20 minutes in the water bath and then refrigerate for at least 2 hours.

YIELD: Serves 6

ADD IT! Serve garnished with whipped cream and shaved chocolate if desired.

Mocha Pots de Crème

These individual "pots of cream" are just to die for.

> 6 ounces (170 g) **bittersweet chocolate**
>
> 1/2 cup (100 g) **sugar**
>
> 3 **eggs**
>
> 1/4 cup **coffee brandy**
>
> 2 cups (475 ml) **heavy cream**

Preheat the oven to 300°F (150°C, gas mark 2).

Chop the chocolate into small pieces. Put the chocolate into a food processor fitted with the steel blade; add the sugar, eggs, and brandy and briefly process.

Put the cream into a 1-quart saucepan. Heat the cream over high heat until it just boils. Remove from the heat and pour into the food processor with the motor running. Process until the chocolate is melted. Pour into six 6-ounce ramekins and put the ramekins into a shallow baking pan. Fill the baking pan with boiling water halfway up the sides of the ramekins and cover the whole thing with foil, sealing the edges of the baking pan.

Bake for 30 to 35 minutes, until the custard is just set and still wiggles a bit in the middle. Cool for 15 to 20 minutes in the water bath and then refrigerate for at least 2 hours.

YIELD: Serves 6

ADD IT! Serve garnished with additional whipped cream and shaved chocolate if desired.

Eggnog Pots de Crème

A festive ending to a holiday meal.

     1 cup (200 g) **sugar**

     3 **eggs**

     2 cups (475 ml) **heavy cream**

     2 **vanilla beans**

     1 teaspoon **nutmeg**

Preheat the oven to 300°F (150°C, gas mark 2).

Mix the sugar and eggs in a mixing bowl and whisk them well.

Put the cream into a 1-quart saucepan. Cut the vanilla beans in half lengthwise. Scrape the seeds out with a sharp knife and add to the saucepan. Add the beans as well. Heat the cream over high heat until it just boils. Remove from the heat and pour through a fine mesh sieve into the mixing bowl while whisking the eggs. Whisk in the nutmeg. Pour the liquid into six 6-ounce ramekins and put the ramekins into a shallow baking pan. Fill the baking pan with boiling water halfway up the sides of the ramekins and cover the whole thing with foil, sealing the edges of the baking pan.

Bake for 30 to 35 minutes, until the custard is just set and still wiggles a bit in the middle. Cool for 15 to 20 minutes in the water bath and then refrigerate for at least 2 hours.

YIELD: Serves 6

ADD IT! Add 2 teaspoons rum extract to the sugar and eggs.

Chocolate Cardamom Pots de Crème

6 ounces (170 g) **bittersweet chocolate**

1/2 cup (100 g) **sugar**

1/2 teaspoon ground **cardamom**

2 **eggs**

2 cups (475 ml) **half and half**

Preheat the oven to 325°F (170°C, gas mark 3).

Chop the chocolate into small pieces. Put the chocolate, sugar, cardamom, and eggs into the bowl of a food processor fitted with the metal blade.

Bring the half and half to a boil and pour over the chocolate. Run the processor until the chocolate is melted. Pour into six 6-ounce ramekins set in a shallow baking pan. Pour boiling water into the pan until it comes halfway up the sides of the ramekins. Cover with foil.

Bake for 25 to 30 minutes, until the centers of the custards are just set. Remove from the oven, remove the foil, and allow the pots de crèmes to cool in the water bath for 30 minutes. Refrigerate for at least 1 hour.

YIELD: Serves 6

Chocolate Coeurs à la Crème

Coeur à la crème is French for heart with cream, and this dessert is traditionally made in a heart-shaped mold. We're going for individual desserts instead, but we promise that the result will still be delicious, rich, chocolate heaven.

> 1 cup (235 ml) **heavy cream**
> 1/3 cup (30 g) **cocoa powder**
> 2 tablespoons (28 g) butter
> 6 ounces (170 g) **cream cheese**
> 1 cup (120 g) **confectioners' sugar**
> 1 teaspoon **vanilla extract**

Mix 1/2 cup (120 ml) of the cream, the cocoa powder, and the butter in a small saucepan. Cook over medium heat, stirring, until smooth—7 to 8 minutes.

Put the cream cheese, sugar, and vanilla in a mixing bowl and beat on medium speed until smooth and fluffy, about 5 minutes. Add the chocolate mixture and blend well. Add the remaining 1/2 cup (120 ml) cream and blend.

Line eight 4-ounce ramekins or molds with cheesecloth. Spoon the chocolate mixture into the ramekins. Wrap the cheesecloth over the top and turn the molds upside-down on a rack placed on a cookie sheet. Refrigerate for at least 8 hours.

Remove the cheesecloth from the molds and unwrap the coeurs à la crème.

YIELD: Serves 8

ADD IT! The traditional garnish for a coeur à la crème is fresh berries, so slice some ripe strawberries and scatter over each serving. Dust them with additional cocoa powder and serve with whipped cream if desired.

♨ Chocolate-Hazelnut Trifle

This is a twist on the traditional trifle, which is rich in custard, jam, and fruit.

> 4 **egg yolks**
> 1 1/2 cups (300 g) **vanilla sugar** (See "Making Vanilla Sugar" on page 12.)
> 2 cups (475 ml) whole **milk**
> 1 (12 ounce, or 340 g) **angel food cake**
> 1 jar (12 ounce, or 340 g) **Nutella chocolate-hazelnut spread**

Fill a large bowl with ice water and set aside. Whisk the egg yolks in a mixing bowl with the sugar.

Put the milk into a saucepan and scald over medium-high heat. Constantly whisking, pour the milk in a thin stream into the egg mixture. Return to the saucepan and cook, stirring constantly, over medium heat until the custard thickens. Immediately plunge the saucepan into the ice water to stop the cooking. Set the cooled custard aside.

Slice the angel food cake into 1/2-inch slices. Cover the bottom of a glass serving bowl with half the cake slices and smear the cake liberally with the Nutella. Spoon in half the custard and add another layer of cake, more Nutella, and top with the remaining custard.

Refrigerate for at least 4 hours.

YIELD: Serves 8 to 10

ADD IT! Top off this trifle with whipped cream.

Fresh Strawberry Trifle

That's what we're talking about! Trifle is a true food of the gods.

> 4 **egg yolks**
> 1 1/2 cups (300 g) **vanilla sugar** (See "Making Vanilla Sugar" on page 12.)
> 2 cups (475 ml) **half and half**
> 1 (12 ounce, or 340 g) **angel food cake**
> 1 quart (660 g) **strawberries**, hulled, reserving several whole for garnish

Fill a large bowl with ice water and set aside. Whisk the egg yolks in a mixing bowl with 1 cup (200 g) of the sugar.

Put the half and half into a saucepan and scald over medium-high heat. Whisking constantly, pour the hot milk in a thin stream into the egg mixture. Return to the saucepan and cook, stirring constantly, over medium heat until the custard thickens. Immediately plunge the saucepan into the ice water to stop the cooking. Set the cooled custard aside.

Mash the strawberries in a bowl along with the 1/2 cup (100 g) remaining sugar. Allow to sit for 10 minutes.

Slice the angel food cake into 1/2-inch slices. Line the bottom of a glass serving bowl with cake and smear the cake liberally with the mashed berries. Spoon in half the custard and add another layer of cake, more berry mash, and top with the remaining custard. Garnish with the reserved whole berries. Refrigerate for at least 4 hours.

YIELD: Serves 8 to 10

Jam Trifle

The English have certainly been known to soak the cake in sherry. This is an alcohol-free version.

> 4 **egg yolks**
> 1 cup (200 g) **vanilla sugar** (See "Making Vanilla Sugar" on page 12.)
> 2 cups (475 ml) **half and half**
> 1 (12 ounce, or 340 g) **angel food cake**
> 2 cups (640 g) strawberry, raspberry, or other favorite **jam**

Fill a large bowl with ice water and set aside. Whisk the egg yolks in a mixing bowl with the sugar.

Put the half and half into a saucepan and scald over medium-high heat. Pour the hot half and half into the bowl in a thin stream, while whisking. Return to the saucepan and cook, stirring constantly, over medium heat until the custard thickens. Immediately plunge the saucepan into the ice water to stop the cooking. Set the cooled custard aside.

Slice the angel food cake into 1/2-inch slices. Line the bottom of a glass serving bowl with cake and smear the cake liberally with the jam. Spoon in half the custard and add another layer of cake, more jam, and top with the remaining custard. Refrigerate for at least 4 hours.

YIELD: Serves 8 to 10

ADD IT! Pour a little sherry over the cake and serve with fresh strawberries or raspberries to match your jam choice.

🥄 Tiramisu

1 container (8 ounces, or 225 g) **vanilla custard**

1 container (8 ounces, or 225 g) **mascarpone cheese**

2 cups (475 ml) **heavy cream**

2 cups (475 ml) **coffee syrup**

24 **ladyfingers**, cake or cookie type

In a mixing bowl, beat the custard and mascarpone together until smooth.

Whip 1 cup (235 ml) of the cream to stiff peaks and fold it into the custard mixture.

Put the coffee syrup in a bowl or shallow pan. Dip 12 of the ladyfingers in the syrup and line the bottom of a 9-inch square serving dish. Top with half the custard mixture and spread out evenly to cover the ladyfingers. Repeat with the remaining ladyfingers to form another layer, then the remaining custard. Refrigerate for at least 8 hours.

Whip the remaining 1 cup (235 ml) cream to stiff peaks and spread over the top of the tiramisu.

YIELD: Serves 6 to 9

ADD IT! Stir in ¼ cup (60 ml) Marsala wine with the custard. Traditional garnish is a dusting of cocoa powder.

🥄 Kiwi Fool

Another delicious dessert entry from Merry Olde England, fools are made of pureed fruit and whipped cream. Gooseberries are the traditional choice; here, we keep the color but change the fruit to something more easily obtainable.

6 ripe **kiwi fruit**

1 cup (200 g) **sugar**

2 cups (475 ml) **heavy cream**

1 teaspoon **vanilla extract**

1 tablespoon (14 ml) **melon liqueur**

Peel the kiwi fruit and slice them, reserving 8 slices for garnish. Put the kiwi fruit and the sugar in a food processor. Process until smooth.

Combine the cream, vanilla, and liqueur in a mixing bowl and whip to stiff peaks. Fold in the fruit puree and spoon into 8 wine glasses or other individual serving containers. Refrigerate for at least 2 hours. Garnish with the reserved fruit slices.

YIELD: Serves 8

Strawberry Fool

A fool is pureed fruit folded into whipped cream, making a light textured pudding.

> 1 quart (700 g) **strawberries**
> 1 cup (200 g) **sugar**
> 2 cups (475 ml) **heavy cream**
> 1 teaspoon **vanilla extract**
> 1 teaspoon **rum extract**

Hull and slice the strawberries, reserving 8 whole berries for garnish. Put the berries and the sugar in a food processor. Process until smooth.

Combine the cream, vanilla, and rum extract in a mixing bowl and whip to stiff peaks. Fold in the fruit puree and spoon into 8 wine glasses or other individual serving containers. Refrigerate for at least 2 hours. Garnish with the reserved berries.

YIELD: Serves 8

Crème Brûlée

This is one of the most popular desserts sold in restaurants, and with good reason.

8 **egg yolks**

2/3 cup (130 g) **sugar**, plus about 1/2 cup (100 g) for topping

2 2/3 cups (630 ml) **heavy cream**

1 tablespoon (14 ml) **vanilla extract**

1/4 teaspoon **nutmeg**

Preheat the oven to 300°F (150°C, gas mark 2).

Combine the egg yolks and 2/3 cup (130 g) sugar in a stainless steel mixing bowl.

Put the cream in a saucepan and bring it just to a boil over high heat. (Watch out, as the cream loves to boil over.) Whisking lightly, pour the cream into the egg yolks in a thin stream. Try not to create much foam, don't whisk hard. Stir in the vanilla and the nutmeg.

Pour the liquid into six 6-ounce ramekins set in a shallow baking dish. Pour boiling water into the baking pan halfway up the sides of the ramekins. Cover with foil.

Bake for 25 to 30 minutes, until the custards are just set in the middle. Cool in the water bath, then remove the ramekins from the water bath and refrigerate for at least 2 hours. Just before serving, sprinkle 2 teaspoons or so of the remaining sugar on top of each custard. Using a propane torch, or under the broiler, caramelize the sugar.

YIELD: Serves 6

Lemon Crème Brûlée

8 egg yolks

$^2/_3$ cup (130 g) **sugar**, plus about $^1/_2$ cup (100 g) for topping

3 lemons

$2^2/_3$ cups (630 ml) **heavy cream**

1 tablespoon (14 ml) **vanilla extract**

Preheat the oven to 300°F (150°C, gas mark 2).

Combine the egg yolks and $^2/_3$ cup (130 g) of the sugar in a stainless steel mixing bowl. Grate the lemon zest, about 1 tablespoon, and add it to the yolks.

Put the cream in a saucepan and bring it just to a boil over high heat. (Watch out, as the cream loves to boil over.) Pour the cream into the egg yolks in a thin stream, whisking lightly. Try not to create much foam; don't whisk hard. Squeeze the lemons to yield about $^1/_3$ cup (75 ml) juice and stir in the lemon juice, along with the vanilla.

Pour the liquid into six 6-ounce ramekins set in a shallow baking dish. Pour boiling water into the baking pan halfway up the sides of the ramekins. Cover with foil.

Bake for 25 to 30 minutes, until the custards are just set in the middle. Cool in the water bath, then remove the ramekins from the water bath and refrigerate for at least 2 hours. Just before serving, sprinkle 2 teaspoons or so of the remaining sugar on top of each custard. Using a propane torch, or under the broiler, caramelize the sugar.

YIELD: Serves 6

Orange Crème Brûlée

8 egg yolks

2/3 cup (130 g) **sugar**, plus about 1/2 cup (100 g) for topping

1/3 cup (75 ml) **orange liqueur**

2 oranges

2 2/3 cups (630 ml) **heavy cream**

Preheat the oven to 300°F (150°C, gas mark 2).

Combine the egg yolks, sugar, and liqueur in a stainless steel mixing bowl. Grate the zest from the oranges and add to the yolks. Squeeze the oranges and add the juice to the bowl.

Put the cream in a saucepan and bring it just to a boil over high heat. (Watch out, as the cream loves to boil over.) Whisking lightly, pour the cream into the egg yolks in a thin stream. Try not to create much foam; don't whisk hard.

Pour the liquid into six 6-ounce ramekins set in a shallow baking dish. Pour boiling water into the baking pan halfway up the sides of the ramekins. Cover with foil.

Bake for 25 to 30 minutes, until the custards are just set in the middle. Cool in the water bath, then remove the ramekins from the water bath and refrigerate for at least 2 hours. Just before serving, sprinkle 2 teaspoons or so of the remaining sugar on top of each custard. Using a propane torch, or under the broiler, caramelize the sugar.

YIELD: Serves 6

Raspberry Crème Brûlée

If you can't find raspberry puree, put about a cup of raspberries in the blender and puree. Push the pureed berries through a fine sieve to get rid of the seeds, and you're good to go. Framboise is a widely available raspberry liqueur.

8 **egg yolks**

$2/3$ cup (130 g) **sugar,** plus about $1/2$ cup (100 g) for topping

$1/4$ cup (60 ml) **raspberry puree**

$1/4$ cup (60 ml) **Framboise**

$2^2/3$ cups (630 ml) **heavy cream**

Preheat the oven to 300°F (150°C, gas mark 2).

Combine the egg yolks, $2/3$ cup (130 g) of the sugar, raspberry puree, and Framboise in a stainless steel mixing bowl.

Put the cream in a saucepan and bring it just to a boil over high heat. (Watch out, as the cream loves to boil over.) Whisking lightly, pour the cream into the egg yolk mixture in a thin stream. Try not to create much foam; don't whisk hard.

Pour the liquid into six 6-ounce ramekins set in a shallow baking dish. Pour boiling water into the baking pan halfway up the sides of the ramekins. Cover with foil.

Bake for 25 to 30 minutes, until the custards are just set in the middle. Cool in the water bath, then remove the ramekins from the water bath and refrigerate for at least 2 hours. Just before serving, sprinkle 2 teaspoons or so of the remaining sugar on top of each custard. Using a propane torch, or under the broiler, caramelize the sugar to a thin crust.

YIELD: Serves 6

Hazelnut Crème Brûlée

8 **egg yolks**

$2/3$ cup (130 g) **sugar**, plus about $1/2$ cup (100 g) for topping

$1/3$ cup (75 ml) **hazelnut liqueur**

$2^{2}/3$ cups (630 ml) **heavy cream**

1 tablespoon (14 ml) **vanilla extract**

Preheat the oven to 300°F (150°C, gas mark 2).

Combine the egg yolks, $2/3$ cup (130 g) of the sugar, and the hazelnut liqueur in a stainless steel mixing bowl.

Put the cream in a saucepan and bring it just to a boil over high heat. (Watch out, as cream loves to boil over.) Whisking lightly, pour the cream into the egg yolks in a thin stream. Try not to create much foam; don't whisk hard. Stir in the vanilla.

Pour the liquid into six 6-ounce ramekins set in a shallow baking dish. Pour boiling water into the baking pan halfway up the sides of the ramekins. Cover with foil.

Bake for 25 to 30 minutes, until the custards are just set in the middle. Cool in the water bath, then remove the ramekins from the water bath and refrigerate for at least 2 hours. Just before serving, sprinkle 2 teaspoons or so of the remaining sugar on top of each custard. Using a propane torch, or the broiler, caramelize the sugar into a thin crust.

YIELD: Serves 6

Ginger Crème Brûlée

This dessert is refreshing and elegant, and don't forget the high gadget allure of making a crème brûlée. (Tiny propane torch! How cool is that!)

8 **egg yolks**
2/3 cup (130 g) **sugar**, plus about 1/2 cup (100 g) for topping
1/4 cup (60 ml) **ginger brandy**
2 2/3 cups (630 ml) **heavy cream**
2 tablespoons (12 g) minced fresh **ginger**

Preheat the oven to 300°F (150°C, gas mark 2).

Combine the egg yolks, 2/3 cup (130 g) of the sugar, and the ginger brandy in a stainless steel mixing bowl.

Put the cream in a saucepan and add the ginger. Bring the cream just to a boil over high heat. (Watch out, as the cream loves to boil over.) Allow to sit, off heat, for 10 minutes to infuse the ginger into the cream. Strain the cream through a fine mesh strainer and discard the ginger. Gently whisk the cream into the egg yolks in a thin stream. Try not to create much foam; don't whisk hard.

Pour the liquid into six 6-ounce ramekins set in a shallow baking dish. Pour boiling water into the baking pan halfway up the sides of the ramekins. Cover with foil.

Bake for 25 to 30 minutes, until the custards are just set in the middle. Cool in the water bath, then remove the ramekins from the water bath and refrigerate for at least 2 hours. Just before serving, sprinkle 2 teaspoons or so of the remaining sugar on top of each custard. Using a propane torch, or the broiler, caramelize the sugar.

YIELD: Serves 6

Coffee Crème Brûlée

8 **egg yolks**

2/3 cup (130 g) **sugar**, plus about 1/2 cup (100 g) for topping

1/3 cup (75 ml) **coffee liqueur**

2 2/3 cups (630 ml) **heavy cream**

1 tablespoon (14 ml) **vanilla extract**

Preheat the oven to 300°F (150°C, gas mark 2).

Combine the egg yolks, 2/3 cup (130 g) sugar, and coffee liqueur in a stainless steel mixing bowl.

Put the cream in a saucepan and bring it just to a boil over high heat. (Watch out, as the cream loves to boil over.) Whisking lightly, pour the hot cream in a thin stream into the egg mixture. Try not to create much foam; don't whisk hard. Stir in the vanilla.

Pour the liquid into six 6-ounce ramekins set in a shallow baking dish. Pour boiling water into the baking pan halfway up the sides of the ramekins. Cover with foil.

Bake for 25 to 30 minutes, until the custards are just set in the middle. Cool in the water bath, then remove the ramekins from the water bath and refrigerate for at least 2 hours. Just before serving, sprinkle 2 teaspoons or so of the remaining sugar on top of each custard. Using a propane torch, or under the broiler, caramelize the sugar until it forms a crunchy crust.

YIELD: Serves 6

Irish Cream Crème Brûlée

8 **egg yolks**

2/3 cup (130 g) **sugar**, plus about 1/2 cup (100 g) for topping

1/2 cup (120 ml) **Irish cream liqueur**

2 2/3 cups (630 ml) **heavy cream**

1 tablespoon (14 ml) **vanilla extract**

Preheat the oven to 300°F (150°C, gas mark 2).

Combine the egg yolks, 2/3 cup (130 g) of the sugar, and the liqueur in a stainless steel mixing bowl.

Put the cream in a saucepan and bring it just to a boil over high heat. (Watch out, as the cream loves to boil over.) Whisking lightly, pour the cream into the egg yolks in a thin stream. Try not to create much foam, don't whisk hard. Stir in the vanilla.

Pour the liquid into six 6-ounce ramekins set in a shallow baking dish. Pour boiling water into the baking pan halfway up the sides of the ramekins. Cover with foil.

Bake for 25 to 30 minutes, until the custards are just set in the middle. Cool in the water bath, then remove the ramekins from the water bath and refrigerate for at least 2 hours. Just before serving, sprinkle 2 teaspoons or so of the remaining sugar on top of each custard. Using a propane torch, or the broiler, caramelize the sugar.

YIELD: Serves 6

Maple Crème Brûlée

Bob sells a ton of these at the Three Stallion Inn.

> 8 **egg yolks**
>
> 2/3 cup (130 g) **sugar**, plus about 1/2 cup (100 g) for topping
>
> 1/2 cup (120 ml) **maple syrup**
>
> 2 2/3 cups (630 ml) **heavy cream**
>
> 1 tablespoon (14 ml) **vanilla extract**

Preheat the oven to 300°F (150°C, gas mark 2).

Combine the egg yolks, sugar, and maple syrup in a stainless steel mixing bowl.

Put the cream in a saucepan and bring it just to a boil over high heat. (Watch out, as the cream loves to boil over.) Whisking lightly, pour the cream into the egg yolks in a thin stream. Try not to create much foam; don't whisk hard. Stir in the vanilla.

Pour the liquid into six 6-ounce ramekins set in a shallow baking dish. Pour boiling water into the baking pan halfway up the sides of the ramekins. Cover with foil.

Bake for 25 to 30 minutes, until the custards are just set in the middle. Cool in the water bath, then remove the ramekins from the water bath and refrigerate for at least 2 hours. Just before serving, sprinkle 2 teaspoons or so of the remaining sugar on top of each custard. Using a propane torch, or under the broiler, caramelize the sugar.

YIELD: Serves 6

Pumpkin Crème Brûlée

8 **egg yolks**

2/3 cup (130 g) **sugar**, plus about 1/2 cup (100 g) for topping

1/2 cup (135 g) canned spiced and sweetened **pumpkin**

1 teaspoon **pumpkin pie spice**

2 2/3 cups (630 ml) **heavy cream**

Preheat the oven to 300°F (150°C, gas mark 2).

Combine the egg yolks, sugar, pumpkin, and pumpkin pie spice in a stainless steel mixing bowl.

Put the cream in a saucepan and bring it just to a boil over high heat. (Watch out, as the cream loves to boil over.) Whisking lightly, pour the cream into the egg yolks in a thin stream. Try not to create much foam; don't whisk hard.

Pour the liquid into six 6-ounce ramekins set in a shallow baking dish. Pour boiling water into the baking pan halfway up the sides of the ramekins. Cover with foil.

Bake for 25 to 30 minutes, until the custards are just set in the middle. Cool in the water bath, then remove the ramekins from the water bath and refrigerate for at least 2 hours. Just before serving, sprinkle 2 teaspoons or so of the remaining sugar on top of each custard. Using a propane torch, or under the broiler, caramelize the sugar.

YIELD: Serves 6

White Chocolate Crème Brûlée

8 **egg yolks**

$2/3$ cup (130 g) **sugar**, plus about $1/2$ cup (100 g) for topping

$1/3$ cup (75 ml) **white crème de cacao**

$2\,2/3$ cups (630 ml) **heavy cream**

4 ounces (115 g) **white chocolate**

Preheat the oven to 300°F (150°C, gas mark 2).

Combine the egg yolks, $2/3$ cup (130 g) of the sugar, and the liqueur in a stainless steel mixing bowl.

Put the cream in a saucepan and bring it just to a boil over high heat. (Watch out, as the cream loves to boil over.) Whisking lightly, pour the cream into the egg yolk mixture in a thin stream. Try not to create much foam; don't whisk hard.

Melt the chocolate in a stainless steel bowl over simmering water. Stir the melted chocolate into the custard mixture. Pour the custard into six 6-ounce ramekins set in a shallow baking dish. Pour boiling water into the baking pan halfway up the sides of the ramekins. Cover with foil.

Bake for 25 to 30 minutes, until the custards are just set in the middle. Cool in the water bath, then remove the ramekins from the water bath and refrigerate for at least 2 hours. Just before serving, sprinkle 2 teaspoons or so of the remaining sugar on top of each custard. Using a propane torch or the broiler, caramelize the sugar.

YIELD: Serves 6

White Chocolate Crème Brûlée with Raspberries

We love this elegant and beautiful dessert.

> 8 **egg yolks**
> 2/3 cup (130 g) **sugar**, plus about 1/2 cup (100 g) for topping
> 2 2/3 cups (630 ml) **heavy cream**
> 6 ounces (170 g) **white chocolate**
> 1 cup (125 g) **raspberries**

Preheat the oven to 300°F (150°C, gas mark 2).

Combine the egg yolks and 2/3 cup (130 g) of the sugar in a stainless steel mixing bowl.

Put the cream in a saucepan and bring it just to a boil over high heat. (Watch out, as the cream loves to boil over.) Whisking lightly, pour the cream into the egg yolks in a thin stream. Try not to create much foam; don't whisk hard.

Melt the chocolate in a stainless steel bowl over simmering water and stir the melted chocolate into the custard mixture. Pour the liquid into six 6-ounce ramekins set in a shallow baking dish. Divide the raspberries among the ramekins. Pour boiling water into the baking pan halfway up the sides of the ramekins. Cover with foil.

Bake for 25 to 30 minutes, until the custards are just set in the middle. Cool in the water bath, then remove the ramekins from the water bath and refrigerate for at least 2 hours. Just before serving, sprinkle 2 teaspoons or so of the remaining sugar on top of each custard. Using a propane torch, or the broiler, caramelize the sugar into a thin crust.

YIELD: Serves 6

Crème Caramel

We are making this crème caramel (also known as flan) recipe as individual flans, but you can also make this as one large custard in a 4 x 9-inch loaf pan.

> 1 1/2 cups (300 g) **sugar**
> About 4 tablespoons (60 ml) water
> 4 **eggs**
> 1 1/2 cups (355 ml) whole **milk**
> 1 cup (235 ml) **half and half**
> 2 teaspoons **vanilla extract**

Preheat the oven to 325°F (170°C, gas mark 3).

Put 1/2 cup (100 g) of the sugar in a 1-quart heavy bottomed saucepan. Add the water, or enough so that the sugar resembles "wet sand." Cook over high heat, not stirring, until the sugar is a deep golden brown. Remove from the heat immediately and pour the caramel evenly among six 6-ounce ramekins.

Whisk the eggs in a mixing bowl with the remaining 1 cup (200 g) sugar.

Put the milk and half and half into a saucepan and scald over medium-high heat. Whisking, pour the hot milk into the eggs in a thin stream. Stir in the vanilla.

Put the ramekins into a baking dish large enough to hold them without touching. Divide the custard among the ramekins. Pour boiling water into the baking dish about halfway up the sides of the ramekins.

Bake for 35 to 40 minutes, until the custards are set. Remove from the oven and allow to cool in the water bath for 30 minutes. Refrigerate overnight.

To serve, slip a sharp knife around the inner wall of the ramekin and turn the crème caramels onto dessert plates, allowing the caramel sauce to flow over the custard and to pool on the plate.

YIELD: Serves 6

Crème Catalan with Strawberries

This has a crisp topping like a crème brûlée, but it's a much lighter dessert.

> 5 **eggs**, separated
>
> 3 teaspoons **flour**
>
> 1 cup (235 ml) **light cream**
>
> $2/3$ cup (130 g) **sugar**, plus another $1/3$ cup (60 g) for finishing
>
> $1/4$ cup (60 ml) water
>
> 1 pint (350 g) **strawberries**, hulled and quartered

Put the egg yolks into a stainless steel mixing bowl. Whisk until pale, then whisk in the flour until smooth.

Heat the cream in a saucepan over medium-high heat until it just boils. (Be careful; it will try to boil over.) Whisk the cream into the yolks in a thin stream. Return the mixture to the saucepan and cook over medium heat, stirring constantly until the mixture boils. Reduce the heat to low and whisk for 2 to 3 minutes, then remove from the heat.

Put the egg whites into a large stainless steel bowl and beat them until stiff peaks form. Set them aside. Combine the $2/3$ cup (130 g) sugar and the water in a small saucepan. Cook over high heat until the mixture is syrup, but still clear. Remove from the heat. Whisking constantly and pouring in a thin stream, add the hot syrup to the egg whites.

Fold the egg whites into the cream mixture. Divide the strawberries among six 6-ounce ramekins. Spoon the custard over the berries to fill each ramekin. Refrigerate, covered with plastic, for at least 8 hours, preferably overnight.

To serve, sprinkle some of the reserved sugar on the top of each custard and caramelize it using a propane torch or under the broiler. Allow to cool briefly.

YIELD: Serves 6

ADD IT! Serve garnished with additional berries if desired.

Raspberry Crème Sucre

1/2 cup (120 ml) water

1 envelope (1/4 ounce, or 7.5 g, each) **unflavored gelatin**

1 cup (200 g) **sugar**

2 cups (460 g) **sour cream**

1 cup (235 ml) **heavy cream**

1 cup (125 g) **raspberries**

Put the water in a small saucepan. Sprinkle the gelatin over the water and allow the gelatin to soften for 5 minutes. Heat the gelatin and water over low heat until the gelatin is completely dissolved. Add the sugar and turn up the heat to medium. Cook, stirring, until the sugar is dissolved.

Put the sour cream in a mixing bowl and whisk in the sugar mixture.

Whip the cream to stiff peaks and fold into the sour cream. Fold in the raspberries. Spoon the cream into a mold or serving dish and refrigerate for at least 4 hours. Unmold if you wish.

YIELD: Serves 6 to 8

ADD IT! Garnish with additional berries and/or whipped cream.

CHAPTER NINE

Fruit Desserts

Many people believe that fruit does not rightfully belong in any discussion pertaining to dessert. And we must admit that as children, we groaned in spirit (and sometimes in voice) when our polite inquiries about dessert choices were met with a sprightly, "We have apples, oranges, or bananas." We weren't fooled by our Mom's cheery voice. She was trying to disguise virtue as reward.

But nowadays, we are more apt to think fondly of a juicy, sweet peach as an after dinner sweet, and we are not alone. At Chez Panisse, the San Francisco restaurant renowned for its celebration of fresh, organic, local produce, the menu will sometimes feature a perfect piece of fruit as a dessert item.

In truth, fruit is amazingly versatile. It can be gussied up with poaching, baking, and grilling; snuggled under a layer of sweet cobbler crust; or served under a drift of whipped cream. There's nothing spartan or second-rate about fruit recipes taking center stage on the dessert menu these days; just try them and see!

♥ Ambrosia

This popular Southern dish is nearly as divisive as clam chowder when it comes to agreeing on how it is best made. Some people claim that pecans and marshmallows are de rigueur, while others scorn the thought. We're trying to walk the path of moderation here and as a result will probably please nobody.

1 fresh **pineapple**

3 medium **oranges**

2 medium **bananas**

1 cup (50 g) **mini marshmallows**

1/2 cup (35 g) **sweetened shredded coconut**

Prepare the pineapple by cutting off the top and bottom and carefully cutting away the rind. Split the pineapple in half lengthwise and remove the core. Slice into 1-inch chunks. Peel and section the oranges and slice into chunks. Slice the bananas into disks.

In a large bowl, combine the pineapple, oranges, bananas, marshmallows, and coconut. Cover and refrigerate.

YIELD: Serves 6 to 8

ADD IT! Depending on your stance on ambrosia, other add-ins include chopped pecans, maraschino cherries, and grapes.

🍎 Roasted Plum and Mascarpone Parfait

Here's a little known rule of fine dining: Any dessert served in a glass is automatically bestowed the status of swanky and elegant. Nobody needs to know how easy they are to make, though, do they?

> 6 **plums**
>
> 1 1/2 cups (300 g) **sugar**
>
> 1 teaspoon **cinnamon**
>
> 12 ounces (340 g) **mascarpone cheese**
>
> 12 **amoretti cookies**

Preheat the oven to 350°F (180°C, gas mark 4).

Split the plums and remove the pits. Cut each plum half into 3 wedges and put them in a mixing bowl.

In a separate bowl, mix together 1/2 cup (100 g) of the sugar and the cinnamon and add to the plums. Toss to coat the plums and spread them on a baking sheet.

Roast in the oven for 20 to 25 minutes, until the plums have begun to wilt a bit. Remove from the oven and cool completely on the baking sheet.

In a mixing bowl, stir the mascarpone and the remaining 1 cup (200 g) sugar together until the sugar is dissolved.

In another bowl, crumble the cookies into coarse crumbs.

Spoon 2 to 3 tablespoons of mascarpone into each of 4 white wine or champagne glasses. Top with a couple of pieces of plum and some cookie crumbs. Repeat for 3 to 4 layers, until the glasses are full almost to the top. Finish with some mascarpone and cookie crumbs. Refrigerate for 1 or more hours.

YIELD: Serves 4

Strawberries with Grand Marnier and Black Pepper

Freshly ground pepper is a key.

> 1 quart (700 g) **strawberries**
> 1/4 cup (60 ml) **Grand Marnier**
> 1 teaspoon freshly ground black **pepper**
> 1/2 cup (100 g) **sugar**, plus 2 tablespoons (25 g)
> 1 cup (235 ml) **heavy cream**

Hull and halve the berries. Toss gently with the Grand Marnier, pepper, and 1/2 cup (100 g) of the sugar. Allow to sit for 15 to 20 minutes, then divide among 4 bowls, being sure to include the juices.

Whip the cream and remaining 2 tablespoons (25 g) sugar until soft peak stage and spoon over the berries.

YIELD: Serves 4

Lavender Peaches Poached in Riesling

You can use any sweet white dessert wine for this dish.

> 4 **peaches**
> 2 cups (475 ml) **Riesling wine**—not dry
> 2 teaspoons dried **lavender**
> 1/2 cup (100 g) **sugar**

Bring a large pot of water to a boil. Drop the peaches in for 15 to 20 seconds, then plunge them into cold water. Drain the peaches and peel them, then cut them in half and remove the pits.

Mix the wine, lavender, and sugar in a 2-quart saucepan. Cook over medium heat until the sugar is dissolved, then add the peaches. Reduce the heat to low and poach for about 25 minutes. Remove the peaches with a slotted spoon and cool them in the refrigerator.

Return the cooking liquid to a boil over medium-high heat and reduce to a syrup consistency. Strain to remove the lavender. Place the peaches on four plates and pour the syrup over.

YIELD: Serves 4

ADD IT! This is great with some raspberry sorbet.

🍑 Citrus Poached Peaches

4 ripe **peaches**

2 cups (400 g) **vanilla sugar** (See "Making Vanilla Sugar" on page 12.)

3 cups (705 ml) **orange juice**

1 teaspoon **cinnamon**

1 pint (285 g) **lemon sorbet**

Boil a large pot of water. Drop the peaches in for 10 seconds, remove them, and plunge them into a bowl of ice water. Peel the peaches carefully, split them, and remove the pits.

In a 12-inch skillet (not cast iron) combine the sugar, orange juice, and cinnamon. Bring to a simmer over medium heat until the sugar is melted. Add the peaches, adding enough orange juice so that they are just covered. (You may need a little more, or a little less, than 3 cups.) Poach for 10 to 12 minutes. Refrigerate in the poaching liquid for at least 2 hours.

Remove the peaches from the poaching liquid and drain on paper towels. Reheat the poaching liquid and reduce by half, stirring. Set aside and let cool.

Ladle a puddle of sauce on four plates. Put two peaches on each plate and fit a small scoop of sorbet into the hollow of each peach half. Serve immediately.

YIELD: Serves 4

Poached Peaches with Melba Gelée

Here is another fancy, kind of complicated dessert that could come out of an upscale restaurant kitchen. Your friends don't have to know that it was easy to make and has only 5 ingredients.

> 4 ripe **peaches**
>
> 3 cups (600 g) **sugar**
>
> 4 cups (950 ml) water
>
> 3 cups (375 g) fresh **raspberries**
>
> 1 envelope ($^1/_4$ ounce, or 7.5 g) **unflavored gelatin**
>
> 1 sheet frozen **puff pastry dough** (6 x 9 inch, or 15 x 22$^1/_2$ cm), thawed

Boil a large pot of water. Drop the peaches in for 10 seconds, remove them, and plunge them into a bowl of ice water. Peel the peaches carefully, split them, and remove the pits.

In a 12-inch skillet (not cast iron), combine 1 cup (200 g) of the sugar with 3 cups (705 ml) of the water. Bring to a simmer over medium heat until the sugar is melted. Add the peaches, adding enough water so that they are just covered, adding a bit more water if needed. Poach for 10 to 12 minutes. Refrigerate in the poaching liquid for at least 2 hours.

Put 2 cups (250 g) of the raspberries into a 1-quart saucepan. Add 1 cup (200 g) of the sugar and 1 cup (235 ml) water. Bring to a simmer over medium heat and cook for 12 to 15 minutes, until the raspberries have broken apart. Push the liquid through a fine sieve and discard the seeds. Return the liquid to a saucepan and sprinkle the gelatin over the liquid. Allow the gelatin to soften for a few minutes, then heat over low heat until the gelatin is dissolved. Pour the liquid into a 9-inch square baking pan. The liquid should be $^1/_4$-inch or so deep. Refrigerate for at least 2 hours until firmly set.

Preheat the oven to 400°F (200°C, gas mark 6). Roll out the pastry very thin and put it onto a parchment-lined baking sheet. Brush the pastry with water and sprinkle with the remaining 1 cup (200 g) sugar. Invert a roasting rack that is as large as the pastry onto the pastry. This will prevent the puff pastry from rising while baking and will result in a thin, crisp sheet.

Bake for 15 to 20 minutes, until golden brown. Remove the rack and cool on the pan. Using a serrated knife, or a pizza cutter, cut the dough into 8 rectangles 1 x 6 inches (2.5 x 15 cm).

Remove the peaches from the poaching liquid and drain them on paper towels. Cut the gelée into diamond-shaped pieces and, using a thin spatula, transfer 3 pieces to each of 4 plates. Place 2 peach halves on top of the gelée pieces on each plate. Garnish with the puff pastry crisps and remaining 1 cup raspberries. Serve immediately.

YIELD: Serves 4

ADD IT! Accompany the poached peach with a scoop of lemon sorbet.

Red Wine–Poached Pears

This is an easy and elegant dessert that can be made ahead of time.

> 6 firm-ripe **pears**, such as Bartlett or Anjou
>
> 2 cups (400 g) **sugar**
>
> 1 bottle (750 ml) **red wine**, such as Merlot, Pinot Noir, or Shiraz
>
> 2 **cinnamon sticks**
>
> 1 **orange**
>
> Water

Peel the pears leaving the stem intact. Using a melon baller, scoop out the core from the bottom of the pears.

Combine the sugar, wine, and cinnamon sticks in a saucepan large enough to snugly hold the pears standing. Cook over high heat until the sugar dissolves. Reduce the heat to low. Slice the orange, skin on, and add to the saucepan. Place the pears in the poaching liquid, standing, and add water as needed to bring the liquid just to the top of the pears.

Poach the pears over low heat for 40 to 45 minutes, until they are easily pierced by a knife, but not mushy. Remove the pears from the poaching liquid and refrigerate them for 1 hour.

Turn the heat to high. Strain the poaching liquid and discard the cinnamon sticks and orange slices, as well as all but 2 cups (475 ml) of the liquid. Put the 2 cups remaining liquid over high heat and reduce to a syrup consistency. (You can make the syrup ahead of time and reheat as needed.)

Put the pears on each of 6 plates and spoon some of the syrup on and around them.

YIELD: Serves 6

ADD IT! Melt 6 ounces (170 g) semisweet chocolate and spoon over the pears after poaching. Refrigerate.

🍎 Apple Charlotte

A Charlotte is a classy and comforting way to end a fall dinner.

> 2 pounds (1 kg) **apples**, such as Granny Smith (about 5 to 6 apples)
> 1 cup (200 g) **sugar**
> 1 teaspoon **cinnamon**
> 1/4 cup (60 ml) water
> Juice of 1 **lemon**
> 1/2 cup (1 stick, or 112 g) butter, softened
> 1 loaf (16 ounces, or 455 g) brioche or challah **bread**

Peel and core the apples and cut them into 1-inch chunks. Put the apples, sugar, and cinnamon into a saucepan. Add the water and cook, stirring occasionally, over medium heat until the apples begin to break down and the sugar and juice forms a syrup—20 to 25 minutes. Stir in the lemon juice. Set aside.

Preheat the oven to 350°F (180°C, gas mark 4). Use 1/4 cup of the butter to coat the inside of a 2-quart soufflé dish thoroughly.

Remove the crust from the bread and slice into 1/2-inch thick slices. Cut the bread as needed to fit slices into the bottom of the dish, then line the sides of the dish with pieces of bread roughly 1 x 4 inches, standing up. Press the bread right into the butter. Fill the center of the bread with the apple mixture and cover with remaining bread strips.

In a saucepan, melt the remaining 1/4 cup butter. Brush the top of the bread with butter.

Bake for 40 to 45 minutes, until the bread is nicely toasted on the side facing the pan. Remove from the oven and allow to cool for 10 minutes, then flip the charlotte out onto a serving platter.

YIELD: Serves 4 to 6

Pear-Cranberry Charlotte

2 pounds (1 kg) **pears**, such as Bartlett or Anjou

2 cups (220 g) fresh or frozen **cranberries** (If frozen, do not thaw.)

1 cup (200 g) **sugar**

1 teaspoon **cinnamon**

1/4 cup (60 ml) water

1/2 cup (1 stick, or 112 g) butter, softened

1 loaf (16 ounces, or 455 g) brioche or challah **bread**

Peel and core the pears and cut them into 1-inch chunks. Put the pears, cranberries, sugar, and cinnamon into a saucepan. Add the water and cook, stirring occasionally, over medium heat until the pears begin to break down and the sugar and juice forms a syrup—20 to 25 minutes. Set aside.

Preheat the oven to 350°F (180°C, gas mark 4). Using 1/4 cup of the butter, thoroughly coat the inside of a 2-quart soufflé dish or flat-bottomed oven safe mixing bowl.

Remove the crust from the bread and slice 1/2-inch thick. Cut the bread as needed to fit slices into the bottom, then line the sides of the dish with overlapping pieces of bread roughly 1 x 4 inches, standing up. Press the bread right into the butter. Fill the center of the bread with the pear mixture and cover with remaining bread strips.

Melt the remaining 1/4 cup butter. Brush the top of the bread with butter.

Bake for 40 to 45 minutes, until the bread is nicely toasted on the side facing the pan. Remove from the oven and allow to cool for 10 minutes, then flip the charlotte out onto a serving platter.

YIELD: Serves 4 to 6

☙ Summer Plum Charlotte

This is a spectacular finish to a summer dinner out on the deck.

>   2 pounds (1 kg) **plums**
>   1 cup (200 g) **sugar**
>   1 teaspoon **cinnamon**
>   1/4 cup (60 ml) water
>   Juice of 1 **lemon**
>   1/2 cup (1 stick, or 112 g) butter, softened
>   1 loaf (16 ounces, or 455 g) brioche or challah **bread**

Split the plums, pit them, and cut each into 8 wedges. Put the plums, sugar, and cinnamon into a saucepan. Add the water and cook, stirring occasionally, over medium heat until the plums begin to break down and the sugar and juice forms a syrup—20 to 25 minutes. Stir in the lemon juice. Set aside.

Preheat the oven to 350°F (180°C, gas mark 4). Using 1/4 cup of the butter, coat the inside of a 2-quart soufflé dish or ovenproof flat-bottomed mixing bowl thoroughly.

Remove the crust from the bread and slice 1/2-inch thick. Cut the bread as needed to fit slices into the bottom, then line the sides of the dish with overlapping pieces of bread roughly 1 x 4 inches, standing up. Press the bread right into the butter. Fill the center of the bread with the plum mixture. Cover with remaining bread strips.

Melt the remaining 1/4 cup butter. Brush the top of the bread with butter.

Bake for 40 to 45 minutes, until the bread is nicely toasted on the side facing the pan. Remove from the oven and allow to cool for 10 minutes, then flip the charlotte out onto a serving platter.

YIELD: Serves 4 to 6

Rhubarb Charlotte

Any of these charlottes can also be done as individual charlottes using 8-ounce ramekins.

> 2 pounds (1 kg) **rhubarb**
> 1 1/2 cups (300 g) **sugar**
> 1 teaspoon **cinnamon**
> 1/2 teaspoon **nutmeg**
> 1/4 cup (60 ml) water
> 1/2 cup (1 stick, or 112 g) butter, softened
> 1 loaf (16 ounces, or 455 g) brioche or challah **bread**

Cut the rhubarb into 1/2-inch pieces. Put the rhubarb, sugar, cinnamon, and nutmeg into a saucepan. Add the water and cook, stirring occasionally, over medium heat until the plums begin to break down and the sugar and juice forms a syrup—20 to 25 minutes. Set aside.

Preheat the oven to 350°F (180°C, gas mark 4). Using 1/4 cup of the butter, coat the inside of a 2-quart soufflé dish thoroughly.

Remove the crust from the bread and slice 1/2-inch thick. Cut the bread as needed to fit slices into the bottom, then line the sides of the dish with pieces of bread roughly 1 x 4 inches, standing up. Press the bread right into the butter. Fill the center of the bread with the rhubarb mixture and cover with remaining bread.

Melt the remaining 1/4 cup butter. Lightly brush the top of the bread with butter.

Bake for 40 to 45 minutes, until the bread is nicely toasted on the side facing the pan. Remove from the oven and allow to cool for 10 minutes, then flip the charlotte out onto a serving platter.

YIELD: Serves 4 to 6

ADD IT! Whip 1 cup (235 ml) heavy cream and use as garnish.

Individual Banana Charlottes with Chocolate Rum Ganache

2 ripe **bananas**

1/2 cup (1 stick, or 112 g) butter, softened

1 loaf (16 ounces, or 455 g) brioche or challah **bread**

4 ounces (115 g) **semisweet chocolate**

2 tablespoons (28 ml) **dark rum**

1 cup (235 ml) **heavy cream**

Peel the bananas and cut them into 1-inch chunks. Put the bananas into a bowl and mash them, leaving some chunks.

Preheat the oven to 350°F (180°C, gas mark 4). Coat the insides of four 8-ounce ramekins thoroughly with 1/4 cup of the butter.

Remove the crust from the bread and slice 1/2-inch thick. Cut the bread as needed to fit a round into the bottom of each ramekin, then line the sides of the dishes with pieces of bread roughly 1/2 x 2 inches, standing up. Press the bread right into the butter. Fill the centers of the ramekins with the banana mixture and cover with remaining bread strips.

Melt the remaining 1/4 cup of butter. Brush the top of the bread with butter.

Bake for 30 to 35 minutes, until the bread is nicely toasted on the side facing the pan. Remove from the oven and allow to cool for 10 minutes.

While the ramekins are baking, chop the chocolate and put it into a stainless steel bowl. Add the rum. Bring 1/2 cup (120 ml) of the cream just to a boil and pour over the chocolate. Allow to stand for 2 minutes, then stir until the chocolate is melted. If all of the chocolate is not melted, place the bowl over simmering water and stir until it is.

When the charlottes are briefly cooled, pool some of the chocolate ganache onto each of 4 plates. Flip out each charlotte from its ramekin and transfer with a spatula onto the chocolate.

Whip the remaining 1/2 cup (120 ml) cream to soft peaks and spoon on top of the charlottes.

YIELD: Serves 4

🍎 Apple Crisp

This is perhaps the classic New England fall dessert; serve with ice cream or whipped cream.

For the apples:

> 2 pounds (1 kg) **apples**, such as Cortland, Macintosh, or Granny Smith (about 5 to 6 apples)
>
> 1 cup (200 g) **sugar**
>
> 1 teaspoon **nutmeg**
>
> 1 tablespoon **cinnamon**

For the streusel:

> 1 cup (120 g) **all-purpose flour**
>
> 1 cup (200 g) **sugar**
>
> 1/4 teaspoon salt
>
> 3 teaspoons **cinnamon**
>
> 1 teaspoon **nutmeg**
>
> 1/2 cup (1 stick, or 112 g) butter, cut into small pieces

To make the apples:

Preheat the oven to 350°F (180°C, gas mark 4).

Peel and core the apples and cut them into wedges. Mix together the sugar, nutmeg, and cinnamon in a large bowl and add the apples, tossing them in the sugar until they are coated. Pour the mixture into a 9 x 14-inch baking pan.

To make the streusel:

In a mixing bowl blend the flour, sugar, salt, cinnamon, and nutmeg. Cut the butter into the dry ingredients, until the mix resembles a coarse meal. Sprinkle the streusel over the apples.

Bake for 35 to 40 minutes, until the streusel is golden brown and the apples are soft and bubbling. Cool for a few minutes and serve.

YIELD: Serves 10 to 12

ADD IT! Mix 1/2 cup (40 g) quick cooking oats into the streusel mix.

Cherry Crisp

For the cherries:

> 2 pounds (1 kg) tart **cherries**
>
> 1 cup (200 g) **sugar**
>
> 1 teaspoon **nutmeg**
>
> 3 teaspoons **cinnamon**

For the streusel:

> 1 cup (120 g) **all-purpose flour**
>
> 1 cup (200 g) **sugar**
>
> 1/4 teaspoon salt
>
> 3 teaspoons **cinnamon**
>
> 1 teaspoon **nutmeg**
>
> 1 cup (2 sticks, or 225 g) butter, cut into small pieces

Preheat the oven to 350°F (180°C, gas mark 4).

To make the cherries:

Pit the cherries and mix them with the sugar, nutmeg, and cinnamon in a large bowl, tossing until they are coated. Pour into a 9-inch square baking pan.

To make the streusel:

In a mixing bowl, blend the flour, sugar, salt, cinnamon, and nutmeg. Using a pastry blender or two knives, cut the butter into the dry ingredients until the mix resembles a coarse meal. Cover the cherries with the streusel.

Bake for 35 to 40 minutes, until the streusel is golden brown and the cherries are soft and bubbling. Cool for a few minutes and serve.

YIELD: Serves 10 to 12

ADD IT! Add 1/2 cup (40 g) quick cooking oats to the streusel mix.

🍎 Rhubarb Crisp

For the rhubarb:

> 2 pounds (1 kg) **rhubarb**
>
> 1 cup (200 g) **sugar**
>
> 3 teaspoons **cinnamon**

For the streusel:

> 1 cup (120 g) **all-purpose flour**
>
> 1 cup (200 g) **sugar**
>
> 1/4 teaspoon salt
>
> 3 teaspoons **cinnamon**
>
> 1/2 cup (1 stick, or 112 g) butter, cut into small pieces

To make the topping:

> 1 cup (230 g) **sour cream**
>
> 1/2 cup (100 g) **sugar**

To make the rhubarb:

Preheat the oven to 350°F (180°C, gas mark 4).

Cut the rhubarb into 1/2-inch pieces, peeling first if the outside is tough. Mix together the sugar and cinnamon in a large bowl and add the rhubarb, tossing them in the sugar until they are coated. Pour into a 9 x 14-inch baking pan.

To make the streusel:

In a mixing bowl, blend the flour, sugar, salt, and cinnamon. Cut the butter into the dry ingredients, until the mix resembles a coarse meal. Cover the rhubarb with the streusel.

Bake for 35 to 40 minutes, until the streusel is golden brown and the rhubarb is soft and bubbling. Cool for a few minutes.

While the dish is cooling, whisk together the sour cream and sugar. Serve the crisp with a dollop of the sour cream on top.

YIELD: Serves 6

ADD IT! Toss 1 cup (165 g) sliced ripe fresh strawberries in with the rhubarb.

Peach-Blueberry Crisp

As with any self-respecting crisp, this is delicious when paired with vanilla ice cream.
Or even better, cinnamon ice cream.

For the fruit:

> 1 1/2 (700 g) pounds **peaches**
>
> 1 cup (200 g) **sugar**
>
> 1 teaspoon **apple pie spice**
>
> 2 cups (290 g) **blueberries**

For the streusel:

> 1 cup (120 g) **all-purpose flour**
>
> 1 cup (200 g) **sugar**
>
> 1/4 teaspoon salt
>
> 3 teaspoons **apple pie spice**
>
> 1 cup (2 sticks, or 225 g) butter, cut into small pieces

Preheat the oven to 350°F (180°C, gas mark 4).

To make the fruit:

Peel and pit the peaches and cut them into wedges. Mix together the sugar and
apple pie spice in a large bowl and add the peaches and blueberries, tossing them
in the sugar until they are coated. Pour into a 9-inch square baking pan.

To make the streusel:

In a mixing bowl, blend the flour, sugar, salt, and apple pie spice. Using a pastry
cutter or knives, cut the butter into the dry ingredients until the mix resembles a
coarse meal. Cover the fruit with the streusel.

Bake for 35 to 40 minutes, until the streusel is golden brown and the peaches
are soft and bubbling. Cool for a few minutes and serve.

YIELD: Serves 8

ADD IT! Add 1/2 cup (40 g) quick cooking oats to the streusel mix.

🍎 Apple Fritters

While these make a delicious dessert, they also make a pretty good breakfast, too.

> Oil for deep frying
>
> 3 **apples**, such as Cortland, Macintosh, or Granny Smith
>
> 1 cup (120 g) **self-rising flour**, plus 1/2 cup (60 g)
>
> 1/2 cup (100 g) **vanilla sugar** (See "Making Vanilla Sugar" on page 12.)
>
> 1/4 teaspoon salt
>
> 1 **egg**
>
> 1 cup (235 ml) whole or 2% **milk**
>
> 2 tablespoons (28 ml) vegetable oil

Heat the oil for deep frying in a fryer or in a deep saucepan to 350°F (180°C, gas mark 4).

Peel and core the apples and cut them into 1/2-inch pieces.

In a mixing bowl, combine 1 cup (120 g) of the flour, sugar, and salt.

In another bowl, whisk together the egg, milk, and oil. Stir the wet ingredients into the dry to form a loose batter. Do not over mix; a few lumps are okay.

Dredge the apple pieces in the remaining 1/2 cup (60 g) flour, then stir into the batter. Fry, in batches if necessary, for 4 to 5 minutes, until golden brown. Drain the fritters on paper towels and continue frying the rest.

YIELD: Serves 4

ADD IT! Serve with some maple syrup for dipping.

🍎 Banana Fritters

Fritters are great in either sweet or savory form. Here they make a delicious way to use up misfit bananas that have been deemed too brown by the Finicky Food Patrol.

> Oil for deep frying
>
> 2 **bananas**
>
> 1 cup (120 g) **self-rising flour**, plus 1/2 cup (60 g)
>
> 1/2 cup (100 g) **vanilla sugar** (See "Making Vanilla Sugar" on page 12.)
>
> 1/4 teaspoon salt
>
> 1 **egg**
>
> 1 cup (235 ml) **milk**
>
> 2 tablespoons (28 ml) vegetable oil

Heat the oil for deep frying in a fryer or in a deep saucepan to 350°F (180°C, gas mark 4).

Peel and cut the bananas into 1/2-inch pieces.

In a mixing bowl, combine 1 cup (120 g) of the flour and the sugar and salt.

In another bowl, whisk together the egg, milk, and oil. Stir the wet ingredients into the dry to form a loose batter. Do not over mix; a few lumps are okay.

Dredge the bananas in the 1/2 cup (60 g) flour, then mix into the batter. Fry, in batches if necessary, for 4 to 5 minutes, until golden brown. Drain the fritters on paper towels and continue frying the rest of the fritters.

YIELD: Serves 4

ADD IT! Serve with some Chocolate Sauce (page 492) for dipping.

🍒 Cherry Fritters

Oil for deep frying

1 cup (120 g) **self-rising flour**, plus 1/2 cup (60 g)

1/2 cup (100 g) **vanilla sugar** (See "Making Vanilla Sugar" on page 12.)

1/4 teaspoon salt

1 **egg**

1 cup (235 ml) **milk**

2 tablespoons (28 ml) vegetable oil

1/2 pound (225 g) **bing cherries**, pitted

Heat the oil for deep frying in a fryer or in a deep saucepan to 350°F (180°C, gas mark 4).

In a mixing bowl, combine 1 cup (120 g) of the flour, sugar, and salt.

In another bowl, whisk together the egg, milk, and oil. Stir the wet ingredients into the dry to form a loose batter. Do not over mix; a few lumps are okay.

Dredge the cherries in the 1/2 cup (60 g) flour, then stir into the batter. Fry, in batches if necessary, for 4 to 5 minutes, until golden brown. Drain the fritters on paper towels and continue frying the rest.

YIELD: Serves 4

🍎 Peach Fritters

If you've ever gone peach picking, you come home with a basket full of gloriously ripe peaches and a slight feeling of panic: How are you going to eat them all before they spoil? After the peach pie, cobbler, and crisp, try fritters!

Oil for deep frying

3 **peaches**

1 cup (120 g) **self-rising flour**, plus 1/2 cup (60 g)

1/2 cup (100 g) **vanilla sugar** (See "Making Vanilla Sugar" on page 12.)

1/4 teaspoon salt

1 **egg**

1 cup (235 ml) **milk**

2 tablespoons (28 ml) vegetable oil

Heat the oil for deep frying in a fryer or in a deep saucepan to 350°F (180°C, gas mark 4).

Peel and pit the peaches, then cut them into 1/2-inch cubes.

In a mixing bowl, combine 1 cup (120 g) of the flour, sugar, and salt.

In another bowl, whisk together the egg, milk, and oil. Stir the wet ingredients into the dry to form a loose batter. Do not over mix; a few lumps are okay.

Dredge the peaches in the remaining 1/2 cup (60 g) flour, then stir into the batter. Fry, in batches if necessary, for 4 to 5 minutes, until golden brown. Drain the fritters on paper towels and continue frying the rest.

YIELD: Serves 4

🍎 Pineapple Fritters

Oil for deep frying

1 can (13 ounces, or 370 g) **pineapple** chunks, drained

1 cup (120 g) **self-rising flou**r, plus 1/2 cup (60 g)

1/2 cup (100 g) **vanilla sugar** (See "Making Vanilla Sugar" on page 12.)

1/4 teaspoon salt

1 **egg**

1 cup (235 ml) whole or 2% **milk**

2 tablespoons (28 ml) vegetable oil

Heat the oil for deep frying in a fryer or in a deep saucepan to 350°F (180°C, gas mark 4).

In a mixing bowl, combine 1 cup (120 g) of the flour, sugar, and salt.

In another bowl, whisk together the egg, milk, and oil. Stir the wet ingredients into the dry to form a loose batter. Do not over mix; a few lumps are okay.

Dredge the pineapple pieces in the remaining 1/2 cup (60 g) flour, then stir into the batter. Fry, in batches if necessary, for 4 to 5 minutes, until golden brown. Drain the fritters on paper towels and continue frying the rest.

YIELD: Serves 4

Lemon-Ricotta Fritters

This is a wonderful finish to an authentic Italian meal.

> 1 cup (120 g) **all-purpose flour**
> 1 cup (200 g) **sugar**
> Pinch salt
> 1 **egg**
> 1 cup (250 g) **ricotta cheese**
> Zest and juice of 3 **lemons**
> Oil for deep frying

In a mixing bowl, combine the flour, sugar, and salt.

In another bowl, whisk together the egg and the ricotta. Stir the wet ingredients into the dry to form a loose batter. Stir in the lemon zest and juice. Do not over mix; a few lumps are okay.

Heat the oil for deep frying in a fryer or in a deep saucepan to 350°F (180°C, gas mark 4).

Drop spoonfuls of the batter into the hot oil. Fry, in batches if necessary, for 4 to 5 minutes, until golden brown. Drain the fritters on paper towels and continue frying the rest.

YIELD: Serves 4

ADD IT! Drizzle with wildflower honey just before serving.

🍎 Apple Strudel

Strudel, the classic German pastry made with very fine layers of pastry, has a reputation as an intimidating dessert. Although it does take time, making a strudel is not really hard at all and can be a fun project to do with a friend or family member.

> 2 1/2 cups (310 g) **all-purpose flour**, plus more for kneading
>
> 1 **egg**
>
> 1/2 cup (120 ml) warm water
>
> 1/4 cup (60 ml) vegetable oil, plus more for dough
>
> 1/4 teaspoon salt
>
> 2 pounds (1 kg) **apples**, such as Granny Smith or Cortland (5 or 6 apples)
>
> 1 cup (200 g) **cinnamon sugar** (See "Making Cinnamon Sugar" on page 12.)
>
> 1/2 cup (25 g) fresh **bread crumbs**

Place the flour in a mixing bowl. Make a well in the center and add the egg, water, oil, and salt. Stir with a spoon or fork. Turn out onto a floured surface and knead, adding slight flour as necessary. Knead about 10 minutes or more. (It will stick to your hands and to the board, but keep kneading and adding very little flour. You should have a soft and elastic dough. You can more easily make this dough in a mixer fitted with a dough hook or in a bread machine.) Place the dough a bowl, brush with a little vegetable oil, cover, and let rest at room temperature for 1 hour.

Preheat the oven to 325°F (170°C, gas mark 3).

Peel and core the apples, then cut them into 10 to 12 wedges each. In a mixing bowl, stir together well the apples and the sugar, until the apples are coated.

Spread a clean tablecloth or sheet on a table and dust with flour. Roll out the dough on another surface to an 8 x 12-inch rectangle. Carefully pick up the dough using your knuckles and, with a friend, gently stretch the dough until it is a thin sheet (translucent) 18 x 18 inches. Carefully lay the dough onto the floured cloth. Sprinkle the bread crumbs along one side of the dough, leaving a 6-inch border. Pile the apples on top of the crumbs in a line. Cover the apples with the border dough and using the cloth, roll the strudel up into a log, ending with the seam side down. Pinch the ends and fold them under the log. Transfer the strudel to a baking sheet.

Bake for 40 to 45 minutes, until golden brown and some syrup is bubbling out a bit. Cool and slice and serve warm or cold.

YIELD: Serves 12 to 14

Plum Strudel

A classic European dessert—imagine yourself by the Danube.

2 1/2 cups (310 g) **all-purpose flour**
1 **egg**
1/2 cup (120 ml) warm water
1/4 cup (60 ml) vegetable oil, plus more for brushing dough
1/4 teaspoon salt
2 pounds (1 kg) **plums**
1 cup (200 g) **cinnamon sugar** (See "Making Cinnamon Sugar" on page 12.)
1/2 cup (25 g) fresh **bread crumbs**

Place the flour in a mixing bowl. Make a well in the center and add the egg, water, oil, and salt. Stir with a spoon or fork then turn out onto a floured surface and knead for about 10 minutes or so, adding minimal flour as necessary. (It will stick to your hands and to the board, but keep kneading and adding very little flour. You should have a soft and elastic dough. You can more easily make this dough in a mixer fitted with a dough hook, or in a bread machine.)

Place the dough in a bowl, brush with a little vegetable oil, cover and let rest at room temperature for 1 hour.

Preheat the oven to 350°F (180°C, gas mark 4).

Split the plums, remove the pits, and cut each of them into 10 to 12 wedges.

In a mixing bowl, stir together the plums and sugar, until the plums are coated.

Spread a clean tablecloth or sheet on a table and dust with flour. Roll out the dough on another surface to an 8 x 12-inch rectangle. Carefully pick up the dough using your knuckles and with a friend gently stretch the dough until it is a thin sheet (translucent) 18 x 18 inches. Carefully lay the dough onto the floured cloth. Sprinkle the bread crumbs along one side of the dough, leaving a

6-inch border. Pile the plums on top of the crumbs in a line. Cover the plums with the border dough and using the cloth, roll the strudel up into a log, ending with the seam side down. Pinch the ends and fold them under the log. Transfer the strudel to a baking sheet.

Bake for 35 to 40 minutes, until golden brown and some syrup is bubbling out a bit. Cool and slice. It's great served warm or cold.

YIELD: Serves 12 to 14

Blueberry Biscuit Cobbler

Cobblers are homey baked desserts that feature fruit covered with sweet biscuit dough. One of the classic variations is blueberry cobbler. Make this dessert after you've taken the kids out foraging for local wild berries or picked them at a farm. They'll eat more than they put in the bucket, but you should still end up with plenty for pie and cobblers.

> 4 cups (580 g) **blueberries**
> 1 1/4 cups (250 g) **sugar**
> 3 tablespoons (25 g) **cornstarch**
> 1/4 cup (1/2 stick, or 55 g) butter
> 2 cups (240 g) **biscuit mix**
> 1/2 cup (100 g) **sugar**
> 1 cup (235 ml) **milk**

Preheat the oven to 350°F (180°C, gas mark 4).

In a saucepan, mix together the berries, 3/4 cup (150 g) of the sugar, and the cornstarch. Heat over medium heat until the sugar is dissolved and the mixture thickens—about 10 minutes. Stir in the butter until melted. Pour the berries into a 9 x 9-inch baking pan.

In a mixing bowl, combine the biscuit mix and the remaining 1/2 cup (100 g) sugar. Stir in the milk. Drop by spoonfuls over the berries.

Bake for 25 to 30 minutes, until the biscuits are golden.

YIELD: Serves 6 to 8

🍎 Blackberry Cobbler

Ideally, you have an empty lot near your house that has filled with a wild tangle of blackberry brambles, providing the neighborhood (and the pesky birds) with a sweet and juicy Mecca every summer. If not, there are plenty of blackberries available at your local grocer. Desserts like this are one of the things that make late summer so special.

> 1/2 cup (1 stick, or 112 g) butter
> 1 1/2 cups (180 g) **self-rising flour**
> 1/4 teaspoon salt
> 1 1/2 cups (300 g) **sugar**
> 1 teaspoon **cinnamon**
> 1 1/2 cups (355 ml) **milk**
> 2 cups (290 g) **blackberries**

Preheat the oven to 350°F (180°C, gas mark 4).

Melt the butter and pour it into a 9 x 13-inch baking pan.

Mix together the flour, salt, 1 cup (200 g) of the sugar, and the cinnamon in a mixing bowl. Stir in the milk to make a thin batter. Pour the batter on top of the butter.

Mix together the berries and the remaining 1/2 cup (100 g) sugar. Pour over the batter.

Bake for 40 to 45 minutes, until a tester inserted into the center of the cobbler comes out clean. Serve warm or room temperature.

YIELD: Serves 12.

🍎 Peach Cobbler

As with any beloved food, there is a great deal of discussion as to what constitutes a cobbler. There are those who insist on pie pastry, and those who scorn the very idea. Others declare authoritatively that the fruit goes on the bottom, while their opponents plump for fruit on the top. We're going with an old-fashioned cobbler recipe that we think is delicious regardless of the Great Cobbler Debate.

> $1/2$ cup (1 stick, or 112 g) butter
> $1 1/2$ cups (180 g) **self-rising flour**
> $1/4$ teaspoon salt
> $1 1/2$ cups (300 g) **sugar**
> 1 teaspoon **cinnamon**
> $1 1/2$ cups (355 ml) **milk**
> 3 cups (600 g) sliced peeled **peaches**

Preheat the oven to 350°F (180°C, gas mark 4).

Melt the butter and pour it into a 9 x 9-inch baking pan.

Mix together the flour, salt, 1 cup (200 g) of the sugar, and the cinnamon in a mixing bowl. Stir in the milk to make a thin batter. Pour the batter on top of the butter.

Mix together the peaches and the remaining $1/2$ cup (100 g) sugar. Pour over the batter.

Bake for 40 to 45 minutes, until a tester inserted into the center of the cobbler comes out clean. Serve warm or room temperature.

YIELD: Serves 12.

Poached Pear Praline Napoleon

Napoleons are a very dressy dessert, but the advent of frozen puff pastry makes them relatively simple to prepare. There are a lot of steps, but nothing is particularly complicated to execute.

For the poached pears:

> 4 firm-ripe **pears**, such as Bartlett or Anjou
>
> 2 cups (400 g) **vanilla sugar** (See "Making Vanilla Sugar" on page 12.)
>
> 4 cups (950 ml) water

For the praline puff pastry:

> 1 sheet frozen **puff pastry dough** (6 x 9 inch, or 15 x 22¹/₂ cm), thawed
>
> 1 cup (200 g) **vanilla sugar** (See "Making Vanilla Sugar" on page 12.)
>
> ¹/₂ cup (120 ml) **heavy cream**

For the custard:

> 3 **egg yolks**
>
> ¹/₂ cup (100 g) **vanilla sugar** (See "Making Vanilla Sugar" on page 12.)
>
> 1 cup (235 ml) **heavy cream**

For the whipped cream:

> 1 cup (235 ml) **heavy cream**
>
> 2 tablespoons (25 g) **vanilla sugar** (See "Making Vanilla Sugar" on page 12)

To make the poached pears:

Peel the pears, removing the stem. Halve the pears lengthwise and use a melon baller to scoop out the core. Mix the sugar and water in a saucepan or sauté pan large enough to just accommodate the pears. Heat over high heat until the sugar is dissolved, then reduce to low heat and add the pears. Poach the pears until they are easily pierced with a sharp knife—about 30 minutes. Refrigerate in the poaching liquid.

To make the praline puff pastry:

Preheat the oven to 400°F (200°C, gas mark 6).

Roll out the pastry very thin and put it onto a parchment-lined baking sheet.

Invert a roasting rack that is as large as the pastry onto the pastry. (This will prevent the puff pastry from rising while baking and will result in a thin, crisp sheet.)

Bake for 15 to 20 minutes, until golden brown. Remove the rack and cool on the pan. Using a serrated knife or a pizza cutter, cut the dough into 8 rectangles 2 x 4 inches.

In a 1-quart heavy bottomed saucepan, mix the sugar with enough water to resemble wet sand. Place on high heat and cook, not stirring, until golden brown. Be careful, as once it begins to brown it will burn quickly. Remove from the heat and add the cream (a spluttery process). Stir until the cream is incorporated into the caramel and the sauce is smooth.

Drizzle the caramel sauce over the puff pastry rectangles.

To make the custard:

Put the egg yolks and sugar into a mixing bowl. Heat the cream just to a boil and whisk into the egg yolks in a thin stream. Return all to the saucepan and cook over medium heat, stirring, until the mixture thickens. Refrigerate in a bowl with plastic wrap directly on the surface of the custard.

To make the cream:

Whip the cream with the vanilla sugar to stiff peaks.

Put one piece of the puff pastry on a plate. Remove a pear half from the poaching liquid and blot dry with a towel. Slice the pear half so that it is still attached at the top and you can fan it out. Put a pear half on the pastry, top with 2 tablespoons of custard, another rectangle of pastry, another pear and more custard. Garnish the pastry with the whipped cream. Repeat with the remaining ingredients.

YIELD: Serves 4

🍎 Quince Tart Tatin

Quinces are practically inedible raw, but cooked they are a delight. They also make terrific natural air freshener. They shrivel but do not rot, and they have a delicious aroma.

- 4 **quinces** (about 2 pounds)
- 1/2 cup (1 stick, or 112 g) butter
- 1 cup (200 g) **sugar**
- 1 teaspoon **cinnamon**
- 2 tablespoons (28 ml) **Calvados** or brandy
- 1 sheet frozen **puff pastry dough**, (6 x 9 inch, or 15 x 22 1/2 cm), thawed

Peel and core the quinces and cut them into 10 to 12 wedges each.

Coat an ovenproof 12-inch sauté pan with the butter. In a small bowl, combine the sugar and cinnamon and sprinkle over the butter. Arrange the quince pieces in overlapping circles in the pan and pour the brandy over.

Cook over medium heat for 25 to 30 minutes, until the quince pieces are softened and the sugar has just begun to darken and lightly caramelized. (Do not allow to over caramelize, as the sugar will quickly burn.)

Preheat the oven to 350°F (180°C, gas mark 4).

Roll out the puff pastry so that it will cover the top of the sauté pan. Drape the dough over the pan, cut off the excess leaving 1/4 inch overhang and tuck the overhang into the pan.

Bake for 20 to 25 minutes, until the puff pastry is golden brown. Remove from the oven, let stand in the pan for 3 to 4 minutes, then flip the tart out onto a serving platter. Rearrange any quince pieces that fall out of place and pour any caramel syrup from the pan over the fruit.

YIELD: Serves 6 to 8

🍎 Strawberry Shortcake

Forget those spongey hockey pucks from the supermarket—a proper shortcake is a biscuit that has been slightly sweetened. They are a snap to make, and boy, does it make a difference. If you're really feeling decadent, try serving these individual shortcakes as dinner one night. You will promptly be nominated for sainthood by your children.

For the biscuits:

> 1 1/2 cups (180 g) **biscuit mix**
> 1/4 cup (50 g) **sugar**
> 3/4 cup (175 ml) whole or 2% **milk**

For the berries:

> 1 quart (575 g) **strawberries**
> 1/2 cup (100 g) **sugar**, plus 1/4 cup (50 g)
> 2 cups (475 ml) **heavy cream**

To make the biscuits:

Preheat the oven to 375°F (190°C, gas mark 5).

In a mixing bowl, combine the biscuit mix and sugar. Stir in the milk. Roll out to 1/2-inch thick and cut out six 2-inch round biscuits. Place them on a baking sheet.

Bake for 12 to 15 minutes, until golden brown. Allow to cool.

To make the berries:

Hull the berries and slice them, reserving 6 nice big berries. Sprinkle 1/2 cup (100 g) of the sugar over and gently mash the berries a bit with a fork or a potato masher. Allow to macerate for 15 to 20 minutes.

Combine the cream and remaining 1/4 cup (50 g) sugar in a bowl and beat on high speed until fluffy.

To serve, split each biscuit and put the bottom on each of 6 plates. Spoon some of the berry mixture over and top with some whipped cream. Cover with the top half of the biscuit, spoon more berries over, top with more cream and garnish with the reserved whole berries.

YIELD: Serves 6

🍎 Grilled Fruit with Chocolate

Here's a good ending for a cookout. Hey, the grill is hot anyhow, right?

- 2 **bananas**
- 4 fresh **figs**
- 4 fresh **apricots**
- 1 cup (235 ml) **Chocolate Sauce** (page 492) or store-bought chocolate sauce
- 1 cup (235 ml) **heavy cream**

Wipe the grill surface with an oiled cloth and turn onto high. (You want a hot grill for this.)

Peel the bananas and slice each into 4 pieces on the bias. Split the figs in half. Split the apricots and remove the pits. Grill the bananas on each side until just marked—1 to 2 minutes. Grill the cut sides of the figs and apricots. Pool some of the chocolate sauce on each of 4 plates and arrange the fruit on top of the chocolate sauce.

Whip the cream to soft peaks and spoon on top of the fruit.

YIELD: Serves 4

🍎 Tropical Grilled Pineapples

This is a really nice dessert to have when there is a grill going anyhow, say at a barbecue, or when camping.

> 1 **pineapple**, preferably golden
>
> 1 pint (285 g) **coconut ice cream**
>
> 1 cup (235 ml) **Caramel Sauce** (page 486) or store-bought caramel sauce
>
> 1 cup (135 g) **macadamia nuts**, rough chopped
>
> 1/2 cup (35 g) sweetened **shredded coconut**, toasted

Clean and oil the grill grate and heat the grill on high.

Prepare the pineapple by cutting off the top and bottom and carefully cutting away the rind. Split the pineapple in half lengthwise and remove the core. Slice each half across into 6 slices. Grill the pineapple slices for 4 to 5 minutes per side. Place 2 slices on each of 6 plates.

Top the pineapple with a scoop of ice cream, then drizzle the caramel sauce over. Sprinkle with the nuts and coconut flakes. Serve immediately.

YIELD: Serves 6.

🍎 Sautéed Apples with Apple Mousse

This one takes a bit of forethought and a little last minute action, but it is a wonderful ending to a fall meal. Granny Smith apples are good for this.

For the mousse:

> 1 pound (455 g) **apples** (about 3 apples)
>
> 1/2 cup (100 g) **sugar**
>
> 1/4 cup (60 ml) water
>
> 3 teaspoons **unflavored gelatin**
>
> 1/4 cup (60 ml) **ginger brandy**
>
> 1 cup (235 ml) **heavy cream**

For the sautéed apples:

> 1 pound (455 g) **apples** (about 2 apples)
>
> 2 tablespoons (¹/4 stick, or 28 g) butter
>
> ¹/2 cup (100 g) **sugar**
>
> ¹/4 cup (60 ml) **ginger brandy**

To make the mousse:

Peel and core the apples. Cut the apples into wedges and put them into a heavy bottomed 2-quart saucepan. Add ¹/2 cup (100 g) of the sugar and the water. Cook over medium-high heat, covered, until the apples are soft and dissolving. Remove from the heat and mash with a potato masher until fairly smooth. Set the applesauce aside.

Sprinkle the gelatin over the brandy in a small saucepan and let soften for 5 minutes. Heat the brandy over low heat until the gelatin dissolves and stir into the applesauce. Refrigerate the applesauce until just cool.

Whip the cream to stiff peaks and fold into the applesauce. Refrigerate the mousse for at least 2 hours. This part can be made up to 2 days in advance and kept refrigerated.

To make the sautéed apples:

Peel and core the apples and slice them into wedges. Heat a 12-inch sauté pan over high heat and add the butter. As soon as the butter melts, add the apples and the sugar. Sauté, tossing for 1 to 2 minutes; add the brandy and continue to sauté the apples for another 3 to 4 minutes.

To serve, divide the apples among 4 plates. Top the apples with a large spoonful of the mousse. Serve immediately.

YIELD: Serves 4

ADD IT! Stir 1 teaspoon cinnamon into the applesauce.

🍎 Sautéed Cherries on Almond Meringues

For the meringues:

> 4 **egg whites**
> 1/2 cup (100 g) **sugar**
> 1 cup (145 g) blanched **almonds**, finely grated

For the cherries:

> 1 pound (455 g) **bing cherries**
> 2 tablespoons (1/4 stick, or 28 g) butter
> 1 cup (200 g) **sugar**
> 1/4 cup (60 ml) **brandy**

To make the meringues:

Preheat the oven to 250°F (120°C, or gas mark 1/2). Line a baking sheet with parchment paper.

In a stainless steel mixing bowl, beat the egg whites, adding the sugar in three stages after the eggs begin to froth. Whip until you have a meringue with glossy firm peaks. Fold in the almonds. Put the meringue in a piping bag fitted with a plain tip (If you don't have a piping bag, put the meringue in a large resealable plastic freezer bag and snip off a corner.). Pipe the meringue in eight 4-inch circles onto the prepared baking sheet.

Bake for 25 to 30 minutes, then turn off the oven and leave the pan inside, without opening the door of the oven for 2 hours, until the meringues are crisp all the way through.

To make the cherries:

Pit the cherries. Heat a 12-inch sauté pan over medium-high heat. Add the butter and when melted add the cherries and the sugar. Cook, stirring, for 5 to 6 minutes, until the cherries wilt a bit and give off some juice, and the sugar is dissolved and makes a syrup with the juice. Add the brandy and continue to cook for 4 to 5 minutes.

Put 1 meringue circle on each of 4 plates and spoon some hot cherries over, then top with another meringue.

YIELD: Serves 4

Maple-Baked Apples

Maple syrup and apples—the essence of a New England harvest. Serve these on a November evening when the wind howls around the eaves and there's a cozy fire in the fireplace.

6 **apples**, such as Cortland, Empire, or McIntosh

1/2 cup (110 g) packed **light brown sugar**

1 teaspoon powdered **ginger**

1 teaspoon **cinnamon**

1/4 cup (1/2 stick, or 55 g) butter

1 cup (235 ml) **maple syrup**

Preheat the oven to 325°F (170°C, gas mark 3).

Core the apples (do not peel) and place them in a baking dish that fits them snugly, but not touching.

Mix together the sugar, ginger, and cinnamon. Sprinkle over the apples, making sure plenty goes into the holes. Divide the butter into 6 pieces and put a piece on top of each apple. Pour the maple syrup over the apples.

Bake for 40 to 45 minutes, until the apples are golden and soft. Serve with the syrup accumulated in the pan as a sauce.

YIELD: Serves 6

Baked Peaches

    3 large ripe **peaches**

    1 cup (225 g) packed **light brown sugar**

    1 teaspoon **cinnamon**

    2 tablespoons ($1/4$ stick, or 28 g) butter, cut into small pieces

    1 cup (230 g) **sour cream**

    $1/4$ cup crushed **gingersnaps** (about 4 cookies)

Preheat the oven to 350°F (180°C, gas mark 4).

Halve each peach and remove the pits. Put into a baking pan that fits the peaches snugly and sprinkle with the sugar, cinnamon, and butter.

Bake for about 30 minutes, basting the peaches occasionally with accumulated syrup.

Remove and put a dollop of sour cream in each peach half; sprinkle with crumbled gingersnaps. Serve warm.

YIELD: Serves 6

🍒 Baked Brandied Cherries

1 pound (455 g) **bing cherries**, pitted
1/4 cup (50 g) **sugar**
1/4 cup (60 ml) water
Zest of 1/2 **lemon**
Juice of 1 lemon
1/3 cup (75 ml) **brandy**
1 quart (570 g) **vanilla ice cream**

Preheat the oven to 375°F (190°C, gas mark 5).

Pour the cherries into a 9-inch square baking pan.

Combine the sugar, water, lemon zest, and lemon juice in a saucepan and heat until the sugar dissolves. Remove from heat and add the brandy. Ladle the hot syrup over the cherries.

Bake for 30 minutes. Remove from the oven and ladle the cherries over dishes of the ice cream.

YIELD: Serves 4 to 6

🍎 Baked Apple with Blackberry Sauce and Sweetened Mascarpone

The blackberry sauce and the mascarpone can be made up to 2 days in advance and stored, refrigerated.

For the baked apples:

> 6 **apples**, such as Cortland, Empire, or McIntosh
> 1/2 cup (100 g) **sugar**
> 1 teaspoon **cinnamon**
> 1/4 cup (1/2 stick, or 55 g) butter

For the blackberry sauce:

> 1 pint (290 g) **blackberries**
> 1 cup (200 g) **sugar**

For the topping:

> 1 cup (240 g) **mascarpone cheese**
> 1/4 cup (50 g) **sugar**
> 1/2 teaspoon **cinnamon**

To make the baked apples:

Preheat the oven to 325°F (170°C, gas mark 3).

Core, but do not peel the apples. Place them snugly in a shallow 1-quart baking dish. Mix the sugar and cinnamon and sprinkle over the apples, then top each with some of the butter.

Bake for 35 to 40 minutes, until the apples are golden brown and soft. Remove and let them sit until they are only warm.

To make the blackberry sauce:

While the apples are baking, combine the blackberries and sugar in a saucepan. Place over medium-high heat and cook, stirring, for 10 to 12 minutes, until the sugar is dissolved and the berries have broken up. Push the mixture through a fine sieve and discard the seeds. Cool the sauce.

To make the topping:

In a small mixing bowl, whisk together the mascarpone, sugar, and cinnamon. Allow to sit for 10 minutes.

To serve, pool some of the blackberry sauce onto each of 6 plates. Top with an apple and spoon some of the mascarpone over.

YIELD: Serves 6

Baked Fruit Compote

1 or 2 **oranges**
^{1}/2 cup (150 g) frozen **mixed berries**
^{1}/4 cup (55 g) packed **light brown sugar**
2 tablespoons (12 g) chopped crystallized **ginger**
4 cups sliced, peeled **nectarines**
2 tablespoons (^{1}/4 stick, or 28 g) butter, cut into small pieces

Preheat the oven to 375°F (190°C, gas mark 5).

Grate the oranges to yield 1 teaspoon zest. Halve and squeeze the oranges to yield ^{1}/2 cup (120 ml) orange juice. Put the zest and orange juice into a mixing bowl.

Thaw the berries and drain any liquid that accumulates. Combine them with the orange juice and zest and add the sugar, ginger, and nectarines. Toss to combine. Pour into a 2-quart baking dish and dot with the butter. Cover with foil or with casserole dish cover.

Bake for 35 to 45 minutes. Serve warm.

YIELD: Serves 6

ADD IT! Spoon this over a dish full of vanilla or fruit ice cream for a delicious sauce.

Tropical Fruit Compote

Good any time of the year, but this is especially welcome on a mid-winter's day.

    2 **bananas**

    1 **mango**

    1 **pineapple**, preferably golden

    1 cup (75 g) sweetened **shredded coconut**

    2 **limes**

Peel the bananas and cut them into 1/2-inch pieces into a large mixing bowl. Peel the mango and cut out the pit. Cut the flesh into 1/2-inch cubes and add to the bowl. Cut the top and bottom off the pineapple. Stand the pineapple up on a cutting board and using a chef's knife, remove the skin. Split the pineapple lengthwise and remove the core. Cut the pineapple into 1-inch cubes and add them to the bowl. Add the coconut and mix well. Halve and squeeze the limes and sprinkle the juice over the fruit and gently mix the fruit.

YIELD: Serves 6 to 8

Bananas Foster

Carol's husband, Don, loves this dessert so much that he's been known to eagerly drive to the nearest store at 9 p.m. to fetch bananas, just to get this dish.

    1/3 cup (5 tablespoons, or 75 g) butter

    1/3 cup (75 g) packed **dark brown sugar**

    3 **bananas**, cut into quarters

    2 tablespoons (28 ml) **banana liqueur**

    1/4 cup (60 ml) **dark rum**

    8 scoops **vanilla ice cream**

Heat a large sauté pan and melt the butter. Add the sugar and stir until the sugar is melted. Add the bananas and cook, turning occasionally, for 2 or 3 minutes. Add the liqueur and the rum and light the rum with a match or long-handled lighter. Swirl the pan gently.

Put two scoops of ice cream on each of four plates. Place the bananas next to the ice cream and spoon sauce over both. Serve immediately.

YIELD: Serves 4

Banana-Toffee Roll-Ups

6 slices **cinnamon swirl bread**

3 ripe **bananas**

1 cup (175 g) **Heath Bar bits**

2 **eggs**

1 cup (235 ml) **heavy cream**

3 tablespoons (45 g) butter

Cut the crust off the bread. Lay out a piece of plastic wrap about 14-inches (35 cm) long. Lay the bread slices, overlapping, to make a rectangle 3 slices across by 2 tall. Press the bread down some at the seams to seal.

Peel and mash the bananas. Spread the banana mash evenly over the bread. Sprinkle the toffee bits over the bananas.

Using the plastic wrap, roll the bread up into a pinwheel inside of the plastic. Twist the ends of the plastic and holding the ends, roll the tube on the counter to tighten the plastic. Tuck in the ends of the wrap under the tube and refrigerate for at least 1 hour.

Whisk together the eggs and 1/2 cup (120 ml) of the cream. Whip the remaining cream to soft peak and refrigerate. Remove the plastic wrap from the tube and slice into 8 pinwheels. Heat a sauté pan over medium heat. Add the butter and when it is just melted, dip the pinwheels in the egg mixture. Sauté like French toast, turning after the first side is browned. When the second side is browned, put two slices on each of four plates. Top each serving with some of the whipped cream.

YIELD: Serves 4

Chocolate-Banana Quesadillas

6 soft flour **tortillas**

$1/4$ cup (60 g) melted butter

3 **bananas**, sliced into $1/4$-inch disks

$3/4$ cup (130 g) **semisweet chocolate chips**

6 scoops **vanilla ice cream**

1 cup **Hot Fudge Sauce** (page 487) or store-bought

Preheat the oven to 450°F (230°C, gas mark 8).

Brush both sides of each tortilla with the butter; place in single layer on ungreased cookie sheet. Layer half of each banana in slices on the center of each tortilla, followed by a handful of chocolate chips. Fold each tortilla in half to form half-moon shape.

Bake for 4 to 6 minutes or until golden brown. Remove from oven and put on plates. Top each with a scoop of vanilla ice cream and drizzle hot fudge sauce over all.

YIELD: Serves 6

Fruit Pizza

1 bag (16 ounces, or 455 g) refrigerated prepared **pizza dough**

$2^1/2$ cups (425 g) skinned, chopped **peaches**

About 3 tablespoons (45 ml) water

$1/2$ cup (75 g) **blueberries**

$1^1/4$ cups (280 g) packed **light brown sugar**

3 tablespoons (45 g) butter

2 tablespoons (15 g) **all-purpose flour**

Preheat the oven to 400°F (200°C, gas mark 6).

Roll out the pizza dough on a lightly floured work surface and put onto a pizza stone or cookie sheet. Bake for about 15 minutes, or until golden brown.

While the dough is baking, put the peaches and water in a small saucepan. Cook on medium heat until the peaches are soft—5 to 8 minutes . Remove from the heat and stir in the blueberries.

In a food processor, combine the sugar, butter, and flour until the mixture resembles coarse meal.

When the dough has cooled a little (but not completely), spoon the warm fruit mixture over the pizza crust and sprinkle the sugar mixture over the top. Put the pizza back in the oven and bake for about 5 minutes more, until the sugar is melted and bubbly. Remove and slice; serve while warm.

YIELD: Serves 6 to 8

ADD IT! Sprinkle chopped almonds over all.

Crêpes Suzette

This classic dish is a show stopper to make.

> 1 cup (200 g) **sugar**
> 1/2 cup (1 stick, or 112 g) butter
> Zest and juice from 1 large **orange**
> 1/2 cup (120 ml) **Grand Marnier** or other orange liqueur
> 8 store-bought dessert **crepes**

Put the sugar, butter, orange zest, and orange juice in a 10-inch sauté pan and heat over high heat until the sugar is dissolved and a syrup forms. Add the liqueur and carefully flame the liqueur. When the flames subside, using tongs, dip a crepe into the syrup and fold into quarters. Repeat until you have 2 crepes on each of 4 plates. Spoon the remaining sauce over.

YIELD: Serves 4

ADD IT! Garnish with a sprinkle of powdered sugar.

Chilled Blueberry Soup

This is a wonderful and unusual summer dessert.

2 pints (580 g) **blueberries**, preferably wild

3/4 cup (150 g) **sugar**

1 cup (235 ml) water, plus more for blending

1 **lemon**

1 **cinnamon stick**

1/2 cup (120 ml) **crème fraîche**

Put the blueberries into a 2-quart saucepan. Add the sugar and water. Zest the lemon and add the zest and the cinnamon stick. Put the pan on medium-high heat and bring to a boil, then lower the heat to a simmer and cook to soup for 15 minutes. Remove from the heat and allow to stand for 30 minutes.

Remove the cinnamon stick and puree the soup in a blender, adding water as needed to achieve a soup consistency. Refrigerate until chilled, up to overnight.

To serve, divide the soup among 4 shallow soup bowls. Whisk the crème fraîche in a small bowl and drizzle over the soup.

YIELD: Serves 4

ADD IT! Use white wine, ruby port, or white grape juice in place of the water.

🍎 Honeydew Melon with Lime-Basil Sorbet

> 3 cups (600 g) **sugar**
>
> 3 3/4 cups (780 ml) water
>
> 1 1/4 cups (295 ml) fresh **lime juice** (about 6 to 7 limes)
>
> 1/4 cup (10 g) fresh **basil leaves**, chopped fine
>
> 1 **honeydew melon**

In a large saucepan, combine the sugar and 3 cups (705 ml) of the water and bring to a boil. Simmer for a few minutes and remove from heat and cool completely. Pour 2 1/2 cups (355 ml) of the sugar syrup, along with the lime juice and 3/4 cup (75 ml) water into an ice cream machine. Stir in the basil leaves and process according to ice cream maker's directions.

Cut the honeydew melon into quarters and scoop out the seeds. Place a melon section on each of four plates; add one or two scoops of sorbet to the hollow of the melon and serve.

YIELD: Serves 4

🍎 Fried Cream with Sautéed Bing Cherries

Fried cream (crema fritta) is a traditional Italian dessert. It is delicious, and much of the work can be done in advance, except for the frying.

For the fried cream:

> 2 cups (475 ml) whole **milk**
>
> 4 egg yolks, plus 2 **eggs**, beaten
>
> 1/2 cup (100 g) **vanilla sugar** (See "Making Vanilla Sugar" on page 12.)
>
> 1/2 cup (60 g) **all-purpose flour**, plus extra for dredging
>
> Vegetable oil for frying

For the cherries:

> 1/4 cup (1/2 stick, or 55 g) butter
>
> 1 pound (455 g) **bing cherries**, pitted
>
> 1/2 cup (100 g) **vanilla sugar** (See "Making Vanilla Sugar" on page 12.)

To make the cream:

Lightly grease a 9-inch square baking dish pan.

In a saucepan over high heat, bring the milk to a boil. In a mixing bowl, combine the egg yolks, the eggs, and sugar and beat until frothy. Add 1/2 cup (60 g) of the flour and stir until smooth. Once the milk begins to boil, remove it from the heat. Whisk hot milk into the egg mixture in a stream then return the mixture to the saucepan and heat over high heat. Whisking constantly, return to a boil. As soon as it boils, remove the pan from the heat and pour and scrape into the baking pan. The milk should be about 1-inch thick. Refrigerate 2 hours or overnight.

To make the cherries:

Heat a 12-inch sauté pan over high heat. Add the butter and when just melted add the cherries. Sprinkle the sugar over the cherries and sauté, stirring for 4 to 5 minutes, until the cherries are heated through and the sugar is dissolved into a syrup. Set aside and keep warm.

Heat the vegetable oil for frying to 350°F (180°C, gas mark 4) in a deep pot or a deep fryer. Cut the refrigerated cream into 2-inch cubes or other shape you choose (diamonds are traditional). Working with a few squares at a time, dip them in the 2 remaining eggs and dredge with flour. Shake off the excess and drop in the hot oil. Fry about 1 minute or until golden brown. Remove with a slotted spoon and drain briefly on paper towels.

To serve, divide the fried cream squares among 4 plates and spoon the cherries over them.

YIELD: Serves 4

ADD IT! Pour in 2 tablespoons (28 ml) kirsch in both the cream (with the milk) and with the cherry sauté (when adding the sugar).

CHAPTER TEN

Candy

Our great aunts Sadie and Ruth Smith kept a candy store in their home in Marblehead, Massachusetts, and it was a popular stop for townsfolk heading to the beach. The sisters made their own ice cream, and, famously homemade fudge that is still remembered fondly when you gather a certain generation of Marbleheaders together.

We inherited the fudge pans, but not the time and energy to make candy. And as we discovered when researching this book, that's our loss. Like so much about food, candy making can be just as much about the process as the product. Try having an old-fashioned taffy pull or have your kids make a pan of fudge with friends. Like many things today, buying a bar of candy is certainly faster, but it doesn't rest on the warm memories of time spent with the people you love.

Caramels

Store-bought caramels are all right, but when you taste these homemade delights you will be hooked. Homemade caramels taste like butter and sunshine mixed together.

2 cups (400 g) **sugar**

Pinch salt

1/2 teaspoon **white vinegar**

About 1/4 cup (60 ml) water

1/4 cup (60 ml) **brandy**

2 teaspoons **vanilla extract**

1 cup (235 ml) **heavy cream**

1/4 cup (1/2 stick, or 55 g) butter

Grease a 9-inch square baking pan.

Put the sugar, salt, and vinegar in a heavy bottomed 2-quart saucepan. Add enough water to make a "wet sand." Cook over high heat, not stirring, until the sugar becomes a deep golden color. Remove from heat and immediately add the brandy and vanilla, then the cream. Watch out, as the mixture will sputter and boil. Stir in the butter until melted. Pour into the prepared pan. Refrigerate until hardened and cut into 1/2-inch cubes.

YIELD: Makes about 60 pieces

Pralines

2 cups (400 g) **sugar**

1/2 cup (120 ml) **light corn syrup**

2 cups (200 g) **pecan pieces**

8 ounces (235 ml) evaporated **milk**

Pinch salt

2 tablespoons (1/4 stick, or 28 g) butter

1/2 teaspoon vanilla extract

Line a baking sheet with waxed paper.

Combine the sugar, corn syrup, pecans, and the evaporated milk in a heavy 2-quart saucepan. Stir together, then boil until soft ball stage—238°F (114°C) on a candy thermometer, or when small amount dropped into a glass of cold water forms a soft ball. Remove from the heat and stir in the butter and vanilla until the butter is melted. Beat until glossy, then drop by spoonfuls onto the baking sheet.

YIELD: Makes about 40 pieces

Divinity

This must be called divinity because it tastes so heavenly. Basically, divinity is an Italian meringue with a twist. A candy thermometer is helpful, but not vital for success.

3 cups (600 g) **sugar**

Water

1/2 cup (120 ml) **corn syrup**

2 **egg whites**

1 teaspoon **vanilla extract**

1 1/2 cups (150 g) **pecan pieces**

Line a baking sheet with waxed paper.

Put the sugar in a heavy bottomed saucepan and add enough water to make "wet sand." Stir in the corn syrup. Cook over high heat until a candy thermometer reads 238°F (114°C), or a bit of the syrup dropped into water forms a soft ball.

While the syrup is cooking, whip the egg whites to stiff peaks. With the mixer on, pour half of the syrup into the whites in a thin stream. Return the pan to the stove and continue cooking to 255°F (125°C), or until a bit of the syrup dropped into cold water forms a hard ball. Again, with the mixer running, slowly incorporate the remaining syrup into the egg whites. Add the vanilla and beat until the candy is thick enough to be dropped from a spoon. Stir in the pecans. Drop by the spoonful onto the baking sheet. Allow to cool.

YIELD: Makes 35 to 40 pieces

Maple-Caramel Corn

Leave it loose or stick it together to make balls. We associate these with Halloween, as our elderly neighbors used to hand them out to all the visiting ghouls and ghosts.

1 cup (200 g) **sugar**

About 2 tablespoons (28 ml) water

1/2 cup (120 ml) **maple syrup**

1/2 teaspoon salt

1/2 cup (120 ml) **heavy cream**

1/4 cup (1/2 stick, or 55 g) butter

1 teaspoon **vanilla extract**

8 cups (65 g) plain popped **popcorn**

Put the sugar in a heavy 2-quart saucepan and add enough water to form a "wet sand." Heat over medium-high heat, not stirring, until the sugar is deep golden brown. Remove from the heat immediately (watch out, once the sugar begins to caramelize it can burn very quickly). Stir in the maple syrup, salt, cream, and butter—this can be a somewhat spluttery process. Stir in the vanilla.

Toss the mixture with the popcorn in a large mixing bowl, then lay out on baking sheets to cool or form into balls.

YIELD: Serves 10 to 12

ADD IT! For some more flavor, add 2 cups (290 g) peanuts tossed with the caramel and popcorn.

Maple-Walnut Candy

Bob lives in Vermont, and we would be sorely remiss not to include this Northern confection.

3 cups (705 ml) **maple syrup**

1 cup (235 ml) **light cream**

1/4 cup (1/2 stick, or 55 g) butter

1 cup (125 g) chopped **walnuts**

1 tablespoon (14 ml) **lemon juice**

Grease a 9-inch square Pyrex baking pan.

Combine the maple syrup, cream, and butter in a heavy 2-quart saucepan. Bring to a boil and cook to soft ball stage, 238°F (114°C) on your candy thermometer. Remove from the heat and stir in the walnuts and the lemon juice. Pour into the pan and allow to solidify, then cut into 1-inch squares.

YIELD: Makes 36 pieces

Old-Fashioned Peanut Brittle

This is an old-fashioned favorite that still brings a smile.

2 cups (400 g) **vanilla sugar** (See "Making Vanilla Sugar" on page 12.)

1 cup (235 ml) light **corn syrup**

1 teaspoon **cider vinegar**

1/2 cup (120 ml) water

2 cups (290 g) unsalted dry roasted **peanuts**

2 teaspoons **baking soda**

1 teaspoon salt

2 tablespoons (1/4 stick, or 28 g) butter, plus more to coat baking sheet

Butter a baking sheet.

Combine the sugar, corn syrup, vinegar, and water in a heavy bottomed 2-quart saucepan. Bring to a boil over high heat. Stir in the peanuts and continue cooking until the sugar is at hard crack stage—300°F (150°C) on a candy thermometer. Remove from the heat and thoroughly stir in the baking soda, salt, and butter. Pour onto the prepared baking sheet. Allow to harden, then break into pieces.

YIELD: Makes about 2 pounds

Crystallized Ginger

This old-fashioned recipe has a wonderful spicy kick to it.

> 1 pound, or 455 g, fresh **ginger**
> 2 cups (400 g) **sugar,** plus 1/4 cup (50 g) to coat
> Water to cover

Peel and thinly slice the ginger root. Put the ginger in a heavy 1-quart saucepan and just cover with water. Heat on medium heat; when it boils, lower to simmer and cook until the ginger pierces easily with a fork, about 25 to 30 minutes.

Drain the ginger and reserve 3 tablespoons (45 ml) of the water.

Place in a saucepan with 2 cups sugar and the reserved water. Bring to a boil, stirring often, until the ginger is transparent and the liquid has nearly disappeared. Reduce to low heat and cook, stirring constantly, until almost dry. Remove from heat. Toss the cooked ginger in sugar to coat. Crystallized ginger will keep up to 3 months if stored in an airtight container.

YIELD: Makes about 1/2 pound

Date Nut Balls

We associate these with Christmastime open houses, but they're good any time of year.

> 1 cup (175 g) candied **dates**, chopped fine
> 1 cup (75 g) sweetened **shredded coconut**, plus 1 cup (75 g) for rolling
> 1/2 cup (60 g) **walnuts**, chopped fine
> Juice of 1 **lemon**
> 1/2 cup (60 g) **confectioners' sugar**

Combine the dates, the 1 cup (75 g) coconut, walnuts, lemon juice, and sugar in a mixing bowl and stir them together thoroughly. Form into 1-inch balls and roll in the remaining 1 cup (75 g) coconut.

YIELD: Makes about 20 balls

Tropical Fruit and Nut Crunch

2 cups (350 g) milk **chocolate chips**

1/2 cup (1 stick, or 112 g) butter

1/2 cup (100 g) **sugar**

1/4 cup (60 ml) **light corn syrup**

1 cup (135 g) unsalted **macadamia nuts**

1 cup (225 g) dried **banana chips**

Line a 9-inch square baking pan with waxed paper. Spray the waxed paper with nonstick cooking spray.

Spread the chocolate chips over the bottom of the prepared pan.

Combine the butter, sugar, and corn syrup in a heavy bottomed 2-quart saucepan. Cook over medium-high heat, stirring, until the butter is melted. Continue cooking until the mixture becomes syrupy and golden brown. Stir in the macadamia nuts and the banana chips. Pour the mixture over the chocolate chips and spread to evenly cover the chips. Cool, then refrigerate the pan for 2 hours. Remove the candy from the pan, peel off the waxed paper, and cut the candy into pieces.

YIELD: Makes about 1 1/2 pounds, about 20 to 25 pieces

Orange Balls

This is an easy candy that requires almost no cooking, let alone messing with a candy thermometer.

1 box (16 ounces, or 455 g) **vanilla wafers**

1/2 cup (115 g) margarine

6 ounces (170 g) frozen **orange juice concentrate**, thawed

1 pound (455 g) **confectioners' sugar**

1 cup (75 g) sweetened **shredded coconut**

1/4 cup (25 g) **candied orange peel**, finely minced

Line a baking sheet with waxed paper.

Using a food processor or rolling pin, crush the vanilla cookies into fine crumbs. Reserve 2 cups (about 6 ounces, or 170 g) of the crumbs and put the rest into a mixing bowl.

Melt the margarine over low heat and stir in the orange juice concentrate. Remove from the heat. Add the sugar, coconut, and orange peel to the bowl and mix with the crumbs. Stir into the margarine and orange juice mixture thoroughly.

Roll 1-inch balls out of the mixture, then roll the balls in the reserved cookie crumbs. Place on the cookie sheet. Repeat until all the dough is used. Refrigerate for at least 1 hour.

YIELD: Makes 30 to 40 balls

Fruit and Nut Mounds

It has chocolate, so it's certified candy, but it also has raisins and almonds for an ostensible healthful component.

1 pound (455 g) **milk chocolate**

1 teaspoon **rum extract**

1 cup (75 g) sweetened **shredded coconut**

1 cup (145 g) **raisins**

1 cup (145 g) slivered unblanched **almonds**

Line a baking sheet with waxed paper.

Chop the chocolate into small pieces and put it into a small stainless steel mixing bowl. Place the bowl over a pan of simmering water until the chocolate is melted. Add the rum extract and stir until the chocolate is smooth. Remove from the heat.

Stir in the coconut, raisins, and almonds, mixing thoroughly. Drop the mixture onto the baking sheet by spoonfuls. Allow to harden at room temperature.

YIELD: Makes about 30 pieces

Assorted Fruit Dipped in Chocolate

We think this is an elegant way to end a meal, a fun gift to make, and a great addition to any festive buffet.

  8 ounces (225 g) **semisweet chocolate**

  2 tablespoons (25 g) shortening

  1 pound (455 g) stem **strawberries**

  1/2 pound (225 g) dried **apricots**

  3 **bananas**

  4 **pears**, such as Bosc

Chop the chocolate into small pieces and put it into a small stainless steel mixing bowl. Place the bowl over a pan of simmering water and stir until the chocolate is melted and smooth. Stir in the shortening until fully melted. Remove from the heat.

Cover a baking sheet with waxed paper. Dip the strawberries into the chocolate, leaving the upper third of the berries bare and place them on the waxed paper. Half dip the apricots. Peel the bananas, cut them into 2-inch pieces and half dip them. Finally, cut the pears into wedges, core the wedges, and dip them in the chocolate.

YIELD: Serves 15 to 30 (50 to 60 pieces of dipped fruit)

ADD IT! Kiwi fruit, sliced star fruit, cherries, and pretzels are all good too

Chocolate Toffee

These are addictively good.

>   1 cup (200 g) **sugar**
>   1 cup (235 ml) dark **corn syrup**
>   1 tablespoon (14 ml) **cider vinegar**
>   1 tablespoon (15 g) **baking soda**
>   6 ounces (170 g) **semisweet chocolate**

Butter a baking sheet.

Stir together the sugar, corn syrup, and vinegar in a heavy bottomed 2-quart saucepan. Boil over high heat to 300°F (150°C), using a candy thermometer. Remove from the heat and stir in the baking soda. Pour the candy onto the baking sheet and allow to cool completely.

Chop the chocolate into small pieces and put it into a small stainless steel mixing bowl. Place the bowl over a pan of simmering water until the chocolate is melted. Stir until the chocolate is smooth. Remove from the heat.

Line a baking sheet with waxed paper. Break the toffee into bite-sized pieces and dip them halfway into the melted chocolate. Lay them on the waxed paper. Allow the chocolate to harden.

YIELD: Makes 20 to 30 pieces.

Chocolate Mice

4 ounces (115 g) **semisweet chocolate**

1/3 cup (75 g) **sour cream**

1 1/3 cups finely crushed **Nabisco Famous Chocolate Wafer cookies** (about 18 cookies)

1/4 cup (25 g) **sliced almonds**

12 long red **licorice whips**

Melt the chocolate in a stainless steel bowl set over simmering water. Stir until smooth, and combine with the sour cream. Stir in 1 cup of the chocolate crumbs and mix well. Cover and refrigerate until firm.

Roll by spoonfuls into balls. Mold to a slight point at one end to make the nose.

Roll each mouse body in the remaining 1/3 cup cookie crumbs. On each mouse, place snippet of licorice in appropriate spot for eyes, almond slices for ears, and a licorice string for the tail.

Refrigerate for at least 2 hours until firm.

YIELD: Makes 12 pieces

ADD IT! You can roll half the mice in confectioners' sugar instead of cookie crumbs to make white mice.

Marge's Peanut Butter-Filled Chocolates

Our Mom has been making these for years. We get them as hearts on Valentine's Day, and the Easter Bunny used to bring them in egg-shaped form every year, too.

> 3/4 cup (195 g) creamy **peanut butter**
>
> 1 teaspoon salt
>
> 1 can (15 ounces, or 440 ml) sweetened **condensed milk**
>
> 1 pound (455 g) **confectioners' sugar**, plus more for kneading
>
> 8 ounces (225 g) **semisweet chocolate**
>
> 2 ounces (55 g) **paraffin wax**, shaved

Line a baking sheet with waxed paper.

Using a mixer on medium speed, cream together the peanut butter, salt, and condensed milk until smooth.

Sift the sugar. Add the sugar to the peanut butter mixture gradually, blending well after each addition, until the mixture becomes stiff. Turn out the mixture onto a kneading surface coated with confectioners' sugar and knead the mixture until it is smooth and not sticky. Cut into about 20 pieces and form them into balls with the palms of your hands. Place the balls on the baking sheet and freeze for 1 hour.

Melt the chocolate and wax in a double boiler, stirring smooth. Remove from the heat and dip each piece of peanut butter candy using 2 forks, then place the candy on the baking sheet. Stir the chocolate after each piece is dipped. Refrigerate the candies for at least 2 hours.

YIELD: Makes 20 candies

Mocha-Hazelnut Balls

We find the coffee syrup right next door to the bottled chocolate syrup at the supermarket.

> 1 1/2 cups (175 g) blanched **hazelnuts**
> 1 cup (120 g) **confectioners' sugar**
> 1 cup **Nabisco Famous Chocolate Wafer cookies** (about 9 cookies)
> 1/4 cup (25 g) **candied lemon peel**, finely chopped
> 1/2 cup (120 ml) **coffee syrup**

Put the hazelnuts in a food processor fitted with the metal blade and process until you have a fine meal. Take about one-third of the ground nuts out of the bowl and set them aside. Add the sugar, cookies, and lemon peel to the processor and run it until the cookies are crumbs. With the machine running, add enough of the coffee syrup for the mixture to form a dough-like consistency.

Roll into 1-inch balls and roll the balls in the reserved ground hazelnuts.

YIELD: Makes about 20 to 25 pieces

Coconut Filled Bon-Bons

These are a perfect Valentine's Day gift. It takes more time than buying a box of chocolates at the drug store, but boy, will you get brownie points.

> 2 cups (150 g) sweetened **shredded coconut**
> 1/2 cup (100 g) shortening
> 8 ounces (235 ml) **sweetened condensed milk**
> 2 cups (240 g) **confectioners' sugar**
> 8 ounces (225 g) **semisweet chocolate**
> 2 ounces (55 g) **paraffin wax**, shaved

Line a baking sheet with waxed paper.

Using a mixer on medium speed, cream together the coconut, shortening, and milk. Add the sugar in thirds, beating well after each addition. Continue to beat until smooth and fluffy—about 10 minutes. Turn out the mixture onto a kneading surface coated with confectioners' sugar and knead the mixture until it is smooth and not sticky. Cut into about 20 pieces and form them into balls with the palms of your hands. Place the balls on the baking sheet and freeze for 1 hour.

Melt the chocolate and wax in a double boiler, stirring smooth. Remove from the heat. Using two forks, dip each piece of coconut candy into the chocolate, then place the candy on the waxed paper to dry. Stir the chocolate after each piece is dipped. Refrigerate the candies for at least 2 hours.

YIELD: Makes 20 candies

Haystacks

Since these are easy to make—with no need for a candy thermometer—haystacks make a great rainy day project for small children.

> 1/2 cup (130 g) creamy **peanut butter**
> 1 cup (175 g) **butterscotch chips**
> 2 cups (100 g) **mini marshmallows**

1 container (16 ounces, or 455 g) fried **Chinese noodles**

1 cup (175 g) **semisweet chocolate chips**

Combine the peanut butter, butterscotch chips, and marshmallows in a 2-quart saucepan. Heat over medium heat, stirring, until the chips and marshmallows are melted and the mixture is smooth.

Put the noodles in a large mixing bowl. Gently stir in the melted butterscotch mixture, so that the noodles are coated.

Line a baking sheet with waxed paper. Butter your hands and drop little stacks of sticky noodles onto the paper. Allow to harden for 30 minutes at room temperature.

Melt the chocolate chips and drizzle the melted chocolate over the stacks. Allow the chocolate to harden at room temperature.

YIELD: Makes 25 to 30 pieces

Raspberry Truffles

16 ounces (455 g) **semisweet chocolate**

1/2 cup (160 g) **seedless raspberry jam**

1/4 cup (60 ml) **heavy cream**

2 tablespoons (1/4 stick, or 28 g) butter

2 **egg yolks**

Chop 12 ounces (340 g) of the chocolate into small pieces.

Combine the jam, cream, chopped chocolate, and butter in a stainless steel bowl set over a pan of simmering water. Stir until the butter and chocolate are melted and the mixture is smooth. Whisk in the egg yolks and continue cooking for 2 minutes. Refrigerate for at least 2 hours, until firm, then roll into 1-inch balls.

Grate the remaining 4 ounces (115 g) chocolate and roll the truffles in it.

YIELD: Makes about 20 to 25 truffles

Grand Marnier Truffles

Chocolate truffles have an elegant reputation, but once you make them, you'll realize that they are a snap.

> 5 ounces (140 g) **semisweet chocolate**
> 1/2 cup (1 stick, or 112 g) butter
> 2 **egg yolks**
> 1 1/2 cups (180 g) **confectioners' sugar**
> 3 tablespoons (45 ml) **Grand Marnier liqueur**
> 1 cup (135 g) **hazelnuts**, finely chopped

Chop the chocolate into small pieces and put it into a small stainless steel mixing bowl. Place the bowl over a pan of simmering water and stir until the chocolate is smooth. Remove from the heat.

In a mixing bowl, using a mixer on medium speed, beat the butter and the egg yolks together until smooth—4 to 5 minutes. Add the sugar and beat until blended. Stir in the melted chocolate and the liqueur. Refrigerate until firm enough to shape. Roll into 1-inch balls and then roll in the hazelnuts.

YIELD: Makes 20 to 25 truffles

Irish Cream Truffles

> 16 ounces (455 g) **semisweet chocolate**
> 1/4 cup (60 ml) **Irish cream liqueur**
> 1/4 cup (60 ml) **heavy cream**
> 2 tablespoons (1/4 stick, or 28 g) butter
> 2 **egg yolks**

Chop 12 ounces (340 g) of the chocolate into small pieces. Combine the liqueur, cream, chopped chocolate, and butter in a stainless steel bowl set over simmering water. Stir until the butter and chocolate are melted and the mixture is smooth. Whisk in the egg yolks and continue cooking for 2 minutes.

Refrigerate for at least 2 hours, until firm, then roll into 1-inch balls.

Grate the remaining 4 ounces (115 g) chocolate and roll the truffles in it.

YIELD: Makes about 20 to 25 truffles

Old-Fashioned Chocolate Fudge

We have the very fudge pans that our great aunts Sadie and Ruth used to make fudge for their candy store; we think they bring us good confectionary luck. At any rate, our candy-making forebears would approve of this fudge.

A note about fudge: If it happens that your fudge doesn't harden, take heart. It's still excellent warmed and poured over ice cream.

> 3 cups (600 g) **sugar**
> 1 cup (235 ml) **whole milk**
> 3 tablespoons (45 ml) **light corn syrup**
> 1/2 cup (45 g) **cocoa powder**
> 1 tablespoon (14 ml) **vanilla extract**
> 2 tablespoons (1/4 stick, or 28 g) butter

Grease a 9-inch square baking pan.

Combine the sugar, milk, and corn syrup in a 2-quart saucepan and cook over medium-high heat until the liquid comes to a rolling boil. Stir in the cocoa powder. Continue cooking to soft ball stage—238°F (114°C) on the candy thermometer. Remove from the heat and let sit for 2 minutes, then stir in the vanilla and butter. Beat until the mixture becomes thick and creamy. Pour into the prepared pan. Cool until solidified and cut into squares.

YIELD: Makes about 25 pieces

ADD IT! If you are a person who needs nuts in fudge, by all means stir in a handful of your preferred nut.

Peanut Butter Fudge

For people who think that fudge is not a proper vehicle for chocolate, here's the classic variation.

    2 cups (400 g) **sugar**
    1 cup (235 ml) whole **milk**
    1/4 cup (60 ml) **light corn syrup**
    1 cup (260 g) creamy **peanut butter**
    1 tablespoon (14 ml) **vanilla extract**

Grease a 9-inch square baking pan.

Combine the sugar, milk, and corn syrup in a 2-quart saucepan and cook over medium high heat until the liquid comes to a rolling boil. Stir in the peanut butter. Continue cooking to soft ball stage—238°F (114 °C) on the candy thermometer. Remove from the heat and let sit for 2 minutes, then stir in the vanilla. Beat until the mixture becomes thick and creamy. Pour into the prepared pan. Cool until solidified and cut into squares.

YIELD: Makes about 25 pieces

CHAPTER ELEVEN

Soufflés

Soufflés have a reputation for being finicky, risky things to attempt, but if you pull aside the curtain, they stand revealed as a simple dessert: egg whites, air, flavorings.

There are a few tricks to a foolproof soufflé. (See "Making Soufflés" on page 19.) But they're simple to do, and once you master them, you'll have a dessert in your repertoire certain to elicit the much-coveted "Oooh" and "Aaaah" from dinner guests. And then you won't have to break the bank ordering that special soufflé when you go out for a festive dinner—you'll know how to make them just as well at home!

All hot soufflés are great with crème anglaise passed on the side.

Basic Dessert Soufflé Base

This is a basic recipe that is used as the base for all of the dessert soufflé recipes in this book. You can make it up to 3 days in advance. Store it refrigerated with plastic wrap directly on the surface. This recipe will make enough soufflé base for 8 to 10 individual soufflés or one large soufflé.

$^1/_4$ cup ($^1/_2$ stick, or 55 g) butter

$^1/_2$ cup (60 g) **all-purpose flour**

1 $^1/_2$ cups (355 ml) whole **milk**

1 cup (200 g) **sugar**

4 **egg** yolks (Save the whites for making the soufflés.)

Melt the butter in a saucepan over low heat and stir in the flour, mixing until you have a smooth paste. Add the milk in a stream, whisking. Add the sugar. Turn up the heat to medium-high and continue to cook, stirring constantly, until the mixture boils and thickens. Turn the heat to medium-low and cook for another 8 to 10 minutes, stirring all the time.

Put the hot base into a mixing bowl and, while mixing, add the egg yolks one at a time. Be sure each yolk is thoroughly incorporated before adding the next one. Continue beating until the base is cooled to room temperature—about 20 minutes. Refrigerate for at least 1 hour

Hazelnut Soufflé

Sugar for the ramekins

Butter for the ramekins

6 **egg whites**

$1/2$ cup (100 g) **sugar**

1 recipe **Basic Dessert Soufflé Base** (page 470)

$1/4$ cup (60 ml) **Frangelica liqueur**

Preheat the oven to 450°F (230°C, or gas mark 8). Prepare eight 6-ounce ramekins or one 1-quart soufflé dish as follows: Thoroughly grease the bottom and sides of the dish with softened butter. Add a little sugar to the pan and tilt and rotate the dish so that the bottom and sides are coated all over with the sugar. Tip and dump out the excess sugar.

In a stainless steel mixing bowl, beat the egg whites until they begin to froth. Add one-third of the sugar and continue beating, adding the sugar in two more additions, until the whites are glossy and hold stiff peaks.

In another mixing bowl, whisk together the soufflé base and the liqueur until smooth. Fold in the egg whites gently, but thoroughly. Fill the prepared ramekin(s). Knock the bottom of the ramekin(s) against the counter gently to release any trapped air. Clean the rim of each ramekin with a paper towel.

Bake for 14 to 16 minutes for individual and for 18 to 22 minutes for a large soufflé. Serve immediately.

YIELD: Serves 8

Apricot Soufflé

Sugar for the ramekins

Butter for the ramekins

6 egg whites

1/2 cup (100 g) **sugar**

1 recipe **Basic Dessert Soufflé Base** (page 470)

3/4 cup (240 g) **apricot jam**

Preheat the oven to 450°F (230°C, or gas mark 8). Prepare eight 6-ounce ramekins or one 1-quart soufflé dish as follows: Thoroughly grease the bottom and sides of the dish with softened butter. Add a little sugar to the pan and tilt and rotate the dish so that the bottom and sides are coated all over with the sugar. Tip and dump out the excess sugar.

In a stainless steel bowl, beat the egg whites until they begin to froth. Add 1/3 of the sugar and continue beating, adding the sugar in two more additions, until the whites are glossy and hold stiff peaks.

Put the jam in a food processor and process until smooth. In another mixing bowl, whisk together the soufflé base and the jam. Fold in the egg whites gently, but thoroughly. Fill the prepared ramekin(s). Knock the bottom of the ramekin(s) against the counter gently to release any trapped air. Clean the rim of each ramekin with a paper towel.

Bake for 14 to 16 minutes for individual and for 18 to 22 minutes for a large soufflé. Serve immediately.

YIELD: Serves 8

Banana Soufflé

Sugar for the ramekins

Butter for the ramekins

6 **egg whites**

1/2 cup (100 g) **sugar**

1 recipe **Basic Dessert Soufflé Base** (page 470)

1 cup (225 g) mashed **banana** (about 2 bananas)

Preheat the oven to 450°F (230°C, or gas mark 8). Prepare eight 6-ounce ramekins or one 1-quart soufflé dish as follows: Thoroughly grease the bottom and sides of the dish with softened butter. Add a little sugar to the pan and tilt and rotate the dish so that the bottom and sides are coated all over with the sugar. Tip and dump out the excess sugar.

In a stainless steel mixing bowl, beat the egg whites until they begin to froth. Add one-third of the sugar and continue beating, adding the rest of the sugar in two more additions, until the whites are glossy and hold stiff peaks.

In another mixing bowl, whisk together the soufflé base and the banana until smooth. Fold in the egg whites gently, but thoroughly. Fill the prepared ramekin(s). Knock the bottom of the ramekin(s) against the counter gently to release any trapped air. Clean the rim of each ramekin with a paper towel.

Bake for 14 to 16 minutes for individual and for 18 to 22 minutes for a large soufflé. Serve immediately.

YIELD: Serves 8

Key Lime Soufflé

Sugar for the ramekins

Butter for the ramekins

6 **egg whites**

1/2 cup (100 g) **sugar**

1 recipe **Basic Dessert Soufflé Base** (page 470)

1/3 cup (75 ml) **key lime juice**

Preheat the oven to 450°F (230°C, or gas mark 8). Prepare eight 6-ounce ramekins or one 1-quart soufflé dish as follows: Thoroughly grease the bottom and sides of the dish with softened butter. Add a little sugar to the pan and tilt and rotate the dish so that the bottom and sides are coated all over with the sugar. Tip and dump out the excess sugar.

In a stainless steel mixing bowl, beat the egg whites until they begin to froth. Add one-third of the sugar and continue beating, adding the sugar in two more additions, until the whites are glossy and hold stiff peaks.

In another mixing bowl, whisk together the soufflé base and the key lime juice until smooth. Fold in the egg whites gently, but thoroughly. Fill the prepared ramekin(s). Knock the bottom of the ramekin(s) against the counter gently to release any trapped air. Clean the rim of each ramekin with a paper towel.

Bake for 14 to 16 minutes for individual and for 18 to 22 minutes for a large soufflé. Serve immediately.

YIELD: Serves 8

Lemon Soufflé

Sugar for the ramekins

Butter for the ramekins

6 **egg whites**

1/2 cup (100 g) **sugar**

1 recipe **Basic Dessert Soufflé Base** (page 470)

Zest and juice of 4 **lemons**

Preheat the oven to 450°F (230°C, or gas mark 8). Prepare eight 6-ounce ramekins or one 1-quart soufflé dish as follows: Thoroughly grease the bottom and sides of the dish with softened butter. Add a little sugar to the pan and tilt and rotate the dish so that the bottom and sides are coated all over with the sugar. Tip and dump out the excess sugar.

In a stainless steel mixing bowl, beat the egg whites until they begin to froth. Add one-third of the sugar and continue beating, adding the sugar in two more additions, until the whites are glossy and hold stiff peaks.

In another mixing bowl, whisk together the soufflé base and the lemon zest and lemon juice until smooth. Fold in the egg whites gently, but thoroughly. Fill the prepared ramekin(s). Knock the bottom of the ramekin(s) against the counter gently to release any trapped air. Clean the rim of each ramekin with a paper towel.

Bake for 14 to 16 minutes for individual and for 18 to 22 minutes for a large soufflé. Serve immediately, with Crème Anglaise (page 482) on the side.

YIELD: Serves 8

⏏ Raspberry Soufflé

To make raspberry puree, thaw 1 package (10 ounces, or 280 g) frozen raspberries in syrup, puree in a blender or food processor, and pass through a fine mesh sieve. Discard the seeds.

Sugar for the ramekins
Butter for the ramekins
6 **egg whites**
$1/2$ cup (100 g) **sugar**
1 recipe **Basic Dessert Soufflé Base** (page 470)
$1/2$ cup **raspberry puree** (See recipe note.)

Preheat the oven to 450°F (230°C, or gas mark 8). Prepare eight 6-ounce ramekins or one 1-quart soufflé dish as follows: Thoroughly grease the bottom and sides of the dish with softened butter. Add a little sugar to the pan and tilt and rotate the dish so that the bottom and sides are coated all over with the sugar. Tip and dump out the excess sugar.

In a stainless steel mixing bowl, beat the egg whites until they begin to froth. Add one-third of the sugar and continue beating, adding the sugar in two more additions, until the whites are glossy and hold stiff peaks.

In another mixing bowl, whisk together the soufflé base and the raspberry puree until smooth. Fold in the egg whites gently, but thoroughly. Fill the prepared ramekin(s). Knock the bottom of the ramekin(s) against the counter gently to release any trapped air. Clean the rim of each ramekin with a paper towel.

Bake for 14 to 16 minutes for individual and for 18 to 22 minutes for a large soufflé. Serve immediately.

YIELD: Serves 8

⌂ Currant Soufflé

Sugar for the ramekins
Butter for the ramekins
6 egg whites
$1/2$ cup (100 g) **sugar**
1 recipe **Basic Dessert Soufflé Base** (page 470)
$1/2$ cup (120 ml) **black currant concentrate**

Preheat the oven to 450°F (230°C, or gas mark 8). Prepare eight 6-ounce ramekins or one 1-quart soufflé dish as follows: Thoroughly grease the bottom and sides of the dish with softened butter. Add a little sugar to the pan and tilt and rotate the dish so that the bottom and sides are coated all over with the sugar. Tip and dump out the excess sugar.

In a stainless steel mixing bowl, beat the egg whites until they begin to froth. Add one-third of the sugar and continue beating, adding the sugar in two more additions, until the whites are glossy and hold stiff peaks.

In another mixing bowl, whisk together the soufflé base and the black currant concentrate until smooth. Fold in the egg whites gently, but thoroughly. Fill the prepared ramekin(s). Knock the bottom of the ramekin(s) against the counter gently to release any trapped air. Clean the rim of each ramekin with a paper towel.

Bake for 14 to 16 minutes for individual and for 18 to 22 minutes for a large soufflé. Serve immediately.

YIELD: Serves 8

Chocolate Soufflé

Sugar for the ramekins

Butter for the ramekins

6 **egg whites**

1/2 cup (100 g) **sugar**

4 ounces (115 g) **bittersweet chocolate**

1 recipe **Basic Dessert Soufflé Base** (page 470)

Preheat the oven to 450°F (230°C, or gas mark 8). Prepare eight 6-ounce ramekins or one 1-quart soufflé dish as follows: Thoroughly grease the bottom and sides of the dish with softened butter. Add a little sugar to the pan and tilt and rotate the dish so that the bottom and sides are coated all over with the sugar. Tip and dump out the excess sugar.

In a stainless steel mixing bowl, beat the egg whites until they begin to froth. Add one-third of the sugar and continue beating, adding the sugar in two more additions, until the whites are glossy and hold stiff peaks.

Melt the chocolate in a stainless steel bowl set over a pot of simmering water. Whisk together the soufflé base and the melted chocolate until smooth. Fold in the egg whites gently, but thoroughly. Fill the prepared ramekin(s). Knock the bottom of the ramekin(s) against the counter gently to release any trapped air. Clean the rim of each ramekin with a paper towel.

Bake for 14 to 16 minutes for individual and for 18 to 22 minutes for a large soufflé. Serve immediately.

YIELD: Serves 8

Coffee Soufflé

Sugar for the ramekins

Butter for the ramekins

6 **egg whites**

$^1/_2$ cup (100 g) **sugar**

1 recipe **Basic Dessert Soufflé Base** (page 470)

$^1/_4$ cup (60 ml) **coffee liqueur**

Preheat the oven to 450°F (230°C, or gas mark 8). Prepare eight 6-ounce ramekins or one 1-quart soufflé dish as follows: Thoroughly grease the bottom and sides of the dish with softened butter. Add a little sugar to the pan and tilt and rotate the dish so that the bottom and sides are coated all over with the sugar. Tip and dump out the excess sugar.

In a stainless steel mixing bowl, beat the egg whites until they begin to froth. Add one-third of the sugar and continue beating, adding the sugar in two more additions, until the whites are glossy and hold stiff peaks.

In another mixing bowl, whisk together the soufflé base and the coffee liqueur until smooth. Fold in the egg whites gently, but thoroughly. Fill the prepared ramekin(s). Knock the bottom of the ramekin(s) against the counter gently to release any trapped air. Clean the rim of each ramekin with a paper towel.

Bake for 14 to 16 minutes for individual and for 18 to 22 minutes for a large soufflé. Serve immediately.

YIELD: Serves 8

Grand Marnier Soufflé

This is a classic of French cooking and a wonderful finish to a formal dinner.

Sugar for the ramekins

Butter for the ramekins

6 egg whites

1/2 cup (100 g) sugar

1 recipe Basic Dessert Soufflé Base (page 470)

1/4 cup (60 ml) Grand Marnier liqueur

Preheat the oven to 450°F (230°C, or gas mark 8). Prepare eight 6-ounce ramekins or one 1-quart soufflé dish as follows: Thoroughly grease the bottom and sides of the dish with softened butter. Add a little sugar to the pan and tilt and rotate the dish so that the bottom and sides are coated all over with the sugar. Tip and dump out the excess sugar.

In a stainless steel mixing bowl, beat the egg whites until they begin to froth. Add one-third of the sugar and continue beating, adding the sugar in two more additions, until the whites are glossy and hold stiff peaks.

In another mixing bowl, whisk together the soufflé base and the liqueur until smooth. Fold in the egg whites gently, but thoroughly. Fill the prepared ramekin(s). Knock the bottom of the ramekin(s) against the counter gently to release any trapped air. Clean the rim of each ramekin with a paper towel.

Bake for 14 to 16 minutes for individual and for 18 to 22 minutes for a large soufflé. Serve immediately.

YIELD: Serves 8

CHAPTER TWELVE

Sauces and Frostings

Also known as the "gilding the lily" chapter, here we offer recipes of sweet stuff that one can use to further adorn already sweet items. And sometimes, that's a good thing.

Crème Anglaise

The basic custard sauce—use to decorate plates, to serve with hot soufflés, and over bread pudding.

> 4 **egg yolks**
> $1/2$ cup (100 g) **sugar**
> 2 cups (475 ml) whole **milk**
> $1/2$ teaspoon **vanilla extract**

Fill a large mixing bowl halfway with ice water. Whisk together the egg yolks and sugar in a stainless steel mixing bowl.

In a saucepan, scald the milk and whisk into the egg mixture in a thin stream. Return to the saucepan and cook over medium heat, stirring constantly, until the custard thickens enough to coat the back of a spoon. Immediately put the pan into the ice water. Stir in the vanilla. When cooled, strain through a fine mesh strainer. Keeps, refrigerated, for up to 1 week.

YIELD: Makes about $2^1/2$ cups

Peanut Sauce

Try this sauce with chocolate ice cream.

> 1 cup (260 g) chunky **peanut butter**
> 1 cup (50 g) **mini marshmallows**
> $1/2$ cup (120 ml) whole or 2% **milk**

Combine all ingredients in the top of a double boiler and cook, stirring occasionally, until smooth.

YIELD: Makes about 2 cups

Strawberry Sauce

What better over vanilla ice cream?

> 2 cups (600 g) frozen **strawberries**
> 1 cup (200 g) **sugar**
> 1 cup (235 ml) water
> 2 tablespoons (15 g) **cornstarch**

Combine the strawberries, sugar, and water in a saucepan. Bring to a simmer over medium-high heat and cook, stirring every few minutes, for about 20 minutes, until the berries are softened and begin to break up into the sauce. Stir the cornstarch with just enough water to make a slurry and stir the slurry into the sauce. Cook for 3 to 4 minutes more, stirring all the time, until the sauce loses its cloudiness and thickens. Cool.

YIELD: Makes about 2½ cups

Blueberry Sauce

This is a great match for vanilla pudding or ice cream.

> 2 cups (290 g) frozen **blueberries**
> 1 cup (200 g) **sugar**
> 1 cup (235 ml) water
> 2 tablespoons (15 g) **cornstarch**

Combine the blueberries, sugar, and water in a saucepan. Bring to a simmer over medium-high heat and cook, stirring every few minutes, for about 20 minutes, until the blueberries are softened. Stir the cornstarch with just enough water to make a slurry and stir the slurry into the sauce. Cook for 3 to 4 minutes more, stirring, until the sauce loses its cloudiness and thickens. Cool.

YIELD: Makes about 2½ cups

Raspberry Sauce

    2 cups (500 g) frozen **raspberries**

    1 cup (200 g) **sugar**

    1 cup (235 ml) water

    $1/4$ cup (30 g) **cornstarch**

Combine the raspberries, sugar, and water in a 2-quart saucepan. Cook over medium heat to a simmer, until the raspberries break apart. Strain through a fine mesh strainer and discard the seeds. Return the resulting liquid to the saucepan. Mix the cornstarch with just enough water to form a slurry, then whisk into the raspberry liquid. Return the pan to medium heat and cook, stirring, until the liquid clarifies and thickens. Chill. Keeps for 2 to 3 weeks in the refrigerator.

YIELD: Makes about 2 cups

Peach Sauce

This is perfect over a basic bread pudding.

    2 cups (500 g) frozen **peaches**

    1 cup (200 g) **sugar**

    1 cup (235 ml) water

    2 tablespoons (15 g) **cornstarch**

Combine the peaches, sugar, and water in a saucepan. Bring to a simmer over medium-high heat and cook, stirring every few minutes, for about 20 minutes, until the peaches are softened and the pieces are dissolving into the sauce. Stir the cornstarch with just enough water to make a slurry and stir the slurry into the peach sauce. Cook for 3 to 4 minutes more, stirring, until the sauce loses its cloudiness and thickens. Cool.

YIELD: Makes about $2^{1/2}$ cups

Warm Lemon Sauce

$1/3$ cup (60 g) **sugar**

$1/8$ teaspoon salt

$1/8$ teaspoon **nutmeg**

$3/4$ cup (175 ml) water

Zest of $1/2$ **lemon**

Juice of 1 **lemon**

2 tablespoons (15 g) **cornstarch**

1 tablespoon butter or margarine

In a small saucepan, combine the sugar, salt, and nutmeg. Gradually whisk in the water, lemon zest, and lemon juice. Cook over low heat. Stir the cornstarch with just enough water to make a slurry and stir the slurry into the sauce. Add the butter and cook for 3 to 4 minutes more, stirring, until the sauce thickens. Cool to warm.

YIELD: Makes about $1\,1/2$ cups sauce

Butterscotch Sauce

This tastes way better than any bottled sauce from the store.

$1/2$ cup (110 g) packed **light brown sugar**

$1/4$ cup (60 ml) **light corn syrup**

$1/2$ cup (120 ml) **heavy cream**

2 teaspoons **vanilla extract**

2 tablespoons ($1/4$ stick, or 28 g) butter

In a 2-quart saucepan, over medium heat, melt together the sugar and the corn syrup. Bring to a boil and allow to boil for 2 minutes. Add the cream and vanilla and stir until smooth. Stir in the butter until melted.

YIELD: Makes about $1\,1/2$ cups

Caramel Sauce

2 cups (400 g) **sugar**
Few drops **lemon juice**
About $1/4$ cup (60 ml) water
$1/4$ cup (60 ml) **rum**
$1 1/2$ cups (355 ml) **heavy cream**

Put the sugar into a heavy bottomed saucepan. Add the lemon juice and enough water to make a "wet sand." Put the pan on high heat and allow to cook until the liquid becomes a rich brown. Immediately remove from the heat and add the rum, then the cream. Be careful, as the liquid will boil up. Stir until smooth, returning the pan briefly to the heat if needed to melt the caramel. Will keep, refrigerated, for up to 1 month. Warm slightly to make the sauce runnier before using.

YIELD: Makes about 3 cups.

Coffee Sauce

This is wonderful as a pool of sauce under a dark chocolate cake.

1 cup (235 ml) **coffee syrup**
2 tablespoons (15 g) **cornstarch**
$1/2$ cup (120 ml) water

Whisk together the syrup, cornstarch, and water in a small saucepan. Cook, stirring, over medium heat until the liquid clears and thickens— 8 to 10 minutes. Keeps, refrigerated, for up to 1 month.

YIELD: Makes about $1 1/2$ cups

Mocha Sauce

Perfect over ice cream, or you could try this as a sauce for a chocolate dessert.

> 8 ounces (225 g) **semisweet chocolate chips**
> 1 cup (235 ml) **half and half**
> 1/2 cup (120 ml) **coffee syrup**

Put the chocolate in a small stainless steel mixing bowl.

In a small saucepan, bring the half and half to a scald over high heat. Pour over the chocolate and allow to sit for 2 minutes. Stir in the coffee syrup, stirring until smooth. Keeps in the refrigerator for up to 1 month and can be melted in the microwave.

YIELD: Makes about 2 cups

Hot Fudge Sauce

This is the best on ice cream.

> 1 cup (200 g) **sugar**
> 1/4 cup (30 g) **cornstarch**
> 1/4 cup (25 g) **cocoa powder**
> 8 ounces (235 ml) **evaporated milk**
> Pinch salt
> 1 cup (235 ml) water
> 1 teaspoon **vanilla extract**
> 2 tablespoons (1/4 stick, or 28 g) butter

Sift together the sugar, cornstarch, and cocoa powder into a 2-quart saucepan. Stir in the evaporated milk, salt, and water. Cook over medium heat, stirring, until thickened and creamy—8 to 10 minutes. Stir in the vanilla and butter. Will keep, refrigerated, for up to 1 month. Just reheat to use.

YIELD: Makes about 2 1/2 cups

Marshmallow Sauce

This is perfect for ice cream sundaes or over a chocolate cake.

> 2 cups (100 g) **mini marshmallows**
> 1/2 cup (120 ml) **half and half**

Combine the marshmallows and half and half in a 2-quart saucepan. Cook over medium-low heat, stirring, until the marshmallows are melted and the sauce is smooth. Cool.

YIELD: Makes about 2 cups

Flora Dora Sauce

This sauce is essential to Molasses Pudding (page 363).

> 1/3 cup (75 g) butter
> 1 cup (120 g) **confectioners' sugar**
> 1/2 teaspoon **vanilla** or rum flavor or 1/2 teaspoon dark rum
> 1 to 2 tablespoons (14 to 28 ml) whole **milk**

Melt the butter in a saucepan over low heat. Whisk in the sugar, followed by the flavoring and milk. Whisk until smooth.

YIELD: Makes about 2/3 cup

Vinegar Sauce

This is a very old-fashioned dessert sauce, but really tasty with apple pie.

> 1/2 cup (100 g) **sugar**
> 2 tablespoons (15 g) **all-purpose flour**
> 1/2 teaspoon **nutmeg**
> 1 cup (235 ml) water
> 2 tablespoons (28 ml) **cider vinegar**

Combine the sugar, flour, nutmeg, water, and vinegar in a 1-quart saucepan. Cook over medium heat until the liquid boils and thickens to coat the back of a spoon. Serve warm.

YIELD: Makes about 1 1/2 cups

Hard Sauce

This is the classic sauce for plum pudding.

> 1 1/4 cups (2 1/2 sticks, or 280 g) butter, softened
> 2 cups (240 g) **confectioners' sugar**
> Pinch salt
> 1 teaspoon **vanilla extract**
> 1/4 cup (60 ml) **brandy**

Using a mixer on medium speed, cream the butter, sugar, and salt together until fluffy—3 to 5 minutes. Add the vanilla and brandy and beat until smooth. Refrigerate until about 1 hour before serving.

YIELD: Makes about 2 cups

Whiskey Sauce

It's the classic combination with warm bread pudding.

  1 cup (235 ml) **light cream**

  $1/4$ cup (50 g) **sugar**

  2 teaspoons **cornstarch**

  1 tablespoon (14 ml) **bourbon whiskey**

  1 teaspoon **vanilla extract**

Combine the cream and sugar in a small saucepan. Heat, stirring, over medium heat until almost to a boil. Remove from the heat.

Stir together the cornstarch, whiskey, and vanilla to make a slurry. Whisk into the hot cream and cook, stirring constantly, until thickened. Remove from the heat. Cool slightly or refrigerate until cold.

YIELD: Makes about $1 1/4$ cups

Lemon Glaze

This is a good glaze for pound cakes.

  2 cups (240 g) **confectioners' sugar**

  $1/4$ cup (60 ml) **lemon juice**

  $1/2$ cup (120 ml) water

  1 teaspoon **vanilla extract**

Combine the sugar with the lemon juice and water in a small saucepan. Cook over medium-high heat until just boiling. Remove from the heat and stir in the vanilla. Allow to cool, then spoon over cake.

YIELD: Makes about 2 cups

Kiwi Coulis

The term coulis refers to a thick sauce or puree.

> 4 ripe **kiwi fruit**
> 1 cup (200 g) **sugar**
> 1 cup (235 ml) water
> 1/4 cup (30 g)**cornstarch**

Peel the kiwi fruit and cut the flesh into 1/2-inch pieces. Combine the kiwi pieces and the sugar in a 2-quart saucepan and add the water. Cook over medium heat to a simmer, until the kiwi fruit is mushy—about 5 minutes. Strain through a fine mesh strainer and discard any seeds. Return the resulting liquid to the saucepan. Mix the cornstarch with just enough water to form a slurry, then whisk into the kiwi liquid. Return the pan to medium heat and cook, stirring, until the liquid clarifies and thickens. Chill. Keeps for 2 to 3 weeks in the refrigerator.

YIELD: Makes about 2 cups

Mango Coulis

> 2 **mangos**
> 1 cup (200 g) **sugar**
> 1 cup (235 ml) water
> 2 tablespoons (15 g) **cornstarch**

Peel the mangos and cut the flesh into 1/2-inch cubes. Combine the mango and the sugar in a 2-quart saucepan and add the water. Cook over medium heat to a simmer, until the mango softens and begins to break down. Strain through a fine mesh strainer. Return the resulting liquid to the saucepan. Mix the cornstarch with just enough water to form a slurry, then whisk into the mango liquid. Return the pan to medium heat and cook, stirring, until the liquid clarifies and thickens. Chill. Keeps for 2 to 3 weeks in the refrigerator.

YIELD: Makes about 2 cups

Sabayon

Wonderful over fresh summer fruits as a light dessert, this is known in Italy as "zabaglione."

> 2 **egg yolks**
> 1/2 cup (100 g) **sugar**
> 1/2 cup (120 ml) **Marsala wine**

Bring a saucepan half full of water to a simmer. Combine all the ingredients in a stainless steel mixing bowl and set over the simmering water. Whisk constantly until the sauce is fluffy, tripled in volume, and you can see streaks of the bottom of the bowl as you whisk. Serve immediately.

YIELD: Makes about 2 cups

Chocolate Sauce

This is a good basic chocolate sauce for everything from desserts to ice cream to glazing cakes and tortes.

> 8 ounces (225 g) **semisweet chocolate chips**
> 1 cup (235 ml) **half and half**

Put the chocolate in a small stainless steel mixing bowl.

In a small saucepan, bring the half and half to a scald over high heat. Pour over the chocolate and allow to sit for 2 minutes. Stir until smooth. Keeps in the refrigerator for up to 1 month and can be melted in the microwave.

YIELD: Makes about 2 cups

Whipped Chocolate Ganache

This makes for an elegant and rich mouthful of smooth chocolate flavor.

    1 cup (235 ml) **whipping cream**

    12 ounces (340 g) **semisweet chocolate**, chopped into small pieces

Bring the cream to a boil in a small saucepan over medium-high heat. Put the chocolate in a stainless steel bowl and pour the hot cream over. Allow to sit for 2 to 3 minutes, then stir until smooth. If chunks of chocolate remain unmelted, set the bowl over simmering water and stir until melted. Refrigerate for 30 minutes.

Whip the cooled ganache until tripled in volume and lightened in color. Store any leftover cake frosted with this in the refrigerator.

YIELD: Makes about 4 cups, enough for a 2-layer cake

Caramel Icing

    1 cup (200 g) granulated **sugar**

    About ¼ cup (60 ml) water

    4 **egg whites**

    1 cup (120 g) **confectioners' sugar**

    1 cup (2 sticks, or 225 g) butter, softened

    1 teaspoon **vanilla extract**

Combine the granulated sugar in a small, heavy-bottomed saucepan with enough water to make "wet sand." Cook on medium high heat, not stirring, until the sugar is a deep golden color. Remove from the heat and allow to cool for 2 to 3 minutes.

While the sugar is cooking, whip the egg whites, adding the confectioners' sugar in 3 stages after the eggs begin to foam, to soft peak. With the mixer running, slowly pour in the granulated sugar. Whip until the mixture is cooled. Cut the butter into small pieces and add them, a few at a time, with the mixer running. Add the vanilla.

YIELD: Makes enough to frost a 2-layer cake—about 3 cups

Chocolate Butter Icing

This icing sets up pretty quickly, so you have to frost fast.

> 3 ounces (85 g) **unsweetened chocolate**
>
> 2 to 3 tablespoons (28 to 45 g) butter
>
> 1/4 cup (60 ml) hot water, **cream**, or **coffee** (you choose!)
>
> 1/8 teaspoon salt
>
> 2 cups (240 g) **confectioners' sugar**, sifted

Melt the chocolate in a double boiler, stirring until smooth. Add the butter and stir to melt. Remove from heat and add the water, cream or coffee, as well as the salt. Gradually stir in the sugar as needed to make a spreadable consistency. (You may not need the entire 2 cups.)

YIELD: Frosts a single-layer cake or torte

Cream Cheese Frosting

It's a classic with carrot cake.

> 8 ounces (225 g) **cream cheese**
>
> 1/4 cup (1/2 stick, or 55 g) butter
>
> 1 **egg white**
>
> 3 cups (360 g) **confectioners' sugar**
>
> 2 teaspoons **vanilla extract**

Using a mixer on medium speed, combine the cream cheese and butter in a mixing bowl and beat until smooth. Add the egg white and beat until fluffy— 3 to 4 minutes. Add the sugar and vanilla and mix until the frosting is smooth and of spreading consistency.

YIELD: Makes about 3 cups, enough to frost a 2-layer cake

Vanilla Buttercream Frosting

There are people who swear that no chocolate layer cake is complete without basic butter frosting.

> 1 cup (2 sticks, or 225 g) butter
>
> 3 cups (360 g) **confectioners' sugar**
>
> 3 teaspoons **vanilla extract**

Using a mixer on medium speed, cream the butter and sugar together for 7 to 8 minutes. Add the vanilla. Mix until smooth and of spreading consistency, adding a bit more sugar if the icing is too thin.

YIELD: Makes about 3 cups, enough to frost a 2-layer cake

Maple Buttercream Frosting

This is excellent on a spice cake.

> 1 cup (2 sticks, or 225 g) butter
>
> 4 cups (480 g) **confectioners' sugar**
>
> 1/2 cup (120 ml) **maple syrup**

Using a mixer on medium speed, cream the butter and sugar together for 7 to 8 minutes until fluffy. Add the maple syrup and mix until smooth and of spreading consistency, adding a bit more sugar if the icing is too thin.

YIELD: Makes about 3 cups, enough to frost a 2-layer cake

Italian Buttercream Frosting

This is a bit more difficult to make, but the result is a real bakery-quality icing.

> 1 1/2 cups (300 g) **sugar**
>
> About 1/4 cup (60 ml) water
>
> 4 **egg whites**
>
> 1/8 teaspoon **cream of tartar**
>
> 1/2 cup (1 stick, or 112 g) butter, softened
>
> 2 teaspoons **vanilla extract**

Combine the sugar in a small, heavy-bottomed saucepan with enough water to make "wet sand." Cook on medium-high heat until the sugar reaches 238°F (114°C) on a candy thermometer.

While the sugar is cooking, whip the egg whites with the cream of tartar to soft peaks. With the mixer running, slowly pour in the hot sugar. Whip until the mixture is cooled. Cut the butter into small pieces and add them, a few at a time, with the mixer running. Add the vanilla.

YIELD: Makes enough to frost a 2 layer cake—about 3 cups

Chocolate Buttercream Frosting

> 1 cup (2 sticks, or 225 g) butter
>
> 3 cups (360 g) **confectioners' sugar**
>
> 4 ounces (115 g) **bittersweet chocolate**, cut into small pieces
>
> 1 teaspoon **vanilla extract**

Using a mixer on medium speed, cream the butter and sugar together for 7 to 8 minutes.

Melt the chocolate in a small stainless steel bowl set over simmering water. Stir the vanilla into the chocolate and stir these into the butter mixture. Mix until smooth and of spreading consistency, adding a bit more sugar if the icing is too thin.

YIELD: Makes about 3 cups, enough to frost a 2-layer cake

Mocha Buttercream Frosting

1 cup (2 sticks, or 225 g) butter

3 cups (360 g) **confectioners' sugar**

1/4 cup (25 g) **cocoa powder**

1/4 cup (60 ml) **coffee**

1 teaspoon **vanilla extract**

Using a mixer on medium speed, cream the butter and sugar together for 7 to 8 minutes. Sift the cocoa powder and stir it in. Add the coffee and vanilla. Mix until smooth and of spreading consistency, adding a bit more sugar if the icing is too thin.

YIELD: Makes about 3 cups, enough to frost a 2-layer cake

Coffee Buttercream Frosting

1 cup (2 sticks, or 225 g) butter

3 cups (360 g) **confectioners' sugar**

1/4 cup (60 ml) **coffee**

1 teaspoon **vanilla extract**

Using a mixer on medium speed, cream the butter and sugar together for 7 to 8 minutes. Add the coffee and vanilla. Mix until smooth and of spreading consistency, adding a bit more sugar if the icing is too thin.

YIELD: Makes about 3 cups, enough to frost a 2-layer cake

Sea Foam Frosting

> 2 cups (450 g) packed **light brown sugar**
>
> 3 **egg whites**
>
> 1/3 cup (75 ml) water
>
> Pinch salt
>
> 1/4 cup (60 ml) **almond liqueur**, such as amaretto

Combine the sugar, egg whites, water, and salt in the top of a double boiler set over simmering water. Stir until the sugar dissolves. Beat, still on the heat, until the frosting forms soft peaks—7 to 9 minutes. Beat in the almond liqueur.

YIELD: Makes about 3 cups, enough to frost a 2-layer cake

Stabilized Whipped Cream

This is great for frosting a cake that is not being served immediately. Tastes like whipped cream, but will not melt away quickly.

> 2 teaspoons **unflavored gelatin**
>
> 1/4 cup (60 ml) water
>
> 1 1/2 cups (355 ml) **heavy cream**
>
> 1/2 cup (60 g) **confectioners' sugar**
>
> 1 teaspoon **vanilla extract**

Combine the gelatin with the water in a small saucepan. Allow the gelatin to soften for a few minutes, then heat over low heat until the gelatin is dissolved. Allow to cool for 8 to 10 minutes.

Combine the cream, sugar, and vanilla in a mixing bowl. Stir in the gelatin. Whip to stiff peaks.

YIELD: Makes about 3 cups, enough to cover a 2-layer cake

Vegan Whipped "Cream"

This recipe may not fool you into thinking you are eating whipped cream, but it is good in its own right. (By the way, Cool Whip is vegan.)

> $1/2$ pound (225 g) firm **tofu**, well drained
>
> $1/2$ cup (100 g) **sugar**
>
> 1 teaspoon **vanilla extract**
>
> Pinch salt
>
> $1/2$ teaspoon **lemon juice**
>
> $1/2$ cup (120 ml) **soy milk**

Combine all of the ingredients except the soy milk in a mixing bowl and beat until smooth. Add the soy milk and beat until fluffy.

YIELD: Makes about 2 cups

INDEX

ACKNOWLEDGMENTS

We are deeply grateful to the families, friends, and colleagues who provided a heaping measure of support, patience, advice, and feedback. In this case, it required a cadre of cooks to help get this cookbook written

As always, our families provided oodles of help and humor, and we'd like to thank Don, Sarah, Olivia, Nicholas, Erica, and Sam for tasting, stirring, baking and measuring right along with us—even when the desserts didn't come out quite right the first try. Our parents, George and Marge Hildebrand, as always were thick in the fray, as were our siblings and their lovely spouses: Amy and Darrell, Charles and Jerrie. Thank you!

Then there are those who put their figures on the line for a good cause. It's a sad thing when people run away from a neighbor bearing cake, but we had a lot of recipes to test, and our friends and neighbors took the brunt. From neighborhood tasting parties to friends who lent their time and kitchens to test recipes, we appreciate all the help we had. In particular, we'd like to thank Susan Crockett for her fabulous pie-making weekend; Leslie and Geol Barnes, Mai and John Ciolfi, Kara and Matt Kressy, Peter Frykman and Kate O'Brien, Alice "There's no such thing as too much chocolate" Kelly, Barbara Bilodeau, and Chris and Margaret Lindquist. Taste-testers extraordinaire, all of you.

Also, we'd like to thank our team of recipe testers for adding yet another task to their already busy lives, and providing us with helpful, thoughtful, and useful feedback. Mary Harris waded through the cookie recipes with energy, skill, and grace; Erin Mohica and her friends did yeoman's duty with the brownies and bars. Finally, many and heartfelt thanks to Laurie Brustlin, Lois Conroy, Muriel Beahm, Madeline Celletti, Susan Young, Betty Obernesser, and June Baldwin.

ABOUT THE AUTHORS

Robert Hildebrand is the executive chef at the Three Stallions Inn in Randolph, Vermont. His work has been featured in *Bon Appetit*, as well as several newspapers.

Carol Hildebrand is an award-winning writer and editor. Her work has appeared in *Boston Magazine, The Old Farmer's Almanac, CIO, Darwin*, and many others.